ART EDUCATION RESOURCE CENTRE

ART EDUCATION
RESOURCE
CENTRE

A HISTORY OF

ART & MUSIC

ART

A HISTORY OF

& MUSIC

H. W. JANSON
Professor of Fine Arts, New York University,
with Dora Jane Janson

JOSEPH KERMAN
Professor of Music, University of California (Berkeley)

Prentice-Hall, Inc., Englewood Cliffs, N. J.

and Harry N. Abrams, Inc., New York

Patricia Egan • *Editor*

Library of Congress Catalog Card Number: 68-26864

Printed and bound in Japan

A HISTORY OF

ART & MUSIC

C O N T

E N T S

FOREWORD

This book has been written to fill a need—the need for a history-in-brief of art and music designed as an introduction to these fields in the framework of a general humanities course. This can be done in several ways, and all of them have their dangers. At one extreme is the integrated treatment of both subjects under common headings, at the other complete independence. The first tends to encourage facile generalizations or forced attempts to demonstrate unity of development at any price, while the second is likely to produce two separate histories without a common denominator.

We have chosen a middle way. Each author has been solely responsible for his own area, so that art and music are presented as separate entities; but, as a glance at the table of contents will show, we have adopted a common pattern of organization for the major subdivisions of both fields, inviting the reader to compare the exposition chapter by chapter. As aspects of the history of civilization, art and music both reflect the major developments that determine the way we divide the flow of the past into periods—such as the rise of towns in the later Middle Ages, the secularism and individualism of the Renaissance, or the dominant role of science and technology in modern life. We have attempted to analyze these reflections wherever we discern them clearly and to correlate and cross-reference our materials whenever we could do so without trespassing on the other's territory.

At the same time, readers need not expect to find a one-to-one correspondence at every point. The consensus of scholarly opinion does not support such a view of things. For art and music often respond to the major changes in the human condition in very different ways; we find the contrasts as revealing as the similarities—and we hope the reader too will find them so. Each field has an internal dynamic of its own that cushions the impact of outside forces, so that the history of art and the history of music are "inner-directed" as well as "other-directed." By tracing each history continuously, we mean to give due weight to the forces of tradition, the exigencies of technique, the special pressures of social expectation, and all the other "inner-directed" forces operative on the two fields individually.

Still another reason made us decide to keep our two accounts separate: although art and music are both as old as mankind, the *known* history of art covers a great deal more ground than the known history of music. From the Old Stone Age to the Greeks—that is, from about 20,000 to about 2,500 years ago—the history of music consists entirely of the history of musical instruments (see, for example, the harp in fig. 17). Of the music played on them we know nothing. The Greeks invented music theory as well as a system of notation, enabling us to know something of their music and of their ideas about music. But it was not until about 1000 A.D. that musical notation became precise enough for modern scholars to reconstruct with reasonable accuracy the sound of actual compositions. In contrast, the history of art during the time span since the Greeks offers a great wealth of material, much of it so fascinating to the modern beholder that he may respond to it more readily than to many works of more recent date.

Yet the Western World—somewhat paradoxically, it would seem—has ranked music far above the visual arts ever since the Greeks. Classical antiquity and the Middle Ages placed music among the "liberal arts" (that is, the intellectual disciplines reserved for free men as against slaves or serfs) because it had a theoretical basis that linked it with both mathematics and philosophy (see below, pp. 215–216). Meanwhile architecture, painting, and sculpture were classed with the "mechanical arts" or crafts, which are based on practice rather than on reason. When, in the Renaissance, the visual arts acquired their own background of theory and rose to the status of "liberal arts," they attributed the superiority of music to its unique power over the emotions. Music was *comes laetitiae, medicina dolorum,* "joy's companion, the cure of sorrows."

During the first century of the modern era, from about 1760 to 1860, the prestige of music as the noblest of the arts received further impetus. Several generations of composers of genius brought about a shift of emphasis from vocal to instrumental music and greatly enlarged its expressive range. At the same time, painters and sculptors grew more and more dissatisfied with traditional subject matter, based on the

Bible and other literary sources, and either made up their own or turned to such themes as landscape, still life, and scenes from contemporary life. They were increasingly concerned with the "how" rather than the "what" of their work, with its emotional effect or harmony of form rather than the significance of the subject. Thus music (especially in what was then its "purest" form, instrumental music) seemed to them the ideal art, free from any external associations. "All art aspires to the condition of music," as one famous critic put it. Painters began to borrow musical titles for their works, calling them "symphonies," "compositions," "improvisations," until some of them, in the early years of this century, drew the ultimate conclusion and rejected representation altogether as an alien, "literary" element.

The difference between the two subjects of our book, then, is not confined to the quantity and range of the works available to us. Art and music play different roles in our cultural life, past and present, and their historical development follows distinctive patterns, sometimes parallel, sometimes complementary.

There is, finally, a difference in the way the two fields lend themselves to discussion in book form. The art historical section is "fully illustrated"—all the works referred to in the text are reproduced, thirty-one of them in color.

But it was not possible, for obvious reasons, to apply the same rule to music; the musical illustrations on the accompanying phonograph record are necessarily limited in number and physically separate from the book itself. On the other hand, they come infinitely closer to the live experience of music than any color reproduction does to the original work of art, even though most of them are "details"—segments of longer pieces. Our miniature recorded anthology concentrates on those periods of music history that would be hardest for the reader to fill in from his own experience or from his record library; the Middle Ages, the Renaissance, and the twentieth century.

The book can be read with profit, we hope, without the record, but it can be read more profitably with musical illustrations to match the visual ones. Those who obtain the record should supplement it with recordings—many are available—of certain well-known longer compositions discussed in the text. They are Bach's Brandenburg Concerto No. 2; Mozart's *Eine kleine Nachtmusik;* and at least one of the following "second-period" Beethoven works: the *Eroica* Symphony, the Fifth Symphony, the *Appassionata* Sonata, and the *Leonore* Overture No. 3. In addition, lists of records suggested for supplementary listening are added at the end of each section of Book Two.

H. W. J.
J. K.

SYNOPSIS OF
ART AND MUSIC TERMS

The following list of terms is drawn from both parts of this book. Cross references are indicated by words in SMALL CAPITALS. *For further information, the reader should consult the appropriate dictionaries and encyclopedias.*

ABSOLUTE MUSIC. Music having form and expression through exclusively musical (i.e., not ILLUSTRATIONAL) elements; used in contrast to PROGRAM MUSIC.

ABSTRACT, ABSTRACTION. Of or pertaining to the formal aspect of art, emphasizing lines, colors, generalized or geometrical forms, etc., especially with reference to their relationship to one another; pertaining to the non-representational art styles of the twentieth century (*colorplate 30*).

ACADEMY. A learned society. (*Art*) In the Renaissance, art academies were private associations of artists; official academies developed in the seventeenth century with leaders claiming authority in establishing standards, stipulating methods, and specifying types of subject matter. (*Music*) One of the HUMANISTIC societies which fostered the MADRIGAL in sixteenth-century Italy.

ACOUSTICS. The science pertaining to sound; commonly used with reference to the properties of a building or room.

AERIAL PERSPECTIVE: see ATMOSPHERIC PERSPECTIVE.

ALLEGORY. In art, the presentation of one subject under the guise of another, or a symbolic narrative (*fig. 161*).

ALLEGRO (Ital., cheerful). In music, means lively, fast; may refer to the character or speed of a MOVEMENT.

ALLELUIA. An elaborate type of PLAINSONG sung by CHOIR and soloists at MASS (*Recorded Example 1*).

AMBULATORY. A passageway, especially around the CHANCEL of a church. An ambulatory may also be outside a church, as in a CLOISTER.

AMPHORA. A Greek vase having an egg-shaped body, a narrow cylindrical neck, and two curving handles joined to the body at the shoulder and neck.

ANTHEM. A short Anglican church composition.

ANTIPHON. A simple type of PLAINSONG sung at the OFFICE.

APSE. A large semicircular or polygonal niche. See BASILICA.

ARCADE. A series of ARCHES and their supports (*figs. 77, 126*).

ARCH. An architectural construction, often semicircular, built of wedge-shaped blocks (voussoirs) to span an opening; it requires support from walls, piers, or columns, and BUTTRESSING at the sides. The form of the arch may also be derived from the ellipse or parabola.

ARCHAIC. A relatively early style, as Greek sculpture of the seventh and sixth centuries B.C.; or any style adopting characteristics of an earlier period.

ARCHITRAVE. The main horizontal beam, and the lowest part of an ENTABLATURE; i.e., a series of LINTELS, each spanning the space from the top of one support to the next.

ARCHIVOLT. The molding, sometimes multiple, on the face of an ARCH and following its contour. In medieval architecture, their ornamentation may be elaborate (*fig. 75*).

ARIA. In OPERA, ORATORIO, etc., a regular song clearly set off from the rest of the music (*Recorded Example 9*).

ARS ANTIQUA, ARS NOVA (Lat.). Fourteenth-century terms for music from the periods after c. 1250 and after c. 1300 respectively.

ATHEMATIC. Without THEMES.

ATMOSPHERIC PERSPECTIVE. A means of showing distance or depth in a painting by modifying the TONE of objects that are remote from the picture plane, especially by reducing in gradual or marked stages the contrast between lights and darks to a uniform light bluish-gray color; contours may also become less distinct. This technique, also known as AERIAL PERSPECTIVE, was first used systematically by the Van Eycks (*colorplate 12*).

ATONAL (twentieth-century). Not tonal; not composed on the basis of the TONAL SYSTEM.

ATRIUM. The rectangular open court in front of a church, usually surrounded by PORTICOS.

AXIAL PLAN. A PLAN in which the parts of a building are disposed symmetrically on a longitudinal axis.

BALLETT, FA-LA. A type of light, dancelike MADRIGAL (sixteenth century).

BARREL VAULT. A semi-cylindrical VAULT (*colorplate 13; figs. 41, 150*).

BAS RELIEF: see RELIEF.

BASE. The lowest element of a COLUMN, wall, DOME, etc.; occasionally of a statue.

BASILICA, BASILICAN. In the Roman period, the word refers to the function of the building —a large meeting hall—rather than to its form, which may vary according to its use; as an official public building, the Roman basilica had certain religious overtones. It often had, but did not require, a longitudinal axis; its entrance and its APSE (or apses) might be on the long or the short side, or on both. The Early Christian basilica adopted some of these features: the longitudinal axis with oblong plan, the flat timber ceiling, trussed roof, and the terminating tribunal which was rectangular or in the shape of an APSE. The entrance was on one short side (usually west) and the apse projected from the opposite (usually east) side, at the farther end of the building.

BASS. The lowest part of a musical composition; see HARMONIC BASS, also BASSO CONTINUO.

BASSO CONTINUO (Ital.). In Baroque CONTINUO TEXTURE (*diagrams 4, 5*), the BASS line, often provided with numbers to facilitate improvisation of fill-in CHORDS on a HARPSICHORD, LUTE, or ORGAN. Figured bass and thorough-bass are alternate terms.

BAYS. Compartments into which a building may be subdivided, usually formed by the space between consecutive architectural supports (*fig. 74*).

BLIND ARCADE. A decorative ARCADE applied to a wall surface, and having no structural function.

BOOK OF HOURS. A book for individual private devotion with prayers for different hours of the day; frequently elaborately ILLUMINATED, and often presenting local variations (*fig. 112*).

BRASSES. Wind instruments made of metal, such as trumpets, horns, trombones, tubas, as distinguished from WOODWINDS, instruments originally made of wood.

BUFFO BASS. A special type of singer or role developed in eighteenth-century comic OPERA.

BURIN. A pointed steel cutting tool. See ENGRAVING.

BUTTRESS, BUTTRESSING. A masonry support that counteracts the lateral pressure (THRUST) exerted by an ARCH or VAULT. See FLYING BUTTRESS; PIER BUTTRESS.

CACCIA (Ital.), CHACE (Fr.). Fourteenth-century POLYPHONIC hunting song.

CADENCE. The ending of a musical phrase, section, or complete work; more exactly, the pattern of two or three NOTES or CHORDS that gives the feeling of termination. SEMITONE CADENCE; a pattern which has a SEMITONE between its last two notes and which sounds very conclusive (e.g., B → C).

CAMERATA (Ital. *camera*, room). A group of literary men, artists, and musicians who met in Florence shortly before 1600 to discuss a new musical style to be based on ancient Greek drama.

CAMPANILE (Ital.). Bell tower; it can be either freestanding or attached to the building (*figs. 54, 78, 95*).

CANON. (*Art*) A fixed set of proportions for the human figure, to be used as a guiding principle of representation. (*Music*) A POLYPHONIC piece in which the voice-lines have the same MELODY but present it at different times (e.g., the tenor voice following the soprano voice one bar later, with the identical music).

CANTATA (Ital.). A relatively short and semidramatic work resembling an OPERA scene. CHURCH CANTATA: a composition in cantata style for the Lutheran church.

CANTUS FIRMUS (Lat., fixed melody). An existing MELODY used as the basis of a POLYPHONIC composition for contrapuntal voices.

CAPITAL. The crowning member of a COLUMN, PIER, or PILASTER, on which the lowest element of the ENTABLATURE rests. See DORIC COLUMN, IONIC COLUMN, CORINTHIAN COLUMN.

CARVING: see SCULPTURE.

CASTING. A method of reproducing a three-dimensional object or RELIEF (*figs. 71, 131*). Casting in bronze or other metal is often the final stage in the creation of a piece of sculpture; casting in plaster is a convenient and inexpensive way of making a copy of an original. A type of bronze casting is the "lost wax" method (*cire perdu*): this produces a single cast, for in the process both the wax mold and the clay model are destroyed. By using a plaster cast as an intermediate step it is possible to make a number of bronze casts. See SCULPTURE.

CENTRAL PLAN. A PLAN in which the main parts of a building, more or less equal in size, are arranged symmetrically around a given point; an important type of non-basilican church design.

CHAMBER MUSIC. Music for a small group of performers, up to about eight in number; usually one performer to each part.

CHANCEL. In a church, the space reserved for the clergy and CHOIR, set off from the NAVE by steps, and occasionally by a screen.

CHANSON (Fr., song). Usually applied to POLYPHONIC French songs of the fourteenth to sixteenth centuries (*Recorded Example 4*).

CHANT. Unaccompanied musical recitation of certain liturgical texts, mainly on a monotone, with slightly elaborated beginning, ending, and punctuating formulas (end of *Recorded Example 1*). The terms Byzantine chant, Syrian chant, Gregorian chant, etc., are used loosely to denote all the service music—chant and song—employed in the Byzantine, Syrian, and early Roman churches.

CHIAROSCURO (Ital., light and dark). In general, the distribution of lighted and shadowed areas in a painting, drawing, or print (*colorplates 14, 19*). Also used specifically to achieve MODELING (*figs. 138, 167*).

CHOIR. (*Art*) See CHANCEL. (*Music*) A group of church singers, as opposed to a CHORUS; also, the instrumental groups within an ORCHESTRA.

CHORALE (Ger., hymn). Hymn tunes of the German Protestant Church. CHORALE-PRELUDE: a work for organ, incorporating a chorale tune.

CHORD. The simultaneous sounding of two or more NOTES.

CHORUS. A group of secular singers.

CHROMATIC, CHROMATICISM. (*Art*) Coloring; see HUE. (*Music*) Musical style involving extensive and "colorful" use of all twelve NOTES of the CHROMATIC SCALE, i.e., the seven notes of the DIATONIC SCALE plus the five SHARPS and FLATS.

CITTERN. A simple type of LUTE (*colorplate 20*).

CLASSIC. (*Art*) Used specifically to refer to Greek art of the fifth century B.C. (*Music*) Used specifically to refer to music of the eighteenth century A.D.

CLASSICAL. (*Art*) Used generally to refer to the art of the Greeks and the Romans. (*Music*) Used commonly for "traditional music" in opposition to "popular."

CLAVICHORD. A small KEYBOARD instrument, forerunner of the piano; its quite expressive tone is produced by striking the strings with little levers (fifteenth to eighteenth centuries).

CLEF. The sign at the beginning of the STAFF which indicates the PITCH of the NOTES.

CLERESTORY. A row of windows in a wall that rises above the adjoining roof; frequently used in churches having NAVE walls higher than the side aisle roofs (*colorplates 4, 8*).

CLOISTER. A covered passageway around an area or court, open (usually with an ARCADE or COLONNADE) on the sides facing the court; generally located south of the NAVE of a church and west of the TRANSEPT, connecting the church with other parts of an adjoining monastery.

CODA (Ital., tail). Ending section; in particular, the ending section of a SONATO-ALLEGRO FORM.

CODEX. A series of manuscript pages held together by stitching. The codex, the earliest form of the book, gradually replaced the scrolls of earlier times.

COLLAGE. A composition made by pasting cut-up textured materials, such as newsprint, wallpaper, wood veneer, etc., to form all or part of a work of art; may be combined with painted or drawn representations, or with three-dimensional objects (*figs. 246, 254*).

COLONNADE. A series of COLUMNS spanned by LINTELS.

COLOR. In general, a quality of visual phenomena; specifically, the choice and treatment of the HUES in a painted representation. See also VALUE, TINT.

COLORATURA (Ital., colored). Type(s) of singing involving many runs, turns, and other extensive melodic ORNAMENTS.

COLUMN. A vertical architectural support, usually consisting of a BASE (except in the Greek DORIC COLUMN), a rounded SHAFT, and a CAPITAL.

COMPOSITION. (*Art*) The arrangement of FORM, COLOR, CHIAROSCURO, LINE, etc., in any given work of art. (*Music*) In general, any piece of work. In particular, the art of putting together the component parts, such as RHYTHM, MELODY, HARMONY, etc., to form an expressive whole.

CONCERTO. An instrumental composition in which an orchestra is contrasted with a single soloist or small solo group (*Recorded Example 12*). CONCERTO GROSSO: the main Baroque type of concerto, employing a small group of soloists.

CONDUCTUS. A type of "NEW PLAINSONG"; also, a form of twelfth- to thirteenth-century POLYPHONY which is not built on a PLAINSONG (see also ORGANUM).

CONSONANCE, CONCORD. The quality of blending detected by the ear at the simultaneous sounding of pairs of NOTES at certain INTERVALS, i.e., an octave (such as low C and high C) or a fifth (C and G). Note-pairs that do not seem to blend are termed DISSONANT; this is to some degree a relative matter.

CONTINUO: see BASSO CONTINUO.

CONTOUR. The outline of a shape which is drawn to suggest its VOLUME (*colorplates 1, 9, 22*).

CONTRATENOR. One type of voice-line used in fourteenth- and fifteenth-century POLYPHONY.

CORINTHIAN COLUMN. First appeared in fifth-century Greece, apparently as a variation of the IONIC. The CAPITAL differentiates the two: the Corinthian capital has an inverted bell shape, decorated with acanthus leaves, stalks, and volute scrolls. The Corinthian ORDER became increasingly popular after the later fourth century B.C.; it was widely used by the Romans (*figs. 39, 40*).

CORNETTO (Ital.). A wind instrument, somewhat like a recorder with a trumpet mouthpiece (fifteenth to seventeenth centuries).

CORNICE. The crowning, projecting architectural feature, especially the uppermost part of an ENTABLATURE.

COUNTERPOINT. The technique or study of combining voice-lines to make POLYPHONY.

COUNTER REFORMATION. The movement within the Roman Catholic Church which followed the Protestant REFORMATION of the sixteenth century; it had notable effects on the art and music of the time.

CROSSING. In a cruciform church, the area where the NAVE and the TRANSEPT intersect.

CUNEIFORM. The wedge-shaped writing of the Sumerians, Assyro-Babylonians, and other ancient Near Eastern peoples.

CUPOLA. A rounded, convex roof or ceiling, usually hemispherical on a circular BASE. The more or less continuous BUTTRESSING required by a cupola may be provided in a number of different ways.

DA CAPO FORM. The strict A B A form employed in late seventeenth-century ARIAS, etc.

DECLAMATION. The manner of setting words to music; the kinds of RHYTHMS and PITCHES used on the various syllables.

DEVELOPMENT. The second section of the SONATA-ALLEGRO FORM.

DIATONIC SCALE: see SCALE.

DIPTYCH (Gr., two folds). Two panels, often hinged together, designed as a single composition or two related compositions (*colorplate 12*).

DISSONANCE, DISSONANT: see CONSONANCE.

DIVERTIMENTO (Ital., amusement). A light genre of CLASSIC instrumental music.

DOME. A large CUPOLA supported by a circular wall or DRUM (*fig. 40*), or, over a non-circular space, by corner structures (see PENDENTIVES).

DOMINANT. The fifth NOTE of any major or minor DIATONIC SCALE.

DORIC COLUMN. The Doric COLUMN stands without a BASE directly on the top of the stepped platform of a temple. Its SHAFT has twenty shallow FLUTES. The Doric CAPITAL curves outward from the top of the shaft to meet the abacus, a square slab forming the uppermost part of the capital on which the ARCHITRAVE rests (*fig. 27*).

DRAWING. A sketch, design, or representation by lines. Drawings are usually made on paper with pen, pencil, charcoal, pastel, chalk, etc.; these techniques may be combined with brush and ink WASH.

DRONE. A long held NOTE.

DRUM. (*Art*) One of several sections composing the SHAFT of a COLUMN; also, a cylindrical wall supporting a DOME. (*Music*) See PERCUSSION INSTRUMENTS.

DYNAMICS. The expressive design of a musical piece in terms of loudness and softness.

ELEVATION. A schematic drawing of one face of a building, either its FAÇADE or one side.

ENAMEL. A colored glass paste which solidifies when fired at high temperature (*figs. 63, 86*).

ENCAUSTIC. A method of painting in colors mixed with wax and applied with a brush, generally while the mixture is hot. The technique was practiced in ancient times and in the Early Christian period, and has been revived by some modern painters (*fig. 52*).

ENGAGED COLUMN, HALF-COLUMN. A COLUMN that is part of a wall and projects somewhat from it. Such a column often has no structural purpose (*figs. 12, 38*).

ENGRAVING. A design, text, or musical score incised in reverse with a BURIN on a copper plate; this is coated with printer's ink, which remains in the incised lines when the plate is wiped off. Damp paper is placed on the plate, and both are put into a press; the paper soaks up the ink and produces a print of the original. The amount of pressure exerted on the burin determines the thickness of the line on the copper plate (*figs. 119, 134, 161*).

ENSEMBLE. In OPERA, a musical number involving several characters at once (*Recorded Example 14*).

ENTABLATURE. The upper part of an architectural ORDER.

EQUAL TEMPERAMENT. The system of tuning which spaces the twelve NOTES of the CHROMATIC SCALE exactly evenly (eighteenth to twentieth centuries).

ETCHING. Like ENGRAVING, etching is an incising (or intaglio) process. However, the design is drawn in reverse with a needle on a plate (often of copper) thinly coated with wax or resin. The plate is placed in a bath of nitric acid; the etched lines are produced on the plate by the corrosion of the acid where the needle has pierced the coating. Wide tonal variety is made possible by exposing different parts of the plate to the acid for varying lengths of time. The coating is then removed, and the prints are made as in engraving (*fig. 181*).

EXPOSITION. The first section of SONATA-ALLEGRO FORM.

FABURDEN, FAUXBOURDON. A medieval English type of improvised POLYPHONY.

FAÇADE. The front of a building.

FIDDLE. A medieval bowed string instrument, forerunner of the violin.

FIFTH, FIFTHS: see INTERVAL.

FLAT: see NOTE.

FLUTE, FLUTES. (*Art*) Vertical channels on a column SHAFT; see DORIC COLUMN, IONIC COLUMN. (*Music*) Instruments belonging to the WOODWIND group.

FLYING BUTTRESS. An ARCH that springs from the upper part of the PIER BUTTRESS of a Gothic church, spans the aisle roof, and abuts the upper NAVE wall to receive the THRUST from the nave VAULTS; it transmits this thrust to the solid pier buttresses (*fig. 88*).

FORESHORTENING. A method of representing objects as if seen at an angle and receding or projecting into space; not in a frontal or profile view (*colorplate 11; figs. 125, 144*).

FORM. (*Art*) The external shape or appearance of a representation, considered apart from its COLOR or material. (*Music*) The "shape" of music in time; among the shaping elements are repetitions of large sections, CADENCES, THEMES, and TONALITIES; more loosely, a category or type of COMPOSITION, e.g. MOTET, LAUDA, SYMPHONY.

FOURTH, FOURTHS: see INTERVAL.

FREESTANDING. Used of a work of SCULPTURE in the round, i.e., in full three-dimensionality; not attached to architecture and not in RELIEF.

FRENCH OVERTURE: see OVERTURE.

FRESCO (Ital., fresh). Fresco is a technique of wall painting known since antiquity; the PIGMENT is mixed with water and applied to a freshly plastered area of a wall. The result is a particularly permanent form of painted decoration (*colorplates 9, 13*).

FRIEZE. In CLASSICAL architecture and its derivatives, an architectural element that rests on the ARCHITRAVE and is immediately below the CORNICE; also, any horizontal band decorated with moldings, RELIEF sculpture, or painting (*figs. 26, 33*).

FROTTOLA. A type of late fifteenth-century Italian song, largely HARMONIC in style.

FUGAL IMITATION, IMITATION. A POLYPHONIC texture in which melodic fragments are systematically echoed through all the voice-lines (*diagram 3*). POINT OF IMITATION: a section of fugal imitation dealing with a single fragment. FUGUE: a COMPOSITION consisting of fugal imitation on (typically) one MELODIC fragment, the fugue subject, treated at considerable length and often in different ways (*Recorded Example 11*).

FUGUE: see FUGAL IMITATION.

FUNCTION. (*Art*) The use or purpose of a building or object. (*Music*) See TONAL SYSTEM.

GABLE. The triangular part of a wall, enclosed by the lines of a sloping roof. See PEDIMENT.

GENRE (Fr., type, class). (*Art*) Subject matter of a particular type, usually portraying aspects of everyday life. (*Music*) A particular type of COMPOSITION.

GESSO (Ital., plaster). The layer of plaster of Paris used in preparing the ground for a painting in TEMPERA.

GOSPEL. (*Music*) A PROPER section of MASS which is performed in CHANT (end of *Recorded Example 1*).

GOSPELS, GOSPEL book. (*Art*) Contains the four Gospels of the New Testament that tell the life of Christ, ascribed to the evangelists Matthew, Mark, Luke, and John. Often profusely illustrated (*colorplates 5, 6, 7; figs. 65, 69*).

GRADUAL. An elaborate type of PLAINSONG sung by CHOIR and soloists at MASS (*Recorded Example 3*).

GREGORIAN CHANT: see CHANT, PLAINSONG.

GROIN. The sharp edge formed by the intersection of two VAULTS.

GROIN VAULT. A VAULT formed by the intersection at right angles of two BARREL VAULTS of equal height and diameter, so that the GROINS form a diagonal cross.

GROUND PLAN: see PLAN.

HALF-COLUMN: see ENGAGED COLUMN.

HARMONY. A CHORD; the chordal aspect of music, as distinct from the MELODIC or RHYTHMIC. Harmonic style or TEXTURE often refers to one in which the harmonic aspect is stressed over the POLYPHONIC. Thus HARMONIC BASS: a BASS line without autonomous melodic character, that exists merely as a support for CHORDS (eighteenth century), as distinct from BASSO CONTINUO (*diagram 7*).

HARPSICHORD, VIRGINAL. A KEYBOARD instrument, forerunner of the piano; its bright tone is produced by plucking the strings with quills (sixteenth to eighteenth centuries).

HIERATIC. Used of certain styles of art where the type of representation is fixed by religious tradition.

HIEROGLYPHICS. The characters and picture-writing used by the ancient Egyptians.

HUE. The property of COLOR by which the various sections of the visible spectrum are distinguished as red, blue, etc.

HUMANISM, HUMANISTIC. (*Art*) Generally refers to the Renaissance revival of interest in, and study of, Roman and Greek culture (*fig. 136*); its earliest significant appearance is in the fourteenth century. (*Music*) Music of the sixteenth century which shows the influence of this revival.

"IDEALIZED" DANCE: see "STYLIZED" DANCE.

IDÉE FIXE (Fr., fixed idea). A tune recurring in the various MOVEMENTS of a PROGRAM SYMPHONY (e.g., Berlioz), and associated with one main personage in the program.

ILLUMINATION. A term used generally for manuscript paintings. Illuminated manuscripts may contain separate ornamental pages, marginal illustrations, ORNAMENT within the text (e.g., around an initial letter), entire MINIATURE paintings, or any combination of these.

ILLUSIONISM, ILLUSIONISTIC. The effort of an artist to represent the visual world with deceptive reality.

ILLUSTRATION, ILLUSTRATIONAL. (*Art*) The representation of a thought, scene, or text by artistic means. (*Music*) The representation of a thought, scene, or text by musical means; see MADRIGAL, PROGRAM.

IMITATION. see FUGAL IMITATION.

IMPASTO. Paint thickly applied.

INTERVAL. Relation between the PITCHES of two NOTES, expressed either as a ratio of their pitch-frequencies (such as 2 : 3) or by a term indicating the number of DIATONIC SCALE notes comprising them (e.g., THIRD, FOURTH, FIFTH, OCTAVE).

INVERSION. Of a MELODY or TWELVE-TONE series, presented upside down (*diagram 10*). See also RETROGRADE INVERSION.

IONIC COLUMN. The Ionic COLUMN stands on a molded BASE. The SHAFT normally has

twenty-four FLUTES, more deeply cut than Doric flutes. The Ionic CAPITAL is identified by its pair of volute scrolls that extend from the sides of the concave bolster (*fig. 30*).

ISORHYTHM. A fourteenth-century compositional system by which MOTETS were written in several large sections, each section identical or nearly identical in over-all RHYTHM but different in actual NOTES.

JONGLEUR (Fr., juggler). A medieval instrumental musician.

KEY. On harpsichords, pianos, organs, etc., the visible part of the action which the player depresses. Also see TONALITY.

KEYBOARD. The whole set of KEYS on a harpsichord, piano, organ, etc.

KEY-NOTE: see TONIC.

KEYSTONE. The central topmost voussoir of an ARCH, often decorated and usually heavier than the other blocks of the arch.

KITHARA. An ancient (especially Greek) harp-like instrument (*colorplate 2*).

KORE (pl. KORAI; Gr., girl or maiden). Designates an ARCHAIC Greek statue of a draped maiden.

KOUROS (pl. KOUROI; Gr., youth). Designates an ARCHAIC Greek statue of a standing nude youth.

KYLIX. A Greek drinking cup shaped as a shallow bowl with two horizontal handles projecting from the sides; often on a stem terminating in a round foot. The inside of the cup often had fine painted decoration (*fig. 23*).

LANTERN. A small structure crowning a DOME, roof, or tower, with openings to admit light; a lantern may also be erected above the CROSSING of a church.

LAUDA. An Italian popular religious song, especially a late fifteenth-century type.

LEITMOTIF (Ger. *Leitmotiv*, leading motive). An orchestral MOTIF which recurs many times during an OPERA in association with some definite feeling, object, or idea (e.g., Wagner).

LEKYTHOS. In the Greek Classic period, a vase characterized by its cylindrical body curving inward at the foot, which is squat and cylindrical; a tall, thin neck with an inverted bell-shaped lip; one curved handle.

LIBRETTO (Ital., little book). The text of an OPERA or ORATORIO.

LIED (Ger. *Lied*, song). A German song.

LINE. (*Art*) A mark made by a moving tool such as a pen or pencil; more generally, an outline, CONTOUR, or SILHOUETTE. (*Music*) Sequence of NOTES, MELODY.

LINEAR PERSPECTIVE. A mathematical system for representing three-dimensional objects and space on a two-dimensional surface. All objects are represented as seen from a single viewpoint. The system is based on the principle of geometric projection; all lines at right angles to the visual plane appear to converge toward a single point in the distance, the vanishing point (*colorplate 13*).

LINTEL. A horizontal beam that spans an opening; see POST AND LINTEL.

LITURGICAL DRAMA. A type of "NEW PLAINSONG" cast in simple dramatic form.

LITURGY. The ritual or form of public worship.

LUNETTE (Fr. *lune*, moon). A semicircular window or wall space.

LUTE. A guitarlike instrument, especially important in the sixteenth century (*figs. 122, 162*). LUTE AIR: a song accompanied by lute (Elizabethan England).

LYRE. An ancient harplike instrument.

MADRIGAL. A sixteenth-century Italian (or English) song for three to eight voices; half POLYPHONIC and half HARMONIC in style, featuring careful DECLAMATION and word ILLUSTRATION (*Recorded Example 7*).

MAESTÀ (Ital., majesty). A relatively elaborate representation of the Virgin Mary (Madonna) and Child enthroned.

MAJOR, MINOR. Two types of diatonic SCALE, distinguished mainly by their third INTERVAL. In the major scale, this is a major third (i.e., C → E); in the minor scale, this is a minor third (i.e., C → E-flat).

MARIAN. Having to do with the Virgin Mary, in her honor.

MASS. The main Catholic service; music for this service (*Recorded Examples 1, 2, 6, 10*). POLYPHONIC MASS: a musical setting of the five main ORDINARY sections of the Mass (fifteenth and sixteenth centuries).

MASS. The expanse of COLOR that defines a painted shape; the three-dimensional volume of a sculptured or architectural form.

MASTABA. A particular kind of Egyptian Old Kingdom tomb. The portion above ground was generally rectangular in plan, with sloping walls and a flat roof. The interior was solid except for the chapel; below was the burial chamber, reached by a vertical SHAFT.

MAZURKA. A Polish dance "STYLIZED" by Chopin.

MEDIUM. The material with which an artist works, such as marble, TERRACOTTA, OIL PAINT, WATERCOLOR, etc.

MELODY. The aspect of music concerned with the relative PITCH of the NOTES, as distinct from RHYTHM. MELODIC: sometimes means "with a clearly defined melody."

MINIATURE. A painting or drawing in an ILLU-

MINATED manuscript; also a very small portrait, frequently painted on ivory.

MINNESINGERS (Ger. *Minne*, love). German courtly poet-composers of the twelfth to fourteenth centuries.

MINOR: see MAJOR.

MINUET. A seventeenth-century French dance; in "STYLIZED" form, frequently used as a MOVEMENT in the Baroque SUITE, and later as a movement in the Classic SYMPHONY, etc.

MODE, MODAL. (a) MODAL MELODIES: melodies (e.g., PLAINSONG) in which no single note seems very central, at least as compared to TONAL MELODIES. (b) MODAL HARMONY: (sixteenth century) a HARMONIC style in which no single TRIAD seems very central, at least as compared to HARMONY based on the TONAL SYSTEM. (c) MODAL RHYTHM: (twelfth and thirteenth centuries) RHYTHM arranged in one of a few simple standard patterns, called RHYTHMIC MODES.

MODELING. See SCULPTURE. In painting or drawing, the means by which the three-dimensionality of a form is suggested on a two-dimensional surface, usually through variations of COLOR and CHIAROSCURO (*colorplates 13, 20*).

MODULATION. Change of TONALITY in the course of a musical passage or MOVEMENT.

MONUMENTAL. Frequently used to describe works that are larger than lifesize; also used to describe works giving the impression of great size, whatever their actual dimensions.

MOSAIC. A design formed by embedding TESSERAE of stone or glass in cement. In antiquity, large mosaics were used chiefly on floors; from the Early Christian period on, mosaic decoration was increasingly used on walls and vaulted surfaces (*colorplate 4*).

MOTET. Vocal COMPOSITION, typically set to sacred words, having vastly differing characteristics from the thirteenth century to the present (*Recorded Example 5*).

MOTIF. (*Art*) A distinctive and recurrent feature of theme, shape, or figure in a work of art. (*Music*) The smallest coherent musical unit, perhaps no more than two NOTES in a memorable RHYTHM—or four, as in Beethoven's Fifth Symphony (. . . —).

MOVEMENT. (*Art*) In architecture, the planned variety of forms, lines, and decoration of a building (*fig. 173*); in painting and sculpture, the implication of action (*fig. 20*). (*Music*) An autonomous or almost autonomous large section of a multi-sectional work, such as CONCERTO GROSSO, SONATA, or SYMPHONY.

MUSICA FICTA (Lat.). The system by which

medieval and Renaissance performers were expected to supply certain SHARPS and FLATS that were not NOTATED in their music.

MUSICOLOGY. Scholarly research in music and music history.

NARTHEX. The transverse part of a church that forms an entrance; usually having COLONNADES or ARCADES, the narthex may be a vestibule inside the church or a porch in front of the FAÇADE (*fig. 54*).

NATURAL: see NOTE.

NAVE. The central aisle of a BASILICAN church, as distinguished from the side aisles; the part of a church between the main entrance and the CHANCEL.

"NEW PLAINSONG": see PLAINSONG.

NOTATION, NOTATED. A system for preserving music by means of written signs, such as letters, or NOTES on a five-line STAFF.

NOTE. A musical sound of certain PITCH (frequency), such as middle C, and duration; also, the written sign representing this sound. The pitch can be altered in the written sign by adding before it a FLAT (to lower it a half-tone), a SHARP (to raise it a half-tone), or a NATURAL (to remove either a flat or a sharp previously indicated).

OCTAVE: see INTERVAL.

OEUVRE (Fr., work). Used to denote an artist's entire production.

OFFICE. The set of eight monastic daily services (in addition to MASS).

OIL PAINTING. Though known to the Romans, it was not systematically exploited until the fifteenth century. In the oil technique of early Flemish painters, pigments were ground in an oil (linseed or nut) and fused while hot with hard resins; the mixture was then diluted with other oils (*colorplate 12*). Venetian painters later used freer brushwork because they adopted softer resins, but their color was more opaque. Their technique of painting in oil on a prepared canvas, instead of on a wood panel (see TEMPERA), was made possible by these softer resins, for the hard resins required a wooden support prepared with GESSO and glue. Oil technique offered such possibilities as retouching, varied shading, transparent glazes, and IMPASTO (*colorplates 14, 18*).

OPERA. A stage play in or with music. OPERA BUFFA, OPERA COMIQUE: Italian and French types of comic opera (eighteenth to twentieth centuries). OPERA SERIA: an Italian term for eighteenth-century serious operas.

OPUS (Lat.: abbr. OP.). Work; opus numbers are assigned to many composers' work on publication, and then identify them.

ORATORIO. A lengthy work for solo singers, chorus, and ORCHESTRA on a religious subject, using many of the techniques of OPERA although not designed for performances on the stage.

ORCHESTRA. A relatively large group of instrumental players. For the make-up of the Classic orchestra, see diagram 8.

ORDER. In architecture, a CLASSICAL system of proportion and interrelated parts. These include a COLUMN, usually with BASE, SHAFT, and CAPITAL, and an ENTABLATURE with ARCHITRAVE, FRIEZE, and CORNICE.

ORDINARY. A section of the MASS or the OFFICE that remains the same from day to day.

ORGAN. An instrument having a KEYBOARD that operates a series of pipes connected with a wind chest (*fig. 114, right*); this chest is supplied with air by various means.

ORGANIC. In architecture, a design that is an integrated whole and also fulfills the functional requirements of a building. In painting and sculpture, works composed of, or suggesting, irregular shapes that resemble natural forms in an integrated system; often used in contrast to "geometric."

ORGANUM (Lat., organ). An early POLYPHONIC piece, either improvised or composed, in which one or more vocal lines is superimposed upon a PLAINSONG (*Recorded Example 3*).

ORNAMENT, ORNAMENTATION. (*Art*) In particular, the decorative details of a work, especially of architecture. (*Music*) A note or group of notes used as decoration of a principle melodic NOTE, vocal or instrumental. Was originally a spontaneous act on the part of the interpreter.

OVERTURE. In OPERA, ORATORIO, etc., the introductory orchestral number, written in a style that varies greatly over the years. FRENCH OVERTURE: a seventeenth-century type in two sections, the first solemn, the second vigorous.

PAINTING MEDIA: see ENCAUSTIC, FRESCO, OIL PAINTING, TEMPERA, WATERCOLOR.

PARAPHRASE. A free way of treating PLAINSONG within a POLYPHONIC work, whereby the plainsong is decorated with extra NOTES or ORNAMENT, provided with a strict RHYTHM, imitated in other voices, etc. (fifteenth to sixteenth century). PARAPHRASE MASS: A polyphonic MASS using paraphrase technique.

PASSION. A section of certain Easter services in which the story is told of the last days of Christ. (*Art*) Illustrations of this story. (*Music*) A musical setting of such a section.

PEDIMENT. In CLASSICAL architecture; the triangular part of the front or back wall that rises above the ENTABLATURE; it is framed by the horizontal CORNICE and the two raking CORNICES. The pediments at either end of a temple often contained sculpture, in high RELIEF or FREESTANDING (*fig. 29*).

PENDENTIVE. An architectural feature having the shape of a spherical triangle; pendentives are used as a transition from a square GROUND PLAN to a circular PLAN that will support a DOME. The dome may rest directly on the pendentives (*fig. 59*), or indirectly, on an intermediate DRUM.

PERCUSSION INSTRUMENTS. General name for instruments which are sounded by striking or shaking, such as drums and tambourines. Tympani or timpani refer to the big drums or kettledrums.

PERISTYLE. A COLONNADE (or ARCADE) around a building or open court (*figs. 29, 42*).

PERSPECTIVE: see ATMOSPHERIC PERSPECTIVE, LINEAR PERSPECTIVE.

PHRASE. In music, by analogy with speech, a phrase is a small coherent unit—more than a "word" and less than an "sentence."

PIER. A vertical architectural element, usually rectangular in section; if used with an ORDER, often has a BASE and CAPITAL of the same design.

PIER BUTTRESS. An exterior pier in Romanesque and Gothic architecture, buttressing the THRUST of the VAULTS within (*figs. 88, 92*).

PIETA (Ital., compassion). In painting or sculpture, a representation of the Virgin Mary mourning the dead Christ whom she holds (*fig. 102*).

PIGMENT. Dry, powdered substances which, when mixed with a suitable liquid, or vehicle, give color to paint. See OIL PAINTING, FRESCO, ENCAUSTIC, TEMPERA, WATERCOLOR.

PILASTER. A flat vertical element having a CAPITAL and BASE, engaged in a wall from which it projects. Has a decorative rather than a structural purpose (*fig. 128*).

PITCH. "Highness" or "lowness" of a musical sound, measured by the actual frequency of the sound waves (e.g., 440 cycles per second) or by the location of the sound on a total SCALE such as a piano KEYBOARD.

PIZZICATO (Ital.). Plucked with a finger; refers to the playing of a stringed instrument that normally is bowed, such as a violin (*Recorded Example 20*).

PLAINSONG. The unaccompanied service music of the Early Christian and medieval periods, comprising both CHANT and the elaborate songs such as ALLELUIAS, etc. "NEW PLAIN-

SONG": the plainsong composed after c. 850 A.D. (SEQUENCE, TROPE, etc.).

PLAN. The schematic representation of a three-dimensional structure, such as a building or monument, on a two-dimensional plane. A GROUND PLAN shows the outline shape at the ground level of a given building and the location of its various interior parts.

POINT OF IMITATION: see FUGAL IMITATION.

POLYPHONY, POLYPHONIC. Music or musical TEXTURE with two or more simultaneous voice-lines rationally ordered together.

POLYPTYCH: see TRIPTYCH.

PORTAL. An imposing doorway with elaborate ORNAMENTATION in Romanesque and Gothic churches (*fig. 98*).

PORTICO. A covered entrance or vestibule, the roof supported on at least one side by a COLONNADE or ARCADE.

POST AND LINTEL. A system or unit of construction consisting solely of vertical and horizontal elements (*fig. 5*): vertical supports (posts) carry horizontal beams (LINTELS).

PROGRAM. An explicit nonmusical idea, story, poem, etc., which an instrumental COMPOSITION depicts, illustrates, or expresses in some way. Thus, the program music and program symphony of the nineteenth century.

PROPER. The sections of the MASS or the OFFICE that are changed from day to day.

PROPORTION, PROPORTIONS. (*Art*) The relation or numerical ratio of the size of any part of a figure or object to the size of the whole. For the representational arts, see CANON; for architecture, see ORDER. (*Music*) The Pythagorean system of numerical relationships governing INTERVALS, esp. the octave, fifth, and fourth. Also, the system in musical NOTATION of diminishing or augmenting the VALUE of notes by arithmetical ratio.

QUARTET. A combination of four instruments; a work written for four instruments; a concert group of four players. Similarly TRIO, QUINTET, SEXTET, SEPTET, OCTET (*diagram 8*). Quartet is often used to mean "string quartet," the main CLASSIC chamber-music arrangement: violin, violin, viola, cello (*Recorded Examples 13, 20*).

RECAPITULATION. The third section of SONATA-ALLEGRO FORM.

RECITATIVE. A type of musical DECLAMATION, for OPERA, etc., which follows the accent of the words at the expense of purely MELODIC, HARMONIC and RHYTHMIC factors. SECCO RECITATIVE: recitative accompanied only by BASSO CONTINUO and fill-in CHORDS.

REFORMATION. The sixteenth-century religious movement for the reform of the Catholic

Church which led to the establishment of the Protestant Church; it had notable effects on art and music.

RELIEF. Forms in SCULPTURE that project from the background, to which they remain attached. Relief may be carved or modeled shallowly to produce low or bas relief (*fig. 19*), or deeply to produce high relief (*fig. 49*); in very high relief, portions may be entirely detached from the background.

REPRESENTATIONAL. As opposed to ABSTRACT, means a portrayal of an object in recognizable form.

RESPONSORY. An elaborate type of PLAINSONG sung by CHOIR and soloists at the OFFICE.

RETROGRADE. Of a MELODY or a TWELVE-TONE SERIES, presented backward; RETROGRADE INVERSION: presented backward and upside down (*diagram 10*).

RHAPSODY, RHAPSODIC: music relatively free in form.

RHYTHM, RHYTHMIC. (*Art*) The regular repetition of a particular form (*colorplate 30*); also, the suggestion of motion by recurrent forms (*colorplate 31*). (*Music*) The aspect of music concerned with the relative duration of the NOTES, as distinct from MELODY. Rhythmic sometimes means "with a clearly defined rhythm." FREE RHYTHM (as in *plainsong*): rhythm that is not specified by the composer, and can therefore vary within certain limits from performance to performance.

RHYTHMIC MODE: see MODE, MODAL.

RIBBED VAULT. A compound masonry VAULT, the GROINS of which are marked by projecting stone ribs (*fig. 89*).

RUSTICATED STONE. Masonry having indented joinings and, frequently, a roughened surface (*fig. 97*).

SARCOPHAGUS (pl. SARCOPHAGI). A coffin made of stone, marble, terracotta (less frequently, of metal). Sarcophagi are often decorated with paintings or RELIEF (*fig. 57*).

SCALE (Lat. *scala*, ladder, staircase). (*Art*) Generally, the relative size of any object in a work of art, often used with reference to normal human scale; more particularly, a graduated line on a PLAN that shows the PROPORTION which the represented object bears to the original. (*Music*) An artificial (and usually traditional) selection of a number of PITCHES, ranged from low to high, which serves as the basic material for music of a certain broad type. Most Western music is based on the DIATONIC SCALE, which is most easily identified in terms of the white notes on the piano KEYBOARD—C, D, E, F, G, A, B (see also MAJOR, MINOR). WHOLE-

TONE SCALE: experimental scale consisting of the notes C, D, E, F-sharp, G-sharp, A-sharp (Debussy). See also CHROMATIC SCALE.

SCHERZO (Ital., joke). A brusque, jocular type of MOVEMENT developed by Beethoven out of the MINUET.

SCULPTURE. The creation of a three-dimensional form, usually in a solid material. Traditionally, two basic techniques have been used: carving in a hard material (*fig. 142*), and MODELING in a soft material such as clay, wax, etc. Modeled sculpture is rendered permanent by a variety of suitable methods, the most common being firing (see TERRACOTTA) or CASTING in molten metal (*fig. 124*). For types of sculpture, see FREESTANDING and RELIEF.

SECCO RECITATIVE: see RECITATIVE.

SEMITONE. The (equal) INTERVAL between any note on the piano KEYBOARD and the next one, up or down, black or white (e.g., B→C).

SEMITONE CADENCE: see CADENCE.

SEQUENCE, SEQUENTIA (Lat.). A type of "NEW PLAINSONG" (*Recorded Example 2*).

SERENADE. A light GENRE of CLASSIC instrumental music.

SERIAL. Arranged in a series, as NOTES are in the TWELVE-TONE SYSTEM; but serial usually means such arrangement of additional musical elements (RHYTHMS, TIMBRES, etc.).

SERIES. (*Art*) A successive group of works. (*Music*) In the TWELVE-TONE SYSTEM, a fixed ordering of the twelve NOTES of the SCALE; in composing, notes are used only in the order of the series, also in INVERSION, RETROGRADE, or RETROGRADE INVERSION (*diagram 10*).

SHAFT. A cylindrical form; in architecture, the part of a COLUMN or PIER intervening between the BASE and the CAPITAL. Also, a vertical enclosed space, as in a MASTABA.

SHARP: see NOTE.

SILHOUETTE. The outline of any given object or a portrait made by tracing the outline, and, occasionally, filling in the whole with black.

SINFONIA (Ital.). The eighteenth-century type of OVERTURE, the forerunner of the Classic SYMPHONY.

SINGSPIEL. German comic OPERA.

SONATA. A work for one or several instruments (but restricted, after the CLASSIC period, to works for one or for two) written in a style that varies greatly from the seventeenth century to the present, but generally in two to four MOVEMENTS.

SONATA-ALLEGRO FORM. The chief form of

CLASSIC music. Consists normally of the EX-POSITION, DEVELOPMENT, RECAPITULATION, and CODA.

SONG-CYCLE. A group of songs linked together by some sort of literary (perhaps also musical) continuity (nineteenth and twentieth centuries).

STAFF. In present-day usage, a set of five horizontal lines upon and between which musical NOTES are written.

STAINED GLASS. The technique of filling architectural openings with glass colored by fused metallic oxides; pieces of this glass are held in a design by strips of lead (fig. 107).

STELE. An upright commemorative slab, bearing either an inscription or a representational relief, or both (fig. 18).

STILE RAPPRESENTATIVO (Ital.). An early seventeenth-century term for RECITATIVE style.

STILL LIFE. A painting or drawing of an arrangement of inanimate objects (colorplate 24; figs. 183, 194).

STRING QUARTET: see QUARTET.

STRINGS: In the modern ORCHESTRA, the four chief members of the violin family: violin, viola, violoncello, and double bass.

"STYLIZED" DANCE, "IDEALIZED" DANCE. A sophisticated COMPOSITION based on a particular dance, evoking its RHYTHMS, mood, pattern of repetitions, etc.

SUBDOMINANT. The fourth NOTE of any major or minor DIATONIC SCALE.

SUBJECT. (Art) Often termed subject matter; that which is represented in a work of art. (Music) See FUGAL IMITATION.

SUITE. A conventionalized grouping of several "STYLIZED" DANCES to form a larger COMPOSITION.

SYMPHONIC POEM. An orchestral composition based on a PROGRAM, usually in one long MOVEMENT (nineteenth century).

SYMPHONY. A large orchestral composition in several MOVEMENTS (eighteenth to twentieth centuries).

TECHNIQUE. (Art) The method, and often the medium, used by the artist. (Music) The skill of the performer, whether vocal or instrumental.

TEMPERA. A painting process distinguished by its binding medium for the PIGMENT, which is an emulsion of egg yolk and water, or egg and oil. Before tempera is applied to a wooden panel, the panel surface must be prepared with a covering of GESSO mixed with glue or gelatine, followed by layers of smooth gesso (fig. 110). Tempera, the basic technique of medieval and Early Renais-sance painters, dries quickly, permitting almost immediate application of the next layer of paint. A disadvantage in comparison with OIL PAINTING is the difficulty of fusing tones.

TENOR MASS. A POLYPHONIC MASS constructed over a tune repeated (usually in long NOTES) in the tenor voice (fifteenth century).

TERRACOTTA (Ital., baked clay). Clay, modeled or molded, and fired until very hard. Used in architecture for functional and decorative parts, as well as for pottery and SCULPTURE (fig. 206). Terracotta may have a painted or glazed surface.

TESSERA (Lat., pl. TESSERAE). A small piece or pieces of marble, colored glass, or gold-backed glass, usually of square or almost square shape with a flat face; used in making MOSAICS.

TEXTING. A process whereby words are added to the long COLORATURA passages of earlier music, such as PLAINSONG or ORGANUM.

TEXTURE. (Art) The surface structure of a work of art, or the simulation in paint, stone, or other media of the drapery, skin, etc., of the object represented (figs. 164, 170). (Music) The "weave" of POLYPHONIC music, the way the simultaneous voice-lines or "threads" are combined and related (diagrams 1–5, 7).

THEME. (Art) The general subject of the COMPOSITION. (Music) A musical unit, ranging in extent from a small MOTIF to an entire tune, which is treated extensively, restated, developed, etc., in the course of a COMPOSITION.

THIRD, THIRDS: see INTERVAL.

THRUST. The lateral pressure exerted by an ARCH or VAULT, and requiring BUTTRESSING.

TIMBRE. The characteristic quality of the sound produced by a particular voice or instrument.

TINT. Generally, color, but more specifically, a color lightened by mixing it with white.

TOCCATA (Ital. toccare, to touch). A RHAPSODIC work designed to show the characteristics of the ORGAN, HARPSICHORD, or sometimes the LUTE.

TONAL SYSTEM. The system developed in the Baroque period whereby all NOTES and TRIADS are felt to be strongly interrelated, each having its particular function with respect to a central note, the TONIC (diagram 6); it is less an abstract "system" than it is a basis for composing that reflects a certain way of hearing notes and HARMONIES. TONAL MELODY and TONAL HARMONY: MELODY and HARMONY in which one note or triad seems very central, as distinct from MODAL MELODY and MODAL HARMONY.

TONALITY. In the TONAL SYSTEM, the set of re-lationships around one particular NOTE, as distinct from the analogous set around some other note. Thus one can MODULATE from the tonality of C to the tonality of G.

TONE. (*Art*) In general a color, but more specifically an over-all VALUE or shade. (*Music*) A musical sound having a definable PITCH.

TONIC. The first note of any major or minor DIATONIC SCALE, hence the KEY-NOTE.

TRACERY. The ornamental stonework filling all or part of a Gothic window, made of various elements combined to create patterns (*fig. 91*).

TRANSEPT. In a cruciform church, an arm forming a right angle with the NAVE, usually inserted between the latter and the CHANCEL, or APSE (*fig. 73*).

TRIAD. A CHORD of three NOTES (and their OCTAVES *ad lib.*), none of which are adjacent, e.g., C E G, or D F A, or B D F.

TRIO SONATA: see TRIO TEXTURE.

TRIO TEXTURE. An important Baroque TEXTURE involving two similar high instruments (violins, etc.) or voices over a BASSO CONTINUO and fill-in CHORDS (*diagram 4*). Note that four, not three, musicians are required. TRIO SONATA: a Baroque instrumental form in several MOVEMENTS employing trio texture. For a more general use of the term "trio," see QUARTET.

TRIPTYCH (Gr., three folds). Three panels designed as a single composition or three related compositions; it has a large center panel, and two side panels half the size of the center panel (*figs. 110, 243*); occasionally the side panels can be folded to cover the center panel (*colorplate 16; fig. 120*). A work composed of more than three panels is known as a POLYPTYCH (Gr., many folds).

TROPE. (*noun*) A type of "NEW PLAINSONG" that is inserted into an older, established PLAINSONG; (*verb*) To insert words and/or music into an older text.

TROUBADOURS, TROUVÈRES. Courtly poet-composers of southern and northern France respectively (twelfth and thirteenth centuries).

TRUMEAU. A supportive PIER in the center of a Romanesque or Gothic PORTAL, often decorated with RELIEF or a figure (*fig. 80*).

TWELVE-TONE SYSTEM, TWELVE-TONE TECHNIQUE. The basis for composing developed by Schoenberg in place of the TONAL SYSTEM, involving the twelve-tone series or row; see SERIES.

TYMPANUM. (*Art*) The space above the LIN-TEL and enclosed by the ARCH (and ARCHIVOLTS) of a medieval PORTAL or doorway; a church tympanum frequently contains RELIEF sculpture. (*Music*) See PERCUSSION INSTRUMENTS.

VALUE. (*Art*) Degree of lightness or darkness in a color. (*Music*) The relative duration of a TONE.

VARIATION. A musical technique whereby a single element—a tune or a bass MOTIF—is repeated several times, each time with changes that modify its nature but do not entirely obscure it (seventeenth to twentieth centuries).

VAULT. An arched roof or covering, made of brick, stone, or concrete. See BARREL VAULT, GROIN VAULT, RIBBED VAULT.

VERSUS (Lat.) A type of "NEW PLAINSONG"; see PLAINSONG.

VESPERS. One of the main OFFICE services.

VIOL. A bowed string instrument in one of several sizes, forerunner of the violin family (fifteenth to seventeenth centuries; *fig. 114, right*).

VIOLA DA GAMBA. The BASS member of the VIOL family.

VIRGINAL: see HARPSICHORD.

VOLUME. (*Art*) Used to describe the three-dimensional quality, solid or hollow, of a work of art. (*Music*) The degree of loudness of sound; see DYNAMICS.

VOUSSOIR: see ARCH.

WASH. Used especially in WATERCOLOR and brush DRAWING to describe a broad thin layer of highly diluted PIGMENT or ink. Also refers to a drawing made in this technique (*fig. 187*).

WATERCOLOR. PIGMENTS mixed with water instead of oil or other media, or a picture painted with watercolor, often on paper.

WHOLE-TONE SCALE: see SCALE.

WOODCUT. A printing process in which a design or lettering is carved in relief on a wooden block; the areas intended not to print off (i.e., to remain white) are hollowed out (*figs. 118, 162, 232*).

WOODWINDS. Wind instruments originally made of wood, such as FLUTES, clarinets, and oboes, as distinguished from BRASSES, those invariably made of metal.

ZIGGURAT (Assyrian–Babylonian *ziqquratu*, mountain top). An elevated platform, varying in height from several feet to the size of an artificial mountain, built by the Sumerians to support their shrines. Later ziggurats were staged towers, with the shrine on top of the uppermost stage (e.g., the Tower of Babel).

BOOK ONE

ART

by H. W. Janson

ART IN THE ANCIENT WORLD

1. THE ART OF PREHISTORIC MAN

When did man start creating works of art? What did they look like? What prompted him to do so? Every history of art must begin with these questions—and with the admission that we cannot answer them. Our earliest ancestors began to walk on the earth with two feet more than a million years ago, but not until some six hundred thousand years later do we meet the earliest traces of man the toolmaker. He must have been *using* tools all along, for apes will pick up a stick to knock down a banana, or a stone to throw at an enemy. The *making* of tools is a more complex matter. It demands first of all the ability to think of sticks or stones as "fruit knockers" or "bone crackers" even at times when they are not needed for such purposes. Once man was able to do that, he discovered that some sticks and stones had a handier shape than others and put them aside for future use—he "appointed" them as tools because he had begun to link *form* and *function*. Some of these stones have survived; they are large pebbles or chunks of rock showing the marks of repeated use for the same operation, whatever that may have been. The next step was for man to try chipping away at these tools-by-appointment so as to improve their shape. This is the earliest craft of which we have evidence, and with it we enter a phase of human development known as the Old Stone Age.

It is during the late stages of the Old Stone Age, some twenty thousand years ago, that we encounter the earliest works of art known to us. These, however, already show an assurance and refinement far removed from any humble beginnings; they must have been preceded by thousands of years of slow growth about which we know nothing at all. At that time, the last Ice Age was drawing to a close in Europe, and the climate between the Alps and Scandinavia resembled that of present-day Alaska. Reindeer and other large herbivores roamed the plains and valleys, preyed upon by the ancestors of today's lions and tigers—and by our own ancestors. These men lived in caves or in the shelter of overhanging rocks. Many such sites have been discovered, and scholars have divided up the "cavemen" into several groups, each named after a characteristic site. Among these it is the so-called Aurignacians and Magdalenians who stand out as especially gifted artists.

The most striking works of Old Stone Age art are the images of animals painted on the rock surfaces of caves, such as those in the cave of Lascaux, in the Dordogne region of France (fig. 1). Bison, deer, horses, and cattle race across walls and ceiling in wild profusion, some simply outlined in black, others filled in with bright earth colors, but all showing the same uncanny sense of life. Even more impressive is the *Wounded Bison* on the ceiling of the cave at Altamira in northern Spain (fig. 2): the dying animal has collapsed, yet even in this helpless state it has lowered its head in self-defense. We are amazed not only by the keen observation, the assured, vigorous outlines, the subtly controlled shading that lends bulk and roundness to the forms, but even more perhaps by the power and dignity of this creature in its final agony.

How did this art develop? What purpose did it serve? And how did it happen to survive intact over so many thousands of years? The last question can be answered readily enough: the pictures rarely occur near the mouth of a cave, where they would be open to easy view (and destruction), but only in the darkest recesses, as far from the entrance as possible. Hidden away as they are in the bowels of the earth, these images must have served a purpose far more serious than mere decoration. There can be little doubt, in fact, that they were part of a magic ritual to ensure a successful hunt. We gather this not only from their secret location and from the lines representing spears or darts that are often found pointing at the animals, but also from the disorderly way the images are

1. *Frieze of Animals* (wall painting). c.15,000–10,000 B.C. Cave of Lascaux (Dordogne), France

superimposed on each other (as in fig. 1). Apparently, for the men of the Old Stone Age there was no clear distinction between image and reality; by making a picture of an animal they meant to bring the animal itself within their grasp, and in "killing" the image they thought they had killed the animal's vital spirit. Hence every image could serve only once—when the killing ritual had been performed, it was "dead" and could be disregarded. The magic worked, too, we may be sure. Hunters whose courage was thus fortified were bound to be more successful when slaying these formidable beasts with their primitive weapons. Nor has the emotional basis for this kind of magic been lost even today; people have been known to tear up the photograph of someone they have come to hate.

Still, there remains a good deal that puzzles us about the cave paintings. Why are they in such inaccessible places? And why are they so marvelously lifelike? Could not the "killing" magic have been practiced just as effectively on less realistic images? Perhaps the Magdalenian cave pictures are the final phase of a develop-

ment that began as simple killing magic but shifted its meaning when the animals became scarce (apparently the big herds withdrew northward as the climate of Central Europe grew warmer). If so, the main purpose of the Lascaux and Altamira paintings may have been not to "kill" but to "make" animals—to increase their supply. Could it be that the Magdalenians had to practice their fertility magic in the bowels of the earth because they thought of the earth itself as a living thing from whose womb all other life springs? This would help to explain the admirable realism of these images, for an artist who believes he is actually "creating" an animal is more likely to strive for this quality than one who merely sets up an image for the kill. Some of the cave pictures even provide a clue to the origin of this fertility magic: the shape of the animal often seems to have been suggested by the natural formation of the rock, so that its body coincides with a bump or its contour follows a vein or crack. We all know how our imagination can make us see all sorts of images in chance shapes such as clouds or ink blots. A Stone Age hunter, his mind filled with thoughts of the big game on which he depended for survival, would have been quite likely to recognize such animals among the rock surfaces of his cave and to attribute deep significance to his discovery. It is tempting to think that those who were particularly good at finding such images gained a special status as artist-magicians and were permitted to perfect their image hunting instead of having to face the dangers of the real hunt, until finally they learned to make images with little or no aid from chance formations.

Apart from large-scale cave art, Old Stone Age men also produced small hand-size carvings in bone, horn, or stone, cut by means of flint tools. They, too, seem to have originated with chance resemblances. At an earlier stage, Stone Age men had been content to collect pebbles in whose natural shape they saw a "magic" representational quality; the more

2. *Wounded Bison* (ceiling painting). c.15,000–10,000 B.C. Cave of Altamira (Santander), Spain

fully worked pieces of later times still reflect this attitude. Thus the so-called *Venus of Willendorf* in Austria (fig. 3), one of several such fertility figurines, has a bulbous roundness of form that may suggest an egg-shaped "sacred pebble."

The art of the Old Stone Age in Europe marks the highest achievement of a way of life that could not survive beyond the special conditions created by the receding ice of the Ice Age which was ending. Between c. 10,000 and 5,000 B.C., the Old Stone Age gave way to new developments, except in a few particularly inhospitable areas where it continued because there was nothing to challenge or disturb it. The Bushmen of South Africa and the aborigines of Australia are living remnants of this primeval mode of existence. Even their art has the flavor of the Old Stone Age; the painting on tree bark from North Australia (fig. 4), while far less skillful than the cave pictures of Europe, shows a similar interest in movement and a keen observation of detail (including an "x-ray view" of the inner organs), only here it is kangaroos on which the hunting magic is being practiced.

3. *Venus of Willendorf.* c.15,000–10,000 B.C. Stone, height 4⅜". Museum of Natural History, Vienna

The Old Stone Age came to an end when men made their first successful attempts to domesticate animals and food grains—one of the truly revolutionary steps in human history, even though the revolution extended over several thousand years. Old Stone Age man had led the unsettled life of a hunter and food gatherer, reaping where nature sowed and thus at the mercy of forces he could neither understand nor control. Once men had learned how to assure their food supply by their own efforts, they settled down in permanent village communities; a new discipline and order entered their lives. There is, then, a basic difference between the New Stone Age and the Old, even though men still depended on stone as the material of their main tools and weapons. The new mode of life brought forth a number of new crafts and inventions long before the earliest appearance of metals: pottery, weaving and spinning, basic methods of architectural construction. We know all this from New Stone Age settlements that have been uncovered by excavation. But these remains tell us very little, as a rule, of the spiritual condition of New Stone Age men; they include stone implements of ever greater technical refinement and a vast variety of clay vessels covered with abstract ornamental patterns, but hardly anything comparable to the art of the Old Stone Age. Yet the change-over from hunting to husbandry must have brought about profound changes in man's view of himself and

4. *A Spirit Man Spearing Kangaroos.* Aboriginal painting on tree bark, c.1900 A.D. Western Arnhem Land, North Australia

the world, and it seems hard to believe that these did not find expression in art. There may be a vast chapter in the development of art here that is lost simply because New Stone Age artists worked in wood and other impermanent materials.

One exception to this general rule is the great stone circle at Stonehenge in southern England (fig. 5), the best preserved of several such megalithic, or "large stone," monuments. Its purpose was religious; apparently the sustained effort required to build it could be compelled only by faith—a faith that almost literally demanded the moving of mountains. The entire structure is oriented toward the exact point where the sun rises on the longest day of the year, and therefore it must have served a sun-worshiping ritual. Even today, Stonehenge has an awe-inspiring, superhuman quality, as if it were the work of a forgotten race of giants. Whether a monument such as this should be termed architecture is a matter of definition: we tend to think of architecture in terms of enclosed interiors, yet we also have landscape architects, the designers of parks and gardens; nor would we want to deny the status of architecture to open-air theaters or stadiums. Perhaps we ought to consult the ancient Greeks, who coined the word. To them, "archi-tecture" meant something higher than ordinary "tecture" (that is, "construction," or "building"), a structure set apart from the merely practical, everyday kind by its scale, order, permanence, or solemnity of purpose. A Greek would certainly have called Stonehenge architecture. And we, too, shall have no difficulty in doing so once we understand that it is not necessary to *enclose* space in order to define or articulate it. If architecture is "the art of shaping space to human needs and aspirations," then Stonehenge more than meets the test.

There are, as we saw, a few human groups for whom the Old Stone Age lasted until the present day. Modern survivors of the New Stone Age are far easier to find. They include all of the so-called primitive societies of tropical Africa, the Americas, and the South Pacific. "Primitive" is an unfortunate word: it suggests —quite wrongly—that these societies represent the original condition of mankind, and has thus come to be burdened with all sorts of emotional overtones. Still, no other single term will do better. Let us continue, then, to use primitive as a convenient label for a way of life that has passed through the hunting-to-husbandry revolution but shows no signs of developing into a "historic" civilization. Primitive societies are essentially rural and self-sufficient; their social and political units are the village and the tribe rather than the city and the state; they perpetuate themselves by custom and tradition, without the aid of written records, and thus have little awareness of their own history. The entire pattern of primitive life is static rather than dynamic, without the inner drive for change and expansion that we take for granted in our own society. Primitive societies tend to be strongly isolationist and defensive toward outsiders; theirs is a stable but precarious balance of man and his environment, ill equipped to survive contact with urban civilizations. While most of them have proved tragically helpless against encroachment by the West, the cultural heritage of primitive man has enriched our own; his customs and beliefs, his folklore, and his music have been recorded by ethnologists, and primitive art is being collected avidly throughout the Western world.

The rewards of this interest in primitive man have been manifold. Among them is a better understanding of the origins of our own culture. Although the materials on which we base our knowledge of primitive society and its ways are usually of quite recent date, they offer striking analogies with the New Stone Age of the distant past. Primitive art, despite its limitless variety, shares one dominant trait: the imaginative reshaping, rather than the careful observation, of the forms of nature. Its concern is not the visible world but the invisible, disquieting world of spirits. To the primitive mind, everything is alive with powerful spirits—men, animals, plants, the earth, rivers and lakes, the

5. Stonehenge. c.1800–1400 B.C.
Diameter of circle 97', height of stones above
ground 13½'. Salisbury Plain (Wiltshire), England

6. *Male Figure Surmounted by a Bird,*
from the Sepik River, New Guinea.
19th–20th century A.D. Wood, height 48″.
Washington University Art Collection, St. Louis

rain, the wind, sun and moon. All these spirits had to be appeased, and it was the task of art to provide suitable dwelling places for them and thus to "trap" them. Such a trap is the splendid ancestor figure from New Guinea (fig. 6). It belongs to a large class of similar objects, ancestor worship being perhaps the most persistent feature of primitive society. The entire design is centered on the head, with its intensely staring shell-eyes, while the body—as in primitive art generally—has been reduced to a mere support. The bird emerging from behind the head represents the ancestor's spirit or life force. Its soaring movement, contrasted with the rigidity of the human figure, forms a compelling image—and a strangely familiar one, for our own tradition, too, includes the "soul bird," from the dove of the Holy Spirit to the albatross of the Ancient Mariner, so that we find ourselves responding, almost against our will, to a work of art that at first glance might seem both puzzling and repellent.

In dealing with the spirit world, primitive man was not content to do rituals or to present offerings before his spirit traps. He needed to act out his relations with the spirit world through dances and similar dramatic ceremonials in which he himself could temporarily assume the role of the spirit trap by disguising himself with elaborate masks and costumes. Nor has the fascination of the mask died out even today; we still feel the thrill of a real change of identity when we wear one at Hal-

loween or carnival time. Masks form by far the richest chapter in primitive art, and one of the most puzzling. Their meaning is often impossible to ascertain, since the ceremonies they served usually had elements of secrecy that were jealously guarded from the uninitiated. This emphasis on the mysterious and spectacular not only heightened the emotional impact of the ritual, it also encouraged the makers of masks to strive for imaginative new effects, so that masks in general are less bound by tradition than other kinds of primitive art. Our example (fig. 7) shows the symmetry of design and the precision and sharpness of carving characteristic of African sculpture. The features of the human face have not been rearranged but restructured, as it were, with the tremendous eyebrows arching above the rest like a protective canopy.

Compared to sculpture, painting plays a subordinate role in primitive society. Although widely used to color wood carvings or the human body, sometimes with intricate ornamental patterns (see fig. 6), it could establish itself as an independent art only under exceptional conditions. Thus the Indian tribes inhabiting the arid Southwest of the United States

7. Mask, from the Bamenda area, Cameroons.
19th–20th century A.D. Wood, height 26½″.
Rietberg Museum, Zurich (E. v.d.Heydt Collection)

8. Sand Painting Ritual for a Sick Child (Navaho). Arizona

developed the unique art of sand painting (fig. 8). The technique, which demands considerable skill, consists of pouring powdered rock or earth of various colors on a flat bed of sand. Despite (or perhaps because of) the fact that these pictures are impermanent and must be made fresh for each occasion, the designs are rigidly traditional; they are also rather abstract, like any fixed pattern that is endlessly repeated. The compositions may be likened to recipes, prescribed by the medicine man and "filled" under his supervision by the painter, for the main use of sand paintings is in ceremonies of healing. That these are sessions of great emotional intensity on the part of both doctor and patient is well attested by our illustration. Such a close union—or even, at times, identity—of priest, healer, and artist may be difficult to understand today. (Or could it be that all these qualities are present to some degree in the personality and work of Sigmund Freud?) But to primitive man, trying to bend nature to his needs by magic and ritual, the three functions must have appeared as different aspects of a single process. And the success or failure of that process was to him quite literally a matter of life and death.

2. EGYPT AND THE ANCIENT NEAR EAST

History, we are often told, begins with the invention of writing, some five thousand years ago. This makes a convenient landmark, for the absence of written records is surely one of the key differences between prehistoric and historic societies, but it also raises some intriguing problems. How valid is the distinction between "prehistoric" and "historic"? Does it merely reflect a difference in our *knowledge* of the past, or was there a genuine change in the way things happened (or the kinds of things that

happened) after "history" began? Obviously, prehistory was far from uneventful: the road from hunting to husbandry is a long and arduous one. Yet these changes in man's condition, decisive though they are, seem incredibly slow-paced when measured against the events of the past five thousand years. The beginning of history, then, means a sudden increase in the speed of events, a shifting from low into high gear. And we shall see that it also means a change in the *kinds* of events.

Prehistory might be defined as that phase of human evolution during which man as a species learned how to survive in a hostile environment; his achievements were responses to threats of physical extinction. With the domestication of animals and food plants, he had won a decisive battle in this war. But the hunting-to-husbandry revolution placed him on a level at which he might well have remained indefinitely, and in many parts of the globe man was content to stay there. In a few places, however, the balance of primitive society was upset by a new threat, posed not by nature but by man himself: competition for grazing land among tribes of herdsmen or for arable soil among farming communities. In these areas, apparently, the hunting-to-husbandry revolution had been too successful, so that the local population grew beyond the available food supply. Such a situation might be resolved in one of two ways: constant tribal warfare could reduce the population, or the people could unite in larger and more disciplined social units for the sake of group efforts (such as building fortifications, dams, or irrigation canals) that no loosely organized tribal society would have been able to achieve. Conflicts of this kind arose in the Nile valley and that of the Tigris and Euphrates some six thousand years ago and generated enough pressure to produce a new kind of society, very much more complex and efficient than had ever existed before. These societies quite literally *made* history; they not only brought forth "great men and great deeds" but also made them *memorable*. (To be memorable, an event has to be more than "worth remembering"; it must happen quickly enough to be grasped by man's memory. Prehistoric events were too slow-paced for that.) From then on, men were to live in a new, dynamic world where their capacity to survive was threatened not by the forces of nature but by conflicts arising either within society or through competition between societies. These efforts to cope with his human environment have proved a far greater challenge to man than his struggle with nature; they are the cause of the ever-quickening pace of events during the past five thousand years. The invention of writing was an early and indispensable achievement of the historic civilizations of Egypt and Mesopotamia. We do not know the beginnings of its development, but it must have taken several centuries after the new societies were already past their first stage. History was well under way by the time writing could be used to record historic events.

Egyptian civilization has long been regarded as the most rigidly conservative ever known. There is some truth in this belief, for the basic pattern of Egyptian institutions, beliefs, and artistic ideas was formed between 3000 and 2500 B.C. and kept reasserting itself for the next two thousand years, so that all Egyptian art, at first glance, tends to have a certain sameness. Actually, Egyptian art alternates between conservatism and innovation, but is never static. Some of its great achievements had a decisive influence on Greece and Rome. We can thus feel ourselves linked to the Egypt of five thousand years ago by a continuous, living tradition.

The history of Egypt is divided into dynasties of rulers, in accordance with ancient Egyptian practice, beginning with the First Dynasty, shortly before 3000 B.C. This method of counting historic time conveys at once the strong Egyptian sense of continuity and the overwhelming importance of the Pharaoh (king), who was not only the supreme ruler but a god. All kings claim to rule in the name or by the grace of some superhuman authority (that is what makes them superior to tribal chiefs); the Pharaoh transcended them all—his kingship was not delegated to him from above but was absolute, divine. However absurd his status may seem, and however ineffective it was at times, it has particular importance for us because it very largely determined the character of Egyptian art. We do not know exactly how the early Pharaohs established their claim to divinity, but we know that they molded the Nile valley into a single, effective state and increased its fertility by regulating the annual floods of the river waters through dams and canals.

Of these public works nothing remains today. Our knowledge of Egyptian civilization rests almost entirely on the tombs and their contents, since little has survived of ancient Egyptian palaces and cities. This is no accident, for these tombs were built to endure forever. Yet the Egyptians did not view life on this

9. *Palette of King Narmer,* from Hierakonpolis. c.3100 B.C. Slate, height 25″. Egyptian Museum, Cairo

earth mainly as a road to the grave; their cult of the dead is a link with the New Stone Age, but the meaning they gave it was quite devoid of that dark fear of the spirits of the dead which dominates primitive ancestor cults. Their attitude was, rather, that man can provide for his own happy afterlife by equipping his tomb as a kind of shadowy replica of his daily environment for his spirit, the *ka*, to enjoy, and by making sure that the *ka* would have a body to dwell in (his own mummified corpse, or, as a substitute, a statue of himself). There is a blurring of the sharp line between life and death in these mock households; a man who knew that after death his *ka* would enjoy the same pleasures he enjoyed, and who had provided these pleasures in advance, could lead an active and happy life free from fear of the great unknown. The Egyptian tomb, then, was a kind of life insurance, an investment in peace of mind.

At the threshold of Egyptian history stands a work of art that is also a historic document: a carved slate palette (fig. 9) celebrating the victory of Narmer, king of Upper Egypt, over Lower Egypt, the oldest known image of a historic personage identified by name. It already shows most of the features characteristic of Egyptian art. But before we concern ourselves with these, let us first "read" the scene. That we are able to do so is another indication that we have left primitive art behind, for the meaning of the relief is made clear not only by means of the hieroglyphic labels, but also through the rational orderliness of the design. Narmer has seized an enemy by the hair and is about to slay him with his mace; two more fallen enemies are placed in the bottom compartment (the small rectangular shape next to the one on the left stands for a fortified town). In the upper right we see a complex bit of picture writing: a falcon above a clump of papyrus plants holds a tether attached to a human head that "grows" from the same soil as the plants. This image actually repeats the main scene on a symbolic level—the head and the papyrus plants stand for Lower Egypt, while the victorious falcon is Horus, the god of Upper Egypt. Clearly, Horus and Narmer are the same: a god triumphs over human foes. Hence, Narmer's gesture must not be taken as representing a real fight. The enemy is helpless from the very start, and the slaying is a ritual, rather than a physical effort. We gather this from the fact that Narmer has taken off his sandals (the court official behind him carries them in his left hand), an indication that he is standing on holy ground. The same notion recurs in the Old Testament when the Lord commands Moses to remove his shoes before He appears to him in the burning bush.

We have discussed this scene at such length because we must grasp its content in order to understand its formal qualities, its *style*. We have avoided that term until now and it is necessary to comment on it briefly before we proceed. *Style* is derived from *stilus*, the ancient Roman word for writing tool; originally, it referred to distinctive ways of writing. Nowadays, however, style is used loosely to mean the distinctive way a thing is done in any field of human endeavor. Often it is simply a term of praise: "to have style" means to have distinction, to stand out. But there is another implication, too—when we say that something "has no style" we mean that it is not only undistinguished but also undistinguishable: we do not know how to classify it, how to put it in its proper context, because it seems to be pointing in several directions at once. A thing that *has style*, then, must not be inconsistent with itself; it must have an inner coherence, a sense of wholeness, of being all of a piece. And this quality has a way of impressing itself upon us even if we do not know what particular *kind* of style is involved. In art, style means the distinc-

10. *Mycerinus and His Queen,* from Giza. c.2500 B.C. Slate, height 56″. Museum of Fine Arts, Boston

tive way in which the forms that make up a given work are chosen and fitted together. To art historians the study of styles is of central importance; it not only enables them to find out, by careful analysis and comparison, when and where (and by whom) a given work was produced, but it also leads them to understand the artist's intention as expressed through the style of his work. This intention depends on both the artist's personality and the setting in which he lives and works. We thus speak of "period styles" if we are concerned with those features which distinguish, let us say, Egyptian art from Greek art. And within these we in turn distinguish particular phases, or national or local styles, until we arrive at the personal styles of individual artists. Even these may need to be subdivided further into the various phases of an artist's development. The extent to which we are able to do all this depends on how much internal coherence, how much of a sense of continuity, there is in the material we are dealing with. The art of historic civilizations tends to have a much more controlled, tightly knit style than does prehistoric art, hence it seemed best not to introduce the term prematurely.

Let us now return to the Narmer palette. The new inner logic of its style is readily apparent, even though the modern notion of showing a scene as it would appear to a single observer at a single moment is as alien to the Egyptian artist as it had been to his Stone Age predecessors. He strives for clarity, not illusion, and therefore picks the most telling view in each case. But he imposes a strict rule on himself: when he changes his angle of vision, he must do so by 90 degrees, as if he were sighting along the edges of a cube. He thus acknowledges only three possible views: full face, strict profile, and vertically from above. Any intermediate position embarrasses him (note the oddly rubberlike figures of the fallen enemies). Moreover, he is faced with the fact that the standing human figure, unlike that of an animal, does not have a single main profile but two competing profiles, so that, for the sake of clarity, he must combine these views. How he does this is clearly shown in the figure of Narmer: eye and shoulders in frontal view, head and legs in profile. The method worked so well that it was to survive for twenty-five hundred years, in spite—or perhaps because—of the fact that it does not lend itself to representing movement or action. The frozen quality of the image would seem to be especially suited to the divine nature of the Pharaoh; ordinary mortals *act*, he simply *is*. Whenever physical activity demanding any sort of effort must be depicted, the Egyptian artist does not hesitate to abandon the composite view of the body, for such activities are always performed by underlings whose dignity does not have to be preserved (compare fig. 13).

The "cubic" approach to the human form can be observed most strikingly in Egyptian sculpture in the round, such as the splendid group of the Pharaoh Mycerinus and his queen (fig. 10). The artist must have started out by drawing the front and side views on the faces of a rectangular block and then working inward until these views met. Only in this way could he have achieved figures of such overpowering three-dimensional firmness and immobility. What magnificent vessels for the *ka* to inhabit! Both have the left foot placed forward, yet there is no hint of a forward movement. The group also affords an interesting comparison of male and female beauty as interpreted by a fine sculptor, who knew not only how to contrast the structure of the two bodies but also how to emphasize the soft, swelling form of the queen through a thin, close-fitting gown.

When we speak of the Egyptians' attitude to-ward death and afterlife, we must be careful to make it clear that we do not refer to the average man but only to the small aristocratic caste clustered around the royal court. There is still a great deal to be learned about the origin and significance of Egyptian tombs, but the concept of afterlife they reflect apparently applied only to the privileged few because of their association with the immortal Pharaohs. The standard form of these tombs was the *mastaba*, a squarish mound faced with brick or stone, above a burial chamber that was deep underground and linked with the mastaba by a shaft. Inside the mastaba there is a chapel for offerings to the *ka* and a secret cubicle for the statue of the deceased. Royal mastabas grew to conspicuous size and soon developed into pyramids. The earliest is probably that of King Zoser (fig. 11) at Saqqara, a step pyramid suggestive of a stack of mastabas as against the smooth-sided later examples at Giza.

The modern imagination, enamored of "the silence of the pyramids," is apt to create a false picture of these monuments. They were not isolated structures but were linked with vast funerary districts, with temples and other buildings which were the scene of great religious celebrations during the Pharaoh's lifetime as well as after. The most elaborate of these is the funerary district around the pyramid of Zoser: its creator, Imhotep, is the first artist whose name has been recorded in history, and deservedly so, since his achievement—or what remains of it—is most impressive even today. Egyptian architecture had begun with structures made of mud bricks, wood, reeds, and other light materials. Imhotep used cut stone,

11. Step Pyramid, Funerary District of King Zoser. c.2650 B.C. Saqqara

12. Papyrus Half-Columns, North Palace,
Funerary District of King Zoser. c.2650 B.C. Saqqara

but his repertory of architectural forms still reflects shapes and devices developed during that
earlier phase. Thus we find columns—always
"engaged" rather than freestanding—which
echo the bundles of reeds or the wooden supports that used to be set into mud-brick walls
to give them added strength. But the very fact
that these members no longer had their original
function made it possible for Imhotep and his
fellow architects to redesign them so as to make
them serve a new, *expressive* purpose (fig. 12).
The notion that architectural forms can express
anything may seem difficult to grasp at first;
today we tend to assume that unless these
forms serve a clear-cut structural purpose
(such as supporting or enclosing) they are
mere surface decoration. Yet the slender, tapering fluted columns in figure 11, or the papy-
rus-shaped half-columns in figure 12, do not
simply decorate the walls to which they are attached; they interpret them and give them life,
as it were. Their proportions, the feeling of
strength or resilience they convey, their spacing, the degree to which they project, all share
in this task. We shall learn more of the expressive role of columns when we come to know
Greek architecture, which took over the Egyptian stone column and developed it further.

Enterprises of the huge scale of the pyramids
mark the high point of Pharaonic power. The
world has always marveled at their sheer size
as well as at the technical accomplishment they
represent; but they have also come to be regarded as symbols of slave labor—thousands of
men forced by cruel masters to serve the glory

of absolute rulers. Such a picture may well be
unjust; certain records have been preserved
which indicate that the labor was paid for. We
are probably nearer the truth if we think of
these monuments as vast public works providing economic security for a good part of the
population.

Before we leave the realm of Egyptian funerary art, let us cast a brief glance at one of the
scenes of daily life that adorn the offering
chambers of the mastabas. While these depict
typical, recurrent activities rather than events
drawn from the career of the deceased, and
thus share the "timelessness" of all Egyptian
art, they offered the artist a welcome opportunity to widen his powers of observation. Our illustration (fig. 13) shows part of a relief of
cattle fording a river; one of the herders carries a newborn calf on his back, to keep it
from drowning, and the frightened animal
turns its head to look back at its mother, who
answers with an equally anxious glance. Such
sympathetic portrayal of an emotional relationship is fully as delightful as it is unexpected in
Egyptian art.

Politically, Egypt reached its greatest power
during the Empire period (c. 1500–1166 B.C.),
when Egyptian rule extended as far to the east
as Palestine and Syria. The divine kingship of
the Pharaoh was now asserted in a new way: by
association with the god Amen, whose identity
had been fused with that of the sun-god Ra,
and who became the supreme deity, towering
above the lesser gods as the Pharaoh towered
above the provincial nobility. Thus vast architectural energies were devoted to the building
of huge temples of Amen under royal sponsor-
ship, such as that at Luxor (fig. 14). Its plan is
characteristic of the general pattern of later
Egyptian temples. The façade (fig. 14, far

13. *Cattle Fording a River* (detail of painted
limestone relief). c.2400 B.C. Tomb of Ti, Saqqara

14. Court and Pylon of
Ramesses II (c.1260 B.C.),
and Colonnade and Court
of Amenhotep III
(c.1390 B.C.). Temple of
Amen-Mut-Khonsu, Luxor

left) consists of two massive walls, with sloping sides, that flank the entrance; this gateway, or pylon, leads to a court, a pillared hall, a second court, and another pillared hall, beyond which is the temple proper. The entire sequence of courts, halls, and temple was enclosed by high walls that shut off the outside world. Except for the monumental façade, such a structure is designed to be experienced from within; ordinary worshipers were confined to the courts and could but marvel at the forest of columns that screened the dark recesses of the sanctuary. The columns had to be closely spaced, for they supported the stone beams (lintels) of the ceiling, and these had to be short to keep them from breaking under their own weight. Yet the architect has consciously exploited this condition by making the columns far heavier than they need be. As a result, the beholder feels almost crushed by their sheer mass. The overawing effect is certainly impressive, but also rather vulgar when measured against the earlier masterpieces of Egyptian architecture. We need only compare the papyrus columns at Luxor with their ancestors at Saqqara (fig. 12) to realize how little of Imhotep's genius still survives here.

The growth of the Amen cult produced an unexpected threat to royal authority: the priests of Amen grew into a caste of such wealth and power that the king could maintain his position only with their consent. One remarkable Pharaoh, Amenhotep IV, tried to defeat them by proclaiming his faith in a single god, the sun disk Aten. He changed his name to Akhenaten, closed the Amen temples, and moved the capital to a new site. His attempt to place himself at the head of a new monotheistic faith, however, did not outlast his reign (1372–1358 B.C.), and under his successors orthodoxy was speedily restored. During the long

period of Egypt's decline, after 1000 B.C., the country became ever more priest-ridden, until, under Greek and Roman rule, Egyptian civilization came to an end in a welter of esoteric religious doctrines. Akhenaten was a revolutionary not only in his faith but in his artistic tastes as well, consciously fostering a new style and a new ideal of beauty. The contrast with the past is strikingly evident in a low-relief portrait of Akhenaten (fig. 15); compared with works in the traditional style (see fig. 10), this head seems at first glance like a brutal caricature, with its oddly haggard features and overemphatic, undulating lines. What distinguishes

15. *Akhenaten (Amenhotep IV)*. c.1365 B.C.
Stone, height 3⅛″. State Museums, Berlin

the "Akhenaten style" is not greater realism so much as a new sense of form that seeks to unfreeze the immobility of Egyptian art—the contours as well as the plastic shapes are more pliable and relaxed, as if they had been suddenly released from the grip of geometry that underlies Egyptian art.

It is an odd and astonishing fact that man should have emerged into the light of history in two separate places at just about the same time. Between 3500 and 3000 B.C., when Egypt was being united under Pharaonic rule, another great civilization arose in Mesopotamia, the "land between the rivers." And for close to three millennia, the two rival centers retained their distinct character, even though they had contact with each other from their earliest beginnings. The pressures that forced the inhabitants of both regions to abandon the pattern of prehistoric village life may well have been the same. But the valley of the Tigris and Euphrates, unlike that of the Nile, is not a narrow fertile strip protected by deserts; it resembles a wide, shallow trough with few natural defenses, easily encroached upon from any direction. Thus the area proved almost impossible to unite under a single ruler. The political history of ancient Mesopotamia has no underlying theme such as divine kingship provides for Egypt; local rivalries, foreign invasions, the sudden upsurge and equally sudden collapse of military power—these are its substance. Even so, there was a remarkable continuity of cultural and artistic traditions. These are very largely the creation of the founding fathers of Mesopotamian civilization, whom we call

16. Statues, from the Abu Temple, Tell Asmar. c.2700–2500 B.C. Marble, height of tallest figure c.30". Iraq Museum, Baghdad, and Oriental Institute, Chicago

Sumerians after Sumer, the region near the confluence of the Tigris and Euphrates which they inhabited.

The origin of the Sumerians remains obscure. Sometime before 4000 B.C. they came to southern Mesopotamia from Persia, founded a number of city-states, and developed their distinctive form of writing in cuneiform (wedge-shaped) characters on clay tablets. Unfortunately, the tangible remains of this Sumerian civilization are very scanty compared to those of ancient Egypt; for lack of stone, the Sumerians built only in mud brick and wood, so that almost nothing is left of their architecture except the foundations. Nor did they share the Egyptians' concern with the hereafter, although a few richly endowed tombs have been found in the city of Ur. Our knowledge of Sumerian civilization thus depends very largely on chance fragments—including vast numbers of inscribed clay tablets—brought to light by excavation. Still, in recent decades we have learned enough to form a general picture of the achievements of this vigorous, inventive, and disciplined people.

Each Sumerian city-state had its own local god, who was its "king" and owner. He in return was expected to plead the cause of his subjects among his fellow deities who controlled the forces of nature, such as wind and weather, fertility, and the heavenly bodies. The community also had a human ruler, the steward of the divine sovereign who transmitted the god's commands. Nor was divine ownership treated as a pious fiction; the god was quite literally thought to own not only the territory of the city-state but the labor power of the population and its products as well. The result was a "theocratic socialism," a planned society centered on the temple. It was the temple that controlled the pooling of labor and resources for such enterprises as building dikes or irrigation ditches, and it collected and distributed a large part of the harvest. All this required the keeping of detailed written records, hence early Sumerian inscriptions deal mainly with economic and administrative matters, although writing was a priestly privilege.

The temple of the local god stood on a raised platform in the center of the city. These platforms, or ziggurats, soon reached the height of true man-made mountains, great landmarks towering above the featureless plain. The most famous of them, the Biblical Tower of Babel, has been completely leveled, but remnants of others survive. Some have yielded stone statuary, such as the group of figures from Tell

Asmar (fig. 16), contemporary with the Pyramid of Zoser. The tallest represents Abu, the god of vegetation, the second largest a mother goddess, the rest priests and worshipers. What distinguishes the two deities is not only their size but the larger diameter of the pupils of their eyes, although the eyes of all the figures are enormous. Their insistent stare is emphasized by colored inlays. Clearly, the priests and worshipers were meant to communicate with the two gods through their eyes. "Representation" here has a very direct meaning: the gods were believed to be present in their images, and the statues of the worshipers served as stand-ins for the persons they portrayed. Yet none of them indicates any attempt to achieve an individual likeness—the bodies as well as the faces are rigorously simplified and schematic so as to avoid distracting attention from the eyes, the "windows of the soul." If the Egyptian sculptor's sense of form was essentially cubic, that of the Sumerian was based on the cone and the cylinder: arms and legs have the roundness of pipes, and the long skirts worn by all these figures are as smoothly curved as if they had been turned on a lathe. Even in later times, when Mesopotamian sculpture had acquired a far richer repertory of shapes, this quality asserts itself again and again.

The conic-cylindrical simplification of the Tell Asmar statues is characteristic of the carver, who cuts his forms from a solid block. A far more flexible and realistic style prevails among those works that are made by addition rather than subtraction (that is, either modeled in soft materials for casting in bronze or put together from such substances as wood, gold leaf, shell, and lapis lazuli). The tombs at Ur have yielded objects of this kind, including the inlaid panel from a bull-headed harp (fig. 17). Here we catch a tantalizing glimpse of Sumerian mythology. The hero embracing two human-headed bulls was so popular a subject that its design has become a rigidly symmetrical formula, but the other sections show animals performing a variety of human tasks in lively and precise fashion: the wolf and the lion carry food and drink to an unseen banquet, while the ass, bear, and deer provide musical entertainment (the harp is the same type as the instrument to which the panel was attached). At the bottom, a scorpion-man and a goat carry some objects they have taken from a large vessel. The artist who created these scenes was far less constrained by rules than were his contemporaries in Egypt; although, he, too, places his figures on ground lines, he is not afraid of over-

lapping forms or foreshortened shoulders. We must be careful, however, not to misinterpret his purpose—what may strike us as delightfully humorous was probably meant to be viewed with perfect seriousness. If we only knew the context in which these actors play their roles! Nevertheless, we may regard them as the earliest known ancestors of the animal fable that later flourished in the West from Aesop to La Fontaine.

After the middle of the third millennium B.C., the Semitic inhabitants of northern Mesopotamia drifted south in ever larger numbers until they outweighed the Sumerian stock. Although they adopted Sumerian civilization, they were less bound by the tradition of theocratic socialism; it was they who produced the first Mesopotamian rulers who openly called themselves kings and proclaimed their ambition to

17. Soundbox of a Harp, from Ur. c.2600 B.C. Bitumen with shell inlay, height 8½″. The University Museum, Philadelphia

18. Stele Inscribed with Law Code of Hammurabi (upper part). c.1760 B.C. Diorite, height of stele c.7′, height of relief 28″. The Louvre, Paris

conquer their neighbors. Few of them succeeded; the second millennium B.C. was a time of almost continuous turmoil. By far the greatest figure of the age was Hammurabi, under whose rule Babylon became the cultural center of Mesopotamia. His most memorable achievement is his law code, justly famous as the earliest written uniform body of laws and amazingly rational and humane in conception. He had it engraved on a tall stele (an upright stone slab used as a marker) the top of which shows Hammurabi confronting the sun-god Shamash (fig. 18). The ruler's right arm is raised in a speaking gesture, as if "the favorite shepherd" were reporting to the divine king. The relief here is so high that the two figures almost give the impression of statues sliced in half. As a result, the sculptor has been able to render the eyes in the round. Hammurabi and Shamash gaze at each other with a force and directness that recalls the statues from Tell Asmar (see fig. 16), whose enormous eyes indicate an attempt to establish the same relationship between god and man in an earlier phase of Mesopotamian civilization.

The most copious archaeological finds date from the third major phase of Mesopotamian history, that between c. 1000 and 500 B.C., which was dominated by the Assyrians. This people had slowly expanded from the city-state

of Assur on the upper course of the Tigris until they ruled the entire country. At the height of its power, the Assyrian empire stretched from the Sinai peninsula to Armenia. The Assyrians, it has been said, were to the Sumerians what the Romans were to the Greeks. Their civilization depended on the achievements of the South, but reinterpreted them to fit its own distinctive character. Much of Assyrian art is devoted to glorifying the power of the king, either by detailed depictions of his military conquests or by showing the sovereign as the killer of lions. These royal hunts were ceremonial combats (the animals were released from cages within a square formed by soldiers with shields) in which the king re-enacted his ancient role as supreme shepherd who kills the predators menacing the communal flock. Here Assyrian art rises to impressive heights, especially in the splendid reliefs of lion hunts from Nineveh. Strange as it seems, the finest images in these scenes are not the king and his retinue but the lions. By endowing them with magnificent strength and courage, the sculptor exalts the king who is able to slay such formidable adversaries. The dying lioness (fig. 19) stands out not only for the subtle gradations of the carved surface, which convey all the weight and volume of the body despite the shallowness of the relief, but for the tragic grandeur of her final agony. Once again we sense the special genius of ancient Mesopotamian art for the portrayal of animals (see fig. 17). Nor was this genius to be lost when Mesopotamia fell to the Persians in the sixth century B.C.; the new rulers took over not only the Assyrian empire but its artistic traditions as well and eventually transmitted some of them to the West.

19. *Dying Lioness,* from Nineveh (Kuyunjik). c.650 B.C. Stone, height of figure 13¾″. British Museum, London

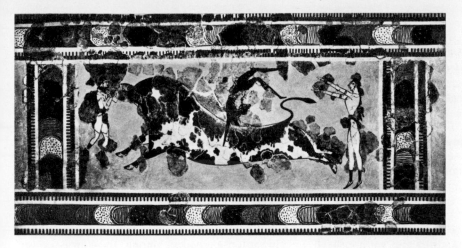

20. *The Toreador Fresco.*
c.1500 B.C. Height c.31½"
(including borders).
Archaeological Museum,
Herakleion

3. GREEK AND ROMAN ART

The two great civilizations discussed in the previous chapter kept their identities for almost three thousand years—half again the length of the Christian Era up to now. Although internal political shifts might shake them from time to time, and foreign invaders temporarily breach their borders, their duration must indeed have seemed without beginning and without end. Yet on the fringes of these giant domains, sheltered from their might but at the same time in communication with them via the Mediterranean Sea, small kingdoms which flourished were founded by other peoples.

A hundred years ago we knew little more about these vest-pocket states than what Homer told us in his account of the Trojan War. Heinrich Schliemann in the 1870s and Sir Arthur Evans at the beginning of our own century made the archaeological finds that proved Homer was describing real people and places, not just inventing a world of heroic adventure.

Of the island-states lying closest to Egypt, Crete was the largest, and the flowering of its civilization—despite certain setbacks and interruptions thought to have been caused by earthquakes—took place at about the same time as that of Egypt. Egyptian artifacts have been found among the Cretan ruins and Cretan pottery in Egypt, so we know that they traded with each other. Out of this commerce, and their own agricultural wealth, the inhabitants of Crete laid the foundations for a way of life that strikes the modern beholder as infinitely livelier and more joyous than anything we have studied so far. This is true even of the deadly game depicted in the *Toreador Fresco* (fig. 20), although it seems an illustration made to order for the blood-chilling legend of the Minotaur (literally "Bull of Minos," the king whose

name is also used to identify this "Minoan" civilization). Every year, the story goes, a group of youths and maidens from such parts of the Greek mainland as the Minoans had conquered were left to perish in the Labyrinth, or maze, where the monster was kept, until a young Greek hero, Theseus, with the help of the Cretan princess Ariadne, managed to slay the Minotaur.

The action shown in the fresco is something between a modern bullfight, where the men are armed, and the outright sacrifice of helpless human beings as told in the legend. Though unarmed, these athletes—boys and girls, differentiated as in Egyptian art by their darker or lighter skin tones—obviously function as an acrobatic team. Each in turn would grasp the horns of the charging bull and be tossed over its back, there to be caught by the other members of the team. In this game of "Minoan roulette" it was the gods who decided whether the sacred bull or the skillful gymnasts would "win." Yet our eyes are charmed long before our minds recoil from the bloody consequences of one miscalculation. Unlike the ponderous permanence of Egyptian figures, all of these—even the bull—have a strangely weightless quality. They seem to float and sway in an atmosphere devoid of gravity where no serious physical shock can occur.

More somber is the corresponding art of the Greek mainland, where warring chiefs were constantly raiding each other's tiny "kingdoms." Whereas no traces of ancient fortifications have been unearthed on Crete, palaces on the peninsula were girt about with walls such as those framing the Lion Gate at Mycenae (fig. 21). So massive are these ramparts that the Greeks of a later time called them "Cyclopean," thinking that such stones could only have been moved by the Cyclopes, a race of giants. The column between the two lions, tapering from top to bottom, is of the same design as those used in Cretan palaces, and from this alone (though there are other evidences as well) we would suspect that there was contact between the Minoans and their neighbors on the Greek mainland. But the artistic ancestry most evident in the two carved lions is Mesopotamian: we have seen symmetrically confronted animals in figure 17; and the *Dying Lioness* (fig. 19) is surely of the same heavy-muscled artistic species as the guardians of the gate.

The works of art we have come to know so far are like fascinating strangers: we approach them fully aware of their alien background and of the "language difficulties" they present. As soon as we come to the sixth century B.C. in Greece, however, our attitude undergoes a change: these are not strangers but relatives, we feel—older members of our own family. It is just as well to remember, as we turn to these "ancestors" of ours, that the continuous tradition that links us to the ancient Greeks is a handicap as well as an advantage: we must be careful, in looking at Greek originals, not to let our memories of their myriad later imitations get in the way.

21. The Lion Gate.
c.1250 B.C. Mycenae

GREEK ART. The Mycenaeans and the other clans described by Homer were the first Greek-speaking tribes to wander into the peninsula, around 2000 B.C. Then, around 1100 B.C., others came, overwhelming and absorbing those who were already there. Some of the late arrivals, the Dorians, settled on the mainland; others, the Ionians, spread out to the Aegean islands and Asia Minor. A few centuries later they ventured into the waters of the western Mediterranean, founding colonies in Sicily and southern Italy. Though the Greeks were united by language and religious beliefs, old tribal loyalties continued to divide them into city-states. The intense rivalry among these for power, wealth, and status undoubtedly stimulated the growth of ideas and institutions; but in the end they paid dearly for their inability to compromise enough, at least, to broaden their concept of state government. The Peloponnesian War (431–404 B.C.) in which the Spartans and their allies defeated the Athenians was a catastrophe from which Greece never recovered.

The destruction of the ancient Mycenaean cities by the Dorians did not, for several centuries, appear to result in anything but retrogression. The new masters seemed content with the meager crafts they had brought with them, chiefly a style of pottery that we call "Geometric" because it was very simply decorated with triangles, checks, or concentric circles. Of monumental architecture and sculpture there was none. Toward 800 B.C. human and animal figures began to appear within the painted bands of the pottery; our example (fig. 22) is a huge vase that served as a grave monument. The bottom of the vase is open so that liquid offerings poured into it could trickle down to the deceased in the grave below, but the scene painted on the outside is commemorative: the dead man is laid out on his bier, with a row of mourners raising their arms in lament on either side; below is a funeral procession of warriors, on foot or in chariots—a hero's funeral. Unlike the Egyptians (see p. 0), the Greeks did not attach much importance to life beyond the grave; although they believed that there was a place to which their "shades" (spirits) went, they counted rather upon their exploits in this world to give them fame and thus immortality. Even at this early stage in the development of Greek painting when the representation of an individual was so far from realistic, his remembrance by posterity was a matter of greater importance than any amount of tomb furnishings.

Toward 700 B.C. Greek art, stimulated by an

Colorplate 1. PSIAX. *Hercules Strangling the Nemean Lion*. Attic Black-Figured amphora (detail).
c.525 B.C. Height of portion shown c. 5¾ ″. Museo Civico, Brescia

Colorplate 2. THE ACHILLES PAINTER. *Muse on Mount Helicon*. White-ground lekythos
(detail, slightly enlarged). c.445 B.C. Private Collection, Lugano

left: 22. Dipylon Vase. 8th century B.C. Height 42½".
The Metropolitan Museum of Art, New York (Rogers Fund)

below: 23. THE FOUNDRY PAINTER. *Lapith Battling a Centaur.*
Attic Red-Figured kylix (interior). c.490–480 B.C.
Diameter 15". Staatliche Antikensammlungen, Munich

increased trade with Egypt and the Near East, began to absorb powerful influences from these regions that put flesh on the bare bones of the Dorians' Geometric images. From the later seventh century to about 480 B.C., this amalgamation produced what we call the "Archaic" style; while it does not yet have the balance and perfection of the "Classic" style, which followed in the later part of the fifth century B.C., the Archaic style has an appealing freshness that makes many persons consider it the most vital phase of Greek art. Ordinarily, decorated pottery, however valuable as an archaeologist's aid, is thought of as an industry or craft, rather than an art; but by about the middle of the sixth century B.C. vase painters were so highly esteemed that the best of them signed their works. Art lovers might collect Psiax (colorplate 1) the way people nowadays collect Picasso. The scene of Hercules strangling the Nemean lion on Psiax's amphora is a far cry from the conventionalized figures of the Geometric style. The two heavy bodies almost seem united forever in their grim struggle; incised line and touches of colored detail have been kept to a minimum so as not to break up the compact black mass, yet both figures show such a wealth of anatomical knowledge and skillful use of foreshortening that they give an amazing illusion of existing in the round.

Like the Hercules amphora, other vase paintings during the sixth century B.C. were done in black pigment against the natural reddish color of the earthenware; but toward the end of the century, vase painters—Psiax among them—experimented with a reversal of the colors, making the backgrounds black and leaving the figures red, the better to simulate flesh tones. By 500 B.C. this new "Red-Figure Style" had completely superseded the earlier "Black-Figure Style." *Lapith Battling a Centaur* (fig. 23) shows the advantage of the reversed color scheme: brushwork replaces the incised lines, so that the artist now has a great deal more freedom in depicting complicated, overlapping shapes; details of costume or facial expression are more precise; and the whole composition seems to expand, since there is no reason to put in more black background than is necessary to set the figures off to advantage.

The Red-Figure Style continued through the fifth century B.C., but alongside it a new method sprang up—possibly in imitation of wall paintings, which have all disappeared since then: these "white-ground lekythoi," as this group of vases is called, seem to have been largely restricted to one purpose, the bottling of oil customarily used as a funerary offering (colorplate 2). The white background permits the artist a wider range of superimposed colors, and we become aware of the subtleties of line drawing that can make shapes seem to recede

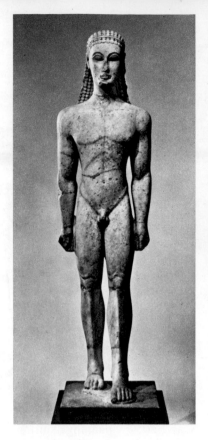

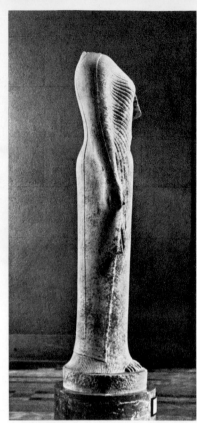

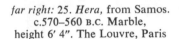

right: 24. *Standing Youth (Kouros).*
c.600 B.C. Marble, height 6′ 1½″.
The Metropolitan Museum of Art,
New York (Fletcher Fund, 1932)

far right: 25. *Hera,* from Samos.
c.570–560 B.C. Marble,
height 6′ 4″. The Louvre, Paris

or come forward, or give us the "feel" of drapery or soft flesh. Further, the white background is easily interpreted as airy space, and
we are less aware of the hard, confining surface
of the vessel itself.

While enough examples of metalwork and
ivory carvings of Near Eastern and Egyptian
origin have been found on Greek soil to account for their influence on Greek vase painting, the origins of monumental sculpture and
architecture in Greece are a different matter.
To see such things, the Greeks had to go to
Egypt or Mesopotamia. There is no doubt that
they did so (we know that there were small
colonies of Greeks in Egypt at the time), but
this does not explain why the Greeks should
have developed a sudden desire during the seventh century B.C., and not before, to have such
things themselves. The mystery may never be
cleared up, for the oldest existing examples of
Greek stone sculpture and architecture show
that Egyptian tradition had already been well
assimilated, and that skill to match was not
long in developing.

Let us begin by comparing a late seventh-
century statue of a Greek youth, called a Kouros (fig. 24), with the statue of Mycerinus (fig.
10). The similarities are certainly striking: in
both we note the same cubic character, as

though the sculptor was still conscious of the
original block of stone; the broad-shouldered
slim, silhouettes; the position of the arms with
their clenched hands; the stance with the left
leg forward; the emphatic rendering of the
kneecaps; and the wiglike curls of the Greek
boy that resemble the headdress worn by the
Pharaoh. Judged by the Egyptian level of accomplishment the Archaic Greek example
seems somewhat awkward—oversimplified,
rigid, less close to nature. But the Greek statue
has some virtues that cannot be measured in
Egyptian terms. First of all, it is freestanding.
In the entire history of art there are no earlier
examples of a sculptor's being daring enough to
liberate a lifesize figure completely from the
surrounding block of stone. What had doubtless started as a timid precaution against break-
age of arms, or the crumbling of the legs under
the weight of the body, became a convention.
Here, however, the artist has carved away
every bit of "dead" stone except for the tiny
bridges that connect the fists to the thighs. This
is a matter not merely of technical daring but
of a new intention: it was important to the
Greek artist to dissociate his statue from inert
matter, the better to approximate the living
being that it represented. Unlike Mycerinus,
who looks as though he could stand in the same

pose till the end of time, the Kouros is tense with a vitality that seems to promise movement. The calm, distant gaze of the Egyptian prince has been replaced by larger-than-life, wide-open eyes that remind us of early Mesopotamian art (see fig. 16).

Statues of the Kouros type were produced in great quantity during the Archaic period, destined for temple offerings or graves. Like the decorated vases of the period, some of them were signed ("So-and-so made me"); but whether they represent gods, or donors, or victors in athletic games, nobody knows for sure. Since they vary but little in their essentials, we assume that they were meant to represent an ideal—a godlike man, or manlike god.

The male figures show best the innovations that give Greek sculpture its particular character, but there is no dearth of female statues of the same period. Since these were invariably clothed, skirts and shawls fill in those empty spaces that make the contrast so clear between Greek sculpture and all that came before it. Nevertheless, the Kore, as the female statue type is called, shows more variations than the Kouros. In part these are due to local differences in dress, but the drapery itself posed a problem—how to relate it to the body—and artists solved it in various ways. The *Hera* (fig. 25), so called because of her impressive size and because she was found in the ruins of the Temple of Hera on the island of Samos, is slightly later than our Kouros (fig. 24). This smooth-skirted figure with the folds of her hem fanning out over a circular base seems to have evolved from a column rather than from a rectangular block. But the majestic effect of the statue depends not so much on its closeness to an abstract shape as on the way the column has blossomed forth with the swelling softness of a living body. Following the unbroken upward sweep of the lower folds of drapery, the eye slows to the gently curving hips, torso, and breast. If we turn back to figure 10, we realize suddenly that Mycerinus' wife, with far more

explicit anatomy, looks squat and lifeless by comparison.

When the Greeks began to build their temples in stone, they fell heir to age-old traditions of architectural sculpture as well. The Egyptians covered the walls and even the columns of their buildings with reliefs (see fig. 13), but these carvings were so shallow that they had no weight or volume of their own. The guardian figures of the Lion Gate at Mycenae are of a different type: although they are carved in high relief on a huge slab, this slab is thin and light compared to the Cyclopean blocks around it. In building the gate, the architect had left an empty triangle above the lintel, for fear that the weight of the wall above would crush it, and then filled the hole with the relief panel. This kind of architectural sculpture is a separate entity, not merely a modified wall surface. The Greeks followed the Mycenaean example—in their temples, stone sculpture is confined to the pediment (the "empty triangle" between the ceiling and the sloping sides of the roof) and to the zone immediately below it (the "frieze") —but they retained the narrative wealth of Egyptian reliefs. The *Battle of Gods and Giants* (fig. 26), part of a frieze, is executed in very high relief with deep undercutting (the hind leg of one of the lions has broken off because it was completely detached from the background). The sculptor has taken full advantage of the spatial possibilities of this bold technique; the projecting ledge at the bottom has become a stage on which to place the figures in depth. As they recede from us, the carving becomes shallower, yet even the furthest plane is not allowed to merge into the background. The result is a condensed but very convincing space that permits a dramatic interplay among the figures such as we have not seen before. Not only in the physical but in the expressive sense, a new dimension has here been conquered.

The Greek achievement in architecture has been identified since ancient Roman times with

26. *Battle of Gods and Giants,* portion of north frieze, Treasury of the Siphnians, Delphi. c.530 B.C. Marble, height 26". Museum, Delphi

27. The Temple of Poseidon (foreground; c.460 B.C.) and the "Basilica" (background; c.550 B.C.). Paestum, Italy

the creation of the three classical architectural orders: the Doric, Ionic, and Corinthian. Of these, the Doric may well claim to be the basic order, being older and more sharply defined than the Ionic; the Corinthian is a variant of the latter. What do we mean by "architectural order"? The term is used only for Greek architecture (and its descendants), and rightly so, for none of the other architectural systems known to us has produced anything like it. Perhaps the simplest way to make clear the unique character of the Greek orders is this: there is no such thing as "the Egyptian temple" or "the Gothic church"—the individual buildings, however much they may have in common, are so varied that we cannot distill a generalized type from them—while "the Doric temple" is a real entity that inevitably forms in our minds as we examine the monuments themselves. This abstraction is not, of course, an ideal against which we may measure the degree of perfection of any given Doric temple; it simply means that the elements of which a Doric temple is composed are extraordinarily constant in number, in kind, and in their relation to one another. Doric temples all belong to the same clearly recognizable family, just as the Kouros statues do; like them, they show an internal

consistency, a mutual adjustment of parts, that gives them a unique quality of wholeness and organic unity.

The term Doric order refers to the standard parts, and their sequence, making up the exterior of any Doric temple. At Paestum (fig. 27), for example, let us note the three main divisions that occur in both temples: the stepped platform, the columns, and the entablature (which includes everything that rests on the columns). The column consists of the shaft, made of sections (drums) and marked with vertical grooves called flutes, and the capital, which supports the horizontal stone blocks of the architrave. Above the architrave is the frieze and the cornice. On the long sides of the temple, the cornice is horizontal; on the short sides (or façades) it is split open so as to enclose the pediment between its upper and lower parts.

The plans of Greek temples are not directly linked to the orders. The basic features of all of them are so much alike that it is useful to study them from a generalized "typical" plan (fig. 28). The nucleus is the cella or naos (the room where the image of the deity is placed), and the entrance porch (pronaos) with two columns flanked by pilasters. Often a second porch is added behind the cella, for symmetry. In large temples, this central unit is surrounded by a row of columns (the colonnade, also called the peristyle).

How did the Doric temple originate? Its essential features were already well established about 600 B.C., but how they developed, and why they congealed so rapidly into a system as it seems they did, remains a puzzle to which we have few reliable clues. The notion that temples ought to be built of stone, with large numbers of columns, must have come from Egypt;

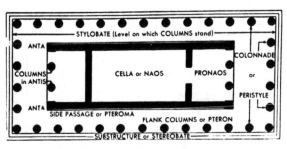

28. Plan of a Typical Greek Temple (after Grinnell)

the fluted half-columns at Saqqara (see fig. 11) strongly suggest the Doric column. Egyptian temples, it is true, are designed to be experienced from the inside, while the Greek temple is arranged so that the exterior matters most (religious ceremonies usually took place out of doors, in front of the temple façade). But might not a Doric temple be interpreted as the columned hall of an Egyptian sanctuary turned inside out? The Greeks also owed something to the Mycenaeans—we have seen an elementary kind of pediment in the Lion Gate, and the capital of a Mycenaean column is rather like a Doric capital (compare fig. 21). There is, however, a third factor: to what extent can the Doric order be understood as a reflection of wooden structures? Our answer to this thorny question will depend on whether we believe that architectural form follows function and technique, or whether we accept the striving for beauty as a motivating force. The truth may well lie in a combination of both these approaches. At the start, Doric architects certainly imitated in stone some features of wooden temples, if only because these features served to identify the building as a temple. But when they became enshrined in the Doric order, it was not from blind conservatism; by then, the wooden forms had been so thoroughly transformed that they were an organic part of the stone structure.

Of the ancient Greek buildings here illustrated, the oldest is the "Basilica" in Paestum (fig. 27, background); near this south Italian town a Greek colony flourished during the Archaic period. The Temple of Poseidon (fig. 27,

foreground) was erected about a hundred years later. How do the two temples differ? The "Basilica" looks low and sprawling—and not only because its roof is lost—while the Temple of Poseidon, by comparison, appears tall and compact. The difference is partly psychological, produced by the outline of the columns which, in the "Basilica," are more strongly curved and are tapered to a relatively tiny top. This makes one feel that they bulge with the strain of supporting the superstructure, and that the slender tops, even though aided by the widely flaring cushionlike capitals, are just barely up to the job. This sense of strain has been explained on the grounds that Archaic architects were not fully familiar with their new materials and engineering procedures, but this is to judge the building by the standards of later temples—and to overlook the expressive vitality of the building, as of a living body, the vitality we also sense in the Archaic Kouros (fig. 24).

In the Temple of Poseidon the exaggerated curvatures have been modified; this, combined with a closer ranking of the columns, literally as well as expressively brings the stresses between supports and weight into more harmonious balance. Perhaps because the architect took fewer risks, the building is better preserved than the "Basilica," and its air of self-contained repose parallels the *Hera* (fig. 25) in the field of sculpture.

As the most perfect embodiment of the Classic period of Greek architecture, the Parthenon (fig. 29) takes us a step further toward harmonious completeness. Although it is only a few

29. The Parthenon, by ICTINUS and CALLICRATES (view from west). 448–432 B.C. Acropolis, Athens

years younger than the Temple of Poseidon, the fact that it was built in Athens, then at the peak of its glory and wealth, ensured it the best of design, material, and workmanship. In spite of its greater size it seems less massive than the earlier temple; rather, the dominant impression is one of festive, balanced grace. A general lightening and readjustment of the proportions accounts for this; the horizontal courses above the columns are not so wide in relation to their length; the framework of the gable projects less insistently; and the columns, in addition to being slenderer, are more widely spaced. The

30. The Propylaea, by MNESICLES
(view from west; 437–432 B.C.), and the Temple of
Athena Nike (upper right; 427–424 B.C.). Acropolis, Athens

31. *Poseidon (Zeus?)*. c.460–450 B.C. Bronze,
height 6′ 10″. National Museum, Athens

curvature of the columns and the flare of the capitals are also discreetly lessened, adding to the new sense of ease. Instead of resembling an Archaic Atlas, straining to hold up the weight of a world placed on his shoulders, the Parthenon performs with apparent facility. Unobtrusive refinements of proportion and line, measurable but not immediately apparent, add to the overall impression of springy vitality: horizontal elements, such as the steps, are not straight, but curve upward slightly toward the middle; the columns tilt inward; and the interval between each corner column and its neighbor is smaller than the standard interval used in the rest of the colonnade. Such intentional departures from strict geometric regularity are not made of necessity; they give us visual reassurance that the points of greatest stress are supported, and provided with a counterstress as well.

Shortly afterward an impressive gateway, the Propylaea (fig. 30), was built upon the rough, irregular hill which one has to climb to reach the Parthenon. It is fascinating to see how the familiar elements of the Doric order are here adapted to a totally different purpose and a difficult terrain. The architect has acquitted himself nobly: not only does the gateway fit the steep and craggy hillside, it transforms it from a rude passage among the rocks into a majestic overture to the sacred precinct above. Next to it (fig. 30, right) is the elegant little Temple of Athena Nike, displaying the slenderer proportions and the scroll capitals of the Ionic order.

Sometimes things that seem simple are the hardest to achieve. Greek sculptors of the late Archaic period (see figs. 24, 26) were adept at representing battle scenes full of struggling, running figures, but their freestanding statues also have an unintentional military air, as of soldiers standing at attention. It took over a century after our Kouros was made before the Greeks discovered the secret of making a figure stand "at ease." Just as in military drill, this is simply a matter of allowing the weight of the body to shift from equal distribution on both legs (as is the case with the Kouros, even though one foot is in front of the other), to one leg. The resulting stance brings about all kinds of subtle curvatures: the bending of the "free" knee results in a slight swiveling of the pelvis, a compensating curvature of the spine, and an adjusting tilt of the shoulders. Like the refined details of the Parthenon, these variations have nothing to do with the statue's ability to maintain itself erect but greatly enhance its lifelike impression: in repose, it will still seem capable

left: 32. PHIDIAS(?).
Three Goddesses,
from east pediment
of the Parthenon. c.438–432 B.C.
Marble, over lifesize.
British Museum, London

below: 33. SCOPAS(?).
Greeks Battling Amazons,
portion of east frieze, Mausoleum,
Halicarnassus. 359–351 B.C.
Marble, height 35".
British Museum, London

of movement; in motion, of maintaining its stability.

This stability in the midst of action becomes outright grandeur in the bronze *Poseidon* (fig. 31), an over-lifesize statue that was recovered from the sea near the coast of Greece some thirty years ago. The pose, to be sure, is that of an athlete, but it is not merely a moment in some continuing exercise; rather, it is an awe-inspiring gesture that reveals the power of the god. Here, the hurling of a weapon (originally, we may be sure, he held a thunderbolt or a trident in his right hand) is a divine attribute, not an act of war.

Battered though it is, the group of *Three Goddesses* (fig. 32) that originally belonged to the scene in the east pediment of the Parthenon, showing the birth of Athena from her father's head, is a good example of that other quality mentioned above: the possibility of action even in repose. Though all are seated, or even half-reclining, the turning of the bodies under the elaborate folds of their costumes makes them seem anything but static. In fact they seem so capable of arising that it is hard to imagine them "shelved" up under the gable. Perhaps the sculptors who achieved such lifelike figures also found this incongruous; at any rate, the sculptural decoration of later buildings tended to be placed in areas where they would seem less boxed in.

This Athenian style, so harmonious both in feeling and form, did not long survive the defeat of Athens by Sparta in the Peloponnesian War. Building and sculpture continued in the same tradition for another three centuries, but without the subtleties of the Classic age whose achievements we have just discussed. The postclassical, or "Hellenistic," style spread far and wide around the Mediterranean shores, but in a sense it turned backward to the scenes of violent action so popular in the Archaic period.

Scopas, who was very probably the sculptor of the frieze showing *Greeks Battling Amazons* (fig. 33), was familiar with the figure style of the Parthenon, but he has rejected its rhythmic harmony, its flow of action from one figure to the next. His sweeping, impulsive gestures require a lot of elbow room. Judged by Parthenon standards, the composition lacks continuity, but it makes up for this in bold innovation (note, for instance, the Amazon seated backward on her horse) as well as heightened expressiveness.

In many more instances than we would like, the most famous works of Greek sculptors of the fifth and fourth centuries B.C. have been lost and only copies are preserved. There is some doubt whether the famous *Hermes* by Praxiteles (fig. 34) is the original, or a copy made some three centuries later. If it is the latter, however, it is a very skillful copy, for it fits perfectly the qualities for which Praxiteles was admired in his own day. The lithe grace, the play of gentle curves, the feeling of complete relaxation (enhanced by an outside support for the figure to lean against) are quite the opposite of Scopas' energetic innovations. The *Hermes*' bland, lyrical charm is further enhanced by the caressing treatment of the surfaces: the meltingly soft, "veiled" features, and even the hair which has been left comparatively rough for contrast, all share a misty, silken quality. Here, for the first time, there is an attempt to modify the stony look of a statue by giving to it this illusion of an enveloping atmosphere.

A hundred years later the effects of the atmosphere surrounding a statue are played up in much more dramatic fashion. The *Nike of Samothrace* (fig. 35)—the goddess of victory—has just alighted on the prow of a warship; her great wings spread wide, she is still partially air-borne by the powerful headwind against which she advances. The invisible force of onrushing air becomes a tangible reality that balances the forward thrust of the figure and shapes every fold of the wonderfully animated drapery. This is not merely a relationship between the statue and the space which the sculptor imagined it inhabiting, but an interdependence more active than we have seen before. Nor shall we see it again for a long time. The *Nike* deserves her fame as the greatest work of Hellenistic sculpture.

By the end of the second century B.C. much of Greek sculpture was made on commission for Rome, the rising power of the Mediterranean region and a center of great admiration

35. *Nike of Samothrace.*
c.200–190 B.C. Marble, height 8'.
The Louvre, Paris

for Greek learning and art. The *Laocoön* group (fig. 36) was dug up in Rome in 1506 A.D., and it made a tremendous impression upon Italian sculptors of that time, notably Michelangelo. Today we tend to find the group (which had special significance for the founding of Rome) somewhat contrived and its pathos and dynamism self-conscious, even though the straining figures remind us of the dramatic style invented by Scopas.

ROMAN ART. The peninsula of Italy did not emerge into the light of history until fairly late. The Bronze Age came to an end there only in the eighth century B.C., about the time the earliest Greek seafarers began to settle along the southern shores of Italy and in Sicily. We know little about the inhabitants of Italy at that time: the classical Greek historian, Herodotus, tells us that they had originally wandered in from Lydia, in Asia Minor, and were called Etruscans. Whether or not they usurped the lands of peoples previously settled there, the homeland of the Etruscans—an area that extends roughly between the cities of Rome and Florence today—is still called Tuscany (from Tusci, or Etrusci). Although they used the Greek alphabet their language was not related to the Greek in any other way, and we understand little of it. Similarly, their art, while owing much to Greek

34. PRAXITELES. *Hermes.* c.330–320 B.C. (or copy?).
Marble, height 7' 1". Museum, Olympia

36. AGESANDER, ATHENODORUS, and POLYDORUS OF RHODES. *The Laocoön Group*. Late 2nd century B.C. Marble, height 7'. Vatican Museums, Rome

techniques and forms, does not "read" as Greek. The famous bronze statue of a she-wolf (fig. 37; the two infants are Renaissance additions), later venerated by the Romans as the nurse of their founding fathers, Romulus and Remus, is actually an Etruscan work. Although the technique of casting large statues in bronze had surely been learned from the Greeks, the wolf has a muscular tautness and an intensity of expression that was, at one time, thought to be medieval. But we shall later see that these Etruscan characteristics continued side by side

with others borrowed from the Greeks, in the art of the Romans who conquered and absorbed the Etruscan state.

More important to the Romans than the sculptural example set by the Etruscans, however, was what they learned from them about the art of building. According to Roman writers the Etruscans were masters of architectural engineering, of town planning, and of surveying. Little remains aboveground of either Etruscan or early Roman architecture; but such works as we have, plus the information collected from recent excavations, show that the Etruscans were, in fact, highly skilled builders. This heritage was to be of particular importance as Rome expanded her rule around the shores of the Mediterranean and toward the less populous north of Europe, building new cities to serve as seats of colonial government. Perhaps the single most important feature of this Etruscan legacy was the true arch, made up of wedge-shaped sections that lock each other securely in place. Not that the Etruscans invented the arch: its use dates as far back as the Egyptians, but they, and the Greeks after them, seem to have considered it merely a useful "beast of burden," and not a form beautiful enough to be used for its own sake. In ancient Mesopotamia it occasionally appeared aboveground in city gates; but it remained for the Etruscans to make it fully "respectable."

The growth of the capital city of Rome is hardly thinkable without the arch and the vaulting systems derived from it: the barrel vault—a half-cylinder; the groin vault, which consists of two barrel vaults intersecting each other at right angles; and the dome.

Greek buildings, however beautiful, were seldom built with a view to accommodating a

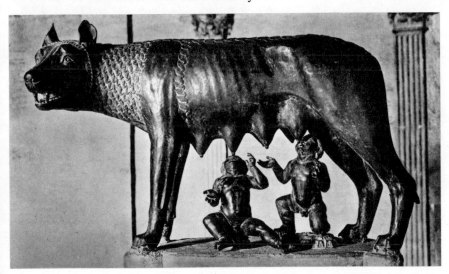

37. *She-Wolf*. c.500 B.C. Bronze, height 33½". Capitoline Museums, Rome

38. The Colosseum. 72–80 A.D. Rome

large crowd of people under one roof; even the temples were considered houses of the gods rather than gathering places for worshipers. Whether the Romans became "indoor people" because of the climate, which seems to have been colder in those days than it is now (forests populated with wolves and bears extended nearly the whole length of the peninsula), or whether the sheer numbers of the population necessitated large administrative buildings and gathering places, the fact remains that Greek models, though much admired, no longer sufficed. Small buildings, such as a votive chapel or a family mausoleum, might imitate a Greek example; but when it came to supplying the citizenry with everything it needed, from water to entertainment on a vast scale, radical new forms had to be invented, and cheaper materials and quicker methods had to be used.

The Colosseum (fig. 38), a huge amphitheater in the center of the old city, which could seat 50,000 spectators, is still one of the largest buildings anywhere. Its core is made of a kind of concrete, and it is a masterpiece of engineering and efficient planning, with miles of vaulted corridors to ensure the smooth flow of traffic to and from the arena. It utilizes the arch, the barrel vault, and the groin vault. The exterior, dignified and monumental, reflects the subdivisions of the interior, but clothed and accentuated in cut stone. There is a fine balance between the vertical and horizontal members that frame the endless series of arches. Reverence for Greek architecture is still visible in the use of half-columns and pilasters reflecting the Greek orders; structurally these have become ghosts—the building would still stand if one stripped them off—but aesthetically they are important, for through them the enormous facade becomes related to the human scale.

The same innovations in engineering and materials permitted the Romans to create vast covered spaces as well. The best preserved of these is the Pantheon (figs. 39, 40), a very large, round temple dedicated, as the name indicates, to all the gods. The portico, originally preceded by a colonnaded forecourt which blocked off the view we now have of the circular walls, looks like the standard entrance to

above: 39. The Pantheon. 118–125 A.D. Rome

right: 40. *The Interior of the Pantheon,* painting by G. P. Pannini, c.1750 A.D. National Gallery of Art, Washington, D.C. (Kress Collection)

41. The Basilica of Constantine.
c.310–320 A.D. Rome

a typical Roman temple (derived from Greek temple façades, with columns in the Corinthian order). All the more breath-taking, then, is the sight as we step through the tall portals, and the great domed space opens before us with dramatic suddenness. That the architects did not have an easy time with the engineering problems of supporting the huge hemisphere of a dome may be deduced from the heavy plainness of the exterior wall. Nothing on the outside gives any hint of the airiness and elegance of the interior; photographs fail to capture it, and even the painting (fig. 40) that we use to illustrate it does not do it justice. The height from the floor to the opening of the dome (called the oculus, or "eye") is exactly that of the diameter of the dome's base, thus giving the proportions perfect balance. The weight of the dome is concentrated on the eight solid sections of wall; between them, with graceful columns in front, niches are daringly hollowed out of the massive concrete, and these, while not connected with each other, give the effect of an open space behind the supports, making us feel that the walls are less thick and the dome much lighter than is actually the case. The multicolored marble panels and paving stones are still essentially as they were, but originally the dome was gilded to resemble "the golden dome of heaven."

Though it is hard to believe, the essential features of this awesome temple were already described (though on a smaller scale) a century earlier, by the architect Vitruvius—for the construction of steam rooms in public baths. In these, the oculus could be covered by a bronze lid that opened and closed to regulate the tem-

perature. Nor was the Pantheon the only huge building to be derived from similar designs for the popular bath establishments that were placed conveniently in various quarters of the city. The Basilica of Constantine (fig. 41), probably the largest roofed space in ancient Rome, is another example. Only one side, consisting of three enormous barrel vaults, still stands today; the center tract (or "nave") was covered by three groin vaults and rose a good deal higher. Since a groin vault is like a canopy, with all the weight concentrated at the four corners, the wall surfaces in between could be pierced by windows, called a "clerestory." Like the niches in the Pantheon, these helped break up the ponderous mass and made it seem less overpowering. We meet echoes of this vaulting system in many later buildings, from churches to railway stations.

In discussing the new forms based on arched, vaulted, and domed construction, we have noted the Roman architects' continued allegiance to the Classic Greek orders. While he no longer relied on them in the structural sense, he remained faithful to their spirit; column, architrave, and pediment might be merely superimposed on a vaulted brick-and-concrete core, but their shape, as well as their relationship to each other, still followed the original grammar of the orders. Only when the Roman Empire was in decline did this reverential attitude give way to unorthodox ideas, as in the Palace of Diocletian (fig. 42) on the coast of present-day Yugoslavia. Here the architrave between the two center columns is curved, echoing the arch of the doorway below; on the left we see an even more revolutionary device—a series of arches resting directly on columns. Thus, on the eve of the victory of Christianity, the marriage of arch and column was finally legitimate.

42. Peristyle, Palace of Diocletian.
c.300 A.D. Split, Yugoslavia

43. *Portrait of a Roman.*
c.80 B.C. Marble, lifesize. Palazzo Torlonia, Rome

44. *Trajan.* c.100 A.D. Marble,
lifesize. Museum, Ostia

Their union, indispensable for the subsequent development of architecture, seems so natural that we wonder why it was ever opposed.

Although there is no doubt that the Romans created a bold new architecture, the question of whether they had anything original to give to the field of sculpture has been hotly disputed, and for quite understandable reasons. A taste for opulent decoration, both exterior and interior, led to wholesale importation of Greek statuary, when it could be obtained, or mass copying of Greek—sometimes even of Egyptian—models. There are entire categories of Roman sculpture which deserve to be called "deactivated echoes" of Greek creations, emptied of their former meaning and reduced to the status of refined works of craftsmanship. On the other hand, certain kinds of sculpture had serious and important functions in ancient Rome, and it is these that continue the living sculptural tradition. Portraiture and narrative reliefs are the two aspects of sculpture most conspicuously rooted in the real needs of Roman society.

The portrait bust in figure 43, dating from the beginning of the Republican era, is probably one of the first permanent embodiments of a much older tradition that we know about from literary sources. When the head of a prominent family died, a wax image was made of his face, and these images were preserved by subsequent generations and carried in the funeral processions of the family. Starting as ancestor worship back in prehistoric times, this custom became a convenient way to demonstrate the importance and continuity of a family —a habit that continues practically unbroken to our own day in the displaying of family portraits. Wax, however, is a very impermanent material, and for some reason—perhaps a crisis of self-confidence—it became important to the patrician families of Rome in the first century B.C. to put these ancestor likenesses into more enduring substance (fig. 43). What differentiates this head from a late, expressive example of Greek sculpture? Can we say that it has any new, specifically Roman qualities? At first it may strike us as nothing more than the detailed record of a facial topography, sparing neither wrinkle nor wart. Yet the sculptor has exercised a choice among which wrinkles to emphasize and which features (the jutting lower lip, for instance) to make a little larger-than-life. The face emerges as a specifically Roman personality—stern, rugged, iron-willed. It is a "father image" of frightening authority;

45. *Equestrian Statue of Marcus Aurelius.* 161–80 A.D.
Bronze, over lifesize. Piazza del Campidoglio, Rome

one that can be imagined to rule not merely a family, but a colony or even an empire. Perhaps this fierce expression is inherited from Etruscan sculpture (see fig. 37); by contrast, even the agonized face of Laocoön (fig. 36) seems lacking in forcefulness.

It may seem surprising that when the Republic, under Julius Caesar, gave way to the Empire (shortly after this head was made), portraiture lost something of its intense individuality. Depictions of the emperors such as Trajan (fig. 44), while not lacking in recognizable personality, set the fashion for more heroic and idealized likenesses. One suspects that as the empire became larger, more complex, and more difficult to keep in rein, the rulers were at pains to give the impression that they were cool in the face of any and all crises. The Greeks had given the world unsurpassable forms in conjuring up gods in the guise of men; the Romans now went back to these forms to elevate the images of men to the level of gods.

A portrait which succeeds in being human, in the noblest sense of the word, is the equestrian statue of the Emperor Marcus Aurelius (fig. 45): a learned man himself, his ideal was the ancient Greek "philosopher-king" who ruled by wisdom rather than by force and cunning. Astride his noble horse (which seems, like its master, to control itself rather than to be controlled) he gazes downward at the passer-by with an expression of lofty calm tinged with compassion.

Alas, the turmoil of the overextended empire had already begun. Soon the ruler's supernatural power, whether conferred by divinity or wisdom, no longer seemed plausible, especially (as was increasingly the case in the third century A.D.) if he had been merely a successful general who attained the throne by overthrowing his predecessor. Such a man was Philippus the Arab (fig. 46), who reigned for five brief years, 244 to 249 A.D. What a portrait it is! For realism, feature by feature, it is as stark as the Republican bust; but here the aim is expressive rather than documentary: all the dark passions of the human mind—fear, suspicion, cruelty—stand revealed with a directness that is almost unbelievable. The face of Philippus mirrors all the violence of the time, yet in a strange way it moves us to pity: there is a psychological nakedness about it that recalls a brute creature, cornered and doomed. Clearly, the agony of the Roman world was not only physical but spiritual.

So, too, were the glories of its dwindling years; or so they must have seemed to Constantine the Great (fig. 47), reorganizer of the Roman State, and the first Christian emperor. No mere bust, this head is one of several remaining fragments of a colossal statue (the head alone is over eight feet tall) that once

46. *Philippus the Arab.* 244–49 A.D. Marble,
lifesize. Vatican Museums, Rome

stood in Constantine's gigantic basilica (see fig. 41). In this head everything is so out of proportion to the scale of ordinary men that we feel crushed by its immensity. The impression of being in the presence of some unimaginable power was deliberate, we may be sure, for it is reinforced by the massive, immobile features out of which the huge, radiant eyes stare with hypnotic intensity. All in all, it tells us less about the way Constantine looked than about his view of himself and his exalted office.

It is almost with the feeling of ridding ourselves of an insupportable weight that we turn back to the early years of the Empire to investigate another type of sculpture, the narrative relief. The *Ara Pacis* (or "peace altar"; fig. 48) was built for Augustus Caesar, nephew and successor to Julius Caesar, and the first to call himself "Emperor." For him, the present and the future looked bright and promising, and he could confidently celebrate Peace, by name and also in spirit. There is a self-assurance about this procession which does not depend upon superhuman intervention, and a kind of joyful

47. *Constantine the Great*. Early 4th century A.D. Marble, height 8'. Capitoline Museums, Rome

dignity that puts us in mind of the Parthenon sculptures when Athens, too, serene in her leadership, could not foresee the bad times so soon to come. But there are also many things that differentiate the *Ara Pacis* from its Greek predecessor: the procession here is a specific occasion rather than a timeless and impersonal event. The participants, at least so far as they belong to the imperial family, were meant to be identifiable portraits, including the children dressed in miniature togas, still too young to understand the solemnity of the occasion (note the little boy tugging at the mantle of the young man in front of him, while turning toward an older child who smilingly tells him to behave). In addition to taking delight in humanizing details, the sculptor has made advances in composition: there is a greater concern to give an illusion of spatial depth than in Greek reliefs, so that some of the faces farthest removed from us (such as the veiled young woman facing the youth whose cloak is being pulled) seem to be embedded in the stone of the background.

This illusion of depth given to a shallow space reached its most complete development in the large narrative panels that formed part of a triumphal arch erected in 81 A.D. to commemorate the victories of the Emperor Titus. One of them (fig. 49) shows the victory procession held after Rome conquered Jerusalem; the booty displayed includes the seven-branched candlestick from the Temple, and other sacred objects. The forward surge of the crowd is rendered with striking success: on the right, the procession turns away from us and disappears through an arch placed obliquely to the background plane so that only the nearer half actually emerges from it—a radical but effective device for conveying the depth of the scene.

Because so little of either Greek or Roman painting has been preserved (and that little is largely thanks to the eruption of Mount Vesuvius in 79 A.D., which buried buildings erected during a relatively short time span—leaving us to wonder what sort of painting came before and after this catastrophe), what does remain is apt to strike the beholder as the most exciting, as well as the most baffling, aspect of art under Roman rule. That famous Greek designs were copied and even Greek painters imported, nobody will dispute; but the number of cases where a direct link can be surely established with the older art is small indeed. A *Battle of Alexander the Great Against the Persians* (fig. 50) may be assumed to have been inspired by

left: 48. *Imperial Procession,*
portion of frieze on the *Ara Pacis.*
13–9 B.C. Marble, height 63″. Rome

below: 49. *Spoils from
the Temple in Jerusalem,*
relief in passageway, Arch of Titus.
81 A.D. Marble, height 7′ 10″. Rome

a Greek work, as well as by Greek history. Actually it is not a painting, but an exceptionally elaborate floor mosaic made out of thousands of tiny colored marble cubes, or tesserae, though we can hardly doubt that it is copied after a Hellenistic picture. But a Hellenistic picture of what date? The crowding, the air of frantic excitement, the powerfully modeled and foreshortened forms, the precisely cast shadows —when did all these qualities reach this particular stage of development? We can only say that we do not know, for even the Laocoön (see fig. 36) seems restrained by comparison.

Movable pictures on panels, such as we think of nowadays when we speak of "paintings," were not frequent in Roman times; or if

50. *Battle of Alexander the Great Against the Persians.* Mosaic, copy of a Hellenistic painting. Width of portion shown c.10½'. National Museum, Naples

they were, they have all disappeared like the wax ancestor images. Rather, pictures were included in the fresco decorations (on more permanent surfaces of hard plaster) of interiors, such as the Ixion Room (fig. 51) from the House of the Vettii in Pompeii. These scenic panels are set into an elaborate ensemble combining imitation (painted) marble paneling, and fantastic architectural vistas seen through make-believe windows. The illusion of surface textures and distant views has an extraordinary degree of three-dimensional reality; but as soon as we try to analyze the relationship of the various parts to each other, we find ourselves con-

fused, and we quickly realize that the Roman painters had no systematic grasp of spatial depth.

When landscapes take the place of architectural features, however, the virtues of the Roman painter's approach outweigh its limitations. This is strikingly demonstrated by the *Odyssey Landscapes*, a continuous stretch of panorama subdivided into eight large panels, each illustrating an episode from the adventures of Odysseus (Ulysses). One of them has been recently cleaned, and is reproduced here in colorplate 3 to show the original brilliance of the tones. The airy, bluish atmosphere creates a wonderful impression of light-filled space that envelops and binds together all the forms within this warm Mediterranean fairyland, where the human figures seem to play no more than an incidental role. Only upon further reflection do we realize how frail the illusion of coherence is: if we were to try mapping this landscape, we would find it as ambiguous as the architectural decorations discussed above.

It would be strange indeed if portraiture, which forms such an outstanding part of Rome's particular contribution to the history of sculpture, had not also existed in painting. Pliny, the Roman historian, mentions it as an established custom in Republican Rome. A few miniatures, painted on glass, have survived from the third century A.D., or later; however, if we want to get some idea of what Roman painted portraits looked like we must turn, strangely enough, to Lower Egypt. There, in

51. The Ixion Room, House of the Vettii. 63–79 A.D. Pompeii

Colorplate 3. *The Laestrygonians Hurling Rocks at the Fleet of Odysseus,*
panel of *Odyssey Landscapes,* wall painting in a house on the Esquiline Hill.
Late 1st century B.C. Vatican Museums, Rome

Colorplate 4. Interior (view toward apse), S. Apollinare in Classe. 533–549 A.D. Ravenna

the region of Faiyum, a strange Romanized version of the traditional Egyptian mummy-case has been found. Before Egypt came under Roman dominion, the heads of mummy-cases were provided with conventionalized masks, modeled in stone, wood, or plaster; now these were replaced by painted portraits of the dead, executed in lifelike colors on wooden panels. The very fine portrait of a boy (fig. 52) is as sparkling and natural as anyone might wish, exhibiting a sureness of touch on the part of the artist that has rarely been surpassed. As in the sculptured busts, the artist has magnified and stressed certain features: the eyes, for example, are exaggeratedly large. But in this happy instance the stylization has not been made with the intention of overawing us (as in the case of Constantine's hypnotic stare, fig. 47), but only to recall the attractive personality of a beloved child.

52. *Portrait of a Boy*, from the Faiyum, Upper Egypt. 2nd century A.D. Encaustic on panel, 13 x 7¼". The Metropolitan Museum of Art, New York (Gift of Edward S. Harkness, 1918)

4. EARLY CHRISTIAN AND BYZANTINE ART

In 323 A.D. Constantine the Great made a fateful decision, the consequences of which are still felt today: he resolved to move the capital of the Roman Empire to the Greek town of Byzantium, which henceforth was to be known as Constantinople. In taking this step, the Emperor acknowledged the growing strategic and economic importance of the eastern provinces (a development that had been going on for some time). The new capital also symbolized the new Christian basis of the Roman state, since it was in the heart of the most thoroughly Christianized region of the Empire. Constantine could hardly foresee that shifting the seat of imperial power would result in splitting the realm, yet within a hundred years the division had become an accomplished fact, even though the emperors at Constantinople did not relinquish their claim to the western provinces. The latter, ruled by western Roman emperors, soon fell prey to invading Germanic tribes—Visigoths, Vandals, Ostrogoths, Lombards. By the end of the sixth century the last trace of centralized authority had disappeared. The Eastern, or Byzantine, Empire, in contrast, survived these onslaughts, and under Justinian (527–565 A.D.) reached new power and stability. With the rise of Islam a hundred years later, the African and Near Eastern parts of the Empire were overrun by conquering Arab armies; in the eleventh century, the Turks occupied a large part of Asia Minor, while the last Byzantine possessions in the West (in southern Italy)

fell to the Normans. Yet the Empire, with its domain reduced to the Balkans and Greece, held on till 1453, when the Turks finally conquered Constantinople itself.

The division of the Roman Empire soon led to a religious split as well. At the time of Constantine, the bishop of Rome, deriving his authority from St. Peter, was the acknowledged head—the Pope—of the Christian Church. His claim, however, soon came to be disputed; differences in doctrine began to develop, and eventually the division of Christendom into a Western, or Catholic, Church and an Eastern, or Orthodox, Church became all but final. The differences between them went very deep: Roman Catholicism maintained its independence from imperial or any other state authority, and became an international institution reflecting its character as the Universal Church. The Orthodox Church, in contrast, was based on the union of spiritual and secular authority in the person of the emperor. It was thus dependent on the State, exacting a double allegiance from the faithful but sharing the vicissitudes of political power. We will recognize this pattern as the Christian adaptation of a very ancient heritage, the divine kingship of Egypt and Mesopotamia; if the Byzantine emperors, unlike their pagan predecessors, could no longer claim the status of gods, they kept a unique and equally exalted role by placing themselves at the head of the Church as well as the State. Nor did the tradition die with the fall of Constantinople. The tsars of Russia claimed the mantle of the Byzantine emperors, and Moscow became "the third Rome"; thus the Russian

Orthodox Church was closely tied to the State, as was its Byzantine parent body.

It is the religious even more than the political separation of East and West that makes it impossible to discuss the development of Christian art in the Roman Empire under a single heading. "Early Christian" does not, strictly speaking, define a style; it refers, rather, to any work of art produced by or for Christians during the time prior to the splitting off of the Orthodox Church—roughly, the first five centuries of our era. "Byzantine art," on the other hand, designates not only the art of the Eastern Roman Empire, but a specific quality of style as well. Since this style grew out of certain tendencies that can be traced back to the time of Constantine, or even earlier, there is no sharp dividing line between the two until after the reign of Justinian, who was not only conversant with artistic currents in both parts of the Empire, but almost succeeded in reuniting them politically as well. Soon after him, however, Celtic and Germanic peoples fell heir to the civilization of late Roman antiquity, of which Early Christian art had been a part, and transformed it into that of the Middle Ages. The East experienced no such break; there, late antiquity lived on, although the Greek and Oriental elements came increasingly to the fore at the expense of the Roman heritage. As a consequence Byzantine civilization never experienced the flux and fusion that created medieval art: "The Byzantines may have been senile," as one historian has observed, "but they remained Greeks to the end."

Before Constantine, Rome was not yet the official center of the faith; older and larger Christian communities existed in the great cities of North Africa and the Near East, such as Alexandria and Antioch, and they probably had artistic traditions of their own of which we seem to catch glimpses in the mainstream of art at a much later date. Actually, our knowledge of them is scanty in the extreme; for the first three centuries of the Christian Era we have little to go on when trying to trace the evolution of art in the service of the new religion. The only exception is the painting found on the walls of catacombs, the underground passages in which the Roman Christians buried their dead.

If the dearth of material from the more flourishing Eastern Christian colonies makes it difficult to judge these pictures in a larger context, they nevertheless tell us a good deal about the spirit of the communities that sponsored them.

53. Painted Ceiling, Catacomb of SS. Pietro e Marcellino. Early 4th century A.D. Rome

The burial rite and safeguarding of the tomb were of vital concern to the early Christians, whose faith rested on the hope of eternal life in paradise. The imagery of the catacombs, as can be seen in the painted ceiling in figure 53, clearly expresses this otherworldly outlook, although the forms are in essence still those of pre-Christian Roman painting. Thus we recognize the compartmental divisions as a late and highly simplified echo of the illusionistic architectural schemes in Pompeian painting; and the modeling of the figures, too, though debased in the hands of an artist of very modest ability, also betrays its descent from the same Roman idiom. But the catacomb painter has used this traditional vocabulary to convey a new, symbolic content, so that to him the original meaning of the forms was a matter of small interest. Even the geometric framework shares in the new task: the great circle suggests the Dome of Heaven, much as the ceiling of the Pantheon was meant to (see p. 31), but here the oculus in the center has been connected to the outer ring by four pairs of brackets, a simple device that forms the cross, the main symbol of the faith. In the central medallion we see a youthful shepherd with a sheep on his shoulders. It is true that this form, too, can be traced as far back as the Archaic Greeks, but here it has become an emblem of Christ the Saviour—the Good Shepherd. The semicircular compartments contain episodes from the legend of Jonah: on the left he is cast from the ship; on the right he emerges from the whale; and at the bottom, safe again on dry land, he meditates upon the mercy of the Lord. This Old Testament miracle enjoyed immense favor in Early Christian art, as proof of the Lord's power to rescue the faithful from the jaws of death. The standing figures, their hands raised in a traditional gesture of prayer, represent members of the Church pleading for divine help.

With the triumph of Christianity as the State religion under Constantine, an almost overnight blossoming of church architecture began in both halves of the Empire. Before that, congregations had not been able to meet in public, and services were held inconspicuously in the houses of the wealthier members; now impressive new buildings were wanted, for all to see. Early Christian basilicas cannot be wholly explained in terms of their pagan Roman predecessors, although the latter served well as a point of departure, combining the spacious interior, necessary for the performing of Christian ritual before a congregation, with imperial associations that proclaimed the exalted status of the new state religion. But the Christian basilica had in addition to be the Sacred House of God; for this reason the entrances, which in Roman secular basilicas had been along the flanks so as to provide many doorways for people bent on a variety of errands, were concentrated at one end, usually facing west. At the opposite end of the long nave was the altar, the focus of the ritual. This emphasis on the longitudinal axis is easily seen in the exterior view of Sant'Apollinare in Classe (fig. 54), a church built on Italian soil during the reign of Justinian. If we except the round bell tower (campanile) on the left, we will find many features to remind us of pagan buildings that have already been discussed: the transverse porch (narthex) which welcomes the visitor to the sacred building, while at the same time obscuring the view of what is to come, is a small-scale, simplified reminder of the portico of the Pantheon (see p. 30). The row of arches, echoed by a matching arcade in the interior, is a form of architecture pioneered under the Emperor Diocletian (p. 32); the clerestory too had appeared earlier in Roman basilicas (p. 31); and turning to the interior view (colorplate 4), we may note that the eastern end, where the altar was placed, is set off from the rest by a frame reminiscent of a Roman triumphal arch (see the one in fig. 49). What is new here, in addition to the more expert use of the column-plus-arch construction, is the astonishing contrast between the plain brick exterior which (unlike classical temples) is merely an envelope for the interior, and the explosion of vivid colors and rich materials within. Having left the workaday world outside, we find ourselves in a shimmering realm of light, where precious marble and glittering mosaics evoke the unearthly splendor of the Kingdom of God.

Although the Romans, too, produced mosaics (see fig. 50), they had used marble tesserae having a limited range of colors; these mosaics were more suitable for floor decoration than for walls. The vast and intricate wall mosaics in Early Christian churches really have no precedent, either for expanse or technique. Instead of stone, the tesserae are made of glass; they are brilliant in color but not rich in tonal gradations, so that they do not lend themselves readily to the copying of painted pictures. Instead, with each tiny square of glass also acting as a reflector, a glittering, screenlike effect is produced, as intangible as it is dazzling. If the exterior of Sant'Apollinare strikes us as unassuming—even antimonumental in comparison with previous building styles—the interior is its perfect complement. Here the dematerialization of the construction is turned to positive account, for the purpose of achieving an "illusion of unreality."

To transport the spectator into realms of glory was not, of course, the only purpose of these mosaics. Like the modest beginnings of Christian art (see fig. 53) they contain symbols of the faith (in Sant'Apollinare the Cross is plainly visible in the oculus that opens onto the starry skies, where Christ presides in the highest

54. S. Apollinare in Classe,
aerial view. 533–49 A.D. Ravenna
(for interior, see colorplate 4)

55. *The Parting of Lot and Abraham.* c.430 A.D. Mosaic.
Sta. Maria Maggiore, Rome

realm of heaven, flanked by the symbols of the
four Evangelists). Sometimes they also illustrate scenes from both Old and New Testaments, thus serving the unlettered as picture-
Bibles. *The Parting of Lot and Abraham* (fig.
55) is one frame of a long series that decorates
the nave of Santa Maria Maggiore in Rome.
The idea of making such a series, as well as
some of the pictorial devices that the mosaicist
has used (such as the "grape clusters" of heads
arising behind the relatively few bodies that occupy the foreground), may well have been derived from Roman narrative reliefs. But the

Early Christian artist was not constrained by
the need to make a specific event look real;
these Biblical scenes, whose stories were known
already to most of the faithful, were not so
much illustrations as symbolic events with a
didactic purpose. Here, for instance, Abraham
and his clan (the left-hand group) are about to
go one way—the way of righteousness; while
Lot and his family, about to exit right, are de-
parting for Sodom, toward depravity and ruin.

For church use and the devotions of the
learned there were also illustrated Bibles. The
development of the book format itself is not
entirely clear: we know that the Egyptians
made a paperlike substance, only more brittle,
out of papyrus reeds. Their "books," however,
were scrolls to be unrolled as one read. This
was not an ideal surface for painted illustration, for the repeated bending and unbending
of each section would tend to make the paint
flake off. The Torah, the sacred scriptures
that are read at each service in synagogues, still
preserves this ancient format. Not until late
Hellenistic times did a better substance become available: parchment, or vellum (thin,
bleached animal hide). It was strong enough to
be creased without breaking, and thus made
possible the kind of bound book (technically
known as a codex) that we still have today.
Between the first and the fourth centuries A.D.
this gradually replaced the scroll, greatly en-
hancing the range of painted illustration (or,
as it is called, illumination) so that it became

56. *Jacob Wrestling with the Angel,* from the *Vienna Genesis.*
Early 6th century A.D. Manuscript illumination. National Library, Vienna

57. Sarcophagus of
Junius Bassus.
c.359 A.D. Marble,
3′ 10½″ x 8′.
Vatican Grottoes,
Rome

the small-scale counterpart of murals, mosaics, or panel pictures. *Jacob Wrestling with the Angel* (fig. 56) comes from one of the oldest extant examples of an Old Testament book, though it must have been preceded by others which have been lost. This codex, called the *Vienna Genesis*, was written in silver (now turned black) on purple-tinted vellum, and adorned with brilliantly colored miniatures; the effect is not unlike that produced by the mosaics which we have discussed. The scene itself does not show a single event, but a whole sequence strung out along a U-shaped path, so that progression in space also becomes progression in time. This method, known as continuous narration, has a long ancestry going back to sculptured relief, and possibly to scroll books. Here it permits the painter to pack a maximum of content into the area of the page at his disposal, and the continuous episodes were probably meant to be "read," like the letters themselves, rather than taken in all at once as a composition.

Compared to painting and architecture, sculpture played a secondary role in Early Christian times. The Old Testament prohibition of "graven images" was thought to apply with particular force to large cult statues—the idols worshiped in pagan temples. To avoid the taint of idolatry, religious sculpture had to develop from the very start in an antimonumental direction. Shallow carving, small-scale forms, and lacelike surface decoration came to be its characteristics. The earliest works of sculpture that can be called "Christian" are sarcophagi made for the wealthier members of the congregation; beginning about the middle of the third

century, they differ from pagan sarcophagi not so much in form as in the subject matter of the decoration. At first this consisted of a somewhat limited repertory, such as we have seen in the catacomb painting: the Good Shepherd, Jonah, etc. (fig. 53). The sarcophagus of Junius Bassus (fig. 57) of a century later, however, shows a richly expanded repertory of subjects, taken from both the Old and the New Testaments, reflecting the new, out-in-the-open position of Christianity now that it was the established State religion and no longer had to allude to the faith in cryptic, symbolic terms. Junius Bassus himself was a Roman prefect.

To those of us who are familiar with only the later formulation of Christ's image, as a bearded and often suffering man, it may at first be difficult to recognize Him at all in these scenes. Youthful and serene, He sits enthroned in heaven (a bearded figure, personifying the sky, holds up His throne) between Saints Peter and Paul (center panel, upper row); nor does He seem troubled in the scene of Christ before Pontius Pilate, which occupies the two panels directly to the right, where He stands, scroll in hand, like some young philosopher expounding his views. This aspect of Christ is in keeping with the Christian thought of the period that stressed His divinity and His power to redeem us from death, rather than the torments that He took on when He became flesh. This dignified conception lent itself well to a revival of some classical features of composition and figures. Such revivals occurred quite frequently during the two centuries after Christianity had become the official religion: paganism still had many adherents (Junius

right: 58. ANTHEMIUS
OF TRALLES
and ISIDORE OF MILETUS.
Hagia Sophia.
532–37 A.D. Istanbul

below: 59. Interior,
Hagia Sophia. Istanbul

Bassus himself was converted only shortly before his death) who may have fostered such revivals; there were important leaders of the Church who favored a reconciliation of Christianity with the classical heritage; and the imperial courts, both East and West, always remained aware of their institutional links with pre-Christian times. Whatever the reasons, we must be glad that the Roman Empire in transition preserved, and thus helped transmit, a treasury of forms and an ideal of beauty that might have been irretrievably lost.

The reign of Emperor Justinian marks the point at which the ascendancy of the Eastern Roman Empire over the Western became complete and final. Justinian himself was an art patron on a scale unmatched since Constantine's day; the works he sponsored or promoted have an imperial grandeur that fully justifies the acclaim of those who have termed his era a golden age. They also display an inner coherence of style which links them more strongly with the future of Byzantine art than with the art of the preceding centuries.

Ironically enough, the richest array of the monuments of this period survives today not in Constantinople, but in the city of Ravenna, in Italy. We have already seen one of them, Sant' Apollinare in Classe, which—better than examples of Early Christian buildings in Rome itself—preserves unaltered the appearance, structural features, and decoration of the earliest churches. But among the surviving buildings of Justinian's reign, by far the greatest is Hagia Sophia (The Church of the Holy Wisdom) in Constantinople (figs. 58, 59). Built in 532–37, it was so famous in its day that even the names of the architects, Anthemius of Tralles and Isidor of Miletus, have come down to us. The design of Hagia Sophia presents a unique combination of elements; it has the longitudinal axis of an Early Christian basilica, but the central feature of the nave is a square compartment crowned by a huge dome abutted at either end by half-domes, so that the effect is that of a huge oval. The weight of the dome is carried on four enormous arches; the walls below the arches have no supporting function at all. The transition from the square formed by the four arches to the circular rim of the dome is made by spherical triangles, called pendentives. This device permits the construction of taller, lighter, and more economical domes than the older method (as seen in the Pantheon). We do not know the ancestry of this useful scheme, but Hagia Sophia is the first example of its use on a monumental scale, and it was epoch-making; henceforth it was to be a basic feature of Byzantine architecture and, somewhat later, of Western architecture as well. The plan and size will recall the Basilica of Constantine (fig. 41), the greatest monu-

ment associated with the ruler for whom Justinian had a particular admiration. Hagia Sophia thus unites East and West, past and future, in a single overpowering synthesis. Although there is nothing unassuming about the grand exterior, as was the case with Sant'Apollinare, the two interiors have in common a feeling of weightlessness (colorplate 4); here, however, it has a new, imaginative aspect, as though the recesses, the pendentives, and the dome were so many sails expanding under the pressure of some great wind. The golden glitter of the mosaics (covered over when the Moslems captured the city, and now only partially restored) must have been even more spectacular when the windows which pierce the walls made the golden sky-dome seem to float on air itself.

It is only fitting that we use, as an example of the mosaics of Justinian's reign, the portrait of the Emperor himself, surrounded by his courtiers, which has survived in good condition in the church of San Vitale in Ravenna (fig. 60). The design, and perhaps the workmen, must have come directly from the imperial workshop. Here we find a new ideal of human beauty: extraordinarily tall, slim figures, with tiny feet, small, almond-shaped faces dominated by large eyes, and bodies that seem capable only of ceremonial gestures and the dis-

60. *Justinian and Attendants.* c.547 A.D. Mosaic. S. Vitale, Ravenna

play of magnificent costumes. Every hint of movement or change is carefully excluded—the dimensions of time and of earthly space have given way to an eternal present amid the golden translucency of heaven, and the solemn frontal images seem to present a celestial rather than a secular court. This union of spiritual and political authority accurately reflects the "divine kingship" of Byzantine emperors.

The majestic images of Justinian's "golden age" continued to pervade all of later Byzantine art as well. But in the *Crucifixion* (fig. 61) of the eleventh century in the church at Daphnē (Greece) we no longer find the youthful, heroic Christ that we saw in the Junius Bassus reliefs; the tilt of the head, the sagging lines of the body, the expression of suffering make a powerful appeal to the beholder's emotions. This compassionate quality was perhaps the greatest achievement of later Byzantine art, even though its full possibilities were to be explored not in Byzantium, but in the medieval West.

Not that it disappeared completely from Byzantine art, but after centuries of repetition, exquisiteness of craftsmanship rather than expressive impact came to dominate such images. The *Madonna Enthroned* (fig. 62) is a work of this kind. The graceful drapery folds, the tender expression are still there; but they have become strangely abstract. The throne (which looks rather like a miniature Colosseum) has lost any semblance of solid three-dimensionality, as have the bodies—though some modeling is still to be found in the faces. With gold as a background, and gold used to pick out all the highlights of the forms, the effect cannot be called either flat or spatial; rather, it is transparent, for everywhere the golden background shines through, as though the picture were lit from behind. Panels such as ours, called icons (sacred images), should be viewed as the aesthetic offspring of mosaics, rather than as the descendants of the classical panel painting tradition from which they spring (see fig. 52).

above: 61. *The Crucifixion.* 11th century. Mosaic. Monastery Church, Daphnē, Greece

right: 62. *Madonna Enthroned.* 13th century. Panel, 32 x 19½". National Gallery of Art, Washington, D.C. (Mellon Collection)

PART TWO

ART IN THE MIDDLE AGES

1. EARLY MEDIEVAL ART

When we think of the great civilizations of our past, we tend to do so in terms of visible monuments that have come to symbolize the distinctive character of each: the pyramids of Egypt, for example; or the Parthenon of Athens; the Colosseum of Rome—all were made famous (or infamous) by the part that they played in the history of their times. In such a review, the Middle Ages would undoubtedly be represented by a Gothic cathedral; we have many to choose from, but whichever one we pick, it will be well north of the Alps, although in territory that formerly belonged to the Roman Empire. And if we spill a bucket of water in front of that cathedral, the water would eventually make its way to the English Channel, rather than to the Mediterranean. This is the most important single fact about the Middle Ages: the center of gravity of European civilization has shifted to what had been the northern boundaries of the Roman world. The Mediterranean, for so many centuries the great highway of commercial and cultural exchange for all the lands along its shores, had become a barrier, a border zone.

In the preceding chapter we became familiar with some of the events that paved the way for the shift: the removal of the imperial capital to Constantinople; the growing split between the Catholic and Orthodox faiths; and the decay of the Western half of the Roman Empire under the impact of invasions by Germanic tribes. Yet these tribes, once they had settled down in their new land, accepted the framework of late Roman, Christian civilization: the new states they founded, on the northern coast of Africa, and in Spain, Gaul, and northern Italy, were Mediterranean-oriented, provincial states along the borders of the Byzantine Empire, subject to the pull of its greater military, commercial, and cultural power. The reconquest of the lost Western provinces remained a serious political goal of Byzantine emperors until the middle of the seventh century. This possibility ceased to exist when a completely unforeseen new force made itself felt in the East: the Arabs, under the banner of Islam, were overrunning the Near Eastern and African provinces of Byzantium. By 732, within a century after the death of Mohammed, they had occupied North Africa as well as most of Spain, and threatened to add southwestern France to their conquests.

It would be difficult to exaggerate the impact upon the Christian world of the lightninglike advance of Islam. With more than enough to do to keep this new force at bay in its own back yard, the Byzantine Empire lost its bases in the western Mediterranean. Left exposed and unprotected, Western Europe was forced to develop its own resources, political, economic, and spiritual. The Church of Rome broke its last ties with the East and turned for support to the Germanic north, where the Frankish kingdom, under the leadership of the energetic Carolingian dynasty, aspired to the status of imperial power in the eighth century. When the Pope, in the year 800, bestowed the title of Emperor upon Charlemagne, he solemnized the new order of things by placing himself and all of Western Christendom under the protection of the King of the Franks and Lombards. He did not, however, subordinate himself to the newly created Catholic emperor; the legitimacy of the latter depended on the pope, whereas hitherto it had been the other way around (the emperor in Constantinople had always ratified the newly elected popes). This interdependent dualism of spiritual and political authority, of Church and State, was to distinguish the West from both the Orthodox East and the Islamic South. Outwardly it was symbolized by the fact that, although the emperor had to be crowned by the pope in Rome, he did not live there; Charlemagne built his capital at the center of his effective power, in Aachen, where Belgium, Germany, and the Netherlands meet today.

THE DARK AGES. The labels we use for historical periods tend to be like the nicknames of people: once established, they are almost impossible to change, even though they may no longer be suitable. Those who coined the term "Middle Ages" thought of the entire thousand years that came between the fifth and fifteenth centuries as an age of darkness, an empty interval between classical antiquity and its revival, the Renaissance in Italy. Since then, our view of the Middle Ages has completely changed; we no longer think of the period as "benighted," but as the "Age of Faith." With the spread of this new, positive conception, the idea of darkness has become confined more and more to the early part of the Middle Ages, roughly between the death of Justinian and the reign of Charlemagne. Perhaps we ought to pare down the Dark Ages even further; there was a great deal of activity in that darkness while the economic, political, and spiritual framework of Western Europe was being established; and as we shall now see, the same period also gave rise to some important artistic achievements.

The Germanic tribes that had entered Western Europe from the east during the declining years of the Roman Empire carried with them, in the form of nomads' gear, an ancient and widespread artistic tradition, the so-called animal style. Examples of it have been found in the form of bronzes in Iran, and gold in southern Russia. A combination of abstract and organic shapes, formal discipline and imaginative freedom, it became an important element in the Celto-Germanic art of the Dark Ages, such as the gold-and-enamel purse cover (fig. 63) from the grave of an East Anglian king who died in 654. Four pairs of motifs are symmetrically arranged on its surface; each has its own distinctive character, an indication that the motifs have been assembled from different

sources. One of them, the standing man between two confronted animals, has a very long history indeed: we first saw it in figure 17—a panel more than three thousand years older. The eagles pouncing on ducks also date back a long way, to carnivore-and-victim motifs. The design just above them, however, is of more recent origin. It consists of fighting animals whose tails, legs, and jaws are elongated into bands forming a complex interlacing pattern. Interlacing bands, as an ornamental device, had existed in Roman and even Mesopotamian art (see fig. 17, bottom row), but their combination with the animal style, as shown here, seems to have been an invention of the Dark Ages.

Metalwork, in a variety of materials and techniques and often of exquisitely refined craftsmanship, had been the principal medium of the animal style. Such objects, small, durable, and eagerly sought after, account for the rapid diffusion of its repertory of forms. They "migrated" not only in the geographic sense, but also technically and artistically into other materials—wood, stone, even manuscript illumination. Wooden specimens, as we might expect, have not survived in large quantities; most of them come from Scandinavia, where the animal style flourished longer than anywhere else. The splendid animal head of the early ninth century (fig. 64) is a terminal post that was found, along with much other equipment, in a buried Viking ship at Oseberg in southern Norway. Like the motifs on the purse cover, it shows a peculiar composite quality: the basic shape of the head is surprisingly realistic, as are certain details (teeth, gums, nostrils), but the surface has been spun over with interlacing and geometric patterns that betray their derivation from metalwork.

This pagan Germanic version of the animal style is reflected in the earliest Christian works of art north of the Alps as well. In order to un-

63. Purse Cover, from the Sutton Hoo Ship-Burial. Before 655 A.D. Gold and enamel. British Museum, London

above: 64. *Animal Head,* from the
Oseberg Ship-Burial. c.825 A.D. Wood, height c.5″.
University Museum of Antiquities, Oslo

right: 65. Cross Page, from *Lindisfarne Gospels.* c.700 A.D.
Manuscript illumination. British Museum, London

derstand how they came to be produced, however, we must first acquaint ourselves with the
important role played by the Irish, who, during
the Dark Ages, assumed the spiritual and cultural leadership of Western Europe. The period
600–800 A.D. deserves, in fact, to be called the
Golden Age of Ireland. Unlike their English
neighbors, the Irish had never been part of the
Roman Empire; thus the missionaries who carried the Gospel to them from the south in the
fifth century found a Celtic society, entirely
barbarian by Roman standards. The Irish readily accepted Christianity, which brought them
into contact with Mediterranean civilization,
but without becoming Rome-oriented. Rather,
they adapted what they had received in a spirit
of vigorous local independence. The institutional framework of the Roman Church, being
essentially urban, was ill suited to the rural
character of Irish life. Irish Christians preferred to follow the example of the desert
saints of North Africa and the Near East who
had left the temptations of the city in order to
seek spiritual perfection in the solitude of the
wilderness. Groups of such hermits, sharing a
common ideal of ascetic discipline, had
founded the earliest monasteries. By the fifth
century, monasteries had spread as far north as
western Britain, but only in Ireland did monas-
ticism take over the leadership of the Church
from the bishops. Irish monasteries, unlike

their desert prototypes, soon became seats of
learning and the arts; they also developed a
missionary fervor that sent Irish monks preaching to the heathen and founding monasteries
in northern Britain as well as on the European mainland. These Irishmen not only
speeded the conversion to Christianity of Scot-
land, northern France, the Netherlands, and
Germany; they also established the monastery
as a cultural center throughout the European
countryside. Although their Continental foundations were taken over before long by the
monks of the Benedictine order, who were advancing north from Italy during the seventh
and eighth centuries, Irish influence was to be
felt within medieval civilization for several
hundred years to come.

In order to spread the Gospel, the Irish monasteries had to produce copies of the Bible and
other Christian books in large numbers. Their
writing workshops (scriptoria) also became
centers of artistic endeavor, for a manuscript
containing the Word of God was looked upon
as a sacred object whose visual beauty should
reflect the importance of its contents. Irish
monks must have known Early Christian illuminated manuscripts, but here again, as in so
many other respects, they developed an independent tradition instead of simply copying
their models. While pictures illustrating Biblical
events held little interest for them, they did de-

Art in the Middle Ages　49

vote much effort to decorative embellishment. The finest of these manuscripts belong to the Hiberno-Saxon style, combining Celtic and Germanic elements, which flourished in those monasteries founded by Irishmen in Saxon England. The Cross Page in the *Lindisfarne Gospels* (fig. 65) is an imaginative creation of breath-taking complexity; the miniaturist, working with a jeweler's precision, has poured into the compartments of his geometric frame an animal interlace so dense and so full of controlled movement that the fighting beasts on the Sutton Hoo purse cover seem childishly simple in comparison. It is as if the world of paganism, embodied in biting, clawing monsters, had here suddenly been subdued by the superior authority of the Cross. In order to achieve this effect our artist has had to impose an extremely severe discipline upon himself. His "rules of the game," for example, demand that organic and geometric shapes must be kept separate; that within the animal compartments every line must turn out to be part of the animal's body, if we take the trouble to trace it back to its point of origin. There are also rules, too complex to go into here, governing symmetry, mirror-image effects, and repetitions of

67. Interior, Palace Chapel of Charlemagne. 792–805 A.D. Aachen

shape and color. Only by working these out for ourselves can we hope to enter into the spirit of this strange, mazelike world.

Of the representational images they found in Early Christian manuscripts, the Hiberno-Saxon illuminators generally retained only the symbols of the four Evangelists, since these could be translated into their ornamental idiom without difficulty. The bronze plaque (fig. 66), probably made for a book cover, shows how helpless they were when given the image of man to copy. In his attempt to reproduce an Early Christian composition, our artist suffered from an utter inability to conceive of the human frame as an organic unit, so that the figure of Christ becomes disembodied in the most elementary sense; head, arms, and feet are separate elements, attached to a central pattern of whorls, zigzags, and interlacing bands. Clearly, there is a wide gulf between the Celto-Germanic and the Mediterranean traditions, a gulf that this Irish artist did not know how to bridge. Much the same situation prevailed elsewhere during the Dark Ages; even the Lombards, on Italian soil, did not know what to do with human images.

CAROLINGIAN ART. The empire built by Charlemagne did not endure for long. His grandsons divided it into three parts, and proved incapable of effective rule even in these, so

66. *The Crucifixion* (from a book cover?). 8th century A.D. Bronze. National Museum of Ireland, Dublin

that political power reverted to the local nobility. The cultural achievements of his reign, in contrast, have proved far more lasting; this very page would look different without them, for it is printed in letters whose shapes derive from the script in Carolingian manuscripts. The fact that these letters are known today as Roman rather than Carolingian recalls another aspect of the cultural reforms sponsored by Charlemagne: the collecting and copying of ancient Roman literature. The oldest surviving texts of a great many classical Latin authors are to be found in Carolingian manuscripts which, until not long ago, were mistakenly regarded as Roman: hence their lettering, too, was called Roman. This interest in preserving the classics was part of an ambitious attempt to restore ancient Roman civilization (see also p. 219), along with the imperial title. Charlemagne himself took an active hand in this revival, through which he expected to implant the traditions of a glorious past in the minds of the semibarbarian people of his realm. To an astonishing extent, he succeeded. Thus the "Carolingian revival" may be termed the first—and in some ways the most important —phase of a genuine fusion of the Celto-Germanic spirit with that of the Mediterranean world.

The fine arts played an important role in Charlemagne's cultural program from the very start. On his visits to Italy, he had become familiar with the architectural monuments of the Constantinian era in Rome, and with those of the reign of Justinian in Ravenna; his own capital at Aachen, he felt, must convey the majesty of empire through buildings of an equally impressive kind. His famous Palace Chapel (fig. 67) is, in fact, directly inspired by the church of San Vitale in Ravenna, from which we have seen the portrait mosaic of Justinian and his courtiers (fig. 60). To erect such a structure on Northern soil was a difficult undertaking: columns and bronze gratings had to be imported from Italy, and expert stonemasons must have been hard to find. The design, by Odo of Metz (probably the earliest architect north of the Alps known to us by name), is by no means a mere echo of its model but a vigorous reinterpretation, with bold structural parts that outline and balance the clear, forthright, divisions of the interior space.

The importance of the monasteries, which were encouraged by Charlemagne, is vividly

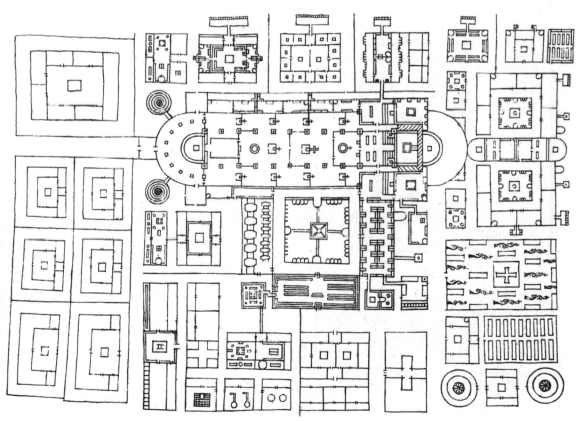

68. *Plan of a Monastery.* 819–30 A.D. Ink on parchment. Chapter Library, St. Gall, Switzerland

suggested by a unique document of the period: the large drawing of a plan for a monastery, preserved in the Chapter Library of St. Gall in Switzerland (fig. 68). Its basic features seem to have been decided upon at a council held near Aachen in 816–17, and then this copy was sent to the abbot of St. Gall for his guidance in rebuilding the monastery. We may regard it; therefore, as a standard plan, to be modified according to local needs. (Our reproduction renders the exact lines of the original, but omits the explanatory inscriptions.) The monastery is a complex, self-contained unit, occupying a rectangle about 500 by 700 feet. The main entry, from the west (left), passes between stables and a hostelry toward a gate which admits the visitor to a colonnaded semicircular portico, flanked by two round towers which must have loomed impressively above the lower outbuildings. It emphasizes the church as the center of the monastic community. The church is a basilica with a semicircular apse and an altar at either end, though the eastern end is given emphasis by a raised choir (with steps leading up to it) preceded by a space, partially screened off from the nave and organized transversally to it, which can be called a transept—a term that we shall meet again in later church plans. The nave and aisles, containing numerous other altars, do not form a single, continuous space but are subdivided into compartments by screens. There are several entrances: two beside the western apse, others on the north and south flanks. This entire arrangement reflects the functions of a monastery church, designed for the devotional needs of the monks, rather than for a congregation of laymen. Adjoining the church to the south, there is an arcaded cloister with a well in the middle; around this are grouped the monks' dormitories (east side), a dining hall and kitchen (south side), and a cellar. The three large buildings to the north of the church are a guest-house, a school, and the abbot's house. To the east are the infirmary, novices' quarters and chapel, the cemetery (marked by a large cross), a garden, and coops for chickens and geese. The south side is occupied by workshops, barns, and other service buildings. There is, needless to say, no monastery exactly like this anywhere—even in St. Gall the plan was not carried out as drawn—yet its layout conveys an excellent notion of the character of such establishments throughout the Middle Ages.

We know from literary sources that Carolingian churches contained murals, mosaics, and relief sculpture, but these have disappeared almost entirely. Smaller, portable works of art, including books, have however survived in considerable numbers. The scriptoria of the various monasteries tended to produce book illuminations which can be grouped into distinct styles, though all of them went back to late classical models. Those that were produced in Aachen itself, under Charlemagne's watchful eye, are very close to the originals; but perhaps more interesting, if somewhat later, is the *Gospel Book of Archbishop Ebbo of Reims* (fig. 69). The St. Mark from this book has many features that will remind us of the Enthroned Christ from the sarcophagus of Junius Bassus (fig. 57) made some five hundred years earlier: the seated "stance," with one foot advanced; the diagonal drape of the upper part of the toga; the square outline of the face; even the hands, one holding a scroll or codex, the other with a quill pen that is added to what must once have been an expository gesture; and the throne on which Christ is seated in the earlier sculpture has exactly the same kind of animal legs as St. Mark's seat. But now the figure is filled with electrifying energy that sets everything in motion; the drapery swirls, the hills heave upward in the background, the vegetation seems tossed about by a whirlwind,

69. *St. Mark,* from the *Gospel Book of Archbishop Ebbo of Reims.* 816–35 A.D. Manuscript illumination. Municipal Library, Épernay, France

and even the acanthus-leaf pattern on the frame assumes a strange, flamelike character. The Evangelist himself has been transformed from a Roman philosopher into a man seized with the frenzy of divine inspiration, an instrument for the recording of the Word of God. This dependence on the Will of the Lord, so powerfully expressed here, marks the contrast between the classical and the medieval image of what Man is. But the means of expression —the dynamism of line that distinguishes our miniature from its classical predecessors—recalls the passionate movement we found in the ornamentation of Irish manuscripts of the Dark Ages.

The influence of the Reims school can still be felt in the reliefs of the bejeweled front cover of the *Lindau Gospels* (colorplate 5), a work of the third quarter of the ninth century. This masterpiece of the goldsmith's art shows how splendidly the Celto-Germanic metalwork tradition of the Dark Ages adapted itself to the Carolingian revival. The main clusters of semiprecious stones are not set directly on the gold ground, but raised on claw feet or arcaded turrets so that light can penetrate beneath them and make them glow. Interestingly enough, the crucified Christ betrays no hint of pain or death, and this, along with His youthful, beardless face, again takes us back to the spirit of the earliest Christian images of the Saviour, as yet untouched by human agony. He seems to 'stand, rather than hang, His arms spread wide in what one might almost call a welcoming gesture. To endow Him with human suffering was not yet conceivable, even though the expressive means were at hand, as we can see in the lamenting figures that surround Him.

OTTONIAN ART. In 870, about the time that the *Lindau Gospels* cover was made, the remains of Charlemagne's empire were ruled by his two surviving grandsons: Charles the Bald, the West Frankish king, and Louis the German, the East Frankish king, whose domains corresponded roughly to the France and Germany of today. Their power was so weak, however, that continental Europe once again lay exposed to attack. In the south, the Moslems resumed their depredations; Slavs and Magyars advanced from the east; and Vikings from Scandinavia ravaged the north and west. These Norsemen (the ancestors of today's Danes and Norwegians) had been raiding Ireland and Britain by sea from the late eighth century on; now they invaded northwestern France as well, occupying the area that has, ever since,

70. *The Gero Crucifix.*
c.975–1000 A.D. Wood, height 6' 2".
Cologne Cathedral

been called Normandy. Once established there, they soon adopted Christianity and Carolingian civilization, and, from 911 on, their leaders were recognized as dukes, nominally subject to the authority of the king of France. During the eleventh century, the Normans assumed a role of great importance in shaping the political and cultural destiny of Europe, with William the Conqueror being crowned King in England, while other Norman nobles expelled the Arabs from Sicily, and the Byzantines from South Italy. In Germany, meanwhile, after the death of the last Carolingian monarch in 911, the center of political power had shifted north to Saxony. The Saxon kings (919–1024) then reestablished an effective central government; the greatest of them, Otto I, also revived the imperial ambitions of Charlemagne. After marrying the widow of a Lombard king, he extended his rule over most of Italy and had himself crowned Emperor by the Pope in 962. From then on, the Holy Roman Empire was to be a German institution. Or perhaps we ought to call it a German dream, for Otto's successors never managed to consolidate their claim to sovereignty south of the Alps. Yet this claim had momentous consequences, since it led the German emperors into centuries of conflict

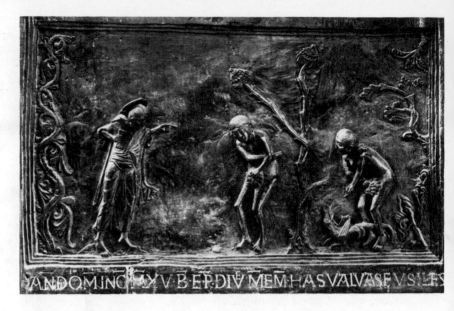

71. *Adam and Eve Reproached by the Lord,* from Doors of Bishop Bernward for Abbey Church of St. Michael. 1015. Bronze, c.23 x 43". Hildesheim Cathedral

with the papacy and local Italian rulers, linking North and South in a love-hate relationship whose echoes can be felt to the present day.

During the Ottonian period, from the mid-tenth century to the beginning of the eleventh, Germany was the leading nation of Europe, politically as well as artistically. German achievement in both areas began as a revival of Carolingian traditions but soon developed new and original traits. These are impressively brought home to us if we compare the Christ on the *Lindau Gospels* cover (colorplate 5) with the *Gero Crucifix* (fig. 70) in the Cathedral of Cologne. The two works are separated by little more than a hundred years' interval, but the contrast between them suggests a far greater span. In the *Gero Crucifix* we meet an image of the Saviour new to Western art, though a restrained beginning toward this interpretation (see fig. 61) was already in the making somewhat earlier in Byzantine art. We do not belittle the genius of the Ottonian sculptor by pointing this out, nor need we be surprised that Eastern influence should have been strong in Germany at this time, for Otto II had married a Byzantine princess, establishing a direct link between the two imperial courts. It remained for the German sculptor to transform the Byzantine image with its gentle pathos into large-scale sculptural terms, imbued with an expressive realism that has been the main strength of German art ever since. How did he arrive at this startling conception? Particularly bold is the forward bulge of the heavy body, which makes the physical strain on arms and shoulders seem almost unbearably real. The

deeply incised, angular features of the face are a mask of agony from which all life has fled. The pervasive presence of Spirit, so new and striking in the St. Mark of the *Ebbo Gospels* (fig. 69), acquires added meaning if paired with this graphic visualization of its departure.

The tutor of Otto II's son and heir, Otto III, was a cleric named Bernward, who later became Bishop of Hildesheim, where he ordered built the Benedictine abbey church of St. Michael. The idea of commissioning a pair of large bronze doors for the church may have come to him as the result of a visit to Rome, where ancient examples, perhaps Byzantine ones too, existed. The Bernward doors, however, differ from these; they are divided into broad, horizontal fields, rather than vertical panels, and each field contains a Biblical scene in high relief. Our detail (fig. 71) shows Adam and Eve after the Fall. Below it, in inlaid letters remarkable for their classical Roman character, is part of the dedicatory inscription, with the date and Bernward's name. In these figures we find nothing of the monumental spirit of the *Gero Crucifix*; they seem far smaller than they actually are, so that one might easily mistake them for a piece of goldsmith's work such as the *Lindau Gospels* cover. The entire composition must have been derived from an illuminated manuscript; the oddly stylized bits of vegetation have a good deal of the twisting, turning movement we recall from Irish miniatures. Yet the story is conveyed with splendid directness and expressive force. The accusing finger of the Lord, seen against a great void of blank surface, is the focal point of the drama; it

Colorplate 5. Upper Cover of binding, the *Lindau Gospels*. c.870 A.D. Gold with jewels,
13¾ x 10½". The Pierpont Morgan Library, New York

Colorplate 6. *Christ Washing the Feet of Peter,* from the *Gospel Book of Otto III.*
c.1000 A.D. Manuscript illumination. Bavarian State Library, Munich

points to a cringing Adam, who passes the blame to his mate, while she, in turn, passes it to the dragonlike serpent at her feet.

The same intensity of glance and gesture characterizes Ottonian manuscript painting, which blends Carolingian and Byzantine elements into a new style of extraordinary power and scope. Perhaps its finest achievement—and one of the great masterpieces of medieval art—is the *Gospel Book of Otto III*, from which we reproduce the scene of Christ washing the feet of the Disciples (colorplate 6). It contains echoes of ancient painting, filtered through Byzantine art; the soft pastel hues of the background recall the illusionism of Roman landscapes (see colorplate 3), and the architectural frame around Christ is a late descendant of the sort of painted architectural perspectives that decorated Pompeian houses (fig. 51). That these elements have been misunderstood by the Ottonian artist is obvious enough; but he has also put them to a new use: what was once an architectural vista now becomes the Heavenly City—the House of the Lord, filled with golden celestial space, as against the atmospheric earthly space without. The figures have undergone a similar transformation: in classical art this composition had been used to represent a doctor treating his patient. Now, St. Peter takes the place of the sufferer, and Christ—still beardless and young here—that of the doctor. A shift of emphasis from physical to spiritual action is conveyed not only through glances and gestures, but also by nonrealistic scale relationships: Christ and St. Peter are larger than the other figures; Christ's "active" arm is longer than the "passive" one; and the eight disciples who merely watch have been compressed into a space so small that we are conscious of them only as so many eyes and hands. Even the Early Christian crowd-cluster from which this derives (see fig. 55) is not quite so literally disembodied.

2. ROMANESQUE ART

Looking back over the ground we have covered in this book so far, a thoughtful reader will be struck by the fact that many of the labels used to designate the art of a given place and period might serve equally well for a general history of civilization. They have been borrowed from technology (e.g., the Stone Age, or the Bronze Age), or from geography, ethnology, or religion, though in our context they also designate artistic styles. There are two notable exceptions to this rule: Archaic and Classical are both primarily terms of style; they refer to qualities of form rather than to the setting in which these forms were created. Why don't we have more terms of this sort? We do, as we shall see—but only for the art of the last nine hundred years. The men who first conceived the history of art as an evolution of styles started out with the conviction that art had already developed to a single climax: Greek art from the age of Pericles to that of Alexander the Great. This style they called Classic (that is, perfect). Everything that came before was termed Archaic—still old-fashioned and tradition-bound, but striving in the right direction. The style that followed this peak did not deserve a special term since it had no positive qualities of its own, being merely an echo or a decadence of Classic art. The early historians of medieval art followed a similar pattern; to them the great climax was the Gothic style (though the term itself was invented by lovers of the classical, and was meant to indicate that medieval art was the work of Goths, or barbarians). This flourished from the thirteenth to the fifteenth century. For whatever was not-yet-Gothic they invented the term "Romanesque"; in doing so they were thinking mainly of architecture; pre-Gothic churches, they noted, were round-arched, solid, and heavy, rather like the ancient Roman style of building, as against the pointed arches and the soaring lightness of Gothic structures.

In this sense, all of medieval art before 1200 could be called Romanesque if it showed any link at all with the Mediterranean tradition. But this usually happened only when an ambitious ruler, like Charlemagne, had dreams of reconstituting the Roman Empire and becoming emperor himself, with all the glorious trappings of old. Such classical revivals rose and fell with the political fortunes of the dynasties that sponsored them. However, the style that is given the name "Romanesque" had a much broader base: it sprang up throughout Western Europe at about the same time, embracing a host of regional styles, distinct yet closely related in many ways, and without a single central source. In this it resembled the art of the Dark Ages which, as we have indicated, wandered with the nomadic tribes that came from Asia, all the way across northern and central Europe, picking up local modifications or putting old forms to new uses.

The welding of all these components into a coherent style during the second half of the eleventh century was not done by any single force, but by a variety of factors that made for

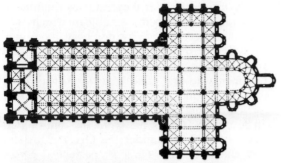

72. Plan, St.-Sernin (after Conant). c.1080–1120

73. St.-Sernin, aerial view. Toulouse

a new burgeoning of vitality throughout the West. Christianity had at last triumphed everywhere in Europe; the threat of hostile invading cultures around its outer edges had been stilled, either because their momentum gave out or because they were conquered or assimilated. There was a growing spirit of religious enthusiasm, reflected in the greatly increased pilgrimage traffic to sacred sites, and culminating, from 1095 on, in the crusades to liberate the Holy Land. Equally important was the reopening of Mediterranean trade routes by the navies of Venice, Genoa, and Pisa, and the revival of trade and manufacturing, with the consequent growth of city life. During the turmoil of the early Middle Ages, the towns of the Western Roman Empire had shrunk greatly (the population of Rome, about one million in 300 A.D.,

fell to less than 50,000 at one time); some were deserted altogether. From the eleventh century on, they began to regain their importance; new towns sprang up everywhere, and an urban middle class of craftsmen and merchants established itself between the peasantry and the landed nobility. In many respects, then, Western Europe between 1050 and 1200 A.D. did indeed become a great deal more "Roman-esque" than it had been since the sixth century, recapturing some of the trade patterns, the urban quality, and the military strength of ancient imperial times. The central political authority was lacking, to be sure (even the empire of Otto I did not extend much farther west than modern Germany does), but the central spiritual authority of the pope took its place to some extent as a unifying force. The international army that responded to Pope Urban II's call to the First Crusade was more powerful than anything a secular ruler could have raised for that purpose.

The quickening of energy in both spiritual and secular enterprise is responsible for the greatest single change that we discern in Romanesque architecture: the amazing number of new buildings which were begun all over Europe at about the same period. An eleventh century monk, Raoul Glaber, summed it up well when he triumphantly exclaimed that the world was "putting on a white mantle of churches." These churches were not only more numerous than those of the early Middle Ages, they were also generally larger, more richly articulated, and more "Roman looking," for their naves now had vaulted roofs instead of wooden ones, and their exteriors, unlike those of Early Christian, Byzantine, Carolingian, and Ottonian churches, were decorated with both architectural ornament and sculpture. Romanesque monuments of the first importance are distributed over an area that might well have represented the world—the Catholic world, that is—to Raoul Glaber: from northern Spain to the Rhineland, from the Scottish-English border to central Italy. The richest crop, the greatest variety of regional types, and the most adventurous ideas are to be found in France. If we add to this group those destroyed or disfigured buildings whose original design is known to us through archaeological research, we have a wealth of architectural invention unparalleled by any previous era. Let us begin our sampling —it cannot be more than that—with St.-Sernin in the southern French town of Toulouse (figs. 72–74). The plan immediately strikes us as much more complex and more fully integrated than the plans of earlier structures, with the possible exception of Hagia Sophia. Its outline is an emphatic Latin cross, of the kind that appears in the mosaic half dome in Sant'Apollinare (colorplate 4), with the stem longer than the three other projecting parts (the Greek cross, used as a symbol in the Eastern Orthodox Church, has all arms of the same length, rather like the cross inscribed in a circle that we saw in our earliest Christian paintings; see fig. 53). The nave is the largest space compartment, but it is extended by the transverse arms (called the transept) where more pilgrims could be accommodated to witness the sacred ritual which was concentrated in the smallest compartment of all, the apse at the east end. Unlike the plan of the monastery church in St. Gall (fig. 68), where altars and chapels for special devotions are scattered fairly evenly throughout the enclosure, and where the transept, though identifiable, tends to merge with the altar space at the east end, this church was plainly meant to accommodate large crowds of lay worshipers. The nave is flanked by two aisles on either side, the inner aisle continuing around the arms of the transept and the apse, thus forming a complete ambulatory (which means "for walking") circuit, anchored to the two towers on either side of the main entrance (these can clearly be seen in the plan, but not

74. Nave and Choir, St.-Sernin. Toulouse

in the superstructure). Chapels extrude from the ambulatory along the eastern edge of the transept arms, and all around the apse; the longest one at the eastern tip was usually dedicated to the Virgin Mary, and is thus often referred to as the Lady Chapel. This type of apse with its elaborations of chapels and ambulatory is called a "pilgrimage choir"; pilgrims could "make the rounds" of the chapels even when there was no Mass being celebrated at the main altar.

The plan shows that the aisles of St.-Sernin were groin-vaulted throughout, and that the measurements of these compartments logically form the basic unit, or module, for all the other dimensions: the width of the central space of the nave, for example, equals twice the width of one compartment in the aisle. On the exterior this rich articulation is further enhanced by the different roof levels of the aisles, set off against the higher gables of nave and transept, and the cluster of semicircular roofs, large and small and at every level, that cover the complex eastern end. Even necessary structural features, such as the thick pier buttresses between the windows, which serve to stabilize the outward thrust of the ceiling vaults, become decorative assets, as is the tower over the crossing (although this was completed in Gothic style, and is taller than originally intended). The two façade towers unfortunately were never completed.

As we enter the nave (fig. 74), we are impressed by its tall proportions, the architectural elaboration of the walls, and the dim indirect lighting, which is filtered through the aisles and the gallery above them, before reaching the nave. The contrast between St.-Sernin and a typical Early Christian basilica, such as Sant' Apollinare (colorplate 4), with its simple "blocks" of space and unobtrusive masonry, does indeed point up the kinship between St.-Sernin and Roman buildings, such as the Colosseum (fig. 38), that have vaults, arches, engaged columns, and pilasters all firmly knit within a coherent order. Yet the forces whose interaction is expressed in the nave of St.-Sernin are no longer the physical, "muscular" forces of Graeco-Roman architecture, but spiritual forces—spiritual forces of the kind that we have seen governing the human body in Carolingian miniatures or Ottonian sculpture. The half-columns running the entire height of the nave wall would appear just as unnaturally drawn-out to an ancient Roman beholder as the arm of Christ in colorplate 6. They seem to be driven upward by some tremendous, unseen pressure, hastening to meet the transverse arches that subdivide the barrel vault of the nave. Their insistent rhythm propels us forward toward the eastern end of the church, with its light-filled apse and ambulatory (now partially obscured by a large altar of later date).

In thus describing our experience we do not, of course, mean to suggest that the architect consciously set out to achieve these effects. For him, beauty and engineering were inseparable; if vaulting the nave so as to eliminate the fire hazards of a wooden roof was a practical aim, it was also a challenge to see how high he could build it (a vault gets more difficult to sustain, the higher it is from the ground) in honor of the Lord, to make His house grander and more impressive. The ambitious height required the galleries over the aisles to carry the thrust of the central barrel vault and ensure its stability. Thus, the "mysterious" semi-gloom of the interior was not a calculated effect, but merely the result of the windows having to be at some distance from the center of the nave. St.-Sernin serves to remind us that architecture, like politics, is "the art of the possible," and that the designer here, as elsewhere, is successful to the extent that he explores the limits of what was possible for him under those particular circumstances, structurally and aesthetically.

Since the west end of St.-Sernin with its towers was never completed, we shall examine

76. West Façade, St.-Etienne. Begun c.1068. Caen

Notre-Dame-la-Grande in Poitiers, a town in the west of France, for a lavish example of the Romanesque church façade (fig. 75). Low and wide, it has elaborately bordered arcades housing large seated or standing figures; below these, deeply recessed within a framework of arches resting on stumpy columns, is the main entrance. A wide band of relief extends from the center arch all across the façade until it is finally terminated by the two towers with their taller bundles of columns and open arcades, looking rather like fantastic chessmen. Their conical helmets match the height of the center gable (which rises above the height of the actual roof behind it). No doubt the columns, with their classical foliage capitals, and the arches are every bit as "Roman" as those used in St.-Sernin. Yet we feel that the whole is neither rational nor organic, even though it provides a visual feast. Perhaps the designer had never studied actual Roman buildings, but had

75. West Façade, Notre-Dame-la-Grande. Early 12th century. Poitiers

received their repertory of forms through Roman sarcophagi (which were abundant through the south of France); examples such as that of Junius Bassus (fig. 57) are decorated with a kind of two-story "doll house" that serves to frame the various Biblical figures.

Further north, in Normandy, the west façade evolved in an entirely different direction. That of the abbey church of St.-Etienne at Caen (fig. 76), founded by William the Conqueror soon after his successful invasion of England, offers a complete contrast to Notre-Dame-la-Grande. Decoration is at a minimum and even contrasts of the lesser architectural members are played down; four huge buttresses divide the front of the church into three vertical sections, and the vertical impetus continues triumphantly in the two splendid towers whose height would be impressive enough even without the tall Early Gothic spires on top. Where St.-Sernin strikes us as full-bodied and "muscular," St.-Etienne is cool and composed: a structure to be appreciated, in all its refinement of proportions, by the mind rather than the visual or tactile faculties. And, in fact, the thinking that went into Anglo-Norman architecture (for William started to build in England, too) is responsible for the next great breakthrough in structural engineering that made possible the soaring churches of the Gothic period.

For an example of Romanesque on English soil, we turn to the interior of Durham Cathedral (fig. 77), just south of the Scottish border, begun in 1093. The nave that we see here is actually one third wider than St.-Sernin, and it has a greater overall length: 400 feet, which places it among the largest churches of medieval Europe. Despite its width, the nave may have been designed from the start to be vaulted; and this vault is of great interest, for it represents the earliest systematic use (the east end vaulting was completed in 1107) of the ribbed groin vault over a three-story nave. The aisles, which we can glimpse through the arcade, consist of the same sort of nearly square groin-vaulted compartments that are familiar to us from St.-Sernin; but the bays of the nave, separated by strong transverse arches, are decidedly oblong. They are groin-vaulted in such a way that the ribs, used at the junctures of the intersections, form a double-X design, dividing the vault into seven sections, rather than the conventional four. Since the nave bays are twice as long as the aisle bays, the heavy transverse arches occur only at the odd-numbered piers of the nave arcade; thus the piers alternate in size, the larger ones, where the

thrust of the vaulting is greatest, being of compound shape (that is, bundles of column shafts and pilaster shafts attached to a square or oblong core), the others cylindrical. But how did the architect come upon this peculiar solution? Let us assume that he was familiar with earlier churches on the order of St.-Sernin, and started out by designing a barrel-vaulted nave with galleries over the aisles, and no windows to light the nave directly. While he was doing so, it suddenly occurred to him that by putting groin vaults over the nave as well as the aisles, he would gain a semicircular area at the ends of each transverse vault; this area, since it had no essential supporting function, could be broken through to make windows. The result would be a pair of Siamese-twin groin vaults, divided into seven compartments, in each bay of the nave. The weight and thrust would be concentrated at six securely anchored points at the gallery level, and thence led down to the piers and columns below. The ribs, of course, were necessary to provide a skeleton, so that the various curved surfaces between them could be filled in with masonry of minimum thickness, thus reducing both weight and thrust.

77. Nave (view toward east), Durham Cathedral. 1093–1130.

We do not know whether this ingenious scheme was actually invented in Durham, but it could not have been created much earlier, for it is still in the experimental stage here; while the transverse arches at the crossing are round, those farther along toward the west end of the nave are slightly pointed, indicating a continuous search for improvements. Aesthetically, the nave of Durham is one of the finest in all Romanesque architecture; the sturdiness of the alternating piers makes a wonderful contrast with the dramatically lighted, sail-like surfaces of the vaults.

Turning to Central Italy, which had been part of the heartland of the original Roman Empire, we might expect it to have produced the noblest Romanesque of them all, since surviving classical originals were close at hand to study. It comes as a slight shock, therefore, to realize that such was not the case: all of the rulers having ambitions to revive "the grandeur that was Rome," with themselves in the role of Emperor, were in the north of Europe. The spiritual authority of the pope, reinforced by considerable territorial holdings, made imperial ambitions in Italy difficult. New centers of prosperity, whether arising from sea-borne commerce or local industries, tended rather to consolidate a number of small principalities, which competed among themselves or aligned

themselves from time to time, if it seemed politically profitable, with the pope or the German emperor. Lacking the urge to re-create the old Empire, and furthermore having Early Christian church buildings as readily accessible as classical Roman architecture, the Tuscans were content to continue what are basically Early Christian forms, but to enliven them with decorative features inspired by pagan Roman architecture. If we take one of the best preserved Tuscan Romanesque examples, the Cathedral complex of Pisa (fig. 78), and compare it on the one hand with the view of Sant' Apollinare in Ravenna (fig. 54), and on the other with the view of St.-Sernin in Toulouse (fig. 73), we are left in little doubt as to which is its closer relation. True, it has grown taller than its ancestor, and a large transept has altered the plan to form a Latin cross, with the consequent addition of a tall lantern rising above the intersection. But the essential features of the earlier basilica type, with its files of flat arcades and even the detached bell tower (the famous "Leaning Tower of Pisa," which was not planned that way but began to tilt because of weak foundations), still continue, much as we see them in Sant'Apollinare.

The only deliberate revival of the antique Roman style was in the use of a multicolored marble "skin" on the exteriors of churches

above: 78. Cathedral, Baptistery, and Campanile. 1053–1272. Pisa

right: 79. Baptistery. c.1060–1150. Florence

(Early Christian examples, we recall, tended to leave the outsides plain). Little of this is left in Rome, a great deal of it having literally been "lifted" for the embellishment of later structures; but the interior of the Pantheon (fig. 40) still gives us some idea of it, and we can recognize the desire to emulate such marble inlay in the Baptistery in Florence (fig. 79). The green and white marble paneling follows severely geometric lines. The blind arcades are eminently classical in proportion and detail; the entire building, in fact, exudes such an air of classicism that the Florentines themselves came to believe, a few hundred years later, that it had originally been a temple of Mars, the Roman god of war. We shall have to return to this Baptistery again, since it was destined to play an important part in the Renaissance.

The revival of monumental stone sculpture is even more astonishing than the architectural achievements of the Romanesque era, since neither Carolingian nor Ottonian art had shown any tendencies in this direction. Freestanding statues, we will recall, all but disappeared from Western art after the fifth century; stone relief survived only in the form of architectural ornament or surface decoration, with the depth of the carving reduced to a minimum. Thus the only continuous sculptural tradition in early medieval art was of sculptures-in-miniature: small reliefs and occasional statuettes, made of metal or ivory. Ottonian art, in works such as the bronze doors of Bishop Bernward, had enlarged the scale of this tradition but not its spirit; and truly large-scale sculpture, represented by the impressive *Gero Crucifix* (fig. 70), was limited almost entirely to wood.

Just when and where the revival of stone sculpture began we cannot say with assurance, but if any one area has a claim to priority it is southwestern France and northern Spain, along the pilgrimage roads leading to Santiago de Compostela. The link with the pilgrimage traffic seems logical enough, for architectural sculpture, especially when applied to the exterior of a church, is meant to appeal to the lay worshiper rather than to the members of a closed monastic community. Like Romanesque architecture, the rapid development of stone sculpture between 1050 and 1100 reflects the growth of religious fervor among the lay population in the decades before the First Crusade. Of course a carved image in stone, being three-dimensional and tangible, is more "real" than a painted one, and to a cleric, steeped in the abstractions of theology and edgy about any

80. South Portal (portion), St.-Pierre. Stone. Early 12th century. Moissac

signs of a revival of idolatry, this might have seemed a frivolous, even dangerous novelty. St. Bernard of Clairvaux, writing in 1127, denounced the sculptured decoration of churches as a vain folly and diversion that tempts us "to read in the marble rather than in our books." His warning was not much heeded, however; to the unsophisticated, any large piece of sculpture inevitably did have something of the quality of an idol, but that very fact is what gave it such great appeal: praying before a statue of a saint made the worshiper feel that his prayers were going in the right direction, not wafting into the thin air that might or might not transmit them to heaven.

Some distance north of Toulouse stands the abbey church of Moissac; its south portal displays a richness of invention that would have made St. Bernard wince. In figure 80 we see the magnificent trumeau (the center post supporting the lintel of the doorway) and the western jamb. Both have a scalloped profile—apparently a bit of Moorish influence—and within these outlines human and animal forms are treated with the same incredible flexibility, so that the spidery Prophet on the side of the trumeau seems perfectly adapted to his precarious perch. He even remains free to cross his legs in a dancelike movement, and to turn his head toward the interior of the church as he unfurls his scroll. But what of the crossed lions that form a symmetrical zigzag on the face of the trumeau—do they have a meaning? So far as we know, they simply "animate" the shaft, as the interlacing beasts of Irish miniatures (whose descendants they are) animated the compartments assigned them. In manuscript illumination, this tradition had never died out; our sculptor has undoubtedly been influenced by it, just as the agitated movement of the Prophet has its ultimate origin in miniature painting. Yet we cannot fully account for the presence of the lions in terms of their effectiveness as ornament. They belong to a vast family of savage or monstrous creatures in Romanesque art that retain their demoniacal vitality even though they are compelled—like our lions —to perform supporting functions. Their purpose, therefore, is also expressive; they embody dark forces that have been domesticated into guardian figures, or banished to a position that holds them fixed for all eternity, however much they may snarl in protest.

In Romanesque churches the tympanum (the lunette inside the arch above the lintel) of the main portal is usually given over to a composition centered on the Enthroned Christ, most often the Apocalyptic Vision of the Last Judgment—the most awesome scene of Christian art. At Autun Cathedral this subject has been visualized with singular expressive force. Our figure 81 shows part of the right half of the tympanum, with the weighing of the souls. At the bottom, the dead rise from their graves, in fear and trembling; some are already beset by snakes or gripped by huge, clawlike hands. Above, their fate quite literally hangs in the balance, with devils yanking at one end of the scales and angels at the other. The saved souls cling, like children, to the hem of the angelic garments, while the condemned are seized by grinning demons and cast into the mouth of Hell. These devils betray the same nightmarish imagination we observed in the pre-Romanesque animal style; but their cruelty, unlike that of the animal monsters, goes unbridled; they enjoy themselves to the full in their grim occupation. No visitor, having "read in the marble" (to speak with St. Bernard), could fail to enter the church in a chastened spirit.

The emergence of distinct artistic personalities in the twelfth century is rarely acknowledged, perhaps because it contravenes the widespread assumption that all medieval art is anonymous. It does not happen very often, of course, but it is no less significant for all that. In the valley of the Meuse River, which runs from northeastern France into Belgium and Holland, there had been a particularly strong awareness of classical sources since Carolingian times (the *Ebbo Gospels*, fig. 69, and the *Lindau Gospels* cover, colorplate 5, originated in this region); it continued to be felt during the Romanesque period. Interestingly enough, the revival of individualism and personality may often be linked with a revival of ancient art, even if the classical influence did not always produce monumental works. "Mosan" Romanesque sculpture excelled in metalwork, such as the splendid bronze baptismal font (fig. 82) of 1107–18 in Liège, which is the masterpiece of the earliest artist of the region whose name we know: Renier of Huy. The vessel rests on twelve oxen (symbolizing the Apostles), like Solomon's basin in the Temple at Jerusalem as

81. *Last Judgment* (detail), west tympanum, Autun Cathedral. Stone. c.1130–35

82. RENIER OF HUY. Baptismal Font.
1107–18. Bronze, height 25″.
St. Barthélemy, Liège

83. Ewer, from Meuse Valley. c.1130.
Gilt bronze, height 7¼″. Victoria & Albert Museum,
London (Crown Copyright Reserved)

described in the Bible. The reliefs make an instructive contrast with those of Bernward's doors (see fig. 71) since they are about the same height. Instead of the rough, expressive power of the Ottonian panel, we find here a harmonious balance of design, a subtle control of the sculptured surfaces, and an understanding of organic structure that, in medieval terms, are amazingly classical. The figure seen from the back (beyond the tree on the left in our picture), with its graceful turning movement and Greek-looking drapery, might almost be mistaken for an ancient work.

Of freestanding bronze sculpture, only one example of the period has survived; but related to it are the countless bronze water ewers, in the shape of lions, dragons, and other monsters, that came into use during the twelfth century for the ritual washing of the priest's hands during Mass. These vessels—another instance of monsters doing menial service for the Lord (see p. 64)—were of Near Eastern inspiration. The beguiling specimen reproduced in figure 83 ultimately goes back, via several intermediaries, to the fanciful performing beasts in figure 17.

Unlike architecture and sculpture, Romanesque painting shows no sudden revolutionary developments that set it apart immediately from Carolingian or Ottonian. Nor does it look any more "Roman." This does not mean that

painting was less important than it had been before: it merely emphasizes the greater continuity of the pictorial tradition, especially in manuscript illumination. Nevertheless, soon after the year 1000 we find the beginnings of a painting style which corresponds to—and often anticipates—the monumental qualities of Romanesque sculpture. As in the case of architecture and sculpture, Romanesque painting developed a wide variety of regional styles; its greatest achievements emerged from the monastic scriptoria of northern France, Belgium, and southern England. The works produced in this area are so closely related in style that at times it is impossible to be sure on which side of the English Channel a given manuscript belongs. Thus, the style of the wonderful miniature of St. John (colorplate 7) has been linked with both Cambrai and Canterbury. The prevalent tendency of Romanesque painting toward uncompromising linearity has here been softened by Byzantine influence, without losing any of the energetic rhythm that it inherited from the Reims school of illumination. But ultimately the style of such a page as this goes back to the Celto-Germanic tradition (see fig. 65), to the precisely controlled dynamics of every contour, both in the main figure and the frame, that unite the varied elements of the composition into a coherent whole, even though in this instance human and floral forms may be copied from Carolingian or Byzantine models. The

84. *The Battle of Hastings,* portion of the *Bayeux Tapestry.* c.1073–83. Wool embroidery on linen, height 20″. Town Hall, Bayeux

85. *The Building of the Tower of Babel,* portion of painted nave vault. Early 12th century. St.-Savin-sur-Gartempe

unity of the page is conveyed not only by style, but by content as well. The Evangelist "inhabits" the frame in such a way that we could not remove him from it without cutting off his ink supply (proffered by the donor of the manuscript, Abbot Wedricus), his source of inspiration (the dove of the Holy Spirit, in the hand of God), or his identifying symbol, the eagle.

The linearity and the simple, closed contours of a painting style such as this lend themselves very well to other media, and to changes in scale (murals, tapestries, stained-glass windows, sculptured reliefs). The so-called Bayeux Tapestry is an embroidered strip of cloth 230 feet long illustrating William the Conqueror's invasion of England; in our detail (fig. 84), which shows the Battle of Hastings, the main scene is enclosed by two border strips performing a function not unlike the frame around the St. John (see above). Partly it is purely decorative (the upper tier with birds and animals), but partly it is integral to the central action (the lower strip is full of dead warriors and horses and thus forms part of the story). Devoid of nearly all the pictorial refinements of classical painting (see fig. 50), it nevertheless manages to give us an astonishingly vivid and detailed account of warfare in the eleventh century; the massed discipline of the Graeco-Roman scene is gone, and this is not due to the artist's ineptitude at foreshortening and overlapping, but to a new kind of individualism that makes of each combatant a potential hero, whether by dint of force or cunning (observe how the soldier, who has just fallen from the horse that is somersaulting with its hind legs in the air, is in turn toppling his adversary by yanking at the saddle girth of his mount).

Firm outlines and a strong sense of pattern are equally characteristic of Romanesque wall painting. The *Building of the Tower of Babel* (fig. 85) is taken from the most impressive surviving cycle, on the nave vault of the church at St.-Savin-sur-Gartempe. It is an intensely dramatic design; the Lord Himself, on the far left, participates directly in the narrative as He addresses the builders of the growing structure. He is counterbalanced, on the right, by the giant Nimrod, the leader of the enterprise, who frantically passes blocks of stone to the masons atop the tower, so that the entire scene becomes a great test of strength between God and Man, a little reminiscent of the hand-to-hand combat in the Bayeux Tapestry.

Soon after the middle of the twelfth century, an important change in style begins to make itself felt in Romanesque painting on either side of the English Channel. *The Crossing of the Red Sea* (fig. 86), one of many enamel plaques that make up a large altarpiece at Klosterneuburg by Nicholas of Verdun, shows that lines have suddenly regained their ability to describe three-dimensional shapes. The drapery folds no longer lead an ornamental life of their own but suggest the rounded volume of the body underneath. Here, at last, we meet the pictorial counterpart of that classicism which we saw earlier in the Baptismal Font of Renier of Huy at Liège (see fig. 82). That the new style should have had its origin in metalwork (which includes not only casting, but also engraving, enameling, and goldsmithing) is not as strange as it might seem, for its essential qualities are sculptural rather than pictorial. In these "pictures on metal," Nicholas straddles the division between sculpture and painting, as well as that between Romanesque and Gothic art. Though the *Klosterneuburg Altar* was completed well before the end of the twelfth century, there is an understandable inclination to rank it as a harbinger of the style to come, rather than the culmination of a style that had been. Indeed, the altarpiece was to have a profound impact upon the painting and sculpture of the next fifty years, when the astonishing humanity of Nicholas' art found a ready response in a Europe that was generally reawakening to a new interest in man and the natural world.

3. GOTHIC ART

Time and space, we have been taught, are interdependent. Yet we tend to think of history as the unfolding of events in time without sufficient awareness of their unfolding in space—we visualize it as a stack of chronological layers, or periods, each layer having a specific depth that corresponds to its duration. For the remote past, where our sources of information are scanty, this simple image works reasonably well. It becomes less and less adequate as we draw closer to the present and our knowledge grows more precise. Thus we cannot define the Gothic era in terms of time alone; we must consider the changing surface area of the layer as well as its depth.

At the start, about 1150, this area was small indeed. It embraced only the province known as the Ile-de-France (that is, Paris and vicinity), the royal domain of the French kings. A hundred years later, most of Europe had "gone Gothic" from Sicily to Iceland, with only a few Romanesque pockets left here and there; through the Crusaders, the new style had even been introduced in the Near East. About 1450 the Gothic area had begun to shrink—it no longer included Italy—and about 1550 it had disappeared almost entirely. The Gothic layer, then, has a rather complicated shape, its depth including nearly four hundred years in some places and a hundred and fifty at the least in others. This shape, moreover, does not emerge with equal clarity in all the visual arts. The term Gothic was coined for architecture, and it is in architecture that the characteristics of the style are most easily recognized. Only during the past hundred years have we become accustomed to speak of Gothic sculpture and painting. There is, as we shall see, some uncertainty even today about the exact limits of the Gothic style in these fields. The evolution of our concept of Gothic art suggests the way the new style actually grew: it began with architecture, and for about a century—from c. 1150 to 1250, during the Age of the Great Cathedrals —architecture retained its dominant role. Gothic sculpture, at first severely architectural in spirit, tended to become less and less so after 1200; its greatest achievements are between the years 1220 and 1420. Painting, in turn, reached a climax of creative endeavor between

86. NICHOLAS OF VERDUN. *The Crossing of the Red Sea,* from *Klosterneuburg Altar.* 1181. Enamel plaque, height 5½". Klosterneuburg Abbey, Austria

1300 and 1350 in Central Italy. North of the Alps, it became the leading art after about 1400. We thus find, in surveying the Gothic era as a whole, a gradual shift of emphasis from architecture to painting, or, better perhaps, from architectural to pictorial qualities (characteristically enough, Early Gothic sculpture and painting both reflect the discipline of their monumental setting, while Late Gothic architecture and sculpture strive for "picturesque" effects rather than clarity and firmness). Overlying this broad pattern there is another one: international diffusion as against regional independence. Starting as a local development in the Ile-de-France, Gothic art radiates from there to the rest of France and to all Europe, where it comes to be known as *opus modernum* or *francigenum* ("modern" or "French" work). In the course of the thirteenth century, the new style gradually loses its "imported" flavor; regional variety begins to reassert itself. Toward the middle of the fourteenth century, we notice a growing tendency for these regional achievements to influence each other until, about 1400, a surprisingly homogeneous "International Gothic" style prevails almost everywhere. Shortly thereafter, this unity breaks apart: Italy, with Florence in the lead, creates a radically new art, that of the Early Renaissance, while north of the Alps, Flanders assumes an equally commanding position in the development of Late Gothic painting and sculpture. A century later, finally, the Italian Renaissance becomes the basis of another international style. With this skeleton outline to guide us, we can now explore the unfolding of Gothic art in greater detail.

The origin of no previous architectural style can be pinpointed as exactly as that of Gothic. It was born between 1137 and 1144 in the rebuilding, by Abbot Suger, of the royal Abbey Church of St.-Denis just outside the city of Paris. If we are to understand how it came to be just there, and just then, we must acquaint ourselves with the special relationship between St.-Denis, Suger, and the French monarchy. The kings of France claimed their authority from the Carolingian dynastic tradition. But their power was eclipsed by that of the nobles who, in theory, were their vassals; the only area they ruled directly was the Ile-de-France, and they often found their authority challenged even there. Not until the early twelfth century did the royal power begin to expand; and Suger, as chief adviser to Louis VI, played a key role in the process. He forged the alliance between the monarchy and the Church, which

brought the bishops of France (and the cities under their authority) to the King's side, while the King, in turn, supported the papacy in its struggles against the German emperors. Suger, however, championed the monarchy not only on the plane of practical politics but on that of "spiritual politics"; by investing the royal office with religious significance, by glorifying it as the strong arm of justice, he sought to rally the nation behind the King. His architectural plans for St.-Denis must be understood in this context, for the church, founded in the late eighth century, enjoyed a dual prestige that made it ideally suitable for Suger's purpose: it was the shrine of the Apostle of France, the sacred protector of the realm, as well as the chief memorial of the Carolingian dynasty (Charlemagne as well as his father, Pepin, had been consecrated there as kings). Suger wanted to make the Abbey the spiritual center of France, a pilgrimage church to outshine the splendor of all the others, the focal point of religious as well as patriotic emotion. But in order to become the visible embodiment of such a goal, the old edifice would have to be enlarged and rebuilt. The great Abbot himself described the campaign in such eloquent detail that we know more about what he desired to achieve than we do about the final result, for the west façade and its sculpture are sadly mutilated today, and the east end (the choir), which Suger regarded as the most important part of the church, has been much altered. Because of the disappointing visual remains of Suger's church today, we must be content here to take note of its importance—and important it was: every visitor, it seems, was overwhelmed by its extraordinary impact, and within a few decades the new style had spread far beyond the confines of the Ile-de-France.

Although St.-Denis was an abbey, the future of Gothic architecture lay in the towns rather than in rural monastic communities. There had been a vigorous revival of urban life, we will recall, since the early eleventh century; this movement continued at an accelerated pace, and the growing weight of the cities made itself felt not only economically and politically, but in countless other ways as well: bishops and the city clergy rose to new importance; cathedral schools and universities took the place of the monasteries as centers of learning (see p. 223), while the artistic efforts of the age culminated in the great cathedrals. That of Notre-Dame ("Our Lady") at Paris, begun in 1163, reflects the salient features of Suger's St.-Denis more directly than any other. Let us begin by comparing the plan (fig. 87) with that of a Romanesque church (fig. 72): it is very much more compact and unified, with the double ambulatory of the choir continuing directly into the aisles, the stubby transept barely exceeding the width of the façade. In preparation for what we shall find in the view of the interior, we may also take note of the vaulting system: each bay (except for the crossing and the apse) along the central axis has an oblong shape, divided by a rib system that we have not met heretofore; outlined by transverse ribs, each compartment is then not only subdivided by two crossed ribs (the groin vault familiar to us from the aisles of St.-Sernin and other churches), but also bisected by a third rib, the ends of each rib corresponding to a column on the floor of the nave. This is known as a sexpartite vault. Although not identical with the vaulting system that we found in Durham Cathedral (fig. 77—the "Siamese-twin" groin vault), it continues the kind of experimentation that was begun in the Norman Romanesque to find ways of lightening the load of masonry between the supports. In the interior (fig. 89) we find other echoes of Norman Romanesque in the galleries above the inner aisles, and the columns used in the nave arcade. Here, also, the use of pointed arches, which was pioneered in the western bays of the nave at Durham, has become systematic throughout the building. The two halves of a pointed arch, by eliminating the part of the round arch that responds the most to the pull of gravity, brace each other; the pointed arch thus exerts less outward pressure than the semicircular arch, and, depending on the angle at which the two sections meet, it can be made as steep as one wishes. The potentialities of the engineering advances that grew out of this discovery are already evident in Notre-Dame; the large clerestory windows, the lightness and slenderness of the forms, which reflect that of the ribs of the vault, create the "weightless" effect that we associate with Gothic interiors. In contrast to the heavily emphasized moldings of St.-Sernin, the walls here are left plain, which makes them seem thinner. Gothic, too, is the "verticalism" of the nave's interior. This depends less on the actual proportions—some Romanesque churches are equally tall, relative to their width—than on the constant accenting of the verticals and on the sense of ease with which the height has been attained.

In Notre-Dame the buttresses (the "heavy bones" of the structure that ultimately take the weight and thrust of the vaulting) are not visible from the inside. The plan shows them as massive blocks of masonry that stick out from the building like a row of teeth. From the outside (fig. 88) we can see that above the level of the aisle compartments, each of these buttresses turns into a diagonally pitched arch that reaches upward to meet the critical spot between the clerestory windows where the outward thrust of the nave vault is concentrated. These arches are called "flying buttresses," and they will remain one of the characteristic features of Gothic architecture. Although they certainly owed their origin to functional considerations, they soon became aesthetically important as well, and apart from supplying actual support, an architect could make them "express" it in a variety of ways.

The most monumental aspect of the exterior of Notre-Dame is the west façade (fig. 90). Except for its sculpture, which suffered heavily during the French Revolution and is for the most part the product of the restorer's art, it retains its original appearance. The design reflects the façade of St.-Denis, which, in turn, had been derived from Norman Romanesque façades such as that of St.-Etienne at Caen (fig. 76), where we find the same basic features: the pier buttresses that reinforce the corners of the towers and divide the façade into three parts; the placing of the portals; the three-story arrangement. The rich sculptural decoration, however, recalls the façades of the west of France (see fig. 75). Much more important than these resemblances are the qualities that distinguish the façade of Notre-Dame from its Romanesque ancestors. Foremost among these is the way all the details have been integrated into a harmonious whole, a formal discipline that also embraces the sculpture, which is no longer permitted the spontaneous (and often uncontrolled) growth that we found on some Romanesque churches. At the same time, the cubic severity of the unadorned front of St.-Etienne has been transformed into its very opposite; lacelike arcades, vast portals and windows dissolve the continuity of the wall surfaces, making a huge, openwork screen of the whole. How rapidly this tendency advanced during the first half of the thirteenth century can be seen by comparing the west façade with the somewhat later portal of the south transept (visible in fig. 88); in the former, the rose window (as the round windows in Gothic churches are called) is deeply recessed, and the stone tracery that makes the pattern is clearly set off from the masonry in which it is imbedded; in the latter, by contrast, we cannot distinguish the

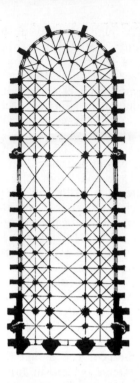

87. Plan, Notre-Dame.
1163–c.1250. Paris

88. Notre-Dame, view from southeast.
1163–c.1250. Paris

89. Interior, Notre-Dame. 1163–c.1200. Paris

90. West Façade, Notre-Dame. c.1200–c.1250. Paris

tracery of the window apart from its frame: a continuous web covers the whole area.

Though we may trace this or that feature of Gothic architecture back to some Romanesque source, the how and why of its success are a good deal more difficult to explain. Here we encounter an ever-present controversy: to the advocates of the functionalist approach, Gothic architecture has seemed the result of advances in engineering that made it possible to build more efficient vaults, to concentrate their thrust at a few critical points, and thus eliminate the solid walls of the Romanesque. But is that all there is to it? We must return briefly to Abbot Suger, who tells us himself that he was hard put to it to bring together artisans from many different regions for his project. This would lend substance to the idea that all he needed was good technicians; yet, if that had been all, he would have found himself with nothing but a conglomeration of different regional styles in the end. Suger's account, however, stresses insistently that "harmony," the perfect relationship among parts, is the source of beauty, since it exemplifies the laws according to which divine reason has constructed the universe; the "miraculous" light flooding through the "most sacred" windows becomes the Light Divine, a mystic revelation of the spirit of God. Whether or not he was the architect of St.-Denis, his was the guiding spirit which made Gothic churches more than just the sum of their parts.

To suggest the fusion of material and spiritual beauty that impressed the visitors to St.-Denis, and which still overwhelms us when we step into the finest Gothic cathedrals, is not easy to do on a printed page. The view inside Chartres Cathedral (colorplate 8) will perhaps supply the dimension that is missing from black-and-white reproductions. Chartres alone, among the major Gothic cathedrals, still retains most of its original stained-glass windows; these act mainly as huge multicolored diffusing filters that change the quality of ordinary daylight, endowing it with the poetic and symbolic values so highly praised by Abbot Suger.

After the basic plan of the Gothic church, as exemplified in the Cathedral of Notre-Dame (fig. 87), had been found satisfactory and the heretofore unimagined flexibility of the groin vault based on the pointed arch had been grasped, the further evolution of Gothic architecture in France became ever more daring in testing the limits to which this kind of construction could be carried. Naves became ever loftier, buttresses lacier, until in a few cases they did collapse. Perhaps the purpose of glorifying

91. West Façade, St.-Maclou.
Begun 1434. Rouen

the divine order, as Abbot Suger had set out to do, imperceptibly turned into a kind of Tower of Babel contest, which as we recall ended disastrously. Still, it is amazing to find that so much Flamboyant ("flame-like") Gothic, as the last phase is called, has stood up. The undulating patterns of curve and countercurve of the pierced-stone ornament in St.-Maclou in Rouen (fig. 91) are so luxuriant that it almost becomes a game of hide-and-seek to locate the "bones" of the building. The architect has turned into a virtuoso who overlays the structural skeleton with a web of decoration so dense and fanciful that structure becomes almost completely obscured.

One of the truly astonishing things about Gothic architecture is the enthusiastic adoption that this "royal French style" found abroad. Even more remarkable was its ability to acclimate itself to a variety of local conditions —so much so, in fact, that the Gothic monuments of England, Germany, and other countries have become objects of intense national pride in modern times. A number of reasons, singly or in combination, might be brought forward to explain this rapid spread: the superior skill of French architects and stone carvers; the vast prestige of French centers of learning, such as the Cathedral School of Chartres or the University of Paris; the vigor of the Cistercian order (founded in France) that built Gothic churches wherever it founded new abbeys. Ultimately, however, the international victory of Gothic art seems to have been due to the extraordinary persuasive power of the style itself, which kindled the imagination and aroused religious feelings even among people who were

92. Salisbury
Cathedral.
1220–70

far removed from the cultural climate of the Ile-de-France.

That England should have proved particularly receptive to the new style is hardly surprising. Yet English Gothic did not grow directly out of the Anglo-Norman Romanesque which had contributed so much of the technical experimentation that went into the realization of St.-Denis. Early English Gothic, though given its start by imported French architects, soon developed its own style, best exemplified in Salisbury Cathedral (fig. 92). We realize at once how different it is from the French example—and also how futile it would be to judge it by French Gothic standards, for its setting, in the middle of the open countryside, does not require it to rise high in order to dominate the clustered core of a city like Paris; nor had it the same mission as St.-Denis, to give spiritual sanction to a royal dynasty. By accepting certain French features, such as the emphasis placed on the main portal by the tall windows above it, it proclaims the new era in architecture—even if these features sometimes look like afterthoughts (note the flying buttresses, which seem structurally unnecessary). With its two strongly projecting transepts and its sprawling façade terminating in stumpy turrets, Salisbury has also retained important features from the Romanesque style. It gives us the impression of spaciousness and ease, as though it were comfortable not only in its setting, but in its links to the Anglo-Norman past.

The spire that rises above the crossing is about a hundred years later than the rest of the building, and it indicates the rapid development of English Gothic toward a more pronounced verticality. The choir of Gloucester Cathedral (fig. 93), in the English Late Gothic ("Perpendicular") style, is more akin to French church interiors, though the repetition of small, identical tracery forms in the great window recalls the repetition of carved motifs on the Salisbury façade. The vaulting displays an innovation which, though it was later adopted on the Continent also, is truly English: the blossoming of the ribs into a multiple-strand ornamental network, obscuring the boundaries between the bays and their subdivisions, and giving the interior a greater visual unity. Though it developed independent of French Flamboyant ornament, there is obviously an artistic kinship between

Colorplate 7. *St. John the Evangelist,* from the *Gospel Book of Abbot Wedricus.*
Shortly before 1147. Manuscript illumination. Société Archéologique, Avesnes, France

Colorplate 8. View of North Clerestory Wall of the Nave.
Chartres Cathedral. 1194–1220

Colorplate 9. GIOTTO. *Christ Entering Jerusalem*. 1305–6. Fresco. Arena Chapel, Padua

Colorplate 10. BOHEMIAN MASTER. *Death of the Virgin*. c.1350–60.
Panel, 39 x 27¾″. Museum of Fine Arts, Boston

these two varieties of intricately worked architectural decoration.

Italian Gothic architecture stands apart from that of the rest of Europe. Judged by the style of the Ile-de-France, most of it hardly can be called Gothic at all. Yet it produced structures of singular beauty and impressiveness. We must be careful to avoid too rigid or technical a standard in approaching these monuments, lest we fail to do justice to their unique blend of Gothic qualities and Mediterranean tradition. The Franciscan church of Santa Croce in Florence (fig. 94) is a masterpiece of Gothic, even though it has wooden ceilings instead of groin vaults. This surely was a matter of deliberate choice rather than of technical or economic necessity, evoking the simplicity of Early Christian basilicas and thereby linking Franciscan poverty with the traditions of the early Church. There is no trace of the Gothic structural system, except for the groin-vaulted choir; the walls remain intact as continuous surfaces (Santa Croce owes part of its fame to its wonderful murals); and there are no flying buttresses, since the wooden ceilings do not require them. Why, then, speak of Santa Croce as Gothic? Surely the use of the pointed arch is not enough to justify the term? Yet we sense immediately that this interior space creates an effect fundamentally different from either Early Christian or Romanesque architecture. The nave walls have the weightless, "transparent" qualities we saw in northern Gothic churches, and the dramatic massing of windows at the eastern end forcefully conveys the dominant role of light. Judged in terms of its emotional impact, Santa Croce is Gothic beyond doubt; it is also profoundly Franciscan—and Florentine—in the monumental simplicity of the means by which this impact is achieved.

If in Santa Croce the architect's main concern was an impressive interior, Florence Cathedral (fig. 95) was planned as a great landmark towering above the entire city. Its most striking feature is the huge octagonal dome (compare Pisa Cathedral, fig. 78), covering a central pool of space that makes the nave look like an afterthought. The actual building of the dome, and the details of its design, belong to the early fifteenth century. Apart from the windows and doorways, there is nothing Gothic about the exterior of Florence Cathedral. The solid walls, encrusted with geometric marble inlays, are a perfect match for the Romanesque Baptistery across the way (see fig. 79); and a separate bell tower, in accordance with Italian tradition (see figs. 54,

93. Choir, Gloucester Cathedral. 1332–57

94. Nave and Choir, Sta. Croce. Begun c.1295. Florence

78), takes the place of the façade towers familiar to us from French Gothic churches. The west façade, so dramatic a feature in French cathedrals, never achieved the same importance in Italy. It is remarkable how few Italian Gothic façades were ever carried near completion (those of Santa Croce and Florence

95. Florence Cathedral. Begun by ARNOLFO DI CAMBIO, 1296; dome by FILIPPO BRUNELLESCHI, 1420–36

Cathedral are both modern). Among those that were, the finest is Orvieto Cathedral (fig. 96); it makes an instructive comparison with Tuscan Romanesque façades (see fig. 78) on the one hand, and French Gothic façades on the other (see fig. 90). Many of its ingredients clearly derive from the latter source, and its screenlike lightness, too, is unmistakably Gothic. Yet these features have been superimposed on what is essentially a basilican façade like that of Pisa Cathedral: the towers have been reduced to turrets so as not to compete with the central gable, and the entire design has a strangely small-scale quality that has nothing to do with its actual size. The Orvieto façade, unlike that of Notre-Dame in Paris, lacks a dominant motif, so that its elements seem "assembled" rather than merged into a single whole. Except for the modest-sized rose window and the doorways, the Orvieto façade has no real openings, and large parts of it consist of framed sections of wall area. Yet we experience these not as solid, material surfaces but as translucent, since they are filled with brilliantly colored mosaics—an effect equivalent to Gothic stained glass in the North.

The secular buildings of Gothic Italy convey as distinct a flavor as the churches. There is nothing in the cities of northern Europe to

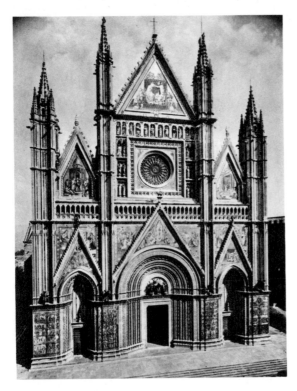

96. LORENZO MAITANI and others. West Façade, Orvieto Cathedral. Begun c.1310

97. Palazzo Vecchio. Begun 1298. Florence

match the impressive grimness of the Palazzo Vecchio (fig. 97), the town hall of Florence. Fortresslike structures such as this reflect the factional strife—among political parties, social classes, and prominent families—so characteristic of life within the Italian city-states. The wealthy man's home (or *palazzo*, a term denoting any large urban house) was quite literally his castle, planned both to withstand armed assault and to proclaim the owner's importance. The Palazzo Vecchio, while larger, follows the same pattern. Behind its battlemented walls, the city government could feel well protected from the wrath of angry crowds. The tall tower not only symbolizes civic pride but has an eminently practical purpose: dominating the city as well as the surrounding countryside, it served as a lookout against enemies from without or within.

The portals of the west façade of St.-Denis were far larger and even more richly decorated than those of Romanesque churches. They paved the way for the admirable west portals of Chartres Cathedral (fig. 98), begun about 1145 under the influence of St.-Denis, but even more ambitious in conception. These probably represent the oldest full-fledged example of Gothic sculpture. Comparing them with a Romanesque portal such as Moissac (fig. 80), we are impressed first by a new sense of order, as if all the figures had suddenly come to attention, conscious of their responsibility to the architectural framework. Symmetry and clarity have taken the place of crowding and frantic movement; figures are no longer entangled with each other, but stand out separately, so that the whole carries much better over a long distance. Particularly striking is the treatment of the door jambs, lined with long figures attached to columns. Instead of being treated essentially as reliefs carved into (or protruding from) the masonry, these are statues, each with its own axis; in theory, at least, they could be detached from their supports. Apparently this first step since the end of classical times toward recapturing monumental stone sculpture in the round could be taken only by "borrowing" the cylindrical shape of the column for the figures. This method traps them into a certain air of immobility, yet the heads already show a gentle, human quality that betokens the search for more realism. It is as though Gothic sculptors had to relive the same experiences as Archaic sculptors in Greece (see fig. 25). Realism is, of course, a relative term whose meaning varies greatly according to circumstances; on the Chartres west portals it appears to spring from

98. West Portals, Chartres Cathedral.
c.1145–70 (for view of interior, see colorplate 8)

a reaction against the demoniacal aspects of Romanesque art, a reaction that may be seen not only in the calm, solemn spirit of the figures, but also in the rational discipline of the underlying symbolic scheme. The subtler aspects of this symbolic program can only be understood by minds well versed in theology; but its main elements are simple enough to be grasped by anyone imbued with the fundamentals of the Bible. The jamb statues, a continuous sequence linking all three portals, represent the prophets, kings, and queens of the Old Testament; their purpose is to acclaim the rulers of France as the spiritual descendants of Biblical rulers, and also—an idea insistently stressed by Abbot Suger—the harmony of secular and spiritual rule. Christ Himself appears enthroned above the main doorway as Judge and Ruler of the Universe, flanked by the symbols of the four Evangelists, with the Apostles assembled below, and the twenty-four Elders of the Apocalypse in the archivolts above. The right-hand tympanum shows His incarnation, with scenes from His life below, and personifications of the liberal arts (human wisdom paying homage to divine wisdom) above. In the left-hand tympanum, finally, we see the timeless Heavenly Christ, the Christ of the Ascension, framed by the signs of the zodiac, and their earthly counterparts, the labors of the months—an ever-repeating cycle of the year.

Instructive programs of this type remained a constant feature of Gothic cathedrals; but styles of sculpture developed rapidly, and varied from region to region. The vast sculptural program for Reims Cathedral had made it necessary to bring together masters and entire workshops from various other building sites, and so we have there a compact sampling of several styles. On the right side of figure 99 we

99. *Annunciation* and *Visitation,* center portal of west façade. Stone, over lifesize. c.1225–45. Reims Cathedral

100. *Melchizedek and Abraham,* interior west wall. Stone. After 1251. Reims Cathedral

see the encounter between the Virgin Mary and St. Elizabeth (the *Visitation*); so expert is the classicism of these works that, at first glance, they seem almost to have stepped out of the *Ara Pacis* relief (see fig. 48). No longer governed, as the Chartres figures were, by the strictly vertical columns, they turn toward each

other with the same human warmth that links the two older children in the *Ara Pacis.*

In the *Annunciation* group (fig. 99, left) the Virgin is in a severe style, with a rigidly vertical body axis and straight, tubular folds meeting at sharp angles. The angel, in contrast, is conspicuously graceful: we note the tiny, round face framed by a cap of curls, the emphatic smile, the strong S-curve of the slender body, the ample, richly accented drapery. This "elegant style," created about 1240 by Parisian masters working for the royal court (see also p. 224), was such a success that it soon became the standard formula for High Gothic sculpture all over Europe.

A slightly later group (fig. 100) in the interior of Reims Cathedral offers a new pictorialism: light and shade now give the deeply recessed figures an atmospheric setting which we have not seen before. Again there is a contrast of styles: Abraham, clad in contemporary armor, is quite bluntly realistic, whereas the priest Melchizedek exhibits a further elaboration of the "courtly" style of the angel in the previous picture. So rich is the intricate drapery that the body almost disappears beneath it —a characteristic that was to become more and more pronounced as Gothic progressed toward its final stage.

Though artists from all over Europe came to be trained in the great cathedral workshops of France, the style that they took home with them rapidly took on some of the character of older native traditions. Thus, the relief showing the *Kiss of Judas* (fig. 101), part of the choir screen of Naumburg Cathedral in Germany, makes us recall the dramatic emotionalism of the much earlier *Gero Crucifix* (see fig. 70), here brought to a theatrical pitch by the contrast of Christ's meekness and the passionate wrath of the sword-wielding St. Peter.

Gothic art, as we have come to know it so far, reflects a desire to endow the traditional themes of Christianity with an ever-greater emotional appeal. It is not surprising, therefore, that Germany played a particular role, near the end of the thirteenth century, in developing a new kind of religious imagery, designed to serve private devotions. The most characteristic and widespread of these images is the so-called *Pietà* (an Italian word derived from the Latin *pietas,* the root word for both "piety" and "pity"), a representation of the Virgin grieving over the dead Christ. No such scene occurs in the Scriptures; it was invented as a counterpart to the familiar Madonna and Child. Our example (fig. 102), like most such

101. *The Kiss of Judas,* on choir screen. c.1250–60. Stone. Naumburg Cathedral

102. *Pietà.* Early 14th century. Wood, height 34½″. Provinzialmuseum, Bonn

103. CLAUS SLUTER. *The Moses Well.* 1395–1406. Stone, height of figures c.6′. Chartreuse de Champmol, Dijon

groups, is carved of wood, vividly painted. Realism here has become purely a vehicle of expression—the agonized faces and Christ's blood-encrusted wounds are enlarged to an almost grotesque degree, so as to arouse an overwhelming sense of horror and pity.

The *Pietà,* with its emaciated, puppetlike bodies, reaches an extreme in the negation of the physical aspects of the human figure. After 1350 a reaction set in, and we again find an in-

terest in weight and volume, coupled with a new impulse to explore tangible reality. The climax was reached about 1400, in the works of Claus Sluter, a Netherlandish sculptor working at the court of Burgundy. His *Moses Well* (fig. 103), so called for the group of Old Testament prophets around the base, including Moses (right) and Isaiah (left), explores sculptural style in two new directions: the Isaiah shows a realism that ranges from the most minute details of the costume to the surprisingly individualized head; the Moses, a new sense of weight and volume. Note that the soft, swinging lines seem to reach out, determined to capture as much of the surrounding space as possible.

Italian Gothic sculpture, like Italian Gothic architecture, stands apart from that of the rest of Europe. It probably began in the extreme south, in Apulia and Sicily, which were part of the domain of the German Emperor, Frederick II. The works made for him have fared badly, but he seems to have favored the classical style of the "Visitation Master" (fig. 99) of Reims Cathedral, which fitted well with the imperial image of himself.

Such was the background of Nicola Pisano, who came to Tuscany from southern Italy about 1250 (the year of Frederick II's death). In 1260 he finished a marble pulpit for the Baptistery of Pisa Cathedral (see fig. 78, foreground), from which we illustrate the *Nativity* (fig. 104); turning back briefly to the Ixion Room decorations (fig. 51) we can spot certain types—the semi-reclining figure, or the crouching one—that have been revived twelve hundred years later. But the treatment of space in our relief is certainly different; instead of the ample, if imprecise, atmosphere that envelops the Roman scenes, this is a kind of shallow box filled to bursting with solid forms that tell not only the story of the Nativity itself, but all the episodes (Annunciation to Mary, Annunciation to the Shepherds) associated with it. There is no precise counterpart of this in Northern Gothic sculpture, and Nicola must have got it from the late Roman style which is also reflected in figure 55, with its crowded space.

Half a century after the Baptistery pulpit, Nicola's son, Giovanni Pisano, made sculpture that was much more in tune with the mainstream of Gothic style. His *Virgin and Child* (fig. 105) still has the rather squat proportions and the Roman facial type that we saw in his father's work, but these have been combined with such up-to-date Gothic traits as the S-curved stance. The weightiness of the classical top half of the figure would make us fear that the Gothic bottom half might collapse under the burden, had Giovanni not used the drapery lines to buttress the top-heavy composition.

By about 1400, at the time of the International Style (see pp. 67, 86), French influence had been thoroughly assimilated in Italy. Its foremost representative was a Florentine, Lorenzo Ghiberti, who, in 1401–2, won a competition for a pair of richly decorated bronze doors for the Baptistery in Florence. We reproduce the trial relief that he submitted, showing the *Sacrifice of Isaac* (fig. 106); the perfection of craftsmanship, which reflects his training as a goldsmith, makes it easy to understand why he won the prize. If the composition seems somewhat lacking in dramatic force, that was in line with the taste of the period, for the realism of the International Style, which developed out of the same courtly art in France that had earlier produced the smiling angel of Reims (see figure at left, fig. 99), did not extend to the realm of the emotions. This also seems to have suited Ghiberti's own lyrical temperament; but however much he may have owed to French influence, Ghiberti remained thoroughly Italian in one respect—his admiration for ancient sculpture, as evidenced by the beautiful nude body of Isaac.

above: 104. NICOLA PISANO. *The Nativity,* panel on pulpit. 1259–60. Marble, 33½ x 43". Baptistery, Pisa

right: 105. GIOVANNI PISANO. *Madonna.* c.1315. Marble, height 27". Prato Cathedral

106. LORENZO GHIBERTI. *The Sacrifice of Isaac.* 1401–2. Gilt bronze, 21 x 17″. National Museum, Florence

Spatial depth, so notably absent in figure 104, has been greatly advanced by Ghiberti; for the first time since classical antiquity, we experience the flat background not as a limiting "wall" but as empty space from which the figures emerge toward the beholder (note especially the angel in the upper right-hand corner). While Ghiberti was no revolutionary himself, he prepares for the great revolution in the arts that we call the Florentine Renaissance, in the second quarter of the fifteenth century.

Though Abbot Suger's St.-Denis had an immediate effect in changing the course of architecture and sculpture, it did not demand any radical change of style in painting. Suger himself places a great deal of emphasis on the miraculous effect of stained glass, which was used in ever-increasing quantities as the new architecture made room for more and larger windows. Yet the technique of stained-glass painting had already been perfected in Romanesque times, and the style of the designs did not change quickly, even though the amount of stained glass required in the new cathedrals caused it to displace manuscript illumination as the leading form of painting. Working in the cathedral workshops, the window designers came to be influenced more and more by the style of the sculptors. The majestic *Habakkuk* (fig. 107), one of a series of windows representing Old Testament prophets, is the direct kin of statues like the *Visitation* group at Reims (fig. 99), and the descendant of Nicholas of Verdun's revival of classicism a genera-

tion before. To create a figure of true monumentality in this medium is something of a miracle in itself: the primitive methods of medieval glass manufacture made it impossible to produce large panes, so that these works are not painting on glass, but "painting with glass," except for linear details that were added in black or brown. More laborious than the mosaicist's technique, that of the window maker involved the fitting together, by means of lead strips, of odd-shaped fragments that followed the contours of his design. Well suited to abstract ornamental pattern, stained glass tends to resist any attempt at three-dimensional effects. Yet in the compositions of a great master the maze of leaded puzzle pieces could resolve itself into figures that have a looming monumentality, such as the *Habakkuk*.

After 1250 architectural activity declined and the demand for stained glass began to slacken. By then, however, miniature painting had caught up with the new style pioneered in stone and glass. However, the centers of production now shifted from monastic scriptoria to urban workshops run by laymen—the ancestors of our modern publishing houses. Some names in this secular breed of illuminators

107. *Habakkuk.* c.1220. Stained-glass window, height c.14′. Bourges Cathedral

now become known to us; an instance is Master Honoré of Paris who did the miniatures in the *Prayer Book of Philip the Fair*. In the scene of *David and Goliath* (fig. 108) the figures do not seem very firmly anchored to the ground, but the attention given to modeling indicates that stone sculpture, such as in figure 100, has been carefully studied. Here, too, a still-timid wish seems to be at work to give the figures a real space of their own to move in. Against the patterned background, Master Honoré has placed a stage-prop landscape; and since the figures obviously cannot step very far to the rear, they assert their mobility by stepping forward onto the frame.

We must now turn our attention to Italian painting, which at the end of the thirteenth century produced an explosion of creative energy as spectacular and far-reaching in its effects as the rise of the Gothic cathedral in France. A single glance at Giotto's mural, *Christ's Entry into Jerusalem* (colorplate 9), will convince us that we are faced with a truly revolutionary development here. How, we wonder, could a work of such monumental power have been produced by a contemporary of Master Honoré? Oddly enough, when we delve into the background of Giotto's art, we find it arose from the same "old-fashioned" attitude that we met in Italian Gothic architecture and sculpture; as a result, panel painting, mosaics, and murals—techniques that had never taken firm root north of the Alps—were kept alive in Italy. At the very same time when stained glass became the dominant pictorial art in the north of Europe, a new wave of Byzantine influence overwhelmed the lingering Romanesque elements in Italian painting. There is a certain irony in the fact that this neo-Byzantine style (or "Greek manner," as the Italians called it) appeared soon after the conquest of Constantinople in 1204 by the armies of the Fourth Crusade—one thinks of the way Greek art had captured the taste of the victorious Romans of old. The Greek manner prevailed until almost the end of the thirteenth century, so that Italian painters were able to absorb the Byzantine tradition far more thoroughly than ever before. In the same years, as we recall, architects and sculptors were assimilating the Gothic style, and toward 1300 this spilled over into painting. It was the interaction of these two currents that produced the new style, of which Giotto is the greatest exponent.

The historical process outlined above will, perhaps, make more sense to us if we consider a fine example of "Greek manner" Italian paint-

108. MASTER HONORÉ. *David and Goliath,* from the *Prayer Book of Philip the Fair*. 1295. Manuscript illumination. Bibliothèque Nationale, Paris

ing, in conjunction with Giotto's *Entry into Jerusalem*. For this purpose, a panel that shows the same subject and was painted about the same time by the Sienese master, Duccio di Buoninsegna, is especially instructive (fig. 109).

In contrast to what we have seen of northern Gothic painting, here the struggle to create pictorial space seems to have been won. Duccio had mastered enough of the devices of Hellenistic-Roman illusionism to know how to create space in depth by the placement of various architectural features which lead the viewer from the foreground and up the path, through the city gate. Whatever the faults of Duccio's perspective, his architecture demonstrates a capacity to contain and define space in a manner vastly more intelligible than anything medieval art had produced, and superior to most classical settings and their Byzantine derivatives. Gothic elements are present, too, in the soft modeling of human forms, and the unmistakable desire on the part of the artist to give his scene lively, even contemporary, touches in order to make us feel that "we are there" (thus, the contemporary costumes and the woebegone expressions in Master Honoré's *David and Goliath*, and the up-to-date Gothic tower, pennant aflutter, in the Duccio panel).

In Giotto, we met an artist of far bolder and more dramatic temper. Giotto was less close to the Greek manner from the start, and he was a wall painter by instinct, rather than a panel painter. His *Entry into Jerusalem* ultimately derives from the same sort of Byzantine composition as Duccio's, though the figure style is another matter entirely, and comes out of the sculpture of Nicola and Giovanni Pisano (see figs. 104, 105). But where Duccio had enriched the traditional scheme, spatially as well as in narrative detail, Giotto subjects it to a

109. DUCCIO. *Christ Entering Jerusalem,* from the back of the *Maestà Altar.* 1308–11. Panel. Cathedral Museum, Siena

radical simplification. The action proceeds parallel to the picture plane; landscape, architecture, and figures have been reduced to the essential minimum; and the limited range and intensity of tones in fresco painting (water colors applied to the freshly plastered wall) further emphasizes the austere quality of Giotto's art, as against the jewel-like brilliance of Duccio's panel (colorplate 10, though slightly later in date, gives some idea of its brightness).

Yet it is Giotto who succeeds in overwhelming us with the reality of the event. How does this come about? First of all, the action takes place in the foreground, much as is the case in the tiny French miniature where we noted that some figures were almost advancing toward us out of the frame (fig. 108). On Giotto's much larger scale, however, and placed so that the beholder's eye level is at the same height as the heads of the figures, the picture space seems to be a continuation of the space we are standing in. Nor does Giotto have to make his characters step in our direction in order to have them

"jump out at us": their forcefully modeled three-dimensionality is so convincing that they seem almost as solid as sculpture in the round. With Giotto, the figures create their own space, and architecture is kept to the minimum required by the narrative. Its depth, consequently, is produced by the combined volumes of the overlapping bodies in the picture, but within these limits it is very persuasive. To those who first saw painting of this sort, the effect must have been as sensational as the first Cinerama films in our own day; and his contemporaries praised him as equal, or even superior, to the greatest of the ancient painters because his forms seemed so lifelike that they could be mistaken for reality itself. His boast was that painting is superior to sculpture—not an idle boast, for Giotto does indeed mark the start of what might be called "the era of painting" in Western art. Yet his aim was not merely to rival statuary; rather, he wanted the total impact of the whole scene to hit the spectator all at once. If we look at earlier pictures, we find our glance traveling at a leisurely pace from detail to detail, until we have surveyed the entire area. But Giotto does not invite us to linger over small things, nor to wander back into the picture space, and even the groups of figures are to be taken as blocks, rather than agglomerations of individuals. Christ stands out alone, in the center, and at the same time bridges the gap between the advancing Apostles on the left, and the bowing townspeople on the right. The more we study the picture, the more we realize that its majestic firmness and clarity harbor great depths of expressiveness.

There are few men in the entire history of art to equal the stature of Giotto as a radical innovator. His very greatness, however, tended to dwarf the next generation of Florentine painters. Siena was more fortunate in this respect, for Duccio had never had the same overpowering impact; so it is there, rather than in Florence, that the next step is taken in the development of Italian Gothic painting. The two brothers Pietro and Ambrogio Lorenzetti coupled the joy in contemporary life that Duccio had included in his works with monumentality of scale and a new interest in solving spatial problems. In the latter regard, Pietro's triptych, *The Birth of the Virgin* (fig. 110), is the boldest of their experiments. The painted architecture has been correlated with the real architecture of the frame in such a way that the two are seen as a single system. Moreover, the vaulted chamber where the birth takes place occupies two panels—it continues unbroken

Art in the Middle Ages 85

110. PIETRO LORENZETTI. *The Birth of the Virgin*. 1342. Panel, 6' 1½" x 5' 11½". Cathedral Museum, Siena

show the life of a well-run city-state, he had to fill the streets and houses with teeming activity; his plausible organization of the many people and buildings comes from a combination of Duccio's panoramic picture space with the immediacy of Giotto's sculptural picture space.

We are now in a position to return to Gothic painting north of the Alps; for what happened there in the latter half of the fourteenth century was determined in large measure by the influence of the great Italians. One of the chief gateways of Italian influence was the city of Prague, which in 1347 became the residence of Emperor Charles IV and rapidly developed into an international center second only to Paris. The *Death of the Virgin* (colorplate 10), which we alluded to for its Sienese-like colors, was nevertheless painted by a Bohemian, about 1360. Although he probably knew the work of the Sienese masters only at second or third hand, the architectural interior betrays its descent from works such as Pietro Lorenzetti's *Birth of the Virgin*. Italian, too, is the vigorous modeling of the heads and the overlapping of the figures that enhance the three-dimensional quality of the composition. Still, the Bohemian master's picture is no mere echo of Italian painting: the gestures and facial expressions convey an intensity of emotion that represents the finest heritage of Northern Gothic art.

The merging of Northern and Italian traditions in an International Gothic style, around the year 1400, has already been mentioned in connection with sculpture; but painters clearly

behind the column that divides the center from the right wing. The left wing represents an anteroom which leads to a vast and only partially glimpsed hall, suggesting the interior of a Gothic church. Here the picture surface begins to assume the quality of a transparent window, which shows the same kind of space that we know from daily experience. The same procedure enabled Ambrogio Lorenzetti, in his fresco *Good Government* in the Siena City Hall, to unfold a comprehensive view of the town before our eyes (fig. 111). In order to

111. AMBROGIO LORENZETTI. *Good Government* (portion). 1338–40. Fresco. Palazzo Pubblico, Siena

112. THE LIMBOURG BROTHERS. *October,*
from *Les Très Riches Heures du Duc de Berry.* 1413–16.
Manuscript illumination. Musée Condé, Chantilly

112 shows the sowing of winter grain during the month of October. It is a bright, sunny day, and—for the first time since classical antiquity—the figures in the foreground cast visible shadows. We marvel at the wealth of minute detail, from the scarecrow in the distance to the footprints that the sower makes in the plowed field. The sower is memorable in other ways as well; his tattered clothing, his sallow unhappy face, go beyond mere description. He is consciously presented as a pathetic figure, to arouse us to the miserable lot of the peasantry in contrast to the life of the aristocracy who live on the far bank of the river Seine in their splendid castle (actually it is a "portrait" of the royal palace of Paris, the Louvre, as it looked in those days). It would be too much to say that the painter was trying to slip in some social criticism. Yet, even if it was to be a long time before anyone thought that such matters as one's station in life were not preordained, the differences are noted here, for the first time, with a sympathetic eye.

Gentile da Fabriano was the finest Italian painter of the International Style. In his *Nativity* (fig. 113) there is a greater sense of weight, of physical substance, than we could hope to find among Northern painters; he is obviously used to working on a larger scale than manuscript illumination. Yet he too commanded the delicate pictorial effects of a miniaturist. The new awareness of light that we first observed in the *October* miniature—light as an independent force, separate from form and color—dominates the entire picture. Even though the main sources of light are the divine radiance of the newborn Child ("the light of the world") and the burst emanating from the angel who brings the glad tidings to the shepherds in the hills, the effect is as natural as if they were sitting around campfires. The poetic intimacy of this night scene opens up a whole new world of artistic possibilities, possibilities that were not to be fully explored until two centuries later.

played the major role in this development. The "realism of particulars" that we first encountered in Gothic sculpture, and later in miniatures, was continued by the workshop of the Limbourg brothers soon after the turn of the fifteenth century. They were Flemings who, like Claus Sluter, the sculptor, had settled in France; but they must have visited Italy as well, for their work includes a great number of motifs, and some entire compositions, borrowed from the great masters of Florence and Siena. The *Book of Hours* that they made for the King of France's brother, the Duke of Berry, contains a group of remarkable calendar pages. Calendar cycles depicting the labors of each month had long been an established part of medieval art (see p. 79). The Limbourg brothers, however, enlarged such examples into panoramas of man's life in nature. Our figure

113. GENTILE DA FABRIANO.
The Nativity, predella panel
of altarpiece
The Adoration of the Magi.
1423. Panel, 12¼ x 29½".
Uffizi Gallery, Florence

PART THREE

ART IN THE RENAISSANCE

In discussing the transition from classical antiquity to the Middle Ages, we were able to point to a great crisis—the rise of Islam—separating the two eras. No comparable event sets off the Middle Ages from the Renaissance. The fifteenth and sixteenth centuries did witness far-reaching developments: the fall of Constantinople and the Turkish conquest of southeastern Europe; the journeys of exploration that led to the founding of overseas empires in the New World, in Africa, and in Asia, with the subsequent rivalry of Spain and England as the foremost colonial powers; the deep spiritual crises of Reformation and Counter Reformation. But none of these can be said to have produced the new era. By the time they happened, the Renaissance was well under way. Thus it is no surprise that scholars debating the causes of the Renaissance disagree like the proverbial blind men trying to describe an elephant. Even if we disregard those few who would deny the existence of the animal altogether, we are left with a vast diversity of views. Every branch of historic study has developed its own image of the period. While these images overlap, they do not coincide, so that our concept of the Renaissance may vary as we focus on its fine arts, music, literature, philosophy, politics, economics, or science. Perhaps the one point on which most experts agree is that the Renaissance had begun when people realized they were no longer living in the Middle Ages.

This statement is not as simple-minded as it sounds; for the Renaissance was the first period in history to be aware of its own existence and to coin a label for itself. Medieval man did not think he belonged to an age distinct from classical antiquity; the past, to him, consisted simply of "B.C." and "A.D."; history, from this point of view, is made in Heaven rather than on earth. The Renaissance, by contrast, divided the past not according to the Divine plan of salvation, but on the basis of human actions. It saw classical antiquity as the era when man had reached the peak of his creative powers, an era brought to a sudden end by the barbarians who destroyed the Roman Empire. In the thousand-year interval of "darkness" which then followed, little was accomplished, but now at last this "time in-between" or "Middle Ages" had given way to a revival of all those arts and sciences that flourished in ancient times. The present could thus be fittingly labeled a "rebirth" —renaissance in French and, by adoption, in English. The origin of this revolutionary view of history can be traced back to the 1330s in the writings of the Italian poet Petrarch (see p. 237), the first of the great men who made the Renaissance. That it should have had its start in the mind of one man is itself a telling comment on the new era, for Petrarch embodies two salient features of the Renaissance: individualism and humanism. Individualism—a new self-awareness and self-assurance—enabled him to claim, against all established authority, that the "age of faith" was actually an era of darkness, and that the "benighted pagans" of antiquity represented the most enlightened stage of history. Humanism, to Petrarch, meant a belief in the importance of what we still call "the humanities" or "humane letters" (as against Divine letters, the study of Scripture): the pursuit of learning in languages, literature, history, and philosophy for its own end, in a secular rather than religious framework. Again he set a pattern, because the humanists, the new breed of scholar following him, became the intellectual leaders of the Renaissance.

Yet Petrarch and his successors did not want to revive classical antiquity lock, stock, and barrel. By interposing the concept of "a thousand years of darkness" between themselves and the ancients, they acknowledged—unlike medieval classicists—that the Graeco-Roman world was now irretrievably dead. Its glories could be revived only in the mind, across the barrier of the "dark ages," by rediscovering the full greatness of ancient achievements in art and thought and by trying to compete with them on an ideal plane. The aim of the Renaissance was not to duplicate the works of antiquity but to equal and perhaps to surpass

114. HUBERT and JAN VAN EYCK. *Singing Angels* (left); *Playing Angels* (right), from side wings of *The Ghent Altarpiece* (open). Completed 1432. Panel, each 63 x 27″. St. Bavo, Ghent

them. In practice, this meant that the authority granted to the ancient models was far from unlimited. The humanists did not become neopagans but went to great lengths seeking to reconcile classical philosophy with Christianity; and architects continued to build churches, not pagan temples, but in doing so they used an architectural vocabulary based on the study of classical structures. Renaissance physicians admired the anatomical handbooks of the ancients, but they discovered errors when they matched the books against the direct experience of the dissection table, and learned to rely on the evidence of their own eyes. It is a fundamental paradox that the desire to return to the classics, based on a rejection of the Middle Ages, brought to the new era not the rebirth of antiquity but the birth of Modern Man.

1. THE FIFTEENTH CENTURY

As we narrow our focus from the Renaissance as a whole to the Renaissance in the fine arts, we are faced with some questions that are still under debate: Did it, like Gothic art, originate in a specific center, or in several places at the same time? Should we think of it as one new, coherent style, or as a new attitude that might be embodied in more than one style? So far as architecture and sculpture are concerned, there is general agreement that the Renaissance began in Florence soon after 1400. In painting, the situation is less clear-cut. Some scholars believe that the first Renaissance painter was Giotto—an understandable claim, since his achievement (and that of his contemporaries in Siena) had revolutionized painting throughout Europe (see p. 84). Nevertheless, it took a second revolution, a century after Giotto, for Renaissance painting to be born, and this revolution began independently both in Florence and in the Netherlands. The twin revolutions were linked by a common aim—the conquest of the visible world beyond the limits of the International Gothic style—yet they were sharply separated in almost every other respect. While the new realism of Florentine painting after about 1420 is clearly part of the Early Renaissance movement, we have no satisfactory name for its counterpart in the North. The label "Late Gothic," often applied to it, hardly does justice to its special character, although the term has some justification. It indicates, for instance, that the creators of the new style in Flanders, unlike their Italian contemporaries, did not reject the International Style; rather, they took it as their point of departure, so that the break with the past was less abrupt in the North than in the South. It also reminds us that fifteenth-century architecture in the North remained firmly rooted in the Gothic tradition. Whatever we choose to call the style of Northern painters at this time, their environment was clearly Late Gothic. How could they create a genuinely post-medieval style in such a setting? Would it not be more reasonable to regard their work, despite its great importance, as the final phase of Gothic painting? If we treat them here as the Northern counterpart of the Early Renaissance, we do so for several reasons. The great Flemish masters whose work we are about to examine were as much admired in Italy as they were at home, and their intense realism had a conspicuous influence on Early Renaissance painting. Moreover, they have a close parallel in the field of music: from about

1420 on, the Netherlands produced a school of composers so revolutionary as to dominate the development of music throughout Europe for the next hundred years (see p. 230). A contemporary said of them that nothing worth listening to had been composed before their time. An analogous claim might well have been made for the new school of Flemish painters.

FLANDERS. The first phase of the pictorial revolution in Flanders is represented by an artist whose name is somewhat uncertain. He was probably Robert Campin, the foremost painter of Tournai, who is recorded there from 1406 until his death in 1444. Among his finest works is the *Annunciation*, the center panel of the *Merode Altarpiece*, done soon after 1425 (colorplate 11). Comparing it with the Franco-Flemish pictures of the International Style (see fig. 112), we recognize that it belongs within that tradition; yet we also find in it a new pictorial experience. For the first time, we have the sensation of actually looking *through* the surface of the panel into a spatial world with all the essential qualities of everyday reality: unlimited depth, stability, continuity, and completeness. The painters of the International Style had never aimed at such consistency; their pictures have the enchanting quality of fairy tales where the scale and relationship of things can be shifted at will, where fact and fancy mingle without conflict. Campin, in contrast, has undertaken to tell the truth, the whole truth, and nothing but the truth. He does not yet do it with ease—his objects, overly foreshortened, tend to jostle each other in space. But, with obsessive determination, he defines every aspect of every last object: its individual shape and size, its color, material, texture; and its way of responding to light (note the surface reflections and sharply defined shadows). The *Merode Annunciation*, in short, transports us quite abruptly from the aristocratic world of the International Style to the household of a Flemish burgher. This is the earliest Annunciation in panel painting that occurs in a fully equipped domestic interior. Campin has here faced a problem no one had met before: how to transfer a supernatural event (the angel announcing to Mary that she will bear the Son of God) from a symbolic setting to an everyday environment, without making it look either trivial or incongruous. He has solved the problem by a method known as "disguised symbolism," which means that any detail within the picture, however casual, may carry a symbolic message. Thus the lilies denote the Virgin's

115. JAN VAN EYCK. *Giovanni Arnolfini and His Bride.* 1434. Panel, 33 x 22½". The National Gallery, London

chastity, and the shiny water basin and the towel on its rack are not merely household equipment but further tributes to Mary as the "vessel most clean" and the "well of living waters." Perhaps the most intriguing symbol is the candle next to the lilies. It was extinguished only moments ago; but why, in broad daylight, had it been lit, and what made the flame go out? Has the divine radiance of the Lord's presence overcome the material light? Or did the flame itself represent the Divine light, now extinguished to show that God has become man, that in Christ "the Word was made flesh"? Clearly, the entire wealth of medieval symbolism survives in our picture, but it is so immersed in the world of everyday appearances that we are often left to doubt whether a given detail demands symbolic interpretation (see p. 232). How, we wonder, could Campin pursue simultaneously what we tend to regard as opposite goals, realism and symbolism? To him, apparently, the two were interdependent, rather than in conflict. He must have felt that he had to "sanctify" everyday reality with the maximum of spiritual significance in order to make it worth painting. This deeply reverential attitude toward the physical universe as a mirror of Divine truths helps us to understand why in our panel even the least conspicuous details

are rendered with the same concentrated attention as the sacred figures; potentially, at least, everything is a symbol, and thus merits an equally exacting scrutiny.

If we compare our colorplate of the *Merode Annunciation* with that of an earlier panel painting (colorplate 10), we become aware of another revolutionary quality of Campin's work. The jewel-like brightness of the older picture, its pattern of brilliant hues and lavish use of gold, have given way to a color scheme far less decorative but much more flexible and differentiated. The subdued tints—muted greens, bluish or brownish grays—show a new subtlety, and the scale of intermediate shades is smoother and has a wider range. All these effects are essential to the realistic style of Campin; they were made possible by the use of oil, the medium he was among the first to exploit. The basic technique of medieval painting had been tempera, in which the powdered pigments were mixed ("tempered") with diluted egg yolk. It produced a thin, tough, quick-drying coat admirably suited to the medieval taste for high-keyed, flat color surfaces. Oil, in contrast, was a viscous, slow-drying medium. It could yield a vast range of effects, from thin, translucent films (called "glazes") to the thickest impasto (a dense layer of creamy, heavy-bodied paint). It also permitted the blending of colors right on the panel, which produced a continuous scale of hues that included rich, velvety dark shades unknown before. Without oil, the Flemish masters' conquest of visible reality would have been much more limited. Thus, from the technical point of view, too, they were the "fathers of modern painting," for oil was to become the painter's basic medium everywhere.

Needless to say, the full range of effects made possible by oil was not discovered all at once, nor by any one man. Campin contributed less than Jan van Eyck, a somewhat younger and much more famous artist, who was long credited with the actual "invention" of oil painting. About Jan's life and career we know a good deal, while his older brother Hubert, apparently also a painter, remains a disputed figure. There are several works that may have been painted by either of the two, including the pair of panels showing the Crucifixion and the Last Judgment (colorplate 12). Scholars agree that their date is between 1420 and 1425, if not on whether Jan or Hubert was the author. The style of these panels has much in common with that of the *Merode Annunciation*—the all-embracing devotion to the visible world, the deep space, the angular drapery folds, less

116. ROGIER VAN DER WEYDEN.
The Descent from the Cross.
c.1435. Panel, 7' 2⅝" x 8' 7⅛".
The Prado, Madrid

graceful but far more realistic than the unbroken loops of the International Style. Yet the individual forms are not so tangible, they seem less isolated, less "sculptural"; and the sweeping sense of space comes not so much from violent foreshortening as from subtle changes of light and color. If we inspect the *Crucifixion* slowly, from the foreground figures to the distant city of Jerusalem and the snow-capped peaks beyond, we see a gradual decrease in the intensity of local colors and in the contrast of light and dark. Everything tends toward a uniform tint of light bluish gray, so that the furthest mountain range merges with the color of the sky. This optical phenomenon is known as "atmospheric perspective," since it results from the fact that the atmosphere is never wholly transparent. Even on the clearest day, the air between us and the things we are looking at acts as a hazy screen that interferes with our ability to see distant shapes and colors clearly; as we approach the limit of visibility, it swallows them altogether. Atmospheric perspective is more fundamental to our perception of deep space than linear perspective, which records the diminution in the apparent size of objects as their distance from the observer increases. It is effective not only in faraway vistas; in the *Crucifixion*, even the foreground seems enveloped in a delicate haze that softens contours, shadows, and colors. The entire scene has a continuity and harmony quite beyond Campin's pictorial range. Clearly, the Van Eycks used the oil medium with extraordinary refinement.

Viewed as a whole, the *Crucifixion* seems singularly devoid of drama, as if the scene had been becalmed by some magic spell. Only when we concentrate on the details do we become aware of the violent emotions in the faces of the crowd beneath the Cross, and the restrained but profoundly touching grief of the Virgin and her companions in the foreground. In the *Last Judgment*, this dual aspect of the Eyckian style takes the form of two extremes: above the horizon, all is order and calm, while below it— on earth and in the realm of Satan—the opposite condition prevails. The two states thus correspond to Heaven and Hell, contemplative bliss as against physical and emotional turbulence. The lower half, clearly, was the greater challenge to the artist's imaginative powers. The dead rising from their graves with frantic gestures of fear and hope, the damned being torn apart by devilish monsters more frightful than any we have seen before, all have the awesome reality of a nightmare—a nightmare "observed" with the same infinite care as the natural world of the *Crucifixion*.

The greatest work of the brothers Van Eyck, the *Ghent Altarpiece*, was begun by Hubert, and completed by Jan in 1432. Of its twenty panels, we must limit ourselves to two, of angels singing and making music (fig. 114). Surely the work of Jan, they show our artist's mastery in presenting large figures at close range. Their realism is so persuasive that they may serve as important visual evidence for the musical practices of the time (see p. 227),

Colorplate 11. Master of Flemalle (Robert Campin?).
The Annunciation, center panel of the *Merode Altarpiece.* c.1425–28. Panel, 25¼ x 24⅞″.
The Metropolitan Museum of Art, New York (The Cloisters Collection, Purchase)

Colorplate 12. HUBERT and/or JAN VAN EYCK.
The Crucifixion (left); *The Last Judgment* (right). c.1420–25. Canvas, transferred from panel,
each 22¼ x 7¾″. The Metropolitan Museum of Art,
New York (Fletcher Fund, 1933)

117. CONRAD WITZ. *The Miraculous Draught of Fishes.* 1444.
Panel, 51 x 61″. Museum, Geneva

118. *St. Dorothy.* c.1420. Woodcut.
Staatliche Graphische Sammlung, Munich

yet they also breathe a deeply devotional spirit.

A renewed interest in realistic portraiture had developed as early as the mid-fourteenth century, but not until Robert Campin did the portrait play a major role in Northern painting. Jan van Eyck produced many, the largest and the most remarkable being *Giovanni Arnolfini and His Bride* (fig. 115). The Flemish cities where the new style of painting flourished—Tournai, Ghent, Bruges—rivaled Florence as centers of international banking and trade. Their foreign residents included many Italian businessmen, such as Giovanni Arnolfini. In the picture, he and his bride are solemnly exchanging marriage vows in the privacy of the bridal chamber. They seem to be quite alone, but as we look at the mirror behind them, we discover in the reflection that two other persons have entered the room. One must be the artist, since the words above the mirror, in florid legal lettering, tell us that "Johannes de eyck fuit hic" (Jan van Eyck was here) and the date, 1434. Jan's role, then, is that of a witness; the panel purports to show exactly what he saw and has the function of a pictorial marriage certificate. Yet the setting, however realistic, is replete with disguised symbolism of the most subtle kind, conveying the sacramental nature of marriage. The single candle in the chandelier, burning in broad daylight, stands for the all-seeing Christ; the shoes which the couple has taken off remind us that this is "holy ground" (see p. 10); even the little dog is an emblem of marital fidelity. Here, as in the *Merode Annunciation*, the natural world is made to contain the world of the spirit in such a way that the two actually become one.

In the work of Jan van Eyck, the exploration of the reality made visible by light and color had reached a limit that was not to be surpassed for another two centuries. Rogier van der Weyden, the third great master of early Flemish painting, set himself a different though equally important task: to recapture, within the framework of the new style created by his predecessors, the emotional drama, the pathos, of the Gothic past. We can see this immediately in his early masterpiece, *The Descent from the Cross* (fig. 116), painted about the same time as the Arnolfini double portrait. The modeling here is sculpturally precise, with brittle drapery folds like those of Campin, while the soft half-shadows show the influence of Jan van Eyck. Yet Rogier is far more than a mere follower of the two older men; what he owes to them he uses for ends that are not theirs but his. The outward events (the lowering of Christ's body from the cross) concern him less than the world of human feeling: the artistic ancestry of these grief-stricken gestures and faces lies in Gothic sculpture such as the Bonn *Pietà* (see fig. 102) and the lamenting angels of Sluter's *Moses Well* (see fig. 103). Indeed, Rogier has staged the scene in a shallow architectural shrine, as if his figures were colored statues, thus focusing our entire attention on the foreground. No wonder that Rogier's art, which has been well described as "at once physically barer and spiritually richer than Jan van Eyck's," set an example for countless other artists. So great was the authority of his style that between 1450 and 1500 he had supreme influence not only in European painting north of the Alps, but in sculpture as well.

Among the countless artists from Spain to the Baltic who turned out provincial adaptations of the new Flemish style, only a few were gifted enough to impress us today. One of the earliest and most original was Conrad Witz of Basel, whose altarpiece for Geneva Cathedral, painted in 1444, includes the remarkable panel shown in figure 117. To judge from the drapery, he must have had close contact with Campin. But it is the setting more than the figures that attracts our interest, and here the influence of the Van Eycks seems dominant. Nevertheless, Witz was an explorer in his own right, who knew more about the optical properties of water than any painter of that time (note especially the bottom of the lakeshore in the foreground). The landscape, too, is an original venture, representing a specific part of the shore of the Lake of Geneva—the earliest "portrait" landscape that we know.

Germany's chief contribution to fifteenth-century art, however, was the development of printing, for pictures as well as books. The ear-

liest type-set printed books were produced in the Rhineland soon after 1450. The new technique spread all over Europe and grew into an industry that had the most profound effect on Western civilization (for music printing, see p. 240). Printed pictures, however, had hardly less importance; without them, the printed book could not have replaced the work of the medieval scribe and illuminator so quickly and completely. The oldest pictorial printing technique is the woodcut, printed from wooden blocks carved in relief (the areas meant to remain white being hollowed out). The earliest examples all show the familiar qualities of the International Style (fig. 118), but they have a flat, ornamental pattern; forms are defined by simple, heavy contours. Since the outlines were meant to be filled in with color, these prints often recall stained glass (see fig. 107) more than the miniatures which they replaced. They were a popular art, on a level that did not attract masters of high ability until shortly before 1500. A single wood block yielded thousands of copies, to be sold for a few pennies apiece, bringing the individual ownership of pictures within everyone's reach for the first time in our history.

Engraving, somewhat younger than woodcuts, was a more sophisticated medium from the start. Unlike woodcuts, engravings are printed not from a raised design but from V-shaped grooves cut into a copper plate with a steel tool known as a burin, so that fine lines are very much easier to achieve. The oldest examples we know, dating from around 1430, already show the influence of the great Flemish painters. Nor do engravings share the anonymity of early woodcuts; individual hands can be distinguished almost from the beginning, dates and initials appear soon after, and the most important engravers of the later fifteenth century are known to us by name. The greatest of them, Martin Schongauer, might be called the Rogier van der Weyden of engraving, since his prints are full of Rogierian motifs and expressive devices. Yet Schongauer had his own powers of invention; his finest prints have a complexity of design, spatial depth, and richness of texture that is fully equivalent to panel paintings. *The Temptation of St. Anthony* (fig. 119) masterfully combines savage expressiveness and formal precision, violent movement and ornamental stability. The longer we look at it, the more we marvel at its range of tonal values, the rhythmic beauty of the engraved line, and the artist's ability to render every conceivable surface texture merely by varying his

119. MARTIN SCHONGAUER. *The Temptation of St. Anthony.* c.1480–90. Engraving. The Metropolitan Museum of Art. New York (Rogers Fund, 1920)

120. JEROME BOSCH. *The Garden of Delights*. c.1500. Panel; center 86½ x 76¾", wings 86½ x 38". The Prado, Madrid

121. JEROME BOSCH. *The Garden of · Delights* (center panel, detail)

122. JEROME BOSCH. *The Garden of Delights* (right wing, detail)

burin's attack upon the plate. He was not to be surpassed by any later engraver in this respect.

Schongauer's engraving of the tormented *St. Anthony* reflects a taste for the gruesome and fantastic that can be found more than once in Northern European art toward the end of the fifteenth century. We encounter its extreme form in the strange works of a Dutch painter, Jerome Bosch, who spent his life in the provincial town of 's Hertogenbosch. His pictures, full of weird and seemingly irrational imagery, have proved so difficult to interpret that many of them still remain a puzzle. We can readily believe this if we study the triptych known as *The Garden of Delights* (figs. 120–22). Of the three panels, only the left one has a clearly recognizable subject: the Lord introducing the newly created Eve to Adam in the Garden of Eden. The landscape, almost Eyckian in its airy vastness, is filled with animals and with hybrid monsters of odd and sinister kinds. The right wing, a nightmarish scene of burning ruins and fantastic instruments of torture, surely represents Hell. But what of the center? Here is a landscape much like that of the Garden of Eden, filled with countless nude men and women performing a variety of peculiar actions: in the middle ground, they parade around a circular basin on the backs of all sorts of beasts; many disport themselves in pools of water; most of them are closely linked with enormous birds, fruit, flowers, or marine animals (fig. 121). Only a few are openly engaged in making love, yet there can be no doubt that the delights in this "garden" are those of carnal desire, however oddly disguised. The birds, fruit, etc., are symbols or metaphors that Bosch uses to depict man's life on earth as an unending repetition of the Original Sin of Adam and Eve, whereby we are all doomed to be the prisoners of our appetites. Nowhere does he so much as hint at the possibility of Salvation; corruption, on the animal level at least, had already asserted itself in the Garden of Eden (witness the monsters in the left wing), and we are all destined for Hell, the Garden of Satan (fig. 122). Despite Bosch's deep pessimism, there is an innocence, even a haunting poetic beauty, in this panorama of sinful mankind. Consciously, he was a stern moralist painting a visual sermon, every detail packed with didactic meaning. Unconsciously, however, he must have been so enraptured by the sensuous appeal of the world of the flesh that the images he coined tend to celebrate what they are meant to condemn. That, surely, is why *The Garden of Delights* still evokes so strong a response today, even though we no longer understand every word of the sermon.

ITALY. When we discussed the new style of painting that arose in Flanders about 1420, we did not try to explain why this revolution took place where and when it did. This does not mean, however, that no explanation is possible. It is simply that we do not yet fully understand the link between the great Flemish painters and the social, political, and cultural setting in which they worked. Regarding the origins of Early Renaissance art in Florence, we are in a better position. In the years around 1400, Florence faced an acute threat to its independence from the powerful Duke of Milan, who was trying to bring all of Italy under his rule. Florence remained the only serious obstacle to his ambition. The successful resistance of the city gave rise to a new, civic-patriotic kind of humanism, which hailed Florence as the "new Athens," the champion of freedom as well as the home of arts and letters. So, in the midst of the crisis, the Florentines embarked upon a vast campaign to embellish their city with monuments worthy of the "new Athens." The huge investment was itself no guarantee of artistic quality, but it provided a splendid opportunity for creative talent of every kind. From the start, the visual arts were considered essential to the resurgence of the Florentine spirit. They had been classed with the crafts, or "mechanical arts," throughout antiquity and the Middle Ages; now, for the first time, they were given the rank of liberal arts. A century later, this claim was to win general acceptance in the Western world. What does it imply? The liberal arts, by a tradition going back to Plato, comprised the intellectual disciplines necessary for a gentleman's education—mathematics (geometry, arithmetic, musical theory), dialectic, grammar, rhetoric, and philosophy; the fine arts were excluded because they were "handiwork," having no basis in theory. Thus, when the artist gained admission to this select group, the nature of his work had to be redefined: he came to be looked upon as a man of ideas, not a mere manipulator of materials, and the work of art was viewed as the visible record of his creative mind. This meant that works of art ought not to be judged by fixed standards of craftsmanship. Soon everything that bore a great master's imprint—drawings, sketches, fragments, unfinished pieces—was eagerly collected. The artist's own outlook, too, underwent a change; now in the company of scholars and poets, he often became a man of learning and literary culture, who might write poems, an autobiography, or treatises on art theory (until then, there had been only "recipe books" for artists). As another consequence of their new social status, artists tended to develop into one of two contrasting personality types: the man of the world, at ease in aristocratic society, or the solitary genius, likely to be in conflict with his patrons. It is remarkable how soon this modern view of art and artists became a living reality in Early Renaissance Florence.

The first half of the fifteenth century is the heroic age of the Early Renaissance. Florentine art, dominated by the original creators of the new style, held an undisputed position of leadership. To trace its beginnings, we must discuss sculpture first, for the great upsurge of civic art patronage had begun with a competition for the Baptistery doors (see p. 82) and for some time involved mainly sculptural projects. One of these was to provide statues for the Gothic niches of the bell tower of Florence Cathedral (see fig. 95), half of which were still empty. Donatello, the founding father of Renaissance sculpture, filled five of them during the decades between 1416 and 1435. The most impressive statue of the series is the unidentified prophet nicknamed *Zuccone* ("pumpkin head"; fig. 123). It has long enjoyed special fame as a striking example of Donatello's realism, and it is indeed realistic—far more so than any an-

cient statue or its nearest rivals, the prophets of the *Moses Well* (see fig. 103). But, we may ask, what *kind* of realism have we here? Instead of following the traditional image of prophets, as Sluter did in the *Moses Well*, Donatello has invented an entirely new type; how did he conceive it? Surely not by observing the people around him. More likely, he imagined the personalities of the prophets from the Biblical accounts of them. He gained the impression, we may assume, of divinely inspired orators haranguing the multitude, and this in turn reminded him of the Roman orators he had seen in ancient sculpture. Hence the classical costume of the *Zuccone*, whose mantle falls from his shoulder like a toga (see fig. 48), and the fascinating head, ugly yet noble, like late Roman portraits (see fig. 46). The Florentines themselves soon forgot that the *Zuccone* was meant to be a prophet, and thought him a portrait of one of their own statesmen. As for Donatello, he seems to have regarded the *Zuccone* with pride as a particularly hard-won achievement; it is the first of his works to carry his signature.

Donatello had learned the technique of bronze sculpture as a youth by working under Ghiberti (see p. 83). It was in this material that, a few years after the *Zuccone*, he produced a *David* (fig. 124), the first freestanding lifesize nude statue since antiquity. It is an

far left: 123. DONATELLO. *Prophet (Zuccone),* on the campanile of Florence Cathedral. 1423–25. Marble, height 6' 5". The original is now in the Cathedral Museum, Florence

left: 124. DONATELLO. *David.* c.1430–32. Bronze, height 62¼". National Museum, Florence

even more revolutionary achievement, for here at one stroke Donatello has recaptured that internal body balance, that "action in repose," which had distinguished the Classic style of Greece (see p. 27). The Middle Ages would surely have regarded the *David* as an idol, and Donatello's contemporaries, too, must have felt uneasy about it; for many years it remained the only work of its kind. Why the artist chose to represent the young victor in this way is a puzzle, unless he wanted to liken a Biblical hero to the nude victorious athletes of antiquity. Be that as it may, nudity is clearly this *David's* natural state; as in ancient statues, the body speaks to us more eloquently than the face.

Meanwhile, Ghiberti, after the great success of his first Baptistery doors, had been commissioned to do a second pair, which were to be dubbed the "Gates of Paradise." Its reliefs, unlike those of the first doors (see fig. 106), were large and set in simple square frames (fig. 125). The hint of spatial depth we saw in *The Sacrifice of Isaac* has now grown in *The Story of Jacob and Esau* into a complete setting for the figures that goes back as far as the eye can reach. We can imagine the figures leaving the scene—the deep, continuous space of this "pictorial relief" in no way depends on their presence. How did Ghiberti achieve this effect? In part by varying the degree of relief, with the forms closest to the beholder being modeled almost in the round—a method familiar to us

125. LORENZO GHIBERTI. *The Story of Jacob and Esau,*
panel of the "Gates of Paradise." c.1435.
Gilt bronze, 31¼" square. Baptistery, Florence

from ancient art (see figs. 26, 48, 49). Far more important, however, is the carefully controlled recession of figures and architecture, causing their apparent size to diminish systematically (rather than haphazardly, as before) as their distance from the beholder increases. This system, which we call scientific perspective, was one of the fundamental innovations that distinguish Early Renaissance art from everything that had gone before as well as from the great Flemish masters of realism, who had achieved the effect of unlimited depth in their pictures by empirical means, through subtle gradations of light and color. Scientific perspective was not discovered by Ghiberti, nor by a painter, but by Filippo Brunelleschi, the creator of Early Renaissance architecture (the building in Ghiberti's relief, figure 125, is designed in this new style). His purpose, apparently, was to find a method of making visual records of architecture on a flat surface in such a way that the depth of the foreshortened flanks of buildings could be measured as precisely as the height or width of the façade. The details of the system need not concern us here, beyond saying that it is a geometric procedure analogous to the way the camera lens projects a perspective image on the film. Its central feature is the vanishing point, toward which any set of parallel lines will seem to converge. If these lines are perpendicular to the picture plane, their vanishing point will be on the horizon, corresponding exactly to the position of the beholder's eye. Brunelleschi's discovery in itself was scientific rather than artistic, but sculptors and painters took it up enthusiastically. Here at last was a theoretical basis for representing the visible world, proving that the fine arts were now indeed "liberal" rather than "mechanical"!

The earliest known picture done according to the new theory is *The Holy Trinity* (colorplate 13) by Masaccio, the young genius who singlehandedly created Early Renaissance painting during his brief life before 1428, when he died at the age of twenty-seven. The new style was by that time well established in sculpture and architecture, making his task easier, but his achievement remains stupendous, nevertheless. Here, as in the case of the *Merode Annunciation* (see colorplate 11), we seem to plunge into a new environment, a realm of monumental grandeur rather than the concrete everyday reality of Robert Campin. What the *Trinity* fresco brings to mind is not the immediate past (see fig. 113) but Giotto's art, with its sense of large scale, its compositional severity and sculptural volume. Yet the differences are as

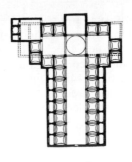

126. FILIPPO BRUNELLESCHI.
Interior and Plan, S. Lorenzo.
1421–69. Florence

striking as the similarities: for Giotto, body and drapery form a single unit, as if both had the same substance, while Masaccio's figures, like Donatello's (see fig. 123), are "clothed nudes," their drapery falling like real fabric. The setting, equally up-to-date, reveals a thorough command of both scientific perspective and Brunelleschi's new architecture. This barrel-vaulted chamber is no mere niche, but a deep space in which the figures could move freely if they wished. And—for the first time in history —we are given all the needed data to measure the depth of this painted interior, to draw its plan, and to duplicate the structure in three dimensions. It is, in a word, the earliest example of a *rational* picture space. For Masaccio, it must also have been a symbol of the universe ruled by Divine reason.

In Masaccio's *Trinity,* as well as in Ghiberti's later relief panel, the new rational picture space is independent of the figures; they inhabit it but do not create it: take away the architecture and you take away the figures' space. We could go even further and say that scientific perspective depends not just on architecture, but on this particular *kind* of architecture, so different from Gothic. In fact, we may well ask what came first in Brunelleschi's mind: the new architectural style, or scientific perspective. Brunelleschi's architecture, as reflected in the *Trinity* and as we see it in actual buildings such as the interior of the church of San Lorenzo (fig. 126), strikes us first of all as a conscious return to the vocabulary of the Greeks and Romans: round arches instead of pointed arches, columns instead of piers, barrel vaults and domes in preference to groin vaults. But Brunelleschi did not revive these forms out of mere

antiquarian enthusiasm. What attracted him to them was what, from the medieval point of view, must have seemed their chief drawback: their inflexibility. A classical column, unlike a medieval column or pier, is strictly defined and self-sufficient, and its shape can be varied only within narrow limits (the ancients, we recall, thought of it as comparable to the human body); the classical round arch has only one possible shape, a semicircle; and the classical architrave and all its details are subject to the strict rules of the "orders" of ancient architecture. Brunelleschi's aim was to rationalize architectural design, and for this he needed the standardized and regular vocabulary of the ancients, based on the circle and the square. The secret of their buildings, he thought, was harmonious proportion—the same ratios of simple whole numbers that determine musical harmony, for they recur throughout the universe and must thus be of Divine origin (see p. 216). The theory of proportions provided him, as it were, with the syntax that ruled the use of his architectural vocabulary. No wonder this stable, rational, and clearly articulated system lent itself so singularly well to scientific perspective! Looking at the interior of San Lorenzo, we immediately sense its cool, controlled quality; unlike a Gothic church interior, which invites us to move forward and explore what seems an architectural miracle, San Lorenzo reveals itself to us completely as soon as we set foot inside it; it is designed to be seen "in scientific perspective," like the chapel in Masaccio's *Trinity.*

San Lorenzo, with its wooden ceiling over the nave, recalls the interior of Santa Croce (see fig. 94) translated into Early Renaissance terms. A similar process of rationalization re-shaped another traditional building type, the *palazzo*. When the Medici, the most powerful family in Florence, had a new palace built for them in the 1440s (fig. 127), their architect, Michelozzo, produced a design recalling the fortresslike older structures (see fig. 97; the windows on the ground floor of the Medici Palace were added a century later). But the three stories are in a graded sequence, each complete in itself: the lowest is built of rough-hewn, "rustic" masonry like the Palazzo Vecchio; the second of smooth-faced blocks with "rusticated" (that is, indented) joints; the surface of the third is unbroken. On top of the structure rests, like a heavy lid, a strongly projecting cornice inspired by those of Roman temples, emphasizing the finality of the three stories.

Brunelleschi's death in 1446 brought to the fore Leone Battista Alberti, whose career as an architect had been long delayed. A highly educated humanist, Alberti was at first interested in the fine arts only as a theorist; he studied the monuments of ancient Rome, composed the earliest treatises on sculpture and painting, and began a third treatise, on architecture. He then started to practice art as a dilettante and developed into an architect of outstanding ability. In his last work, the church of Sant'Andrea in Mantua (fig. 128), he accomplished a seemingly impossible feat: he superimposed a classical temple front on the traditional basilican church façade (see figs. 78, 96). To harmonize this "marriage," he used pilasters instead of columns, thus stressing the continuity of the wall surface. They are of two sizes: the smaller ones sustain the arch over the huge center niche, while the larger ones form what is known as a "colossal" order including all three stories of the façade. So intent was Alberti on harmonious proportions that he inscribed the entire design within a square.

Nevertheless, as a basilican church, Sant' Andrea does not conform to the ideal shape of sacred buildings defined in Alberti's treatise on architecture. He explains there that the plan of such structures should be either circular or of a shape derived from the circle (square, hexagon, etc.), because the circle is the only perfect shape and therefore a direct image of Divine reason. And he points to the Pantheon (see figs. 39, 40) as a precedent. That such a central-plan structure was ill adapted to Catholic ritual made no difference to Alberti; a church, he believed, must be a visible embodiment of "divine proportion," and the central plan alone permitted attainment of this aim. When he formulated these ideas, he could not yet cite any · modern example. Toward the end of the century, however, after his treatise became widely known, the central-plan church gained general acceptance. An early

127. MICHELOZZO. Palazzo Medici-Riccardi. Begun 1444. Florence

128. LEONE BATTISTA ALBERTI. Façade, S. Andrea. Designed 1470. Mantua

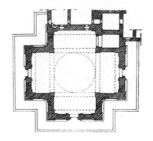

129. GIULIANO DA SANGALLO.
Interior and Plan, Sta. Maria delle Carceri.
1485–92. Prato

with fine precision. Comparing it with Roman heads (see figs. 43, 44, 46), we find that the Florentine doctor radiates a human warmth and individuality far beyond any attained in ancient times. He is linked to his Roman predecessors only by the idea of portrait sculpture in the round as an effective—and enduring—substitute for the sitter's real presence.

The only sculptor of the second half of the century to share some of Donatello's range and ambition was Andrea del Verrocchio, the teacher of Leonardo da Vinci. Even he, however, has left us few monumental works. His crowning achievement, the bronze equestrian monument of Bartolommeo Colleoni (fig. 131), was commissioned by the city fathers of Venice, not of Florence. Colleoni, who had commanded the Venetian army, had requested such a statue in his will and, by way of encouragement, had left a sizable fortune to the Republic of Venice. In Roman times, the bronze equestrian statue had been reserved for emperors; the only surviving example, the Marcus

and distinguished specimen is Santa Maria delle Carceri in Prato (fig. 129), near Florence, by Giuliano da Sangallo. It conforms closely to Alberti's ideal: except for the dome, the entire structure would fit neatly inside a cube, since its height (up to the drum of the dome) equals its length and width. By cutting into the corners of this cube, Giuliano has formed a Greek cross. The dimensions of the four arms stand in the simplest possible ratio to those of the cube: their length is one half their width, their width one half their height. They are barrel-vaulted, and the dome rests on these vaults. There can be no doubt that Giuliano wanted his dome to accord with the age-old tradition of the Dome of Heaven; the single round opening in the center and the twelve on the perimeter clearly refer to Christ and the Apostles.

By 1450 the great civic campaign of art patronage had petered out, and Florentine artists had to depend mainly on private commissions. This put the sculptors at a disadvantage; and since monumental tasks were few, they concentrated on works of moderate size and cost for individual patrons, such as bronze statuettes and portrait busts. A fine early example of this new class of "domestic sculpture" is the marble bust of *Giovanni Chellini* (fig. 130) by Antonio Rossellino, a master who rose to prominence in the 1450s. It represents a highly esteemed aged physician, whose personality—at once sardonic and kindly—has been observed

130. ANTONIO ROSSELLINO. *Giovanni Chellini.* 1456.
Marble, height 20″. Victoria & Albert Museum, London

131. ANDREA DEL VERROCCHIO. *Equestrian Monument of Bartolommeo Colleoni.* c.1483–88. Bronze, height c.13′. Campo SS. Giovanni e Paolo, Venice

effectively contrasted with the rigid surfaces of the armored figure bestriding it. Colleoni looms in the saddle, his legs straight and one shoulder thrust forward, the very embodiment of forceful dominance. His face, which is not a true likeness but an ideal projection of the personality Verrocchio associated with successful leadership in war, radiates an almost frightening sense of power.

What, meanwhile, had been the development of Florentine painting? Masaccio had died too young to found a "school," and his style was too bold to be taken up immediately by his contemporaries. Their work, for the most part, combines his influence with lingering elements of the International Style. There was, in fact, only one painter who fully understood Masaccio's style and made it the basis of his own: Piero della Francesca, who came from southeastern Tuscany; after having been trained in Florence he left the city for his home territory, never to return. Piero's most impressive work, a fresco cycle in the church of San Francesco in Arezzo, dates from 1450 to 1460. Its many scenes tell the legend of the True Cross (the origin and history of the cross used for Christ's crucifixion). The section illustrated in figure 132 shows Helena, the mother of the Emperor Constantine, discovering the True Cross and the two crosses of the thieves crucified on either side of Christ (all three crosses had been hidden by enemies of the Faith). At the left they are being lifted out of the ground, and at the right the True Cross is identified through its power to bring a dead youth back to life. Piero's figures have all the harsh grandeur of Masaccio's (see colorplate 13). They seem to

Aurelius (see fig. 45), was on display throughout the Middle Ages—it was thought to represent Constantine, the first Christian emperor —but it remained for the Early Renaissance to revive the type. For a general like Colleoni, it was a special honor to be so commemorated, and Verrocchio has made the most of his opportunity. The horse, graceful and spirited, its hide revealing every vein, muscle, and sinew, is

132. PIERO DELLA FRANCESCA. *The Discovery and Proving of the True Cross.* c.1460. Fresco. S. Francesco, Arezzo

133. ANDREA DEL CASTAGNO. *David.* c.1450–57. Leather, height 45½″. National Gallery of Art, Washington, D.C. (Widener Collection)

The Florentines must have regarded Piero's style as somewhat outmoded, for in the 1450s a new trend made its appearance in Florentine painting. We see it in the remarkable *David* by Andrea del Castagno (fig. 133), a work contemporary with Piero's Arezzo frescoes. Solid volume and statuesque immobility have given way to graceful movement, conveyed both by the pose and the windblown hair and drapery; the modeling has been minimized, so that the *David* seems to be in relief rather than in the round, with the forms now defined mainly by their undulating outlines. This dynamic linear style has important virtues, but they are far from those of Masaccio. It was to dominate the second half of the century in Florentine art. Antonio del Pollaiuolo, the most vigorous practitioner of this style, had been trained as a goldsmith and metalworker, probably in Ghiberti's workshop, and had worked also as a painter and an engraver. His most famous print, the *Battle of Ten Naked Men* (fig. 134), shows an indebtedness to both Castagno and ancient art. The subject—undoubtedly a classical one—has not yet been convincingly identified, but it does not matter a great deal; the primary purpose of the engraving obviously was to display Pollaiuolo's mastery of the human body in action. This was still a novel problem then, and Pollaiuolo contributed more than any other master to its solution. He realized that a full understanding of bodily movement demands a detailed mastery of anatomy, down to the last muscle and sinew. While we do not know for sure, he may well have been the first artist to dissect human bodies for firsthand knowledge of their structure (a practice then uncommon even in medical schools). The ten naked men do indeed have an oddly "flayed" look, as if

belong to a lost heroic race, beautiful and strong—and silent. Their inner life is conveyed by glances and gestures, not by facial expressions. Above all, they have a gravity, both physical and emotional, that makes them kin to classical Greek sculpture. How did Piero arrive at these memorable images? Using his own testimony, we may say that they were born of his passion for perspective. More than any artist of his day, he believed in scientific perspective as the basis of painting; in a treatise full of rigorous mathematics—the first of its kind—he demonstrated how perspective applied to stereometric bodies and architectural shapes, and to the human form. This mathematical outlook permeates all his work. He saw a head, an arm, or a piece of drapery as variations or compounds of spheres, cylinders, cones, cubes, and pyramids, and he endowed the visible world with the impersonal clarity and permanence of mathematics. We may call him the earliest ancestor of the abstract artists of our own time, for they, too, work with systematic simplifications of natural forms. It is not surprising that Piero's fame today is greater than ever before.

134. ANTONIO DEL POLLAIUOLO. *Battle of Ten Naked Men.* c.1465–70. Engraving. The Metropolitan Museum of Art, New York (Joseph Pulitzer Bequest, 1917)

135. SANDRO BOTTICELLI.
The Birth of Venus. c.1480.
Canvas, 5′ 9″ x 9′ 2″.
Uffizi Gallery, Florence

their skin has been stripped away to reveal the play of muscles underneath. Equally novel are their facial expressions, as strained as their bodily movements. Contorted features are, of course, to be found in earlier art, but the emotional anguish they express does not arise from, or accompany, the extreme physical action of Pollaiuolo's struggling nudes. The integration of motion and emotion seems to have been his particular concern.

Pollaiuolo's style strongly influenced the last great Early Renaissance painter of Florence, Sandro Botticelli, whose best-known pictures were done for the so-called Medici circle. This consisted of the patricians, literati, and scholars surrounding Lorenzo the Magnificent, the head of the Medici family and, for all practical purposes, the ruler of the city. It was for one member of this group that Botticelli did his *Birth of Venus* (fig. 135). The kinship with Pollaiuolo's *Ten Naked Men* is unmistakable: in both, the shallow modeling and the emphasis on outline produce an effect of low relief rather than of solid, three-dimensional shapes; in both we note an unconcern with deep space —the thicket behind the *Ten Naked Men* forms an ornamental screen much like the grove on the right-hand side of the *Venus*. Yet the differences are equally striking. Botticelli evidently does not share Pollaiuolo's passion for anatomy. His bodies are more attenuated, and drained of all weight and muscular power; they appear to float even when they touch the ground. All this seems to deny the basic values of the founding fathers of Renaissance art. Still, the picture does not look medieval: the

bodies, ethereal though they be, retain their voluptuousness, and they enjoy full freedom of movement. To understand this paradox, we must consider the general use of classical subjects in Early Renaissance art. During the Middle Ages, the forms used in classical art had become divorced from classical subject matter; pictures of the pagan gods were based on literary descriptions rather than classical images. Only toward 1450 did classical form begin to rejoin classical content. Botticelli's *Venus* is the first monumental image, since Roman times, of the nude goddess derived from classical statues of Venus. Moreover, the subject is clearly meant to be serious, even solemn. How could such images be justified in a Christian civilization? In the Middle Ages, classical myths had at times been interpreted didactically as allegories of Christian ideas. Europa abducted by the bull, for instance, could be declared to signify the soul redeemed by Christ. But to fuse the Christian faith with ancient mythology required a more sophisticated argument than such forced interpretations. This was provided by the Neo-Platonic philosophers, who enjoyed tremendous prestige in the late fifteenth century and subsequently. They believed that the life of the universe, including that of man, was linked to God by a spiritual circuit continuously ascending and descending, so that all revelation— from the Bible, Plato, or classical myths—was one. Similarly, they proclaimed that beauty, love, and beatitude, being phases of this circuit, were one. Thus the Neo-Platonists could invoke the "celestial Venus" (the nude Venus born of the sea) interchangeably with the Virgin Mary as the source of "divine love." This celestial Venus, it was said, dwells purely in the sphere of mind, while her twin, the ordinary Venus, engenders "human love." Botticelli's picture, then, has a quasi-religious meaning. As baptism is a "rebirth in God," so the birth of Venus evokes the hope for "rebirth" from which the Renaissance takes its name (see p. 88). Thanks to the fluidity of Neo-Platonic doctrine, the possible associations to be linked with our picture are almost limitless. All of them, however, "dwell in the sphere of mind," and Botticelli's Venus would hardly be a fit vessel for them if she were less ethereal.

We must now turn to Early Renaissance art in Northern Italy. It developed only toward 1450, since the Gothic tradition was strong in this area. We shall leave aside North Italian architecture and sculpture between 1450 and 1500, since the major works are by imported Florentines such as Alberti and Verrocchio (see figs. 128, 131). We must, however, take a glance at painting in and around Venice, for during those years a great tradition was born there that was to flourish for the next three centuries. Florentine masters had been carrying the new style to Venice and the neighboring city of Padua since the 1420s, but they evoked only rather timid local responses until, shortly before 1450, the young Andrea Mantegna emerged as an independent master. Next to

137. GIOVANNI BELLINI. *St. Francis in Ecstasy.* c.1485. Panel, 48½ x 55″. The Frick Collection, New York (Copyright)

Masaccio, Mantegna was the most important painter of the Early Renaissance; and he, too, was a precocious genius, fully capable at seventeen of carrying out commissions on his own, such as the frescoes in the Eremitani Church in Padua. They were almost entirely destroyed in 1944—perhaps the most serious artistic loss during World War II. The scene shown in figure 136, *St. James Led to His Execution,* is the most dramatic of the cycle because of its daring "worm's-eye" perspective, which is based on the beholder's actual eye level (the horizon is below the bottom of the picture). The architectural setting looms large, as in Masaccio's *Trinity* (colorplate 13). Its main feature, a triumphal arch, although not a direct copy of any Roman monument, looks so authentic that it might as well be. Mantegna's devotion to the visible remains of antiquity, his desire for almost archaeological authenticity, can also be seen in the costumes of the Roman soldiers. But the tense figures, lean and firmly constructed, are clearly of Florentine ancestry; Mantegna owed most to Donatello, who had spent ten years in Padua. The large crowd of bystanders generates an extraordinary emotional tension, which erupts in real physical violence on the far right; and the great spiral curl of the banner echoes the turbulence below.

If Mantegna's style impresses us with its dramatic force, his brother-in-law in Venice, Giovanni Bellini, was a poet of light and color. Bellini was slow to mature; his finest pictures, such as *St. Francis in Ecstasy* (fig. 137), date from the last decades of the century or later. The saint is here so small in comparison to the

136. ANDREA MANTEGNA. *St. James Led to His Execution.* c.1455. Fresco. Ovetari Chapel, Church of the Eremitani, Padua (destroyed 1944)

setting that he seems almost incidental, yet his mystic rapture before the beauty of the visible world sets our own response to the view that is spread out before us, ample and intimate at the same time. He has left his wooden pattens behind and stands barefoot on holy ground, like Moses in the Lord's presence (see p. 10). Bellini surely knew and admired the work of the great Flemish painters (Venice had strong trade links with the North), and he shared their tender regard for every detail of nature, and their use of oil rather than tempera. Unlike the Northerners, however, he knew how to define the beholder's spatial relationship to the landscape; the rock formations in the foreground are clear and firm, like architecture rendered by the rules of scientific perspective.

2. THE SIXTEENTH CENTURY

It used to be taken for granted that the High Renaissance followed upon the Early Renaissance as naturally as noon follows morning. The great masters of the sixteenth century—Leonardo, Bramante, Michelangelo, Raphael, Titian—were thought to have shared the ideals of their predecessors, but to have expressed them so completely that their names became synonyms of perfection. They represented the climax, the classic phase, of Renaissance art, just as the architects and sculptors of Athens had brought Greek art to its highest point in the later fifth century B.C. This view also explained why these two classic phases were so brief: if art develops along the pattern of a ballistic curve, its highest point cannot be expected to last more than a moment, and must be followed by a decadent phase, "Hellenistic" in the one case, "Late Renaissance" in the other.

Today we have a less assured, but also a less arbitrary, estimate of what, for lack of a better term, we still call the High Renaissance. In some respects, it was indeed the culmination of the Early Renaissance, while in others it represented a departure. Certainly the tendency to view the artist as a sovereign genius was never stronger. Men of genius were thought to be set apart from ordinary mortals by the divine inspiration guiding their efforts, and were called "divine," "immortal," and "creative" (before 1500, *creating*, as distinct from *making*, had been the privilege of God alone). This cult of genius had a profound effect on the artists themselves: it spurred them on to vast and ambitious goals, often unattainable, and their faith in the divine origin of inspiration led them to

138. LEONARDO DA VINCI. *Adoration of the Magi* (detail). 1481–82. Panel, size of area shown c.24 x 30″. Uffizi Gallery, Florence

rely on subjective standards of truth and beauty, rather than on the universally valid rules acknowledged by the Early Renaissance (such as scientific perspective and the ratios of musical harmony). That may be the reason why the great artists of the High Renaissance did not set the pace for a broadly based "period style" that could be practiced on every level of quality. The High Renaissance produced very few minor masters; it died with the men who created it, or even before. Of the great personalities mentioned above, only Michelangelo and Titian lived beyond 1520. In pointing out the limited and precarious nature of the High Renaissance, however, we do not mean to deny its tremendous impact upon later art. For most of the next three hundred years, the great personalities of the early sixteenth century loomed so large that their predecessors seemed to belong to a forgotten era. When they were finally rediscovered, people still acknowledged the High Renaissance as the turning point by referring to all painters before Raphael as "the Primitives."

One of the strange and compelling aspects of the High Renaissance is the fact that its key monuments were all produced between 1495 and 1520, despite the differences in age of the men who created them (Bramante was born in 1444, Titian about 1490). Leonardo, though not the oldest of the group, is the earliest of the High Renaissance masters. Conditions in Florence did not favor him after he had completed his training under Verrocchio; at the age of thirty he went to work for the Duke of Milan —as military engineer, architect, sculptor, and painter—leaving behind unfinished a large *Adoration of the Magi*. The panel's remarkable

—and indeed, revolutionary—feature is the way it is painted. Our detail (fig. 138) shows the area to the right of center, which is more nearly finished than the rest; the forms seem to materialize softly and gradually, never quite detaching themselves from a dusky realm. Leonardo, unlike Castagno or Botticelli, thinks not of outlines, but of three-dimensional bodies made visible in varying degrees by light. In the shadows, these shapes remain incomplete, their contours merely implied. In this method of modeling (called *chiaroscuro*, "light-and-dark") the forms no longer stand abruptly side by side. And there is a comparable emotional continuity as well: the gestures and faces of the crowd convey with touching eloquence the reality of the miracle—the newborn Christ—they have come to behold.

Toward the end of his stay in Milan, Leonardo tried to apply this method of painting to a fresco of the *Last Supper* (fig. 139). Unhappily, the mural began to deteriorate within a few years, since the artist had experimented with an oil-tempera medium that did not adhere well to the wall. Yet what remains is more than enough to explain why the *Last Supper* became famous as the first classic statement of the ideals of the High Renaissance. Viewing the composition as a whole, we see at once its balanced stability; only afterward do we discover that this balance has been achieved by the reconciliation of competing, even conflicting claims. In Early Renaissance art, the architecture often threatens to overpower the figures (see figs. 125, 136). Leonardo, in contrast,

began with the figure composition, and the architecture had merely a supporting role from the start, even though it obeys all the rules of scientific perspective. The central vanishing point is behind the head of Christ in the exact middle of the picture, thus becoming charged with symbolic significance. Equally plain is the symbolic function of the main opening in the rear wall; its pediment acts as the architectural equivalent of a halo. We thus tend to see the setting almost entirely in relation to the figures, rather than as a pre-existing entity. We can test this by covering the upper third of the picture: the composition then looks like a frieze, the grouping of the Apostles is less clear, and the calm triangular shape of Christ becomes merely passive, instead of acting as a physical and spiritual focus. The Saviour, presumably, has just spoken the fateful words, "One of you shall betray me," and the disciples are asking, "Lord, is it I?" But to view the scene as one particular moment in a psychological drama hardly does justice to Leonardo's intentions. The gesture of Christ is one of submission to the Divine will, and of offering. It hints at Christ's main act at the Last Supper, the institution of the Eucharist ("Jesus took bread . . . and said, Take, eat; this is my body. And he took the cup . . . saying, Drink ye all of it; for this is my blood . . ."). And the Apostles are not merely responding; each reveals his own personality, his own relationship to the Saviour. (Note the dark, defiant profile of Judas, that sets him apart from the rest.) They exemplify what the artist wrote in one of his notebooks,

139. LEONARDO DA VINCI. *The Last Supper.* c.1495–98. Mural. Sta. Maria delle Grazie, Milan

140. LEONARDO DA VINCI. *Mona Lisa.* c.1503–5.
Panel, 30¼ x 21″. The Louvre, Paris

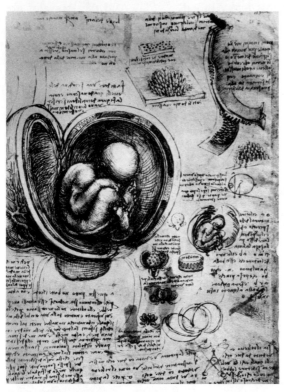

141. LEONARDO DA VINCI. *Embryo in the Womb.* c.1510.
Ink. Royal Library, Windsor Castle (Crown Copyright)

that the highest aim of painting is to depict "the intention of man's soul" through gestures and the movements of limbs—a dictum that refers not to momentary emotional states but to man's inner life as a whole.

In 1499, the duchy of Milan fell to the French, and Leonardo returned to a Florence very different from the city he remembered. The Medici had been expelled, and Florence was briefly a republic again. There Leonardo painted his most famous portrait, the *Mona Lisa* (fig. 140). The chiaroscuro we noted in the *Adoration* is now so perfected that it seemed miraculous to his contemporaries. The forms are built from layers of glazes so gossamer-thin that the entire panel seems to glow with a gentle light from within. But the fame of the *Mona Lisa* comes not from this pictorial subtlety alone; even more intriguing is her psychological fascination. Why, among all the smiling faces ever painted, has this one been singled out as "mysterious"? Perhaps because, as a portrait, the picture does not fit our expectations. The features are too individual for an ideal type, yet the element of idealization is so strong that it blurs the sitter's character. Once again the artist has brought two opposites into harmonious balance. The smile, too, may be read in two ways: as the echo of a mood, and as a timeless, symbolic expression. Clearly, the *Mona Lisa* embodies a quality of maternal tenderness which was to Leonardo the essence of womanhood. Even the landscape, composed mainly of rocks and water, suggests elemental generative forces. In the later years of his life, Leonardo devoted himself more and more to his scientific interests. Art and science had first been united in Brunelleschi's discovery of perspective; Leonardo's work is the climax of this trend. The artist, he believed, must know all the laws of nature, and the eye was to him the perfect instrument for gaining such knowledge. The extraordinary scope of his own inquiries is attested by the hundreds of drawings and notes which he hoped to incorporate into an encyclopedic set of treatises. How original he was as a scientist is still a matter of debate, but in one field his importance is undisputed: he created the modern scientific illustration, an essential tool for anatomists and biologists. A drawing such as the *Embryo in the Womb* (fig. 141) combines vivid observation with the clarity of a diagram, or—to paraphrase Leonardo's own words—sight and insight.

The concept of genius as divine inspiration, a superhuman power granted to a few rare individuals and acting through them, is nowhere exemplified more fully than in Michelangelo. Not only his admirers viewed him in this light; he himself, steeped in Neo-Platonism, accepted the idea of his genius as a living reality, although it seemed to him at times a curse rather than a blessing. Conventions, standards, and traditions might be observed by lesser spirits; he could acknowledge no authority higher than the dictates of his genius. Unlike Leonardo, for whom painting was the noblest of the arts because it embraced every visible aspect of the world, Michelangelo was a sculptor—more specifically, a carver of marble statues—to the core. Art, for him, was not a science but "the making of men," analogous to divine creation. Only the "liberation" of real, three-dimensional bodies from recalcitrant matter could satisfy the urge within him. Painting, he believed, should imitate the roundness of sculptured forms, and architecture, too, must partake of the organic qualities of the human figure. Michelangelo's faith in the image of man as the supreme vehicle of expression gave him a sense of kinship with classical sculpture closer than that of any other Renaissance artist, although he admired Giotto, Masaccio, and Donatello. Yet, as a Neo-Platonist, he looked upon the body as the earthly prison of the soul—noble, surely, but a prison nevertheless. This dualism endows his figures with their extraordinary pathos; outwardly calm, they seem stirred by an overwhelming psychic energy that has no release in physical action.

The unique qualities of Michelangelo's art are fully present in the *David* (fig. 142), the earliest monumental statue of the High Renaissance. Commissioned in 1501, when the artist was twenty-six, the huge figure was put at the left of the entrance to the Palazzo Vecchio as the civic-patriotic symbol of the Florentine republic (see fig. 97; a modern copy has now replaced the original). This role was a suitable one for the *David*. Without the head of Goliath, he looks challenging—not a victorious hero but the champion of a just cause. Nude, like Donatello's bronze *David* (see fig. 124), he boldly faces the world, vibrant with pent-up energy. But the style of the figure proclaims an ideal very different from Donatello's. Michelangelo had just spent several years in Rome, and had been strongly impressed with the emotion-filled, muscular bodies of Hellenistic sculpture. Their heroic scale, their superhuman beauty and power, and the swelling volume of their forms became part of Michelangelo's style, and through him part of Renaissance art in general. Still, the *David* could never be

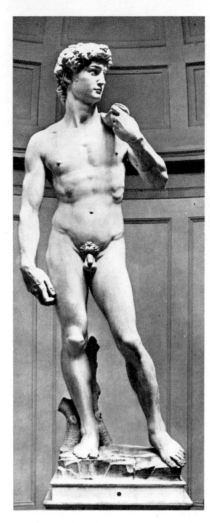

142. MICHELANGELO. *David*. 1501–4. Marble, height 13′ 5″. Academy, Florence

taken for an ancient statue. In the *Laocoön* (see fig. 36) and similar works, the body "acts out" the spirit's agony, while the *David*, characteristically, is both calm and tense.

Soon after, Michelangelo was called to Rome by Pope Julius II, the greatest and most ambitious of Renaissance popes, for whom he designed an enormous tomb. After a few years, however, the Pope changed his mind and set the reluctant artist to work on the ceiling fresco of the Sistine Chapel (fig. 143). Driven by his desire to resume the tomb project, Michelangelo finished the entire ceiling in four years (1508–12). He produced a masterpiece of truly epochal importance. The ceiling is a huge organism with hundreds of figures rhythmically distributed within the painted architectural framework, dwarfing the earlier murals below by its size, and still more by its compelling inner unity. In the central area, subdivided by five pairs of girder arches, are nine scenes from Genesis, from the Creation of the World (at

143. Interior, Sistine Chapel (showing Michelangelo's Ceiling Fresco and *Last Judgment*). The Vatican, Rome

What greater theme could he wish than the Creation, Man's Fall, and his ultimate reconciliation with the Lord? A detailed survey of the Sistine Ceiling would fill a book; we shall have to be content with the *Creation of Adam* (fig. 144), the most famous of the major scenes. It shows not the physical molding of Adam's body but the passage of the divine spark—the soul—and thus achieves a dramatic juxtaposition of Man and God unrivaled by any other artist. The relationship between the earth-bound Adam and the figure of God rushing through the sky becomes even more meaningful when we realize that Adam strains not only toward his Creator but toward Eve, whom he sees, yet unborn, in the shelter of the Lord's left arm. Our illustration also shows the garland-bearing nude youths that accompany the main sections. These wonderfully animated figures play an important role in Michelangelo's design; they form a kind of chain linking the Genesis scenes, yet their significance remains uncertain. Are they images of human souls? Do they represent the world of pagan antiquity? Whatever their symbolic intent, it is overpowered by the wealth of expression Michelangelo has poured into these figures.

the far end of the Chapel) to the Drunkenness of Noah. The theological scheme behind the choice of these scenes and the rich program surrounding them—the nude youths, the medallions, the prophets and sibyls, the scenes in the spandrels—has not been fully explained, but we know that it links the early history of man and the coming of Christ, the beginning of time and its end (the *Last Judgment* on the wall above the altar). How much responsibility did Michelangelo have for the program? He was not a man to submit to dictation, and the subject matter as a whole fits his cast of mind so perfectly that his own desires cannot have conflicted strongly with those of his patron.

When Michelangelo returned to the Sistine Chapel over twenty years later, the Western world was gripped by the spiritual and political crisis of the Reformation (see p. 124). We observe with shocking directness how the mood has changed as we turn from the radiant vitality of the ceiling fresco to the somber vision of the *Last Judgment*. Mankind, Blessed and Damned alike, huddles together in tight clumps, pleading for mercy before a wrathful

144. MICHELANGELO. *The Creation of Adam,* detail of Sistine Ceiling. 1508–12. Fresco. The Vatican, Rome

145. MICHELANGELO. *The Last Judgment*
(detail, with self-portrait). 1534–41. Fresco.
Sistine Chapel, The Vatican, Rome

God (figs. 143, 145). Seated on a cloud below the Lord is the Apostle Bartholomew, holding a human skin to represent his martyrdom (he had been flayed). The face on that skin is not the saint's, however; it is Michelangelo's own. In this grimly sardonic self-portrait the artist has left his personal confession of guilt and unworthiness.

The interval between the Sistine Ceiling and the *Last Judgment* coincided with the papacies of Leo X and Clement VII; both were members of the Medici family and preferred to employ Michelangelo in Florence. His activities centered on San Lorenzo, the Medici church, where Leo X had decided to build a chapel containing four monumental tombs for members of the family. Michelangelo worked on the project for fourteen years, completing the chapel and two tombs. It is the artist's only work where his statues remain in the setting planned specifically for them (fig. 146 shows the tomb of Giuliano). The design of the monument is strangely impersonal: there is no inscription, two allegorical figures (*Day* on the right, *Night* on the left) recline on the sarcophagus, and the statue of Giuliano, in classical military garb, bears no resemblance to the deceased. ("A thousand years from now, nobody will want to know what he really looked like," Michelangelo is said to have remarked.) What is the meaning of the monument? The question, put countless times, has never found a definitive answer. Michelangelo's plans for the Medici tombs underwent so many changes while the work was under way that the present state of the monuments can hardly be the final solution; rather, the dynamic process of design was arbitrarily halted by the artist's departure for Rome in 1534. *Day* and *Night* were certainly planned for horizontal surfaces, not for the curved lid of the present sarcophagus. Perhaps they were not even intended for this particular tomb. Giuliano's niche is too narrow and shallow to hold him comfortably. Other figures and reliefs were planned, but never executed. Yet the tomb of Giuliano remains a compelling visual unit. The great triangle of the statues is held in place by a network of verticals and horizontals whose slender, sharp-edged forms heighten the roundness and weight of the sculpture. In the brooding menace of *Day* and the disturbed slumber of *Night*, the dualism of body and soul is expressed with unforgettable grandeur.

During the last thirty years of his long career, architecture became Michelangelo's main preoccupation. In order to understand his achievement in that field, we must discuss briefly his most important predecessor, Donato Bramante. Bramante had been working for the Duke of Milan in the 1490s, together with

146. MICHELANGELO. Tomb of Giuliano de' Medici.
1524–34. Marble, height of central figure 71″.
New Sacristy, S. Lorenzo, Florence

147. DONATO BRAMANTE. The Tempietto. 1502.
S. Pietro in Montorio, Rome

than in any fifteenth-century structure. Equally striking is the "sculptural" treatment of the walls: deeply recessed niches "excavated" from heavy masses of masonry. These cavities are counterbalanced by the convex shape of the dome and by strongly projecting moldings and cornices. As a result, the Tempietto has a monumental weight that belies its modest size.

The Tempietto is the earliest of the great achievements that made Rome the center of Italian art during the first quarter of the sixteenth century. Most of them belong to the decade 1503–13, the papacy of Julius II. It was he who decided to replace the Early Christian basilica of St. Peter's with a church so magnificent as to overshadow all the monuments of ancient imperial Rome. The task naturally fell to Bramante. His design, of 1506, is known to us mainly from a plan (fig. 148), which bears out the words Bramante reportedly used to define his aim: "I shall place the Pantheon on top of the Basilica of Constantine." (See figs. 39–41.) Bramante's design is indeed of truly imperial magnificence: a huge dome crowns the crossing of the barrel-vaulted arms of a Greek cross, with four lesser domes and tall corner towers filling the angles. This plan fulfills all the demands laid down by Alberti for sacred architecture (see p. 102); based entirely on the circle and the square, it is so rigidly symmetrical that we cannot tell which apse was to hold the high altar. Inside the church, the "sculptured wall" reigns supreme: the plan shows no

Leonardo. After Milan fell, he went to Rome, and there he became the creator of High Renaissance architecture. The new style is fully evident in his Tempietto at San Pietro in Montorio (fig. 147), designed soon after 1500. Its nickname, "little temple," seems well deserved: in the three-step platform, and the severe Doric order of the colonnade, classical temple architecture is more directly recalled

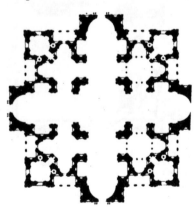

above: 148. DONATO BRAMANTE.
Original Plan for St. Peter's,
Rome (after Geymüller). 1506

right: 149. MICHELANGELO.
St. Peter's, view from west.
1546–64 (dome completed by
Giacomo della Porta, 1590).
Rome

continuous surfaces, only great, oddly shaped "islands" of masonry that have been well described by one critic as giant pieces of toast half-eaten by a voracious space. Their actual size can be visualized only if we compare the measurements of Bramante's church with those of earlier buildings. San Lorenzo in Florence, for instance, is 268 feet long, less than half the length of the new St. Peter's (550 feet). Each arm of Bramante's Greek cross has about the dimensions of the Basilica of Constantine. No wonder the construction of St. Peter's progressed at a snail's pace. At Bramante's death, in 1514, only the four crossing piers had actually been built. For the next three decades the campaign was carried out hesitantly by architects trained under Bramante. A new and decisive phase began only in 1546, when Michelangelo took charge; the present appearance of the church (fig. 149) is largely shaped by his ideas. Michelangelo simplified Bramante's overly complex plan without changing its basic character; he also redesigned the exterior, using a colossal order to emphasize the compact body of the structure, thus setting off the dome more dramatically. Although largely built after his death, the dome reflects Michelangelo's ideas in every important respect. Bramante had planned a stepped hemisphere, somewhat like the dome of the Pantheon, which would have seemed to press down on the church below; Michelangelo's conveys the opposite sensation, a powerful thrust that draws energy upward from the main body of the structure. The high drum, the strongly projecting buttresses accented by double columns, the ribs, the raised curve of the cupola, the tall lantern —all contribute verticality at the expense of the horizontals. We may recall Brunelleschi's Florence Cathedral dome (see fig. 95), from which Michelangelo clearly borrowed a great deal. Yet the effect is immensely different: the Florence dome gives no hint of the internal stresses, while Michelangelo finds a sculptured shape for these contending forces and relates them to those in the rest of the building (the impulse of the paired colossal pilasters below is taken up by the double columns of the drum, continues in the ribs, and culminates in the lantern). The logic of this design is so persuasive that few domes built between 1600 and 1900 fail to acknowledge it.

If Michelangelo exemplifies the solitary genius, Raphael belongs to the opposite type: the artist as a man of the world. Although each had his partisans, both enjoyed equal fame. Today our sympathies are less evenly divided—

In the room the women come and go
Talking of Michelangelo.

(T. S. Eliot)

So do a lot of us, including the authors of historical novels and fictionalized biographies, whereas Raphael is usually discussed only by historians of art. His career is too much of a success story, his work too replete with seemingly effortless grace, to match the tragic heroism of Michelangelo. As an innovator, Raphael contributed less than either Leonardo or Michelangelo, yet he is the central painter of the High Renaissance; our conception of the entire style rests on his work more than on any other master's. His genius was a unique power of synthesis that enabled him to merge the qualities of Leonardo and Michelangelo, creating an art at once lyric and dramatic, pictorially rich and sculpturally solid. At the time Michelangelo began to paint the Sistine Ceiling, Julius II summoned Raphael from Florence to decorate a series of rooms in the Vatican Palace. In the first, the Stanza della Segnatura, Raphael's frescoes refer to the four domains of learning —theology, philosophy, law, and the arts. Of these, *The School of Athens* (fig. 150) has long been acknowledged as the perfect embodiment of the classic spirit of the High Renaissance. Its subject is "the Athenian school of thought"; a group of famous Greek philosophers is gathered around Plato and Aristotle, each in a characteristic pose or activity. Raphael must have already seen the Sistine Ceiling, then nearing completion, for he evidently owes to Michelangelo the expressive energy, the physical power, and the dramatic grouping of his figures. Yet Raphael has not simply borrowed the older master's repertory of gestures and poses; he has absorbed it into his own style, and thereby given it different meaning. Body and spirit, action and feeling, are now balanced harmoniously, and every member of this great assembly plays his role with magnificent, purposeful clarity. *The School of Athens* suggests the spirit of Leonardo's *Last Supper* (fig. 139) rather than that of the Sistine Ceiling (fig. 143). This holds true of the way each philosopher reveals "the intention of his soul," of the formal rhythm linking individuals and groups, of the centralized, symmetrical design, and of the interdependence of the figures and their architectural setting. But compared with the hall of the *Last Supper*, Raphael's classical edifice shares far more of the compositional burden. Inspired by Bramante, it seems like an advance view of the new St. Peter's (fig. 148).

150. RAPHAEL. *The School of Athens.* 1510–11. Fresco. Stanza della Segnatura, Vatican Palace, Rome

151. RAPHAEL. *Galatea.* 1513. Fresco.
Villa Farnesina, Rome

Raphael never again set so splendid an architectural stage. To create pictorial space, he relied increasingly on the movement of human figures, rather than perspective vistas. In his *Galatea* (fig. 151), the subject is again classical —the nymph Galatea, vainly pursued by Polyphemus, belongs to Greek mythology—but here the gay and sensuous aspect of antiquity is celebrated, in contrast to the austere idealism of *The School of Athens.* Its composition recalls *The Birth of Venus* (see fig. 135), which Raphael knew from his Florence days, yet their very resemblance emphasizes their profound dissimilarity. Raphael's full-bodied, dynamic figures take on their expansive spiral movement from the vigorously twisting pose of Galatea; in Botticelli's picture, the movement is not generated by the figures but imposed upon them from without, so that it never detaches itself from the surface of the canvas.

The distinction between Florence and Venice, so marked in the fifteenth century, is as striking in the High Renaissance. Titian, the outstanding Venetian painter of the new style and an artist of prodigious gifts, had as long a career as Michelangelo's. His *Bacchanal,* painted about 1518 (colorplate 14), makes a telling contrast with Raphael's *Galatea.* It, too, is frankly pagan, inspired by an ancient author's description of such a revel, and the figures, active and muscular, move with a joyous abandon not unlike Raphael's. By this time, Titian had already become familiar with the High Renaissance in Florence and Rome through engravings. A number of the celebrants in his *Bacchanal* also reflect the influence of ancient sculpture. Yet Titian's approach to antiquity is very different from Raphael's; he visualizes the realm of classical myths as part of the natural world, inhabited not by animated statues but by beings of flesh and blood. The figures of the *Bacchanal* are idealized just enough beyond everyday reality to persuade us that they belong to a long-lost golden age. They invite us to share their blissful state in a way that makes Raphael's *Galatea* seem cold and remote by comparison. The reason for the difference is not far to seek: Titian is the artistic heir of Giovanni Bellini. His figures move in a landscape as deep, poetic, and warmly sunlit as that of Bellini's *St. Francis* (see fig. 137), although the forms are now painted with far greater breadth and sensuousness. Aside from all his other achievements, Titian also was the greatest portraitist of the century. His *Man with the Glove* (fig. 152), unlike the *Mona Lisa* (see fig. 140), offers no disquieting mysteries but a profound sense of the sitter's individuality. Casually posed and lost in thought, the young man seems quite unaware of us. The dreamy intimacy of this portrait, the hint of melancholy in its mood, the soft outlines and deep shadows, give it a haunting poetic appeal. In Titian's hands, the possibilities of oil technique—rich, creamy highlights, dark tones that are yet transparent and delicately modulated—are now fully realized; the separate brush strokes, hardly visible before, become increasingly free, so that the personal rhythms of the artist's "handwriting" are an essential element of the finished work. In this respect, Titian seems infinitely more "modern" than Leonardo, Michelangelo, or Raphael.

MANNERISM AND OTHER TRENDS. What happened after the High Renaissance? About fifty years ago the answer would have been: the Late Renaissance, which was dominated by shallow imitators of the great masters of the previous generation and lasted until the Baroque style emerged at the end of the century. Today we take a far more positive view of the artists who reached maturity after 1520, but we still have to agree on a name for the seventy-five years separating the High Renaissance from the Baroque. Any one label implies that the period had one style, and nobody has succeeded in defining such a style. But if there was no single style, why should the span 1525–1600 be regarded as a period at all? Perhaps the difficulty can be resolved by thinking of it as a time of crisis that gave rise to several competing tendencies rather than one dominant ideal —or as a time full of inner contradictions, not unlike the present and thus peculiarly fascinating to us. Among these trends, that of Mannerism is the most discussed today. The scope and significance of the term remain problematic: its original meaning was narrow and derogatory, designating a group of painters in Rome and Florence whose self-consciously "artificial" style was derived from certain aspects of Raphael and Michelangelo. More recently, the cold formalism of their work has been recognized as part of a wider movement that placed "inner vision," however subjective and fantastic, above the twin authority of nature and the ancients. Its first signs appear shortly before 1520 in the work of some young painters in Florence. By 1521, Rosso Fiorentino, the most eccentric member of this group, expressed the new attitude with full conviction in *The Descent from the Cross* (colorplate 15). Nothing has prepared us for the shocking impact of this latticework of spidery forms spread out against the dark sky. The figures are agitated yet rigid, as if congealed by a sudden, icy blast; even the

152. TITIAN. *Man with the Glove*. c.1520. Canvas, 39½ x 35″. The Louvre, Paris

draperies have brittle, sharp-edged planes; the acid colors and the brilliant but unreal light reinforce the nightmarish effect of the scene. Here is what amounts to a revolt against the classical balance of High Renaissance art—a profoundly disquieting, willful, visionary style that indicates a deep-seated inner anxiety.

This "anticlassical" style, the first phase of Mannerism, was soon replaced by another aspect of the movement, less expressive of psychological turmoil but equally far removed from the confident, stable world of the High Renaissance. We see it in *The Madonna with the Long Neck* (fig. 153) by Parmigianino, painted when the artist had returned to his native Parma after several years' sojourn in Rome. He had been deeply impressed with the rhythmic grace of Raphael (compare fig. 151), but he has transformed the older master's figures into a remarkable new breed: their limbs, elongated and ivory-smooth, move with effortless languor, embodying an ideal of beauty as remote from nature as any Byzantine figure. Their setting is equally arbitrary, with a gigantic—and apparently purposeless—row of columns looming behind the tiny figure of a prophet; Parmigianino seems determined to prevent us from measuring anything in this picture by the standards of ordinary experience. Here we approach the "artificial" style for which the term Mannerism was originally coined. *The Madonna with the Long Neck* is a vision of unearthly perfection, its cold elegance

no less compelling than is the violence seen in Rosso's *Descent*.

In Venice, Mannerism appeared only toward the middle of the century. Its leading exponent, Tintoretto, was an artist of prodigious energy and inventiveness, combining elements of both "anticlassical" and "elegant" Mannerism in his work. He reportedly wanted "to paint like Titian and to design like Michelangelo," but his relationship to these two masters, though real enough, was as peculiar as Parmigianino's was to Raphael. Tintoretto's last major work, *The Last Supper* (fig. 154), is also his most spectacular; it denies in every possible way the classic values of Leonardo's version of the subject (see fig. 139), painted a century before. Christ, to be sure, still occupies the center of the composition, but now the table is placed at right angles to the picture plane, so that His small figure in the middle distance is distinguishable only by the brilliant halo. Tintoretto has given the scene an everyday setting, cluttering it with attendants, containers of food and drink, and domestic animals. But this serves only to contrast dramatically the natural with the supernatural, for there are also celestial attendants—the smoke from the blazing oil lamp miraculously turns into clouds of angels that converge upon Christ just as He offers His body and blood, in the form of bread and wine, to His disciples. Tintoretto's main concern has been to make visible the institution of the Eucharist, the transubstantiation of earthly into

left: 153. PARMIGIANINO. *The Madonna with the Long Neck.* c.1535. Panel, 7′ 1″ x 4′ 4″. Uffizi Gallery, Florence

below: 154. TINTORETTO. *The Last Supper.* 1592–94. Canvas, 12′ x 18′ 8″. S. Giorgio Maggiore, Venice

Divine food; he barely hints at the human drama of Judas' betrayal (Judas is the tiny figure to the rear on the near side of the table).

The last—and perhaps greatest—Mannerist painter was also trained in Venice. Domenicos Theotocopoulos, nicknamed El Greco, came from Crete. His earliest training must have been under a local master still working in the Byzantine tradition, but in Venice he quickly absorbed the lessons of Titian, Tintoretto, and other Venetian painters. Later, in Rome, he came to know the art of Michelangelo, Raphael, and the Central Italian Mannerists. In 1576/77 he went to Spain, settling in Toledo for the rest of his life. Yet he remained an alien in his new homeland; although the spiritual climate of the Counter Reformation, which was especially intense in Spain, may account for the exalted emotionalism of his mature work, his style had already been formed before he arrived in Toledo. Nor did he ever forget his Byzantine background—until the end of his career, he signed his pictures in Greek. The largest and most resplendent of El Greco's commissions is *The Burial of Count Orgaz* (fig. 155); the huge canvas honors a medieval benefactor of the church who was so pious that St. Stephen and St. Augustine miraculously appeared at his funeral to lower the body into its grave. El Greco represents the burial as a contemporary event, portraying among the attendants many of the local nobility and clergy; the dazzling display of color and texture in the armor and vestments could hardly be surpassed by Titian himself. Directly above, the count's soul (a small, cloudlike figure like the angels in Tintoretto's *Last Supper*) is carried to Heaven by an angel. The celestial assembly filling the upper half of the picture is painted very differently from the lower half: every form—clouds, limbs, draperies—takes part in the sweeping, flamelike movement toward the distant figure of Christ. Here, even more than in Tintoretto's art, the various aspects of Mannerism fuse into a single ecstatic vision. Like an enormous window, the canvas fills one entire wall of its chapel, so that we must look sharply upward to see the upper half of the picture. El Greco's violent foreshortening is calculated to achieve an illusion of boundless space above, while the foreground figures appear as on a stage (note that their feet are cut off by the frame). El Greco's task may be compared to Masaccio's in his *Trinity* mural (see colorplate 13). The contrast measures the dynamic evolution of Western art since the beginning of the Early Renaissance.

155. EL GRECO. *The Burial of Count Orgaz.* 1586. Canvas, 16′ x 11′ 10″. S. Tomé, Toledo, Spain

If Mannerism produced the personalities that today seem most "modern"—El Greco's fame is greater now than it ever was before—its dominance was not uncontested in the sixteenth century. Another trend that also emerged about 1520 anticipated so many features of the Baroque style that it might be labeled Proto-Baroque. Its most important representative, Correggio, was a phenomenally gifted painter who spent most of his brief career in Parma. He absorbed the influence of Leonardo and the Venetians, then of Michelangelo and Raphael, but their ideal of classical balance did not attract him. His art is filled with movement that sweeps through the composition, carrying the figures along with it, such as the nymph Io ecstatically swooning in the embrace of a cloudlike Jupiter (fig. 156). Leonardesque chiaroscuro, combined with a Venetian sense of color and texture, produces an effect of exquisite voluptuousness that far exceed Titian's in the *Bacchanal* (see colorplate 14). Correggio had no immediate successors, but toward 1600 his art began to be widely appreciated. For the next century and a half, he was admired as the equal of Raphael—while the Mannerists, so important before, were now largely forgotten.

A third trend in sixteenth-century Italian painting emerged in the towns located in the

156. CORREGGIO. *Jupiter and Io.* c.1532. Canvas, 64½ x 27¾″. Kunsthistorisches Museum, Vienna

pernatural; at first glance, the picture looks like a High Renaissance work born fifty years too late. Yet we miss one essential—the elevated, ideal conception of man that underlies the work of the High Renaissance masters. Veronese paints a sumptuous banquet, a true feast for the eyes, but not "the intention of man's soul." We are not even sure which event from the life of Christ he originally meant to depict, for he gave the canvas its present title only after he had been summoned by a religious tribunal on the charge of filling his picture with "buffoons . . . and similar vulgarities" unsuited to its sacred character. Veronese's dogged refusal to admit the justice of the charge, his insistence on his right to introduce directly observed details, however "improper," and his indifference to the subject of the picture spring from an attitude so startlingly "extroverted" that it was not generally accepted until the nineteenth century. The painter's domain, Veronese seems to say, is the entire visible world, and in it he acknowledges no authority other than his senses.

Alpine foothills. The artists in towns like Verona worked in a style based on Titian's but with a stronger interest in everyday reality. In the work of Paolo Veronese, this North Italian realism takes on the splendor of a pageant (see also pp. 238-39). Born and trained in Verona, Veronese became, after Tintoretto, the most important painter in Venice; although utterly unlike in style, both found favor with the public. The contrast is strikingly evident if we compare Tintoretto's *Last Supper* (see fig. 154) with Veronese's *Christ in the House of Levi* (fig. 157), which deals with a similar subject. Veronese avoids all reference to the su-

Italian sculptors and architects of the later sixteenth century in general fail to match the achievements of the painters, with one important exception: Andrea Palladio, an architect second in importance only to Michelangelo. Palladio stands in the tradition of the humanist and theoretician Leone Battista Alberti (see p. 102). Although his career centered on his native town of Vicenza, not far from Venice, his buildings and theoretical writings soon brought him international renown. Architecture, according to Palladio, must be governed both by reason and by certain universal rules that were perfectly exemplified by the buildings of the

157. PAOLO VERONESE. *Christ in the House of Levi.* 1573. Canvas, 18′ 2″ x 42′. Academy, Venice

158. ANDREA PALLADIO. Villa Rotonda.
1567–70. Vicenza

ancients. He thus shared Alberti's basic out-look and his firm faith in the cosmic signifi-cance of numerical proportions. They differed in how each man related theory and practice. With Alberti, this relationship had been loose and flexible, whereas Palladio believed quite literally in practicing what he preached. His ar-chitectural treatise is consequently more practi-cal than Alberti's—this helps to explain its huge success—while his buildings are linked more directly with his theories. It has even been said that Palladio designed only what was, in his view, sanctioned by ancient precedent. If the results are not necessarily classic in style, we may call them "classicistic" (to denote a conscious striving for classic qualities); this is indeed the usual term for both Palladio's work and his theoretical attitude. The Villa Rotonda (fig. 158), one of his most famous buildings, perfectly illustrates the meaning of classicism. An aristocratic country residence near Vicenza, it consists of a square block surmounted by a dome and is faced on all four sides with identi-cal porches having the shape of temple fronts. Alberti defined the ideal church as a com-pletely symmetrical, centralized design; Palla-dio evidently found in the same principles the ideal country house. But how could he justify the use of so solemn a motif as the temple front in this context? Surprisingly enough, he was convinced that Roman private houses had por-ticoes such as these (excavations have since proved him wrong). Yet Palladio's use of the temple front here was not mere antiquarianism; he probably persuaded himself that it was legit-imate because he regarded it as desirable for both beauty and utility. In any case, the porches of the Villa Rotonda, perfectly correlated with the walls behind, are an or-ganic part of his design. They lend the struc-ture an air of serene dignity and festive grace that still appeals to us today.

THE RENAISSANCE IN NORTHERN EUROPE. North of the Alps, the majority of fifteenth-century artists had remained indifferent to Italian forms and ideas. Since the time of Robert Campin and the Van Eycks, they had looked to Flan-ders, not Tuscany, for leadership. This isola-tion ends suddenly, toward the year 1500. As if a dam had burst, Italian influence flows north-ward in an ever-widening stream, and Northern Renaissance art begins to replace Late Gothic. That term, however, is much less well defined than Late Gothic, which refers to a single, clearly recognizable stylistic tradition. The di-versity of trends north of the Alps is even greater than in Italy during the sixteenth cen-tury. Nor does Italian influence provide a com-mon denominator, for this influence is itself di-verse: Early Renaissance, High Renaissance, and Mannerist, each in some regional variant from Lombardy, Venice, Florence, or Rome. And its effects may be superficial or profound, direct or indirect, specific or general. More-over, the Late Gothic tradition remained very much alive, if no longer dominant, and its encounter with Italian art resulted in a kind of Hundred Years' War of styles which ended only when, about 1600, the Baroque emerged as an international movement. The course of this "war" was decisively affected by the Ref-ormation, which had a far more immediate im-pact on art north of the Alps than in Italy. Our account, then, must be oversimplified, empha-sizing the heroic phases of the struggle at the expense of the lesser engagements.

Let us begin with Germany, the home of the Reformation, where the main battles of the "war of styles" took place during the first quar-ter of the century. Between 1475 and 1500, it had produced such important masters as Schongauer (see p. 96), but these hardly pre-pare us for the astonishing burst of creative en-ergy that was to follow. The achievements of this period—comparable in its brevity and bril-liance to the Italian High Renaissance—are measured by the contrasting personalities of its greatest artists, Matthias Grünewald and Al-brecht Dürer. Both died in 1528, probably at about the same age. Dürer quickly became in-ternationally famous, while Grünewald re-mained so obscure that his real name, Mathis Gothart Nithart, was discovered only recently. His fame, like El Greco's, is almost entirely of our own century. In Northern art of his time, he alone overwhelms us in his main work, the

159. MATTHIAS GRÜNEWALD.
The Crucifixion, from
The Isenheim Altarpiece (closed).
c.1510–15. Panel,
8′ 10″ x 10′ 1″.
Musée Unterlinden, Colmar
(for the second view
of altarpiece, see colorplate 16)

Isenheim Altarpiece (colorplate 16), with something like the power of the Sistine Ceiling. Painted in 1509–15 for the monastery church of the Order of St. Anthony at Isenheim, in Alsace, it is now in the museum of the nearby town of Colmar. The altarpiece has three stages, or "views." The first, when all the wings are closed, shows *The Crucifixion* (fig. 159) —probably the most impressive ever painted. In one respect it is very medieval: Christ's unbearable agony, and the desperate grief of the Virgin, St. John, and Mary Magdalen, recall older devotional images such as the Bonn *Pietà* (see fig. 102). But the body on the cross, with its twisted limbs, countless lacerations, and rivulets of blood, is on a heroic scale that raises it beyond the merely human: thus the two natures of Christ are revealed. The same message is conveyed by the flanking figures: the three historic witnesses on the left mourn Christ's death as a man, while John the Baptist, on the right, points with calm emphasis to Him as the Saviour. Even the background suggests this duality: this Golgotha is not a hill outside Jerusalem, but a mountain towering above lesser peaks. The Crucifixion becomes a lonely event silhouetted against a deserted, ghostly landscape and a blue-black sky. Darkness is over the land, in accordance with the Gospels, yet brilliant light bathes the foreground with the force of sudden revelation. This union of time and eternity, of reality and symbolism, gives

Grünewald's *Crucifixion* its awesome grandeur.

When the outer wings are opened, the mood of the *Isenheim Altarpiece* changes dramatically (colorplate 16). All three scenes in this second "view"—the *Annunciation,* the *Angel Concert for the Madonna and Child,* and the *Resurrection*—celebrate events as jubilant in spirit as the *Crucifixion* is austere. Most striking is the sense of movement pervading these panels—everything twists and turns as though it had a life of its own. This vibrant energy has thoroughly reshaped the brittle, spiky contours and angular drapery patterns of Late Gothic art; Grünewald's forms are soft, elastic, fleshy. His light and color show a corresponding change: commanding all the resources of the great Flemish masters, he employs them with unexampled boldness and flexibility. His color scale is richly iridescent, its range matched only by the Venetians'. And his exploitation of colored light is altogether without parallel at that time. In the luminescent angels of the *Concert* and, most spectacularly, in the rainbow-hued radiance of the Risen Christ, Grünewald's genius has achieved miracles-through-light that are unsurpassed to this day.

How much did Grünewald owe to Italian art? Nothing at all, we are tempted to reply. Yet he must have learned from the Renaissance in more ways than one: his knowledge of perspective (note the low horizons) and the physical vigor of some of his figures cannot be explained by the Late Gothic tradition. Perhaps the most important effect of the Renaissance on him, however, was psychological. We know little about his career, but apparently he did not lead the settled life of a craftsman-painter controlled by the rules of his guild; he was also an architect, engineer, and entrepreneur who worked for many different patrons without staying anywhere for long. He was in sympathy with Martin Luther (who frowned upon religious images as "idolatrous") even though, as a painter, he depended on Catholic patronage. In a word, Grünewald seems to have shared the free, individualist spirit of Italian Renaissance artists. The daring of his pictorial vision likewise suggests a reliance on his own resources. The Renaissance, then, had a liberating effect on him but did not change the basic cast of his imagination. Instead, it helped him to epitomize the expressive aspects of the Late Gothic in a style of unique intensity and individuality.

For Albrecht Dürer, the Renaissance held a different and richer meaning. He visited Venice as a young journeyman and returned to his native Nuremberg with a new conception of the world and the artist's place in it. The unbridled fantasy of Grünewald's art was to him "a wild, unpruned tree" which needed the discipline of the objective, rational standards of the Renaissance. Taking the Italian view that the fine arts belong among the liberal arts, he also adopted the ideal of the artist as a gentleman and humanistic scholar. By steadily cultivating his mind he came to encompass a vast variety of techniques and subjects. And since he was the greatest printmaker of the time, he had a wide influence on sixteenth-century art through his woodcuts and engravings, which circulated throughout the Western world. The first artist to be fascinated by his own image, Dürer was in this respect more of a Renaissance personality than any Italian. His earliest known work, a drawing made at thirteen, is a self-portrait, and he continued to produce them throughout his career. Most impressive, and peculiarly revealing, is the panel he painted in 1500 (fig. 160): pictorially, it belongs to the Flemish tradition, but the solemn, frontal pose and the Christ-like idealization of the features assert an authority quite beyond the range of ordinary portraits. The picture looks, in fact, like a secularized icon, reflecting not so much Dürer's vanity as the seriousness with which he regarded his mission as an artistic reformer.

The didactic aspect of Dürer's art is evident in many of his greatest prints, such as *Knight,*

160. ALBRECHT DÜRER. *Self-Portrait.* 1500. Panel, 26¼ x 19¼". Pinakothek, Munich

161. ALBRECHT DÜRER. *Knight, Death, and Devil.* 1513. Engraving. Museum of Fine Arts, Boston

Art in the Renaissance 123

Death, and Devil (fig. 161). The knight on his beautiful mount, poised and confident like an equestrian statue, embodies an ideal both aesthetic and moral: he is the Christian Soldier, steadfast on the road of faith toward the Heavenly Jerusalem and undeterred by the hideous horseman threatening to cut him off, or by the grotesque devil behind him. The dog, another symbol of virtue, loyally follows his master despite the lizards and skulls in his path. Italian Renaissance form, united with the heritage of Late Gothic symbolism (whether open or disguised), here takes on a new, characteristically Northern significance. The subject of *Knight, Death, and Devil* seems to have been derived from a book called the *Manual of the Christian Soldier* by Erasmus of Rotterdam, the greatest of Northern humanists. Dürer's own convictions were essentially those of Christian humanism; they made him an early and enthusiastic follower of Martin Luther (see also p. 240), although, like Grünewald, he continued to work for Catholic patrons. In the 1520s he tried to create a monumental art embodying the Protestant faith, but his efforts were doomed by the spiritual leaders of the Reformation, who looked upon them with indifference, or, more often, outright hostility. Dürer thus turned to the theory of art, devoting a good part of his final years to this. His work includes a treatise on geometry based on a thorough study of Piero della Francesca's discourse on perspective. Often, he went beyond his Italian sources; he invented, for instance, a device for producing an image by purely mechanical means, to demonstrate the objective validity of perspective (fig. 162). Two men "draw" the lute as it would appear to us if we looked at it from the spot on the wall marked by a little hook; the string passing through the hook substitutes for the visual rays. The man on the left attaches the end of the string to successive points on the contour of the lute; the other man marks where the string passes through the vertical frame (the picture plane) and makes corresponding dots on the drawing board hinged to the frame. Dürer knew, of course, that such an image was the record of a scientific experiment, not a work of art; nor was he really interested in making pictures without human skill and judgment. Yet his device, however clumsy, is the first step toward the principle of the photographic camera.

Dürer was a pioneer also in transplanting classical subjects to Northern soil. More often than not, however, these were based on literary rather than visual sources, so that the classical content was not cast in classical form. The same is true of his contemporaries, such as the gifted Bavarian painter Albrecht Altdorfer, who did the impressive *Battle of Issus* (fig. 163). Unless we read the text on the tablet suspended in the sky, we cannot possibly identify the subject, Alexander's victory over Darius. Altdorfer has tried to follow ancient descriptions of the actual number and kind of combatants, but this required him to adopt a bird's-eye view whereby the two protagonists are lost in the antlike mass of their own armies (for contrast, see the Hellenistic representation of the same subject, fig. 50). Moreover, the soldiers' armor and the town in the distance are unmistakably of the sixteenth century. The picture might well show some contemporary battle, except for one

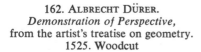
162. ALBRECHT DÜRER.
Demonstration of Perspective,
from the artist's treatise on geometry.
1525. Woodcut

feature: the spectacular sky, with the sun triumphantly breaking through the clouds and "defeating" the moon. The celestial drama above a vast Alpine landscape, obviously correlated with the human contest below, raises the scene to the cosmic level. Altdorfer may be viewed as a later, and lesser, Grünewald; although he, too, was an architect, well acquainted with perspective and the Italian stylistic vocabulary, his paintings show the unruly imagination already familiar from the work of the older master. But, unlike Grünewald, Altdorfer makes the human figure incidental to its spatial setting. The tiny soldiers of the *Battle of Issus* have their counterpart in his other pictures, and he painted at least one landscape with no figures at all—the earliest example of "pure" landscape.

Although greatly gifted, Altdorfer and his German contemporaries evaded the main challenge of the Renaissance that was so bravely faced—if not always mastered—by Dürer: the image of man. Their style, antimonumental and miniaturelike, set the pace for dozens of lesser masters; perhaps the rapid decline of German art after Dürer's death was due to a failure of ambition among artists and patrons alike. The career of Hans Holbein the Younger—the one painter of whom this is not true—confirms the general rule. Younger than Dürer by twenty-six years, Holbein grew up in Augsburg, a city in South Germany particularly open to Renaissance ideas, and then became the leading artist of Basel, in Switzerland. In 1526, when Basel was in the throes of the Reformation crisis, he went to England, hoping for commissions at the court of Henry VIII. On his return two years later, he saw fanatical mobs destroying religious images as "idols," and in 1532 he settled permanently in London as court painter to Henry VIII. His portrait of the king (fig. 164) shares the rigid frontality of Dürer's self-portrait (see fig. 160), but its purpose is to convey the almost divine authority of the absolute ruler: the immobile pose, the air of unapproachability, the display of precisely rendered jewels and gold embroidery, create an overpowering sensation of the monarch's ruthless, commanding presence. Such "class-conscious" portraits were gaining international currency at the courts of Europe during the second quarter of the century, and Holbein's are the most impressive examples of their kind. If they owe something to the icons of religious art, that is perhaps less surprising than it might seem; for in the religious wars following the Reformation, it was the sovereign who, as "Defender of

163. ALBRECHT ALTDORFER. *The Battle of Issus.* 1529. Panel, 62 x 47″. Pinakothek, Munich

164. HANS HOLBEIN THE YOUNGER. *Henry VIII.* 1540. Panel, 32⅛ x 29″. National Gallery, Rome

the Faith," decided whether his subjects were to be Catholic or Reformed.

The Netherlands in the sixteenth century had the most turbulent and painful history of any country north of the Alps. They were then part of the far-flung empire of the Hapsburgs under

Charles V, who was also king of Spain. The Reformation quickly became powerful in the Netherlands, and the attempts of the Crown to suppress it led to open revolt against foreign rule. After a bloody struggle, the northern provinces (today's Holland) gained their independence, while the southern ones (now called Belgium) remained in Spanish hands. The religious and political strife might have had catastrophic effects on the arts, yet this, astonishingly, did not happen. While the Netherlands had no pioneers of the Northern Renaissance comparable to Dürer, they absorbed Italian elements more steadily than did Germany. Between 1550 and 1600, their most troubled time, the Netherlands produced the major painters of Northern Europe, who paved the way for the great Dutch and Flemish masters of the next century. Apart from the assimilation of Italian art, Netherlandish sixteenth-century painters had one main concern: to develop a repertory of subjects to supplement, and eventually replace, the traditional religious themes. The process was gradual, shaped less by individual achievement than by the need to cater to popular taste as church commissions became steadily scarcer. Pieter Bruegel the Elder, the only genius among these painters, explored landscape, peasant life, and moral allegory, such as *The Land of Cockaigne* (fig. 165). It shows a fool's paradise where tables are always laden with tasty dishes, houses have roofs made of pies, and pigs and chickens run about roasted to a turn. The lesson Bruegel teaches us here is philosophical rather than religious: the men under the tree are not sinners in the grip of evil, like those in Bosch's *Garden of Delights* (see fig. 121), they are simply not wise enough to know what is best for them. By becoming slaves to their stomachs, they have given up all ambition, all self-respect, for the sake of a kind of animal happiness—the knight has dropped his lance, the farmer his flail, and the scholar his books. "Beware of the fool's paradise," Bruegel seems to say, "it's more dangerous than hell because people *like* going there." And the monumental design of the painting, in the shape of a great wheel turned on its side, proves that he must have thought his subject serious and important.

In architecture and sculpture, it took the northern countries longer to assimilate Italian forms than in painting. France, more closely linked with Italy than the rest (we recall the French conquest of Milan), was the first to achieve an integrated Renaissance style. In 1546 King Francis I, who had shown his admiration for Italian art earlier by inviting Leonardo to France, decided to replace the old Gothic royal castle, the Louvre (see fig. 112), with a new and much larger structure on the same site. The project, barely begun at the time of his death, was not completed until more than a century later; but its oldest portion, by Pierre Lescot (fig. 166), is the finest surviving example of Northern Renaissance architecture. The details of Lescot's façade are derived from Bramante and his successors and have an astonishing classical purity, yet we would not mistake it for an Italian structure. Its distinctive quality comes not from Italian forms superficially applied, but from a genuine synthesis of the traditional Gothic castle with the Renaissance palace. Italian, of course, are the

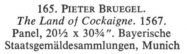

165. PIETER BRUEGEL.
The Land of Cockaigne. 1567.
Panel, 20½ x 30¾ ". Bayerische
Staatsgemäldesammlungen, Munich

Colorplate 13.
MASACCIO. *The Holy Trinity*.
1425. Fresco.
Sta. Maria Novella,
Florence

Colorplate 14. TITIAN. *Bacchanal*. c.1518. Canvas, 5′ 8¾″ x 6′ 4″.
The Prado, Madrid

Colorplate 15. ROSSO FIORENTINO. *The Descent from the Cross.*
1521. Panel, 11′ x 6′ 5½″. Pinacoteca, Volterra

Colorplate 16. MATTHIAS GRÜNEWALD. *The Annunciation* (left);
Angel Concert for the Madonna and Child (center); *The Resurrection* (right),
second view of the *Isenheim Altarpiece*. c.1510–15. Panel; center 8′ 10″ x 11′ 2½″,
side wings each 8′ 10″ x 4′ 8″. Musée Unterlinden, Colmar

Colorplate 17. Balthasar Neumann. The Kaisersaal, Episcopal Palace. 1719–44. Würzburg

Colorplate 18. Diego Velazquez. *The Maids of Honor* (detail). 1656.
Canvas. The Prado, Madrid.

Colorplate 19. REMBRANDT. *The Polish Rider*.
c.1655. Canvas, 46 x 53″. The Frick Collection, New York

166. PIERRE LESCOT.
Square Court, the Louvre.
Begun 1546. Paris

superimposed classical orders, the pedimented window frames, and the arcade on the ground floor. But the continuity of the façade is interrupted by three projecting pavilions which take the place of the castle turrets (compare fig. 112), and the steep roof is also traditionally Northern. The vertical accents thus overcome the horizontal ones (note the broken architraves), their effect reinforced by the tall, narrow windows. Equally un-Italian is the rich sculptural decoration covering almost the entire wall surface of the third story. These reliefs, admirably adapted to the architecture, are by Jean Goujon, the finest French sculptor of the mid-sixteenth century. Unfortunately, they have been much restored. Like Lescot's architecture, Goujon's figures combine classical details with a delicate slenderness that gives them a uniquely French elegance.

3. THE BAROQUE

Baroque has been the term used by art historians for almost a century to designate the style of the period 1600–1750. Its original meaning —"irregular, contorted, grotesque"—is now largely forgotten. There is also general agreement that the new style was born in Rome around 1600. What remains under dispute is the impulse behind it. Thus it has been claimed that the Baroque style expresses the spirit of the Counter Reformation; yet the Counter Reformation, a dynamic movement of self-renewal within the Catholic Church, had already done its work by 1600 (for its effect on music, see p. 236); Protestantism was on the defensive, and neither side any longer had the power to upset the new balance. The princes of the Church who supported the growth of Baroque art were known for worldly splendor rather than piety. Besides, the new style penetrated the Protestant North so quickly that we must be careful not to overstress its Counter Reformation aspect. Equally questionable is the claim that Baroque is "the style of absolutism," reflecting the centralized state ruled by an autocrat of unlimited powers. Although absolutism reached its climax in France in the later seventeenth century, during the reign of Louis XIV, it had been in the making since the 1520s. Moreover, Baroque art flourished in bourgeois Holland no less than in the absolutist monarchies; and the style officially sponsored under Louis XIV was a notably subdued, classicistic kind of Baroque. There are similar difficulties if we try to relate Baroque art to the science and philosophy of the period. Such a link did exist in the Early and High Renaissance: an artist then could also be a humanist and scientist. But now scientific and philosophical thought became too complex, abstract, and systematic for him to share; gravitation, calculus, and *Cogito, ergo sum* could not stir his imagination. Baroque art, then, was not simply the result of religious, political, or intellectual developments. Interconnections surely existed, but we do not yet understand them fully. Until we do, let us think of the Baroque style as one among other basic features—the newly fortified Catholic faith, the absolutist state, and the new role of science—that distinguish the period 1600–1750 from what had gone before.

Rome became the fountainhead of the Baroque, as it had of the High Renaissance a century earlier, by gathering artists from other regions to perform challenging tasks. The papacy once again patronized art on a large scale, aiming to turn Rome into the most beautiful city of the entire Christian world. At first, the artists on hand were late Mannerists of feeble distinction, but the campaign soon attracted ambitious younger masters. They were the ones who created the new style. Foremost was a painter of genius, called Caravaggio after his birthplace near Milan, who did several monumental canvases for the church of San Luigi dei Francesi, including *The Calling of St. Matthew* (fig. 167). The style shown in this extraordinary picture is remote from both Mannerism and the High Renaissance; its realism is so uncompromising that a new term, "naturalism," is needed to distinguish it from the earlier kind. Never have we seen a sacred subject depicted so entirely in terms of contemporary low life. Matthew the tax gatherer sits with some armed men—evidently his agents—in what appears to be a common Roman tavern; he points questioningly at himself as two figures approach from the right. They are poor people, whose bare feet and simple garments contrast strongly with the colorful costumes of Matthew and his companions. Why do we sense a religious quality in this scene? What identifies one of the figures as Christ? Surely it is not the Saviour's halo, an inconspicuous gold band that we might well overlook. Our eyes fasten instead on His commanding gesture, borrowed from Michelangelo's *Creation of Adam* (see fig. 144), which bridges the gap between the two groups. Most important of all, however, is the strong beam of sunlight above Christ that illuminates

his face and hand in the gloomy interior, thus carrying His call across to Matthew. Without this light—so natural yet so charged with symbolic meaning—the picture would lose its magic, its power to make us aware of the Divine presence. Caravaggio here gives moving, direct form to an attitude shared by some of the great saints of the Counter Reformation: that the mysteries of faith are revealed not by intellectual speculation but spontaneously, through an inward experience open to all men. His paintings have a "lay Christianity," untouched by theological dogma, that appealed to Protestants no less than Catholics. Hence his profound—though indirect—influence on Rembrandt, who was the greatest religious artist of the Protestant North.

In architecture, the beginnings of the Baroque style cannot be defined as precisely as in painting. In the vast church-building program that got under way in Rome toward 1600, the most talented young architect was Carlo Maderno; in 1603 he was given the task of completing, at long last, the church of St. Peter's, after the pope had decided to add a nave, converting Bramante's and Michelangelo's central-plan building into a basilica (fig. 168). Maderno's design for the façade follows the pattern established by Michelangelo for the exterior (compare fig. 149), but with a dramatic emphasis on the portals. There is what can only be called a crescendo effect from the corners toward the center: the spacing of the colossal order becomes closer, pilasters turn into columns, and the façade wall projects step by step. This quickened rhythm became the dominant principle of Maderno's façade designs, not only for St. Peter's but for smaller churches as well; it replaced the traditional notion of the church façade as one continuous wall surface with the

above: 167. CARAVAGGIO. *The Calling of St. Matthew.*
c.1597–98. Canvas, 11' 1" x 11' 5".
Contarelli Chapel, S. Luigi dei Francesi, Rome

right: 168. St. Peter's, aerial view. Nave and façade by CARLO MADERNO, 1607–15; colonnade by GIANLORENZO BERNINI, designed 1657. Rome

left: 169. GIANLORENZO BERNINI. *David.* 1623.
Marble, lifesize. Borghese Gallery, Rome

below: 170. BERNINI. *The Ecstasy of St. Theresa.* 1645–
1652. Marble, lifesize. Sta. Maria della Vittoria, Rome

"façade-in-depth," dynamically related to the open space before it. The possibilities implicit in this new concept were not to be exhausted for a hundred and fifty years. Maderno's work on the St. Peter's façade was completed by Gianlorenzo Bernini, the greatest sculptor-architect of the century. It was he who molded the open space in front of the façade into a magnificent oval "forecourt" framed by colonnades which Bernini himself likened to the motherly, all-embracing arms of the Church.

Such a charging of space with active energy is a key feature of Baroque art (see also pp. 244–45). Caravaggio had achieved it, with the aid of a sharply focused beam of light, in his *St. Matthew*; Bernini was a master of it, not only in architecture but in sculpture as well. If we compare his *David* (fig. 169) with Michelangelo's (see fig. 142), and ask what makes Bernini's Baroque, the simplest answer would be: the implied presence of Goliath. Bernini's *David* is conceived not as a self-contained figure but as "half of a pair," his entire action focused on his adversary. Did the artist, we wonder, plan a statue of Goliath to complete the group? He never did, for his David tells us clearly enough where *he* sees the enemy. Thus the space between David and his invisible opponent is charged with energy: it "belongs" to the statue. If we stand directly in front of this

formidable fighter, our first impulse is to get out of the line of fire. Baroque sculpture, then, eschews the self-sufficiency of Early and High Renaissance sculpture for an illusion—the illusion of presences or forces that are implied by the behavior of the sculptured figure. Because of this "invisible complement," Baroque sculpture has been denounced as a tour de force, attempting illusionistic effects that are outside its province. The accusation is pointless, for illusion is the basis of every artistic experience, and we cannot very well regard some kinds or degrees of illusion as less legitimate than others. It is true, however, that Baroque art acknowledges no sharp distinction between sculpture and painting. The two may enter into a symbiosis previously unknown, or, more precisely, both may be combined with architecture to form a compound illusion, like that of the stage. Bernini was at his best when he could merge all three arts in this fashion. His masterpiece is the Cornaro Chapel, containing the famous group called *The Ecstasy of St. Theresa* (fig. 170), in the church of Santa Maria della Vittoria. Theresa of Avila, one of the saints of the Counter Reformation, had described how an angel once pierced her heart with a flaming golden arrow: "The pain was so great that I screamed aloud; but at the same time I felt such infinite sweetness that I wished the pain to

171. GIOVANNI BATTISTA GAULLI.
Triumph of the Name of Jesus.
1672–85. Ceiling fresco.
Il Gesù, Rome

last forever." Bernini has made this visionary experience as sensuously real as Correggio's *Jupiter and Io* (see fig. 156); the angel, in a different context, would be indistinguishable from Cupid, and the saint's ecstasy is palpably physical. Yet the two figures, on their floating cloud, are lit (from a hidden window above) in such a way as to seem almost dematerialized in their gleaming whiteness. The beholder experiences them as visionary. The "invisible complement" here, less specific than David's but equally important, is the force that carries the figures heavenward, causing the turbulence of their drapery. Its nature is suggested by the golden rays, which come from a source high above the altar: in an illusionistic fresco on the vault of the chapel, the glory of heaven is revealed as a dazzling burst of light from which tumble clouds of jubilant angels. It is

this celestial "explosion" that gives force to the thrusts of the angel's arrow and makes the ecstasy of the saint believable. A similar "explosion" (on a much larger scale and hence more easily photographed) may be seen on the nave vault of the church of Il Gesù (fig. 171)—further evidence of Bernini's imaginative daring, although his role was only advisory. The commission for the fresco went to Giovanni Battista Gaulli, his young protégé; his talented assistant, Antonio Raggi, did the stucco sculpture. As we see the ceiling fresco spilling so dramatically over its frame, then turning into sculptured figures, it is clear that the conception must be Bernini's. Such displays, designed to overwhelm the beholder emotionally, may well be termed "theatrical," both in spirit and in some of the devices employed. Bernini himself had a passionate interest in the theater.

172. LODOVICO BURNACINI. Stage Design
for *"La Zenobia di Radamisto,"*
Opera by G. A. Boretti,
Vienna, Hoftheater, 1662
(engraving by F. van den Steen).
Theater Collection, Houghton Library,
Harvard University, Cambridge, Mass.

Looking at a typical Baroque stage with all its illusionistic devices, such as the one in figure 172, we sense its kinship with the ceiling of Il Gesù and the Cornaro Chapel (see also pp. 246–47).

As a personality type, Bernini represents the self-assured, expansive man of the world. His great rival in architecture, Francesco Borromini, was the opposite: a secretive and emotionally unstable genius, he died by suicide. The temperamental contrast between the two would be evident from their works alone, even without the testimony of their contemporaries. Both exemplify the climax of Baroque architecture in Rome, yet Bernini's design for the colonnade of St. Peter's is dramatically simple and unified, while Borromini's structures are extravagantly complex. Bernini himself agreed with those who denounced Borromini for disregarding the classical tradition, enshrined in Renaissance theory and practice, that architecture must reflect the proportions of the human body. We understand this accusation when we look at Borromini's first project, the church of

San Carlo alle Quattro Fontane (fig. 173). The vocabulary is not unfamiliar, but the syntax is new and disquieting; the ceaseless play of concave and convex surfaces makes the entire structure seem elastic, "pulled out of shape" by pressures that no previous building could have withstood. The plan is a pinched oval suggesting a distended and half-melted Greek cross, as if it had been drawn on rubber. In the façade, designed almost thirty years later, these pressures and counterpressures reach their maximum intensity. Characteristically, it incorporates sculpture and even a painting, borne aloft by flying angels. San Carlo alle Quattro Fontane established Borromini's local and international fame. "Nothing similar," wrote the head of the religious order for which the church was built, "can be found anywhere in the world."

The wealth of new ideas introduced by Borromini was exploited not in Rome but in Turin, the capital of Savoy, which became the creative center of Baroque architecture in Italy toward the end of the seventeenth century. In 1666, that city attracted Borromini's most brilliant successor, Guarino Guarini, a monk whose architectural genius was deeply grounded in philosophy and mathematics. His design for the façade of the Palazzo Carignano (fig. 174) repeats on a larger scale the undulating movement of San Carlo alle Quattro Fontane, using a highly individual vocabulary. Incredibly, the exterior of the building is entirely of brick, down to the last ornamental detail. The ultimate development of the style invented by Borromini, however, took place north of the Alps, in Austria and southern Germany. In these countries, ravaged by the Thirty Years' War, there was little building activity until near the end of the seventeenth century; Baroque was an imported

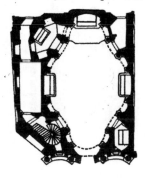

173. FRANCESCO BORROMINI. Façade and Plan, S. Carlo alle Quattro Fontane. 1638–67. Rome

174. GUARINO GUARINI. Palazzo Carignano.
Begun 1679. Turin

175. JOHANN FISCHER VON ERLACH. St. Charles
Borromaeus. 1716–37. Vienna

style, practiced mainly by visiting Italians. Not until the 1690s did native designers come to the fore. There followed a fifty-year period of intense activity that gave rise to some of the most imaginative creations in the history of architecture. We must be content with a small sampling of these monuments, erected for the glorification of princes and prelates who, generally speaking, deserve to be remembered only as lavish patrons of the arts. Johann Fischer von Erlach, the first great architect of the Late Baroque in Central Europe, is linked most directly to the Italian tradition. His design for the Church of St. Charles Borromaeus in Vienna (fig. 175) combines reminiscences of the exterior of St. Peter's and the portico of the Pantheon with a pair of huge columns which here substitute for façade towers. With these inflexible elements of Roman imperial art embedded in the elastic curvatures of his church, Fischer von Erlach expresses, more boldly than any Italian Baroque architect, the power of the Christian faith to absorb and transfigure the splendors of antiquity.

The architects of the next generation, among whom Balthasar Neumann was the most prominent, favored a tendency toward lightness and elegance. Neumann's largest project, the Episcopal Palace in Würzburg, includes the breath-taking Kaisersaal (colorplate 17), a great oval hall decorated in white, gold, and pastel shades—the favorite color scheme of the mid-eighteenth century. The structural members, such as columns, pilasters, and architraves, are minimized; windows and vault segments are framed with continuous, ribbonlike moldings, and the white surfaces are spun over with irregular ornamental designs. This repertory of lacy, curling motifs, invented in France about 1700, is the hallmark of the Rococo style (see p. 153), which is here happily combined with German Late Baroque architecture. The membranelike ceiling so often gives way to illusionistic openings of every sort that we no longer feel it to be a spatial boundary. These openings do not, however, reveal avalanches of figures propelled by dramatic bursts of light, like those of Roman ceilings (compare fig. 171), but blue sky and sunlit clouds, and an occasional winged creature soaring in this limitless expanse. Only along the edges are there solid clusters of figures (fig. 176). Here the last, and most refined, stage of illusionistic ceiling decoration is represented by its greatest master, Giovanni Battista Tiepolo. Venetian by birth and training (see also p. 251), Tiepolo blended the tradition of High Baroque illusionism with the pag-

176. GIOVANNI BATTISTA TIEPOLO. Ceiling Fresco,
Kaisersaal (detail). 1751. Episcopal Palace, Würzburg
(see colorplate 17)

177. PETER PAUL RUBENS. *Marie de' Medici,
Queen of France, Landing in Marseilles.* 1622–23.
Panel, 25 x 19¾". Pinakothek, Munich

eantry of Veronese. His mastery of light and
color, the grace and felicity of his touch, made
him famous far beyond his home territory. In
the Würzburg frescoes his powers are at their
height. He was afterward invited to decorate
the Royal Palace in Madrid, where he spent his
final years.

Although Rome was its birthplace, the Baroque style soon became international. Among
the artists who helped bring this about, the
great Flemish painter Peter Paul Rubens holds
a place of special importance. It might be said
that he finished what Dürer had started—the
breaking down of artistic barriers between
North and South. Rubens grew up in Antwerp,
the capital of the "Spanish Netherlands" (see
p. 126), and remained a devout Catholic all
his life. Trained by local painters, he became a
master in 1598, but developed a personal style
only when, two years later, he went to Italy.
During his eight years' stay he eagerly studied
ancient sculpture, the masterpieces of the High
Renaissance, and the work of Caravaggio, absorbing the Italian tradition far more thoroughly
than had any Northerner before him. He competed, in fact, with the best Italians of his day
on even terms, and could well have made his

career in Italy. He chose instead to settle down
in Antwerp as court painter to the Spanish regent, a special appointment that exempted him
and his workshop from local taxes and guild
rules. Rubens thus had the best of both worlds:
at court, he was valued not only as an artist but
as a diplomat, so that he had entree to the
royal households of the major powers, while he
was also free to carry out a vast volume of
work for the city of Antwerp, for the Church,
and for private patrons. In the 1620s, Rubens'
dynamic style reached a climax in his huge decorative schemes for churches and palaces. The
most famous, probably, is the cycle in the Luxembourg Palace in Paris, glorifying Marie de'
Medici, the widow of Henri IV and the mother
of Louis XIII. Figure 177 shows the artist's oil
sketch for one episode, the young queen landing in Marseilles. Hardly an exciting subject—
yet Rubens has turned it into a spectacle of unprecedented splendor. As Marie de' Medici
walks down the gangplank, Fame flies over-
head sounding a triumphant blast on two trumpets, and Neptune rises from the sea with his
fishtailed crew; having guarded the queen's
journey, they rejoice at her arrival. Everything
flows together here in swirling movement:
heaven and earth, history and allegory—even

drawing and painting, for Rubens used oil sketches like this one to prepare his compositions. Unlike earlier artists, he preferred to design his pictures in terms of light and color from the very start. This unified vision, approached but never fully achieved by the great Venetians of the previous century, was Rubens' most precious legacy to subsequent painters.

Soon after completing the Luxembourg cycle, Rubens spent more than a year in Madrid, where he befriended the recently appointed court painter, Diego Velázquez. The superbly gifted young artist had been deeply impressed with the style of Caravaggio; Rubens helped him to discover the beauty of Titian and develop a new fluency and richness. No picture displays Velázquez' mature style more fully than *The Maids of Honor* (fig. 178, colorplate 18), which is both a group portrait and an everyday scene. It might be subtitled "the artist in his studio," for Velázquez shows himself at work on a huge canvas; in the center is the little Princess Margarita, who has just posed for him, among her playmates and maids of honor. The faces of her parents, the king and queen, appear in the mirror on the back wall. Have

they just stepped into the room, to see the scene exactly as we do, or does the mirror reflect part of the canvas—presumably a full-length portrait of the royal family—on which the artist has been working? This ambiguity is characteristic of Velázquez' fascination with light. The varieties of direct and reflected light in *The Maids of Honor* are almost limitless, and the artist challenges us to find them: we are expected to match the mirror image against the paintings on that wall, and against the "picture" of the man in the open doorway. The side lighting (from the right) and the strong contrasts of light and dark still suggest the influence of Caravaggio, but Velázquez' technique is far more varied and subtle, with delicate glazes setting off the impasto of the highlights, and brushwork even freer and more sketchy than that of Titian or Rubens. The colors, too, have a Venetian warmth and brilliance. Yet Velázquez does not seem interested in catching time on the wing; his aim is to show not figures in motion but the movement of light itself and the infinite range of its effects on form and color. For Velázquez, light *creates* the visible world. Not until two centuries later shall we meet painters capable of realizing the implications of this discovery.

In contrast to Flanders, where painting was overshadowed by the majestic personality of Rubens, Holland produced a bewildering variety of masters and styles. The new nation was proud of its hard-won freedom. Though the cultural links with Flanders remained strong, several factors encouraged the rapid growth of Dutch artistic traditions. Unlike Flanders, where all artistic activity radiated from Antwerp, Holland had many flourishing local schools: besides Amsterdam, the commercial center, we find important groups of painters in Haarlem, Utrecht, Leyden, Delft, and other towns. Holland was a nation of merchants, farmers, and seafarers, and the Reformed faith was its official religion; thus Dutch artists lacked the large-scale public commissions sponsored by State and Church that were available throughout the Catholic world. As a consequence, the private collector now became the painter's chief source of support. There was no shrinkage of output; on the contrary, the Dutch public developed so insatiable an appetite for pictures that the whole country became gripped by a kind of collector's mania. Everyone invested in paintings, just as millions of Americans played the stock market in the 1920s. The comparison is not far-fetched, for pictures became an important commodity in

178. DIEGO VELAZOUEZ. *The Maids of Honor*. 1656. Canvas, 10′ 5″ x 9′. The Prado, Madrid (see colorplate 18)

179. FRANS HALS. *The Jolly Toper*. 1627.
Canvas, 31⅞ x 26¼". Rijksmuseum, Amsterdam

Holland, and their trade followed the law of supply and demand. Many artists produced "for the market" instead of relying on commissions from individual patrons. The mechanism of the art market has been said to raise a barrier between artist and public, and to falsify the "true worth" of the work of art. Such charges, however, are unrealistic: the true worth of a work of art is always unstable, and depends on time and circumstance; even those who believe in timeless values in art will concede that these values cannot be expressed in money. Because the art market reflects the dominant, rather than the most discerning, taste of the moment, works by artists now regarded as mediocre may once have been overpriced; others, highly valued today, seem once to have sold too cheaply. Yet the system that prevailed in antiquity and the Middle Ages, when artists were paid on standards of craftsmanship, was hardly fairer in rewarding aesthetic merit. The market does form a barrier between artist and public, but there are advantages in this as well as drawbacks. To subject the artist to the pressure of supply and demand is not necessarily worse than to make him depend on the favor of princes. The lesser men will tend to become specialists, steadily producing their marketable pictures, while artists of independent spirit, perhaps braving economic hardship, will paint as they please and rely for support on the discerning minority. From the collector's mania in

seventeenth-century Holland came an outpouring of artistic talent comparable only to Early Renaissance Florence, although many Dutchmen were lured into becoming painters by hopes of success that failed to come true. Even the greatest masters were sometimes hard-pressed (it was not unusual for an artist to keep an inn, or run a small business on the side). Yet they survived—less secure, but freer.

The Baroque style came to Holland from Antwerp, through the work of Rubens, and from Rome, through direct contact with Caravaggio and his followers, some of whom were Dutchmen. One of the first to profit from this experience was Frans Hals, the great portrait painter of Haarlem. He was born in Antwerp, and what little is known of his early work suggests the influence of Rubens. His mature style, however, seen in such pictures as *The Jolly Toper* (fig. 179), combines Rubens' robustness and breadth with a concentration on the "dramatic moment" that must be derived from Caravaggio. Everything here conveys complete spontaneity: the twinkling eyes and the half-open mouth, the raised hand, the teetering wine-glass, and—most important of all—the quick way of setting down the forms. Hals works in dashing brush strokes, each so clearly visible as a separate entity that we can almost count the total number of "touches." With this open, split-second technique, the completed picture has the immediacy of a sketch. The impression of a race against time is, of course, deceptive; Hals spent hours, not minutes, on this lifesize canvas, but he maintains the illusion of having done it in the wink of an eye.

Rembrandt, the greatest genius of Dutch art, was also stimulated at the beginning of his career by indirect contact with Caravaggio; his earliest pictures are small, sharply lit, and intensely realistic. From these he developed, in the 1630s, a full-blown High Baroque style. *The Blinding of Samson* (fig. 180) shows us the Old Testament world in oriental splendor and violence, cruel yet seductive. The sudden flood of brilliant light pouring into the dark tent is unabashedly theatrical, heightening the drama. Rembrandt was at this time an avid collector of Near Eastern paraphernalia, which serve as props in these pictures. He was now Amsterdam's most sought-after portrait painter and a man of considerable wealth. This prosperity petered out in the 1640s, although the artist's fall from public favor was less sudden and catastrophic than his romantic admirers would have us believe. Still, the 1640s were a

180. REMBRANDT. *The Blinding of Samson.* 1636.
Canvas, 93 x 119″. Städel Institute, Frankfurt

181. REMBRANDT. *Christ Preaching.* c.1652.
Etching. The Metropolitan Museum of Art, New York
(Bequest of Mrs. H. O. Havemeyer, 1929)

period of crisis, of inner uncertainty and external troubles. Rembrandt's outlook changed profoundly: after about 1650, his style eschews the rhetoric of the High Baroque for lyric subtlety and pictorial breadth. In his later years, Rembrandt often adapted, in a very personal way, pictorial ideas from the Northern Renaissance, as in *The Polish Rider* (colorplate 19). We cannot be sure that the rider is Polish—the title was given to him later—although his costume is of the kind worn by the local troops then fighting the Turks in eastern Europe; nor is Rembrandt's exact purpose clear. But Dürer's famous engraving, *Knight, Death, and Devil* (see fig. 161), which Rembrandt surely admired, may be the key to the picture. Is not the Polish Rider another Christian Soldier bravely making his way through a perilous world? The dangers in this case are ours to im-

agine in the gloomy landscape, but the rider's serious, alert glance suggests unseen threats. With such a relationship of form and content, the differences between the painting and the print make a rewarding study. Dürer's horseman, boxed into the composition, is balanced and stationary like an equestrian statue; Rembrandt's, slightly foreshortened and off center, is in motion—urged on, as it were, by the light from the left. The curving path he follows will soon lead him beyond the frame. This subtle imbalance implies a space far vaster than the compass of the picture and stamps Rembrandt's work as Baroque, despite the absence of the more obvious hallmarks of the style. Much the same may be said of the religious scenes that play so large a part in Rembrandt's later work, such as the etching, *Christ Preaching* (fig. 181). It is a quiet scene, full of the artist's deep feeling of compassion for the poor and outcast who make up Christ's audience. Rembrandt had a special sympathy for the Jews, as the heirs of the Biblical past and as the patient victims of persecution; they were often his models. This print strongly suggests some corner in the Amsterdam ghetto. As in *The Polish Rider*, it is the magic of Rembrandt's light that endows *Christ Preaching* with spiritual significance.

Rembrandt's importance as a graphic artist is second only to Dürer's, although we get no more than a hint from this single example. But we must add a word about his medium. By the seventeenth century, the techniques of woodcut and engraving were employed mainly to reproduce other works. The creative printmakers, including Rembrandt, preferred etching. An etching is made by coating a copperplate with resin to make an acid-resistant "ground," through which the design is scratched with a needle, laying bare the metal surface underneath. The plate is then bathed in an acid that etches ("bites") the lines into the copper. To scratch a design into the resinous ground is, of course, an easier task than cutting it into the copperplate directly, hence an etched line is freer and more individual than an engraved line. The chief virtue of etching is its wide tonal range, including velvety dark shades not possible in engravings or woodcuts. No etcher ever exploited this quality more subtly than Rembrandt.

Rembrandt's religious pictures demand an insight that was beyond the capacity of all but a few collectors. Most art buyers in Holland preferred subjects within their own experience—landscapes, still lifes, scenes of everyday life.

182. JACOB VAN RUISDAEL. *The Jewish Graveyard.*
c.1655. Canvas, 32 x 37½". State Gallery, Dresden

183. WILLEM HEDA. *Still Life.* 1634. Panel, 17 x 22½".
Boymans-van Beuningen Museum, Rotterdam

These were produced in ever greater volume and variety by specialists, so that we can here illustrate only a small sampling. Perhaps the richest of the newly developed "specialties" was landscape, both as a portrayal of familiar views and as an imaginative vision of nature. Of the latter kind is *The Jewish Graveyard* (fig. 182) by Jacob van Ruisdael: the thunderclouds passing over a wild, deserted mountain valley, the medieval ruin, the torrent that has forced its way between ancient graves, all create a mood of deep melancholy. Nothing endures on this earth, the artist tells us—time, wind, and water grind all to dust, the feeble works of man as well as the trees and rocks. Ruisdael's signature on the gravestone nearest us is a final touch of gloomy irony. This view of man's impotence in the face of natural forces has an awe-inspiring quality on which the Romantics, a century later, were to base their concept of the Sublime. Even still life can be tinged with a melancholy sense of the passing of all

earthly pleasures, sometimes through such established symbols as death's-heads and extinguished candles, or by more subtle means. Our example (fig. 183) belongs to a widespread type, the "breakfast piece," showing the remnants of a meal. Food and drink are less emphasized than luxury objects—crystal goblets and silver dishes—carefully juxtaposed for their contrasting shape, color, and texture. But virtuosity was not the artist's only aim: his "story," the human context of these grouped objects, is suggested by the broken glass, the half-peeled lemon, the overturned silver dish; whoever sat at this table has suddenly been forced to abandon his meal. The curtain that time has lowered on the scene, as it were, invests the objects with a strange pathos. Here the disguised symbolism of Late Gothic painting (see p. 90) lives on in a new form.

The pictures of everyday life (also known as "genre" pictures) range from tavern brawls to refined domestic interiors. *The Eve of St. Nicholas* (fig. 184) by Jan Steen is midway between these extremes. St. Nicholas has just paid his pre-Christmas visit to the household, leaving toys, candy, and cake for the children; everybody is jolly except the bad boy on the left, who has received only a birch rod. Steen tells this story with relish, embroidering it with many delightful details. Of all the Dutch painters of daily life, he was the sharpest, and most good-humored, observer. To supplement his

184. JAN STEEN. *The Eve of St. Nicholas.* c.1660–65.
Canvas, 32¼ x 27¾". Rijksmuseum, Amsterdam

earnings he kept an inn, which perhaps explains his keen insight into human behavior. His sense of timing often reminds us of Frans Hals (compare fig. 179), while his storytelling stems from the tradition of Pieter Bruegel (compare fig. 165).

In the genre scenes of Jan Vermeer, by contrast, there is hardly any narrative. Single figures, usually women, engage in simple, everyday tasks; when two are present, as in *The Letter* (colorplate 20), they no more than exchange glances. They exist in a timeless "still life" world, seemingly calmed by some magic spell. The cool, clear light that filters in from the left is the only active element, working its miracles upon all the objects in its path. As we look at *The Letter*, we feel as if a veil had been pulled from our eyes; the everyday world shines with jewel-like freshness, beautiful as we have never seen it before. No painter since Jan van Eyck *saw* as intensely as this. But Vermeer, unlike his predecessors, perceives reality as a mosaic of colored surfaces—or, perhaps more accurately, he translates reality into a mosaic as he puts it on canvas. We see *The Letter* as a perspective "window," but also as a plane, a "field" composed of smaller fields. Rectangles predominate, carefully aligned with the picture surface, and there are no "holes," no undefined empty spaces. These interlocking shapes give to Vermeer's work a uniquely modern quality. How did he acquire it? We know little about him except that he was born in Delft in 1632 and lived and worked there until his death at forty-three. The Dutch followers of Caravaggio had influenced him but this is hardly enough to explain the genesis of his style, so daringly original that his genius was not recognized until a century ago.

185. LOUIS LE NAIN. *Peasant Family*. c.1640. Canvas, 44½ x 62½″. The Louvre, Paris

Our discussion of Baroque art in Flanders, Spain, and Holland has been limited to painting; architecture and sculpture in these countries have no basic importance for the history of art. In France, however, the situation is different. Under Louis XIV France became the most powerful nation of Europe, militarily and culturally; by the late seventeenth century, Paris had replaced Rome as the world capital of the visual arts. How did this astonishing change come about? Because of the Palace of Versailles and other vast projects glorifying the king, we are tempted to think of French art in the age of Louis XIV as the expression of absolutism. This is true of the climactic phase of Louis' reign, 1660–85, but by that time French seventeenth-century art had already formed its distinctive style. Frenchmen are reluctant to call this style Baroque; to them it is the Style of Louis XIV; often they also describe the art and literature of the period as "classic." The term, so used, has three meanings: as a synonym for "highest achievement," it implies that the style of Louis XIV corresponds to the High Renaissance in Italy, or the age of Pericles in Greece; the term also refers to the emulation of the form and subject matter of ancient art; finally, "classic" suggests qualities of balance and restraint, like those of the classic styles of the High Renaissance and of ancient Greece. The second and third of these meanings describe what could be called, more accurately, "classicism." And since the Style of Louis XIV reflects Italian Baroque art, however modified, we must label it either "classicistic Baroque" or "Baroque classicism."

This classicism was the official court style by 1660–85, but its origin was not political. It sprang, rather, from the persistent tradition of sixteenth-century art, which in France was more intimately linked with the Italian Renaissance than in any other Northern country (see p. 126). Classicism was also nourished by French humanism, with its intellectual heritage of reason and Stoic virtue. These factors retarded the spread of the Baroque in France and modified its interpretation. Rubens' Medici cycle, for example, had no effect on French art until the very end of the century; in the 1620s, the young painters in France were still assimilating Caravaggio. Some developed astonishingly original styles, such as Louis Le Nain, whose *Peasant Family* (fig. 185) has a human dignity and a compassion for the poor that seem akin to Rembrandt. Yet Louis Le Nain, like Vermeer, had to be rediscovered in modern times. In his day he was soon forgotten,

left: 186. NICOLAS POUSSIN. *The Rape of the Sabine Women.* c.1636–37. Canvas, 61 x 82½". The Metropolitan Museum of Art, New York (Dick Fund, 1946)

below: 187. CLAUDE LORRAINE. *View of the Campagna.* c.1650. Wash drawing. British Museum, London

because from about 1650 on classicism was supreme in France, and he was no classicist.

The artist who did most to bring about this change of taste was Nicolas Poussin. The greatest French painter of the century, and the earliest French painter to win international fame, Poussin nevertheless spent almost his entire career in Rome. There he formulated the style that was to become the ideal model for French painters of the second half of the century. Its qualities are well displayed in *The Rape of the Sabine Women* (fig. 186): the strongly modeled figures are "frozen in action," likes statues, and many are in fact derived from Hellenistic sculpture (compare fig. 36). Behind them, Poussin has placed reconstructions of Roman architecture that he believed to be archaeologically correct. Emotion is abundantly in evidence, yet it so lacks spontaneity that it fails to touch us. All sensuous appeal has been consciously suppressed from the severe discipline of an intellectual style. Poussin strikes us as a man who knew his own mind only too well, an impression confirmed by the numerous letters in which he expounded his views. The highest aim of painting, he believed, is to represent noble and serious human actions. These must be shown in a logical and orderly way—not as they really happened, but as they would have happened if nature were perfect. To this end, the artist must strive for the general and typical; appealing to the mind rather than the senses, he suppresses such trivialities as glowing color, and stresses form and composition.

In a good painting, the beholder should be able to "read" the exact emotions of each figure, and relate them to the event depicted. These ideas were not new—we recall Leonardo's statement that the highest aim of painting is to portray "the intention of man's soul"—but before Poussin no one had made the analogy between painting and literature so close, nor put it into practice so single-mindedly.

If Poussin, in such pictures as *The Rape of the Sabine Women*, celebrated the heroic aspects of antiquity, the great French landscapist Claude Lorraine brought out its idyllic aspects. He, too, spent almost his entire career in Rome, and explored the countryside nearby—the Campagna—more thoroughly and affectionately than any Italian. Countless drawings,

188. CLAUDE PERRAULT.
East Front, the Louvre.
1667–70. Paris

each made on the spot, such as the miraculously fresh and sensitive example in figure 187, bear witness to his extraordinary powers of observation. These sketches, however, were only the raw material for his paintings, which do not aim at topographic exactitude but evoke the poetic essence of a countryside filled with echoes of antiquity. To modern eyes, these pictures have far less appeal than the drawings, many of which convey a sense of immediacy so striking that they seem to have been made only yesterday.

In France itself, meanwhile, Baroque classicism in architecture became the official "royal style" when young Louis XIV took over the reins of government in 1661. Colbert, the king's chief adviser, built the administrative apparatus supporting the power of the absolute monarch. In this system, aimed at subjecting the thoughts and actions of the entire nation to strict control from above, the visual arts had the task of glorifying the king. That Louis XIV's choice of classicism was deliberate we know from the first great project of his reign, the completion of the Louvre. Work on the palace had proceeded intermittently for over a century, along the lines of Lescot's design (see fig. 166); what remained to be done was to close the court on the east side with an impressive façade. Colbert invited Bernini to Paris, hoping the famous master of the Roman Baroque would do for the French king what he had already done so magnificently for the Church. Bernini submitted three designs, all on a scale that would have dwarfed the existing parts of the palace. After much argument and intrigue, Louis XIV rejected these plans, and turned over the problem to a committee of three: Louis Le Vau, his court architect, who had worked on the project before; Charles Lebrun, his court painter; and Claude Perrault, who was a student of ancient architecture, not a professional architect. All three were responsible for the structure that was actually built

(fig. 188), although Perrault is usually credited with the major share. The design in some ways suggests the mind of an archaeologist, but one who knew how to select those features of classical architecture that would link Louis XIV with the glory of the Caesars and yet be compatible with the older parts of the palace. The center pavilion is a Roman temple front, and the wings look like the flanks of that temple folded outward to form one plane. The temple theme demanded a single order of freestanding columns, yet the Louvre had three stories—a difficulty skillfully resolved by treating the ground story as the base of the temple, and recessing the upper two behind the screen of the colonnade. The entire design combines grandeur and elegance in a way that fully justifies its fame.

Ironically, this great exemplar of classicism proved too pure. Perrault soon faded from the architectural scene, and Baroque features reappeared in the king's vastest enterprise, the Palace of Versailles. Louis XIV himself was less interested in architectural theory and monumental exteriors than in the lavish interiors that would make appropriate settings for himself and his court. The man to whom he really listened was not an architect, but the painter Lebrun, who now became supervisor of all the king's artistic projects. As chief dispenser of royal art patronage, he commanded so much power that for all practical purposes he was the dictator of the arts in France. Lebrun had studied under Poussin in Rome, but the great decorative schemes of the Roman Baroque must also have impressed him. He became a superb decorator, utilizing the combined labors of architects, sculptors, painters, and craftsmen for ensembles of unheard-of splendor, such as the Salon de la Guerre at Versailles (fig. 189). To subordinate all the arts to a single goal—here, the glorification of Louis XIV—was in itself Baroque (see p. 249); if Lebrun went less far than Bernini, he nevertheless drew freely on his memories of Rome. The Salon de la Guerre seems in many ways closer to the Gesù ceiling (see fig. 171) than to Perrault's Louvre façade. And, as in so many Italian Baroque interiors, the separate ingredients are less impressive than the effect of the whole.

The Palace of Versailles, just over eleven miles from the center of Paris, was begun by Le Vau. After his death, the entire project, under Jules Hardouin-Mansart, was vastly expanded to accommodate the ever-growing royal household. The Garden Front, intended as the principal view of the palace, was stretched to enormous length (fig. 190), so that the façade design, a less severe variant of Perrault's Louvre colonnade, looks repetitious and out of scale. The whole center block contains a single room, the famous Hall of Mirrors, with the Salon de la Guerre and its counterpart, the Salon de la Paix, at either end. Apart from its magnificent interior, the most impressive aspect of Versailles is the park extending west of the Garden Front for several miles (the aerial view in figure 190 shows only a small portion). Its design, by André Le Nôtre, is so strictly correlated with the plan of the palace that it becomes a continuation of the architectural space. Like the interior of Versailles, these formal gardens, with their terraces, basins, clipped hedges, and statuary, were meant to provide an appropriate setting for the king's appearances in public. The spirit of absolutism is even more striking in this geometric regularity imposed upon an entire countryside than it is in the palace itself.

Centralized control over the visual arts was exerted by Lebrun not only through the power of the purse; it also included a new system of educating artists in the officially approved style. In antiquity and the Middle Ages, artists had been trained by apprenticeship, and this time-honored practice still prevailed in the Renaissance. But as artists gained a liberal-arts status (see p. 100), they wished to supplement their "mechanical" training with theoretical knowledge. For this purpose, they founded "art academies," patterned after the academies of the humanists (the name is derived from the grove of Academe where Plato met with his disciples). Art academies first appeared in Italy (see also p. 237); they seem to have been private associations of artists who met periodically to draw from the model and discuss questions of art theory. Later, these academies took over some functions from the guilds, but their teaching was limited and far from systematic. Such was the Royal Academy of Painting and Sculpture in Paris, founded in 1648; when Lebrun became its director, in 1663, he established a rigid curriculum of compulsory instruction in practice and theory, based on a system of "rules"; this set the pattern for all later academies, including their modern successors, the art schools of today. Much of this body of doctrine was derived from Poussin's views but carried to rationalistic extremes. The Academy even devised a

189. JULES HARDOUIN-MANSART, CHARLES LEBRUN, and ANTOINE COYSEVOX. Salon de la Guerre, Palace of Versailles. Begun 1678

190. LOUIS LE VAU and JULES HARDOUIN-MANSART. Palace of Versailles, aerial view from west. 1669–85 (Gardens by ANDRE LE NOTRE, 1664–72)

191. ANTOINE WATTEAU.
A Pilgrimage to Cythera. 1717.
Canvas, 51 x 76½".
The Louvre, Paris

method of tabulating, in numerical grades, the merits of artists past and present in such categories as drawing, expression, and proportion. The ancients received the highest marks, needless to say, then came Raphael and Poussin; the Venetians, who overemphasized color, ranked low, and the Flemish and Dutch lower still. Subjects were similarly classified, from history (classical or Biblical) at the top to still life at the bottom.

It is hardly surprising that this strait-jacket system produced no significant artists. Its absurd rigidity generated a counterpressure that vented itself as soon as Lebrun's authority began to decline. Toward 1700, the members of the Academy formed two warring factions over the issue of drawing versus color: the conservatives (or "Poussinistes") against the "Rubénistes." The former defended Poussin's view that drawing, which appealed to the mind, was superior to color, while the latter advocated color as being more true to nature. They also pointed out that drawing, admittedly based on reason, appeals only to the expert few, whereas color appeals to everyone. This argument had revolutionary implications, for it proclaimed the layman to be the ultimate judge of artistic values, and challenged the Renaissance view that painting, as a liberal art, could be appreciated only by the educated mind. In 1717, soon after Louis XIV's death, the "Rubénistes" scored a final triumph when Antoine Watteau was admitted to the Academy on the basis of *A Pilgrimage to Cythera* (fig. 191). This picture violated all academic canons, and its subject did not conform to any established category. But the Academy, now very accommodating, invented for Watteau the new category of *fêtes galantes* (elegant fetes or entertainments). The term refers less to this one canvas than to the artist's work in general, which mainly shows scenes of elegant society, or comedy actors, in parklike settings. He characteristically interweaves theater and real life so that no clear distinction can be made between the two. The *Pilgrimage* includes yet another element, classical mythology: these

192. GERMAIN BOFFRAND. Salon de la Princesse,
Hôtel de Soubise. Begun 1732. Paris

150   *Art in the Renaissance*

Colorplate 20. JAN VERMEER VAN DELFT. *The Letter*. 1666. Canvas, 17¼ x 15¼".
Rijksmuseum, Amsterdam

Colorplate 21. JOSEPH M. W. TURNER. *The Slave Ship.*
1839. Canvas, 35¾ x 48″. Museum of Fine Arts, Boston

young couples have come to Cythera, the island of love, to pay homage to Venus (whose garlanded image appears on the far right). As the enchanted day draws to a close, they are about to go aboard the boat, accompanied by swarms of cupids, and be transported back to the everyday world. The style at once recalls Rubens' (see fig. 177), but Watteau adds a poignant touch, a poetic subtlety of his own. His figures have not the robust vitality of Rubens'; slim and graceful, they move with the studied assurance of actors who play their roles so superbly that they touch us more than reality ever could.

Watteau signals a shift in French art and French society. After the death of Louis XIV, the centralized administrative machine that Colbert had created ground to a stop. The nobility, hitherto attached to the court at Versailles, were now freer of royal surveillance. Many of them chose not to return to their ancestral homes in the provinces, but to live in Paris, where they built themselves elegant town houses, known as *hôtels*. Because these city sites were usually cramped and irregular, they offered scant opportunity for impressive exteriors; the layout and décor of the rooms became the architects' main concern. As the state-sponsored buildings became fewer, the field of "design for private living" took on new importance. The *hôtels* demanded a style of decoration less grandiloquent than Lebrun's—an intimate, flexible style that would give greater scope to individual fancy uninhibited by classicistic dogma. French designers created the Rococo style in response to this need. Rococo was a refinement in miniature of the curvilinear, "elastic" Baroque of Borromini and Guarini, and thus could be happily united with Austrian and German Late Baroque architecture (see p. 140). In France, most examples of the style, such as the Salon de la Princesse in the Hôtel de Soubise, by Germain Boffrand (fig. 192), are smaller in scale and less exuberant than those in Central Europe; the ceiling frescoes and decorative sculpture in palaces and churches are unsuited to domestic interiors, however lavish. We must therefore remember that in France, Rococo painting and sculpture were less closely linked with their architectural setting than in Italy, Austria, and Germany, although they reflect the same taste that produced the Hôtel de Soubise. Characteristic of Rococo sculpture are small, coquettishly erotic groups designed to be viewed at close range, playful echoes of the ecstasies of Bernini. Monumental commissions were few, but the eques-

193. ETIENNE MAURICE FALCONET.
Equestrian Monument of Peter the Great. 1766–82.
Bronze, over lifesize. Leningrad

trian statue of Peter the Great, made for Catherine of Russia by Etienne Maurice Falconet (fig. 193), recaptures the essence of Baroque movement and grandeur. Bernini had proposed such a monument to Louis XIV, who turned him down because he found the rearing horse incompatible with royal dignity.

French Rococo painting follows the "Rubéniste" style of Watteau, intimate in scale and deliciously sensual in style and subject, although without the emotional depth that distinguishes Watteau's art. Yet there were other painters whose style can be termed Rococo only with reservations, such as Jean-Baptiste Siméon Chardin. The "Rubénistes" had cleared the way for a new interest in the Dutch masters as well, and Chardin was the finest painter of still life and genre representing this trend. His still lifes eschew the "object appeal" of their Dutch predecessors. In the example shown in figure 194, we see only the common objects that belong in any kitchen: earthenware jugs, a casserole, a copper pot, a piece of raw meat, smoked herring, two eggs. But how important they seem, each so firmly placed in relation to the rest, each so worthy of the artist's—and our—scrutiny! Despite his concern with formal problems, evident in the beautifully balanced design, Chardin presents these objects with a

194. JEAN-BAPTISTE SIMEON CHARDIN.
Kitchen Still Life. c.1730–35. Canvas, 12½ x 15¼".
Ashmolean Museum, Oxford

respect close to reverence. More than shapes, colors, and textures, they are to him symbols of the life of the common man. In spirit, if not in subject matter, Chardin is more akin to Louis Le Nain than to any Dutch painter.

We have not mentioned English architecture since our discussion of the Perpendicular style (see p. 72). This insular form of Late Gothic proved extraordinarily persistent; it absorbed the stylistic vocabulary of the Italian Renaissance during the sixteenth century, but as late as 1600 English buildings still retained a "Perpendicular syntax." It was the influence of Palladio that finally brought this lingering Gothic tradition to an end, replacing it with an equally strong allegiance to classicism. We can see this classicism in some parts of St. Paul's Cathedral (fig. 195) by Sir Christopher Wren, the great English architect of the late seventeenth century: the dome looks like a vastly enlarged version of Bramante's Tempietto (see fig. 147). St. Paul's is otherwise an up-to-date Baroque design reflecting a thorough acquaintance with contemporary architecture in Italy and France. Sir Christopher came close to being a Baroque counterpart of the Renaissance artist-scientists. An intellectual prodigy, he studied anatomy first, then physics, mathematics, and astronomy, and was highly esteemed by Sir Isaac Newton. His serious interest in architecture did not begin until he was about thirty. There is, however, apparently no direct link between his scientific and artistic ideas. Had not the great London fire of 1666 destroyed the Gothic Cathedral of St. Paul, and many lesser churches, Sir Christopher might have remained an amateur architect. But after that catastrophe he was named to the royal commission for rebuilding the city, and a few years later he began his designs for St. Paul's. On his only trip abroad, he had visited Paris at the time of the dispute over the completion of the Louvre, and he must have sided with Perrault, whose design for the East Front is clearly reflected in the façade of St. Paul's. Yet, despite his belief that Paris provided "the best school of architecture in Europe," Sir Christopher was not indifferent to the achievements of the Roman Baroque. He must have wanted the new St. Paul's to be the St. Peter's of the Church of England, soberer and less large, but equally impressive.

England never accepted the Rococo style in architecture. French Rococo painting, on the other hand, had a decisive—though unacknowledged—effect across the Channel and helped to bring about the first school of English painting since the Middle Ages that had more than local importance. The earliest of these painters, William Hogarth, made his mark in the 1730s with a new kind of picture, which he described as "modern moral subjects . . . similar to representations on the stage." He wished to be judged as a dramatist, he said, even though his "actors" could only "exhibit a dumb show." These paintings, and the engravings he made from

195. CHRISTOPHER WREN. Facade,
St. Paul's Cathedral. 1675–1710. London

them for popular sale, came in sets, with details recurring in each scene to unify the sequence. Hogarth's "morality plays" teach, by horrid example, the solid middle-class virtues: they show a country girl who succumbs to the temptations of fashionable London; the evils of corrupt elections; aristocratic rakes who live only for ruinous pleasure, marrying wealthy women of lower status for their fortunes (which they promptly dissipate). In *The Orgy* (fig 196), from *The Rake's Progress*, the young wastrel is overindulging in wine and women. The scene is so full of visual clues that a full account would take pages, plus constant references to the adjoining episodes. Yet, however literal-minded, the picture has great appeal. Hogarth combines some of Watteau's sparkle with Jan Steen's narrative gusto, and so entertains us that we enjoy his sermon without being overwhelmed by its message. He is probably the first artist in history to become also a social critic in his own right.

Portraiture remained the only constant source of income for English painters. Here, too, the eighteenth century produced a style that differed from the Continental traditions that had dominated this field ever since the days of Holbein. Its greatest master, Thomas Gainsborough, began by painting landscapes, but ended as the favorite portraitist of British high society. His early portraits, such as *Robert Andrews and His Wife* (fig. 197), have a lyrical charm that is not always found in his later pictures. These two people, members of the landed gentry, are naturally, and unpretentiously, at home in their setting. The landscape, although derived from Ruisdael and his school, has a sunlit, hospitable air never achieved (or desired) by the Dutch masters; and the casual grace of the figures indirectly recalls Watteau's style. Gainsborough's great rival on the Lon-

196. WILLIAM HOGARTH. *The Orgy,* Scene III from *The Rake's Progress.* c.1734. Canvas, 24½ x 29½". Sir John Soane's Museum, London

don scene was Sir Joshua Reynolds, the president of the Royal Academy from its founding in 1768. Like his French predecessors, Reynolds formulated in his famous *Discourses* what he felt were necessary rules and theories. His views were essentially those of Lebrun, tempered by British common sense. And, like Lebrun, he found it difficult to live up to his theories in actual practice. The best that can be said of Reynolds is that he almost succeeded in making painting respectable in England as a liberal art (he received an honorary doctorate from Oxford), but at what cost! His *Discourses*, which soon became standard, inhibited the visual capacity of generations of students in England and America. He was generous enough to give praise to Gainsborough, whom he outlived by a few years, and whose instinctive talent he must have envied.

197. THOMAS GAINSBOROUGH. *Robert Andrews and His Wife.* c.1748–50. Canvas, 27½ x 47". The National Gallery, London

PART FOUR

ART IN THE MODERN WORLD

1. ENLIGHTENMENT AND REVOLUTION

The era to which we ourselves belong has not yet acquired a name of its own. Perhaps this does not strike us as peculiar at first, but considering how promptly the Renaissance coined a name for itself, we may well ponder the fact that no such key idea has emerged in the two centuries since our era began. Perhaps "revolution" is a suitable concept, because rapid and violent change has indeed characterized the modern world. Our era began with revolutions of two kinds: the industrial revolution, symbolized by the steam engine, and the political revolution, under the banner of democracy, in America and France. Both revolutions are still going on; industrialization and democracy are goals all over the world. Western science and Western political ideology (and in their wake all the other products of modern Western civilization, from food and dress to art and literature) will soon belong to all mankind. We tend to think of these two movements as different aspects of one process—with effects more far-reaching than any since the New Stone Age revolution (see above, p. 5)—yet the twin revolutions of modern times are not the same. The more we try to define their relationship, the more paradoxical it seems. Both are founded on the idea of progress, and both command an emotional allegiance that was once reserved for religion; but while progress in science and industry during the past two centuries has been continuous and palpable, we can hardly make this claim for man's pursuit of happiness, however we choose to define it.

Here, then, is the conflict fundamental to our era. Man today, having cast off the framework of traditional authority which confined and sustained him before, can act with a latitude both frightening and exhilarating. In a world where all values may be questioned, man searches constantly for his own identity, and for the meaning of human existence, individual and collective. His knowledge about himself is now vastly greater, but this has not reassured him as

he had hoped. Modern civilization thus lacks the cohesiveness of the past; it no longer proceeds by readily identifiable periods, nor are there clear period styles in art or in any other form of endeavor. Instead, we find another kind of continuity, that of movements and countermovements. Spreading like waves, these "isms" defy national, ethnic, and chronological boundaries; never dominant anywhere for long, they compete or merge with each other in endlessly shifting patterns. Hence our account of modern art must be by movements rather than by countries; for, all regional differences notwithstanding, modern art is as international as modern science.

If the modern era was born in the American Revolution of 1776 and the French Revolution of 1789, these cataclysmic events were preceded by a revolution of the mind that had begun half a century earlier. Its standard-bearers were those thinkers of the Enlightenment in England and France—Hume, Voltaire, Rousseau (see p. 258), and others—who proclaimed that all human affairs ought to be ruled by reason and the common good, rather than by tradition and established authority. In the

198. JACQUES GERMAIN SOUFFLOT. The Panthéon (Ste.-Geneviève). 1755–92. Paris

199. THOMAS JEFFERSON.
Garden Façade, Monticello.
1770–84; 1796–1806.
Charlottesville, Va.

200. KARL LANGHANS.
The Brandenburg Gate.
1788–91. Berlin

arts, as in economics, politics, and religion, this rationalist movement turned against the prevailing practice: the ornate and aristocratic Baroque-Rococo. The call went out for a return to reason, nature, and morality in art, and to the mid-eighteenth century this meant a return to the ancients—after all, had not the classic philosophers been the original "apostles of reason"? In 1755, when the German art historian and critic Johann Winckelmann published a famous tract urging the imitation of the "noble simplicity and calm grandeur" of the Greeks, the first great monument of the new style was begun in Paris: the Panthéon (fig. 198) by Jacques Germain Soufflot, built as a church but secularized during the Revolution (see also p. 262). The smooth, sparsely decorated surfaces are abstractly severe, while the huge portico is modeled directly on ancient Roman temples. What distinguishes this cool, precise Neoclassicism from earlier classicisms is less its external appearance than its motivation; instead of merely reasserting the superior authority of the ancients, it claimed to be more rational, and hence more "natural," than the

Baroque. In England and America, the same trend produced the architectural style known as "Georgian." A fine example is Monticello, the home Thomas Jefferson designed for himself (fig. 199). Executed in brick with wooden trim, it is less austere than the Panthéon, except for the use of the Doric order. Jefferson still preferred the Roman Doric, but the late eighteenth century came to favor the heavier and more "authentic" Greek Doric, in what is known as the Greek Revival phase of Neoclassicism. Greek Doric, however, was also the least flexible order, and so was particularly difficult to adapt to modern tasks even when combined with Roman or Renaissance elements. Only rarely could it furnish a direct model for Neoclassic structures, as in the Brandenburg Gate in Berlin (fig. 200), derived from the Propylaea (see fig. 30).

In painting, the anti-Rococo trend was at first a matter of content rather than style. This accounts for the sudden fame, about 1760, of Jean-Baptiste Greuze: The Village Bride (fig. 201), like his other pictures of those years, is a scene of lower-class family life. In contrast to earlier genre paintings (compare fig. 184) it has a contrived, stagelike character, borrowed from the "dumb-show" narratives of Hogarth (see fig. 196). But Greuze has neither wit nor satire. His pictorial sermon illustrates the social gospel of the Enlightenment—that the poor, unlike the immoral aristocracy, are full of "natural" virtue and honest sentiment. Everything is calculated to remind us of this, from the declamatory gestures and expressions of the actors to the hen with her chicks in the foreground: one chick has left the brood and sits alone on a saucer, like the bride who is about to leave *her* "brood." *The Village Bride* was acclaimed as a masterpiece. Here at last was a painter who appealed to the beholder's moral sense instead of merely giving him pleasure like the frivolous artists of the Rococo! The loudest praise came from Diderot, that apostle of Reason and Nature, who accepted such narratives as "noble and serious human action" in Poussin's sense (see p. 147). He modified his views later, when a far more gifted and rigorous "Neo-Poussinist" appeared on the scene— Jacques Louis David. In *The Death of Socrates* (fig. 202) David seems more "Poussiniste" than Poussin himself (compare fig. 186); the composition unfolds like a relief, parallel to the picture plane, and the figures are as solid—and as immobile—as statues. Yet there is one unexpected element: the lighting, with its precise cast shadows, is derived from Caravaggio (see fig. 167), and so is the firmly realistic detail. In consequence, the picture has a quality of life

rather astonishing in so doctrinaire a statement of the new ideal style. The very harshness of the design suggests that its creator was passionately engaged in the issues of his time, artistic as well as political. Socrates, about to drain the poison cup, is shown here not only as an example of Ancient Virtue but as a Christ-like figure (there are twelve disciples in the scene).

David took an active part in the French Revolution, and for some years he practically controlled the artistic affairs of the nation. During this time he painted his greatest picture, *The Death of Marat* (fig. 203). David's deep emotion has made a masterpiece from a subject that would have embarrassed any lesser artist: for Marat, one of the political leaders of the Revolution, had been murdered in his bathtub. A painful skin condition caused him to do his paperwork there, with a wooden board for a desk. One day a young woman named Charlotte Corday burst in with a personal petition and plunged a knife into him while he read it. David has composed the scene with a stark directness that is truly awe-inspiring. In this canvas, a public memorial to the martyred hero, devotional image and historical account coincide. Because classical art could offer little guidance here, the artist has again drawn on the Caravaggesque tradition of religious art.

Later on, David became an ardent admirer of Napoleon and painted several large pictures glorifying the emperor (see also p. 268). But as the chief painter of the Napoleonic myth he was partially eclipsed by younger men. His

201. JEAN-BAPTISTE GREUZE.
The Village Bride. 1761.
Canvas, 36 x 46½".
The Louvre, Paris

202. JACQUES LOUIS DAVID.
The Death of Socrates. 1787.
Canvas, 59 x 78".
The Metropolitan Museum
of Art, New York
(Wolfe Fund, 1931)

203. JACQUES LOUIS DAVID. *The Death of Marat.* 1793.
Canvas, 65 x 50½". Museums of Fine Arts, Brussels

mantle finally descended upon a pupil, Jean-Auguste Ingres. Never an enthusiastic Bonapartist, Ingres went to Italy in 1806 and remained for eighteen years. Only after his return did he become the high priest of the Davidian tradition. What had been a revolutionary style only half a century before, now congealed into rigid dogma, endorsed by the government and

backed by the weight of conservative opinion. Fortunately, Ingres' pictures were far less doctrinaire than his theories. He always held that drawing was superior to painting, yet in a canvas such as his *Odalisque* (fig. 204) he sets off the petal-smooth limbs of this oriental Venus ("odalisque" is a Turkish word for a harem slave girl) with a dazzling array of rich tones and textures. The subject itself, redolent with the enchantment of the *Thousand and One Nights*, is characteristic of Romanticism (see p. 162), which Ingres professed to despise. Nor does this nude embody a classical ideal of beauty. Her proportions, her strange mixture of coolness and voluptuousness, remind us, rather, of Parmigianino (see fig. 153).

History painting as defined by Poussin and David remained Ingres' lifelong ambition, but it gave him great trouble, while portraiture, which he pretended to dislike, was his strongest gift. He was, in fact, the last great professional in a field soon to be monopolized by the camera. Although photography became a practical process only about 1840, its experimental background goes back to the late eighteenth century. The impulse behind these experiments was not so much scientific curiosity as a quest of the True and Natural. The harsh realism of David's *Marat* proclaims this standard of unvarnished truth; so does Ingres' *Cherubini* (fig. 205), which at first glance looks like a kind of "superphotograph," despite the presence of the Muse behind the composer. But this impression is deceptive. If we disregard the incongruous and faintly comic allegory, we realize how much character interpretation the portrait

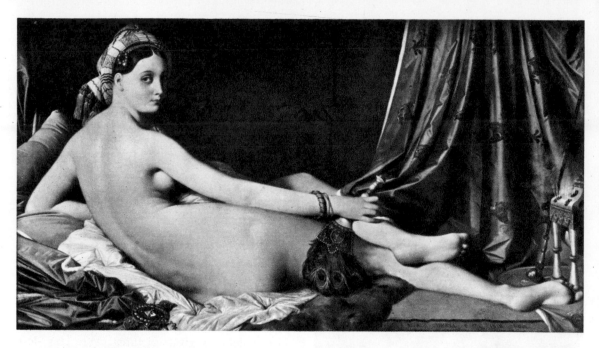

204. JEAN-AUGUSTE DOMINIQUE INGRES.
Odalisque. 1814. Canvas, 35¼ x 63¾".
The Louvre, Paris

205. JEAN-AUGUSTE DOMINIQUE INGRES.
Luigi Cherubini and the Muse of Lyric Poetry. 1842.
Canvas, 41⅜ x 37". The Louvre, Paris

contains (see p. 262). Only Ingres could so unify psychological depth and physical accuracy. His followers concentrated on physical accuracy alone, in vain competition with the camera.

The development of Neoclassic sculpture follows the pattern of architecture and painting but is less venturesome than either. Sculptors were overwhelmed by the authority accorded (since Winckelmann) to ancient statues; how could a modern artist compete with these works, which everyone acclaimed as the acme of sculptural achievement? At the same time, the new standard of uncompromising realistic "truth" embarrassed the sculptor. When a painter renders anatomical detail, clothing, or furniture with photographic precision he produces not a duplicate of reality but a representation of it, while to do so in sculpture comes dangerously close to mechanical reproduction —a handmade equivalent of the plaster cast. As we might deduce from what has just been said, portraiture proved the most viable field for Neoclassic sculpture. Its most distinguished practitioner, Jean Antoine Houdon, has an acute sense of individual character. His fine statue of Voltaire (fig. 206) does full justice to the sitter's skeptical wit and wisdom, and the classical drapery enveloping the famous sage —to stress his equivalence to ancient philosophers—is not incongruous, for he wears it as casually as a dressing gown. The more doctrinaire Neoclassic sculptors often adopted a less happy solution by portraying their sitters in classic nudity. The most famous of them, Antonio Canova, produced a colossal nude statue of Napoleon, inspired by portraits of ancient rulers whose nudity indicates their status as divinities. Not to be outdone, Napoleon's sister Pauline Borghese permitted Canova to sculpt her as a reclining Venus (fig. 207). The statue is so obviously idealized as to still any gossip; we recognize it as a precursor, more classically proportioned, of Ingres' *Odalisque* (see fig. 204). Strange to say, *Pauline Borghese* seems less three-dimensional than the painting. She is designed like a "relief in the round," for front and back view only, and her very considerable charm comes almost entirely from the fluid grace of her outlines. Here we also encounter the problem of representation versus duplication, not in the figure itself but in the pillows, mattress, and couch.

2. ROMANTICISM AND IMPRESSIONISM

The Enlightenment, paradoxically, liberated not only reason but also its opposite; it helped to create a new wave of emotionalism that was to last for the better part of a century and came to be known as Romanticism. Those who, in the mid-eighteenth century, shared the revulsion against the established social order and religion —against established values of any sort—could either try to found a new order on their faith in the power of reason, or they could find release

206. Jean Antoine Houdon. *Voltaire*. 1781. Terracotta model for marble, height 47". Fabre Museum, Montpellier, France

207. Antonio Canova. *Pauline Borghese as Venus*. 1808. Marble, lifesize. Borghese Gallery, Rome

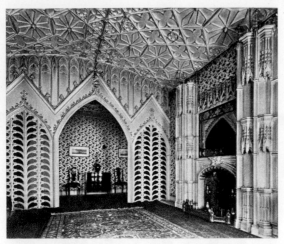

208. HORACE WALPOLE, with WILLIAM ROBINSON and others. Strawberry Hill. 1749–77. Twickenham, England

in a craving for emotional experience. Their common denominator was a desire to "return to Nature." The rationalist acclaimed Nature as the ultimate source of reason, while the Romantic worshiped her as unbounded, wild and ever-changing, sublime and picturesque. If man were only to behave "naturally," the Romantic believed, giving his impulses free rein, evil would disappear. In the name of nature, he exalted liberty, power, love, violence, the Greeks, the Middle Ages, or anything that aroused his response, although actually he exalted emotion as an end in itself. At its extreme, this attitude could be expressed only through direct action, not through works of art. (It has motivated some of the noblest—and vilest—acts of our era.) No artist, then, can be a wholehearted Romantic, for the creation of a work of art demands some detachment and self-awareness. What Wordsworth, the great Romantic poet, said of poetry—that it is "emotion recollected in tranquillity"—applies also to the visual arts. To cast his experience into permanent form, the Romantic artist needs a style. But since he is in revolt against the old order, this cannot be the established style of his time; it must come from some phase of the past to which he feels linked by "elective affinity" (another Romantic concept). Romanticism thus favors the revival, not of one style, but of a potentially unlimited number of styles. In fact, revivals—the rediscovery and utilization of forms hitherto neglected or disliked—became a stylistic principle: the "style" of Romanticism in art (also, to a degree, in literature and music). Neoclassicism, seen in this context, is no more than an aspect of Romanticism.

Given the individualistic nature of Romanticism, we might expect the range of revival styles to be widest in painting, the most personal and private of the visual arts, and least wide in architecture, the most communal and public. Yet the opposite is true. Painters and sculptors were unable to abandon Renaissance habits of representation, and they never really revived medieval art, or preclassic ancient art. Architects were not subject to this limitation, and the revival styles persisted longer in their work than in the other arts. Characteristically, at the time they launched the classic revival, they also started a Gothic revival. England was in the lead here, as it was in the development

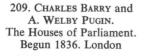

209. CHARLES BARRY and
A. WELBY PUGIN.
The Houses of Parliament.
Begun 1836. London

of Romantic literature and painting. Horace Walpole, influential as a man of letters and an amateur of the arts, set the example for the others when, in 1749, he began to "gothicize" his country house, Strawberry Hill; its dainty, playful interiors (fig. 208) look almost as if decorated with lace-paper doilies. Gothic here is still an "exotic" style. It appeals because it is strange, like the oriental tales of the *Thousand and One Nights*, or the medieval romances (such as the legends of King Arthur) that were being revived in the "Gothick" novels of the time.

After 1800, the choice between the classic and Gothic modes was more often resolved in favor of Gothic. Nationalist sentiment, strengthened in the Napoleonic wars, favored the "native" style, for England, France, and Germany each tended to think that Gothic expressed its particular national genius. Thus, when a spectacular fire gutted the Houses of Parliament in London in 1834, the rebuilding had to be done in Gothic style (fig. 209). As the seat of a vast government apparatus, but at the same time a focus of patriotic feeling, it presents a curious mixture—repetitious symmetry governs the main body of the structure, and "picturesque" irregularity its silhouette. Meanwhile, the stylistic alternatives were continually increased for architects by other revivals. By the middle of the nineteenth century, the Renaissance and then the Baroque returned to favor, bringing the revival movement to full circle. This last phase of Romantic architecture, which lingered on past 1900, is summed up in the Paris Opéra (fig. 210), designed by Charles Garnier. Its Neo-Baroque quality stems more from the profusion of sculpture and ornament than from its architectural vocabulary: the paired columns of the façade, "quoted" from the Louvre (see fig. 188), are combined with a smaller order, in Italian Renaissance fashion (compare fig. 157). The whole building looks "overdressed," its luxurious vulgarity so naïve as to be disarming. It reflects the taste of the beneficiaries of the industrial revolution, newly rich and powerful, who saw themselves as the heirs of the old aristocracy and thus found prerevolutionary styles more appealing than classic or Gothic. This "architecture of conscious display" was divorced from the practical demands of the industrial age—the factories, warehouses, stores, and city apartments that formed the bulk of building construction. There, in the world of commercial architecture, we find soon after 1800 the gradual introduction of new materials

210. CHARLES GARNIER. The Opéra. 1861–74. Paris

211. HENRI LABROUSTE. Reading Room, Bibliothèque Ste.-Geneviève. 1843–50. Paris

and techniques that were to have a profound effect on architectural style by the end of the century. The most important was iron, never before used as an actual building material. Within a few decades of its first appearance, iron columns and arches had become the standard means of supporting the roofs over the large spaces required by railroad stations, exhibition halls, and public libraries. A noted early example is the Bibliothèque Ste.-Geneviève in Paris, built by Henri Labrouste (fig. 211); in the reading room a row of cast-iron columns supports two barrel roofs resting on cast-iron arches. Labrouste chose to leave this iron skeleton uncovered, and to face the difficulty of relating it to the massive Renaissance revival style of his building. If his solution does not fully integrate the two systems, it at least lets them coexist. The iron columns are as slender as the new material permits; their collective effect is that of a space-dividing screen, belying their structural importance, even though Labrouste has tried to make them weightier by putting them on tall pedestals of solid masonry. With the arches, Labrouste has gone to the other extreme: since there was no way to make them look as powerful as their masonry ancestors, he has perforated them with lacy scrolls as if they were pure ornament. This aesthetic use of exposed iron members has a fanciful and delicate air that links it, indirectly, to the Gothic revival.

In sculpture, as we suggested earlier, there was no Gothic revival, despite some isolated essays in that direction. Instead, we find a return to the emotionalism and theatricality of the Baroque, long before the Baroque revival in architecture. By the 1830s, Neo-Baroque sculpture had produced a masterpiece in the splendidly rhetorical *Marseillaise* (fig. 212) on the Arc de Triomphe in Paris, by François Rude. The soldiers, volunteers of 1792 rallying to defend the Republic, are still in classical guise, but the Genius of Liberty above them imparts her great forward-rushing movement to the entire group. She would not be unworthy of Bernini (see figs. 169, 170). It was Rude who inspired the generation of French sculptors that decorated the façade of the Paris Opéra.

Romanticism produced few memorable works in sculpture. The unique virtue of sculpture, its solid, space-filling reality, was no more congenial to the Romantic temperament than the laborious process of translating a sketch into a permanent, finished work. Painting, in contrast, remains the greatest creative achievement of Romanticism in the visual arts, on a par with poetry and second only to music. Literature, both past and present, now became a more important source of inspiration for painters than ever before, and provided them with a new range of subjects, emotions, and attitudes. Romantic poets, in turn, often saw nature with a painter's eye. Many had a strong interest in art criticism and theory; some were capable draftsmen; and William Blake cast his visions in pictorial as well as literary form.

Within the Romantic movement, painting and literature had a complex, subtle, and by no means one-sided relationship.

It is no coincidence that two Americans working in England were among the pioneer contributors to the Romantic movement in painting. The first of these, Benjamin West, came to Rome in 1760 from Pennsylvania and caused something of a sensation, since no American painter had appeared in Europe before. He relished his role of frontiersman and always took pride in his New World background, even after he had settled in London, where he succeeded Reynolds as president of the Royal Academy. We can sense this in his most famous work, *The Death of General Wolfe* (fig. 213). Wolfe's death in the siege of Quebec, during the French and Indian War, had aroused considerable feeling in London. When West decided to paint it, two methods were open to him: he could give a factual account with the maximum of historic accuracy, or he could idealize it in the manner of the "Neo-Poussinist" painters, with the figures in "timeless" classical costume. Although he had absorbed the influence of the Neo-Poussinists in Rome, he did not follow them here; he knew the American locale of the subject too well for that. Instead, he merged the two approaches:

212. FRANÇOIS RUDE. *La Marseillaise.* 1833–36. Stone, c.42 x 26'. Arc de Triomphe, Paris.

left: 213. BENJAMIN WEST.
The Death of General Wolfe.
1770. Canvas, 59½ x 84″.
National Gallery of Canada, Ottawa

below: 214. JOHN SINGLETON COPLEY.
Watson and the Shark. 1778.
Canvas, 72½ x 90¼″.
Museum of Fine Arts, Boston

his figures wear modern dress, and the conspicuous Indian places the event in the New World, yet all of the attitudes and expressions are "heroic." The composition indeed recalls an old and hallowed theme, the lamentation over the dead Christ (see fig. 116), dramatized by Baroque lighting. West thus endowed the death of a modern hero both with the rhetorical pathos of "noble and serious human action" as defined by Poussin, and with the trappings of a real event. He created an image that expresses a phenomenon basic to modern times, the shift of emotional allegiance from religion to nationalism. No wonder his picture had countless successors during the nineteenth century.

John Singleton Copley of Boston moved to London just two years before the American Revolution. Already an accomplished portraitist, he now turned to history painting in the manner of West. His first work in that field, *Watson and the Shark* (fig. 214), is also the most important as a model of Romantic imagery. Watson, a young Englishman attacked by a shark while swimming in Havana harbor, had been dramatically rescued; many years later he commissioned Copley to depict this gruesome experience. Perhaps he thought that only a painter from America could do full justice to the exotic flavor of the subject. Copley, following West's example, has made every detail as authentic as possible (note the Negro, who serves the same purpose as the Indian in West's picture), while making use of all the resources of Baroque painting to invite the emotional participation of the beholder. The shark becomes a monstrous embodiment of evil, the man with the boat hook resembles an Archangel Michael fighting Satan, and the nude youth flounders helplessly between the forces of

doom and salvation. This charging of a private adventure with the emotional and symbolic qualities of myth is entirely characteristic of Romanticism.

It was, however, in landscape rather than in history painting that Romanticism reached its fullest expression. The *Landscape* (fig. 215) by Alexander Cozens, done only a few years after Copley's *Watson*, is so revolutionary that it seems to belong to a different era. Cozens had tired of traditional landscapes; artists using them as models, he felt, could produce only stereotyped variations on standard themes. The direct study of nature could not be the new starting point, since it did not supply the imaginative, poetic quality that for Cozens was the essence of landscape painting. He thus developed what he called "a new method of assisting the invention in drawing original compositions of landscape" which he published, with illustrations such as our figure 215, shortly before his death. Leonardo da Vinci, Cozens noted, had observed that an artist could stimulate his imagination by trying to find recognizable shapes in the stains on old walls; why not produce such chance effects on purpose, to be used in the same way? Crumple a sheet of paper, smooth it; then, while thinking generally of landscape, blot it with ink, using as little conscious control as possible (figure 215 shows an "ink-blot landscape"). The next step is to pick out representational elements in the configuration of blots, and to elaborate them into a finished picture. There is, of course, an essential difference between Leonardo's and Cozens' methods: the blots are not a work of nature but a work of art. They show, if nothing else, a highly individual graphic "handwriting." The Cozens method has far-reaching implications, theoretical as well as practical, but these could hardly have been understood by his contemporaries, who thought the "blot-master" ridiculous. Yet the "method" was never forgotten, its memory kept alive by its very notoriety. The two greatest masters of Romantic landscape in England, John Constable and William Turner, both profited from its liberating effect, however much they differed in other ways.

John Constable admired Ruisdael (see fig. 182), yet he strenuously opposed all flights of fancy. Landscape painting, he believed, must be based on observable facts; it should aim at "embodying a pure apprehension of natural effect." All his pictures show familiar views of the English countryside. Although he painted the final versions in his studio, he prepared them by making countless oil sketches out of doors. In these he was less concerned with concrete detail than with the qualities of light and atmosphere, so that the land often serves as a mere foil for the ever-changing drama of wind, sunlight, and clouds. The sky, to Constable, was "the key note, the standard scale, and the chief organ of sentiment"; he studied it with a meteorologist's precision, the better to grasp its infinite variety as a mirror of those sweeping forces so dear to the Romantic view of nature. Trying to record these effects, he developed a technique as broad, free, and personal as Cozens' "blotscapes," even though his point of departure was the exact opposite. The large pictures of Constable's final years retain more and more of the quality of his oil sketches; in *Stoke-by-Nayland* (fig. 216) the earth and sky seem both to have become "organs of sentiment" that pulsate with the artist's poetic sensibility.

William Turner had meanwhile arrived at

above: 215. ALEXANDER COZENS. *Landscape, from A New Method of Assisting the Invention in Drawing Original Compositions of Landscape.* 1784–86. Aquatint. The Metropolitan Museum of Art, New York (Rogers Fund, 1906)

right: 216. JOHN CONSTABLE. *Stoke-by-Nayland.* 1836. Canvas, 49½ x 66½". The Art Institute of Chicago

a style which Constable, deprecatingly but acutely, called "airy visions, painted with tinted steam." Turner, too, made copious studies from nature (though in water color, not oils), but he chose scenery that satisfied the Romantic taste for the Picturesque and the Sublime —mountains, the sea, or the sites of historic events; in his large pictures he often changed these views so freely that they became quite unrecognizable. Many of his landscapes are linked with literary themes. When exhibiting them, Turner would add appropriate quotations from ancient or modern authors to the catalogue, or he would make up some lines himself and claim to be citing his own unpublished poem, "Fallacies of Hope." Yet these canvases are the opposite of history paintings as defined by Poussin: the titles indeed indicate "noble and serious human actions," but the tiny figures, lost in the seething violence of nature, suggest the ultimate defeat of all endeavor —"the fallacies of hope." *The Slave Ship* (colorplate 21), one of Turner's most spectacular visions, shows how he transmuted his literary sources into "tinted steam." Originally entitled *Slavers Throwing Overboard the Dead and Dying—Typhoon Coming On*, the painting compounds several levels of meaning. In part, it has to do with a specific incident Turner had read about: when an epidemic broke out on a slave ship, the captain jettisoned his human cargo because he was insured against the loss of slaves at sea, but not by disease. Turner also thought of a passage from James Thomson's *The Seasons*, which describes how sharks follow a slave ship during a typhoon, "lured by the scent of steaming crowds, or rank disease, and death." But what is the relation between the slaver's action and the typhoon in the painting? Are the slaves being cast into the sea against the threat of the storm (perhaps to lighten the ship)? Is the typhoon Nature's retribution for the captain's greed and cruelty? Of the many storms at sea that Turner painted, none has quite this apocalyptic quality. A cosmic catastrophe seems about to engulf everything, not merely the slaver but the sea itself with its crowds of fantastic and oddly harmless-looking fish. While we still feel the force of Turner's imagination, most of us today, perhaps with a twinge of guilt, enjoy the tinted steam for its own sake, rather than as a vehicle of the awesome emotions the artist meant to evoke. Perhaps Turner himself sometimes wondered if his tinted steam had its intended effect on all beholders. In Goethe's *Color Theory*, then recently translated into English,

217. GEORGE CALEB BINGHAM. *Fur Traders on the Missouri*. c.1845. Canvas, 29 x 36". The Metropolitan Museum of Art, New York (Morris K. Jesup Fund, 1933)

he could have read that yellow has a "gay, softly exciting character," while orange-red suggests "warmth and gladness." Would *The Slave Ship* arouse the intended emotions in a viewer who did not know the title?

The Romantic view of nature as embodied in English painting and poetry soon spread to the Continent and across the Atlantic. A charming American example, although less daring than either Constable or Turner, is George Caleb Bingham's *Fur Traders on the Missouri* (fig. 217). In the silence of these vast, wide-open spaces, two trappers glide downstream in the misty sunlight, a black fox chained to the prow of their dugout canoe. They remind us of how much Romantic adventurousness went into the westward expansion of the United States.

Before we pursue Romantic painting in France, we must take account of the great Spanish painter Francisco Goya, David's contemporary and the only artist of the age who may be called, unreservedly, a genius. His early works, in a delightful late Rococo vein, reflect the influence of Tiepolo and the French masters (Spain had produced no important painters for a century). During the 1780s, however, Goya absorbed the libertarian ideas of the Enlightenment; even though he was a court painter, he surely sympathized with the Revolution, and not with the king of Spain, who had joined other monarchs in war against the young French Republic. When Napoleon's armies occupied Spain in 1808, Goya and many of his countrymen hoped that the conquerors would bring the liberal reforms so badly needed. The savage behavior of the

French troops crushed these hopes, and generated a popular resistance of equal savagery. Many of Goya's works from 1810–15 reflect this bitter experience. The greatest is *The Third of May, 1808* (fig. 218), commemorating the execution of a group of Madrid citizens. Here the blazing color, broad fluid brushwork, and dramatic nocturnal light are clearly no longer Rococo but Neo-Baroque, based on Velázquez and Rembrandt. The picture has all the emotional intensity of religious art, yet these martyrs are dying for Liberty, not the Kingdom of Heaven; and their executioners are not the agents of Satan but of political tyranny —a formation of faceless automatons, impervious to their victims' despair and defiance. The same scene was to be re-enacted countless times in modern history. With the clairvoyance of genius, Goya created an image that has become a terrifying symbol of our era.

After the defeat of Napoleon, the restored Spanish monarchy brought a new wave of repression, and Goya withdrew more and more into a private world of nightmarish visions. Finally, in 1824, he went into exile in France, where he died. His importance for the French Romantic painters is well attested by the greatest of them, Eugène Delacroix, who said that the ideal style would be a combination of Michelangelo's art with Goya's.

But Goya's influence in France began only after his death. Meanwhile, the reign of Napoleon, with its glamour, its adventurous conquests in remote parts of the world, had given rise to a Baroque revival among the younger painters, who felt the style of David too confining for the excitement of the age. The *Mounted Officer of the Imperial Guard* (fig. 219),

219. THEODORE GERICAULT. *Mounted Officer of the Imperial Guard.* 1812. Canvas, 9′ 7″ x 6′ 4½″. The Louvre, Paris

painted by Théodore Géricault at the astonishing age of twenty-one, renders a vision of the Romantic hero with Rubens-like energy (see fig. 177). For Géricault, politics no longer had the force of a faith. All he saw in Napoleon's campaigns was the thrill—irresistible to the Romantic—of violent action.

The year 1824 was crucial for French painting. Géricault died (in consequence of a riding accident); Goya arrived from Spain; Ingres returned home and had his first public success; the first showing in Paris of works by Constable was a revelation to many French artists; and *The Massacre at Chios* (fig. 220) established Eugène Delacroix as the foremost Neo-Baroque Romantic painter. An early admirer of Géricault, Delacroix had been exhibiting for some years, but the *Massacre*—conservatives called it "the massacre of painting," others acclaimed it enthusiastically—made his reputation. For the next quarter century, he and Ingres were acknowledged rivals, and their polarity, fostered by partisan critics, dominated the artistic scene in Paris. Like West's *Death of General Wolfe* (fig. 213), the *Massacre* was inspired by a contemporary event: the Greek war of independence against the Turks, which stirred a sympathetic response throughout Western Europe (the full title is *Scenes of the Massacre at Chios: Greek Families Awaiting*

218. FRANCISCO GOYA. *The Third of May, 1808.* 1814–15. Canvas, 8′ 9″ x 13′ 4″. The Prado, Madrid

Colorplate 22. EDOUARD MANET. *The Fifer*.
1866. Canvas, 63 x 38¼". The Louvre, Paris

Colorplate 23. CLAUDE MONET. *The River*. 1868. Canvas, 32 x 39½".
The Art Institute of Chicago (Potter Palmer Collection)

Death or Slavery). Delacroix, however, aimed at "poetic truth" rather than at recapturing a specific, actual event. He shows us an intoxicating mixture of sensuousness and cruelty, but he does not succeed in forcing us to suspend our disbelief. While we revel in the sheer splendor of the painting, we do not quite accept the human experience as authentic; we react, in other words, much as we do to Turner's *Slave Ship* (colorplate 21). One reason may be the discontinuity of the foreground, with its dramatic contrasts of light and shade, and the luminous sweep of the landscape (which Delacroix is said to have hastily repainted after seeing Constable's work). Originally, the background of the *Massacre* was probably like that of Géricault's *Mounted Officer*; the Turkish horseman directly recalls the earlier picture. However that may be, we cannot help feeling that for Delacroix there really was no basic distinction between Greeks and Turks—both belong to the exotic world of the Near East, alien, violent, and seductive. In his *Odalisque* (fig. 204), Ingres had celebrated the same environment—but how different the result! The same contrast is found in the portraiture of these perennial antagonists. Delacroix rarely painted portraits on commission; he felt at ease only when portraying his personal friends and fellow victims of the "Romantic agony" such as the Polish composer Frédéric Chopin (fig. 221). Here is the Romantic hero at his purest, consumed by the fire of his genius (see p. 274).

Turner and Delacroix reflect the attitude that eventually doomed the Romantic movement: its growing detachment from contemporary life. It is ironical that Honoré Daumier, the one great Romantic artist who did not shrink from reality, remained in his day practically unknown as a painter. A biting political cartoonist, Daumier contributed masterful satirical drawings to various Paris weeklies for most of his life. He turned to painting in the 1840s, but found no public for his work. Only a few friends encouraged him, and, a year before his death, arranged his first one-man show. Daumier's mature paintings have the full pictorial range of the Neo-Baroque, but the subjects of many of them are scenes of daily life like those he treated in his cartoons. *The Third-Class Carriage* (fig. 222) is such a work. Painted very freely, it must have seemed raw and "unfinished" even by Delacroix's standards. Yet its power is derived from this very freedom, and for that reason Daumier cannot be labeled a realist; his concern is not for the tangible surface of reality but for the emotional meaning

220. EUGENE DELACROIX.
The Massacre at Chios. 1822–24. Canvas,
13' 10" x 11' 7". The Louvre, Paris

221. EUGENE DELACROIX. *Frédéric Chopin*. 1838.
Canvas, 18 x 15". The Louvre, Paris

222. HONORE DAUMIER.
The Third-Class Carriage. c.1862. Canvas, 26 x 35½".
The Metropolitan Museum of Art, New York (Bequest of
Mrs. H.O. Havemeyer, 1929. The H.O. Havemeyer Collection)

behind it. In this picture, he captures a peculiarly modern human condition, "the lonely crowd" composed of people who have nothing in common apart from the fact that they are traveling together in one railway car. Though physically crowded, they take no notice of one another—each is alone with his own thoughts. Daumier explores this state with an insight into character and a breadth of human sympathy worthy of Rembrandt, whose work he revered. His feeling for the dignity of the poor also suggests Louis Le Nain (see fig. 185), who had recently been rediscovered by French critics.

Landscape in French Romantic art was of far less importance than in English art. France did, however, produce one great landscapist, Camille Corot, whose early work has an important place in the development of modern landscape painting. In 1825, Corot went to Italy and explored the countryside around Rome, like a latter-day Claude Lorraine (see fig. 187). But he did not transform his sketches into pastoral visions; what Claude recorded only in his drawings—the quality of a particular place at a particular time—Corot made into paintings, small canvases done on the spot in an hour or two. Such a work is his view of Papigno, an obscure little hill town (fig. 223). In size and immediacy, these pictures are analogous to Constable's oil sketches, yet they stem from a different tradition. If Constable's view of nature, which emphasizes the sky as "the chief organ of sentiment," derives from Dutch seventeenth-century landscapes, Corot's instinct for architectural clarity and stability recalls Poussin and Claude. Yet he, too, insists on "the truth of the moment"; his exactness of

above: 223. CAMILLE COROT.
Papigno. 1826. Canvas,
13 x 15¾". Collection
Dr. Fritz Nathan, Zurich

right: 224. GUSTAVE COURBET.
The Stone Breakers. 1849.
Canvas, 63 x 102".
Formerly State Gallery,
Dresden (destroyed 1945)

225. WINSLOW HOMER.
The Morning Bell. c.1866.
Canvas, 24 x 38".
Yale University Art Gallery,
New Haven
(Stephen C. Clark Collection)

observation, and his readiness to seize any view that attracted him during his excursions, show the same commitment to direct visual experience that we find in Constable.

REALISM. "Can Jupiter survive the lightning rod?" asked Karl Marx, not long after the middle of the century. The French poet and art critic Charles Baudelaire was addressing himself to the same problem when, in 1846, he called for paintings that expressed "the heroism of modern life." At that time, only one painter was willing to make an artistic creed of this demand: Baudelaire's friend Gustave Courbet. Proud of his rural background and a socialist in politics, Courbet had begun as a Neo-Baroque Romantic, but by 1848, under the impact of the revolutionary upheavals then sweeping Europe, he had come to believe that the Romantic emphasis on feeling and imagination was merely an escape from the realities of the time. The modern artist must rely on his own direct experience ("I cannot paint an angel because I have never seen one," he said); he must be a Realist. As a descriptive term, "realism" is not very precise. For Courbet, it meant something akin to the "naturalism" of Caravaggio (see page 136). As an admirer of Louis Le Nain and Rembrandt he had, in fact, strong links with the Caravaggio tradition, and his work, like Caravaggio's, was denounced for its supposed vulgarity and lack of spiritual content. The storm broke in 1849 over *The Stone Breakers* (fig. 224), the first canvas fully embodying Courbet's programmatic Realism. He had seen two men working on a road, and had asked them to pose for him in his studio, where

he painted them lifesize, solidly and matter-of-factly, without pathos or sentiment; the young man's face is averted, the old one's half hidden by a hat. Yet he cannot have picked them casually: their contrast in age is significant—one is too old for such heavy work, the other too young. Endowed with the dignity of their symbolic status, they do not turn to us for sympathy. Courbet's friend, the socialist Proudhon, likened them to a parable from the Gospels.

Courbet's Realism, then, was a revolution of subject matter more than of style. Yet the conservatives' rage at him as a dangerous radical is understandable; his sweeping condemnation of *all* traditional subjects drawn from religion, mythology, allegory, and history only spelled out what many others had begun to feel, but had not dared to put into words. After 1850, Realists sharing all or part of Courbet's convictions appeared everywhere in the Western world, whether or not they were familiar with his work. Winslow Homer was a particularly fine representative of this trend in America. He visited Paris as a young man in the late 1850s, then worked as a pictorial reporter during the Civil War. In the 1860s he also did some of his most remarkable paintings, such as *The Morning Bell* (fig. 225). The fresh delicacy of the sunlit scene is reminiscent of Corot, and the picture has an extraordinarily subtle design as well: the dog and the group of girls turn the footpath into a seesaw, its upward slant balanced by the descending line of the treetops. Despite its idyllic air, *The Morning Bell* is a tribute to "the heroism of modern life"—the building to the left is a cannery, and its bell tolls to announce the working day.

Art in the Modern World 173

IMPRESSIONISM. Courbet's art helps us to understand a picture that shocked the public even more than any of his: Edouard Manet's *Luncheon on the Grass* (fig. 226), which shows a nude model accompanied by two gentlemen in frock coats. Manet was the first to grasp Courbet's full importance—the *Luncheon* is, among other things, a tribute to the older artist. Renaissance masters had often juxtaposed nude and clothed figures in outdoor settings, but when Manet did so, he caused a scandal, since his painting gives no hint of a "higher" significance. Yet the group has so formal a pose that he could not possibly have intended to depict an actual event. Perhaps the meaning of the canvas lies in this denial of plausibility, for the scene fits neither the plane of everyday experience nor that of allegory. The *Luncheon* is a manifesto of artistic freedom, asserting the painter's privilege to combine whatever elements he pleases for aesthetic effect alone. The nudity of the model is "explained" by the contrast between her warm, creamy flesh tones and the cool black-and-gray of the men's attire. Or, to put it another way, the *Luncheon* tells us that the world of painting has an internal logic distinct from the logic of familiar reality, and that the painter's first loyalty is to his canvas, not to the outside world. Here begins an attitude that was to become a bone of contention later under the slogan "art for art's sake" (see p. 176). Manet himself disdained controversy, but his work attests his lifelong devotion to "pure painting"—to the belief that brush strokes and color patches, rather than the things they stand for, are the artist's primary reality. Among the old masters, he found that

Hals, Velázquez, and Goya had come closest to this ideal. He admired their broad, open technique, their preoccupation with light and color values. Many of his canvases are, in fact, "pictures of pictures"—they translate into modern terms those older works that particularly challenged him. Yet he always filtered out the expressive or symbolic content of his models, lest the viewer's attention be distracted from the pictorial structure itself. His paintings have an emotional reticence that can easily be mistaken for emptiness unless we understand its purpose.

Courbet is said to have remarked that Manet's pictures were as flat as playing cards. Looking at *The Fifer* (colorplate 22) we can see what he meant. Done three years after the *Luncheon*, it is a painting without shadows (there are a few, but it takes a real effort to find them), hardly any modeling, and no depth. The figure looks three-dimensional only because its contour renders the forms in realistic foreshortening; otherwise, Manet eschews all the methods devised since Giotto's time for transmuting a flat surface into a pictorial space. The gray background seems as near to us as the figure, and just as solid; if the fifer stepped out of the picture, he would leave a hole, like the cut-out shape of a stencil. Here, then, the canvas itself is no longer a "window," but a screen made up of patches of color. In retrospect, we realize that the revolutionary qualities of Manet's art already appear, less obviously, in the *Luncheon*; the three main figures form a unit almost as shadowless and stencil-like as the fifer. They would be more at home on a flat screen than they are in their Courbet-like landscape setting.

What brought about this "revolution of the color patch"? We do not know, and Manet himself surely did not reason it out beforehand. Perhaps he was impelled to create the new style by the challenge of photography. The "pencil of nature" had vindicated the objective truth of Renaissance perspective (see fig. 162), but it established a standard of representational accuracy that no handmade image could rival. Painting needed to be rescued from competition with the camera. This Manet accomplished by insisting that a painted canvas is, above all, a surface covered with pigments —that we must look *at* it, not *through* it. Unlike Courbet, he gave no name to the style he had created; when his followers began calling themselves Impressionists, he refused to accept the term for his own work. The word was coined in 1874, after a hostile critic had looked

226. EDOUARD MANET. *Luncheon on the Grass*
(*Le Déjeuner sur l'Herbe*). 1863. Canvas, 7' x 8' 10".
The Louvre, Paris

at a picture entitled *Impression: Sunrise* by Claude Monet, and it certainly fits Monet better than it does Manet. Monet had adopted Manet's concept of painting and applied it to landscapes done out of doors, such as *The River* (colorplate 23). It is flooded with sunlight so bright that conservative critics claimed it made their eyes smart. In this flickering network of color patches, the reflections on the water are as "real" as the banks of the river Seine (see also p. 283). Even more than *The Fifer*, Monet's painting is a "playing card"; were it not for the woman and the boat in the foreground, the picture could hang upside down with hardly any difference of effect. This inner coherence sets *The River* apart from earlier "impressions" like Corot's *Papigno* (see fig. 223), even though both share the same on-the-spot immediacy and fresh perception.

Scenes from the world of entertainment—dance halls, cafés, concerts, the theater—were favorite subjects for Impressionist painters. Auguste Renoir, another important member of the group, filled his with the *joie de vivre* of a singularly happy temperament. The flirting couples in *Le Moulin de la Galette* (fig. 227), under the dappled pattern of sunlight and shade, radiate a human warmth that is utterly entrancing, even though the artist permits us no more than a fleeting glance at any of them. Our role is that of the casual stroller, who takes in this slice of life as he passes. By contrast, Edgar Degas makes us look steadily at the disenchanted pair in his café scene (fig. 228), but, so to speak, out of the corner of our eye. The design of this picture, at first glance,

seems as unstudied as a snapshot, yet the longer we look, the more we realize that everything has been made to dovetail precisely—that the zigzag of empty tables between us and the luckless couple reinforces their brooding loneliness. Compositions as boldly calculated as

229. JAMES A. M. WHISTLER. *Nocturne in Black and Gold: The Falling Rocket.* c.1874. Panel, 23¾ x 18⅜″. The Detroit Institute of Arts

this set Degas apart from his fellow Impressionists. A wealthy aristocrat by birth, he had been trained in the tradition of Ingres, whom he greatly admired. Like Ingres, he was a masterful portraitist, although he portrayed only friends and relatives, people with whom he had emotional ties. His profound sense of human character lends weight even to seemingly casual scenes such as that in figure 228.

Courbet, during his later years, enjoyed considerable fame and influence abroad; the Impressionists gained international recognition more slowly. Americans were among their first patrons, responding to the new style more readily than Europeans did. At a time when no French museum would have them, Impressionist works entered public collections in the United States, and American painters were among the earliest followers of Manet and his circle. James McNeill Whistler, who had settled in London in 1859 for the rest of his life, was in close touch with the rising Impressionist movement in France during the 1860s. His best-known picture, *Arrangement in Black and Gray: The Artist's Mother*, reflects the influence of Manet in its emphasis on flat areas. Its rise to fame as a symbol of our latter-day "mother cult" is a paradox of popular psychol-

ogy that would have dismayed Whistler; he wanted the canvas to be appreciated for its formal qualities alone. A witty and sharp-tongued advocate of "art for art's sake," he thought of his pictures as analogous to pieces of music, often calling them "symphonies" or "nocturnes." The boldest of these is *Nocturne in Black and Gold: The Falling Rocket* (fig. 229); if it were not for the explanatory subtitle, we would have real difficulty making it out. No Frenchman had yet dared to produce a picture so "nonrepresentational," so reminiscent of Cozens' blotscapes and Turner's "tinted steam" (see fig. 215, colorplate 21). It was this painting, more than any other, that prompted the British critic John Ruskin to accuse Whistler of "flinging a pot of paint in the public's face." Since Ruskin had highly praised Turner's *Slave Ship*, it would seem that what he really liked was not the tinted steam itself but the Romantic sentiment behind it. During the subsequent libel suit, Whistler stated his aims in words that fit *The Falling Rocket* especially well: "I have perhaps meant rather to indicate an artistic interest alone in my work, divesting the picture from any outside sort of interest. . . . It is an arrangement of line, form, and color, first, and I make use of any incident of it which shall bring about a symmetrical result." The last phrase is particularly significant, since Whistler acknowledges that in utilizing chance effects he does not look for resemblances but for a purely formal harmony. His statement reads like a prophecy of American abstract painting today (see colorplate 31).

POST-IMPRESSIONISM. In 1882 Manet was made a chevalier of the Legion of Honor by the French government. Impressionism by now was gaining wide acceptance, but it had ceased to be a pioneering movement. The future belonged to the "Post-Impressionists." This colorless label designates a group of artists who had become dissatisfied with the limitations of Impressionism and went beyond it in various directions. It is difficult to find a more descriptive term for them, since they did not share a common goal. In any event, they were not "anti-Impressionists." Far from trying to undo the effects of the "Manet Revolution," they wanted to carry it further; Post-Impressionism is in essence just a later stage—though a very important one—of the development that had begun with such pictures as Manet's *Luncheon on the Grass*.

Paul Cézanne, the oldest Post-Impressionist

painter, was born in Aix-en-Provence, near the Mediterranean coast. He came to Paris in 1861, imbued with enthusiasm for the Romantics, especially Delacroix. But he soon discovered Manet as well, and by the early 1870s he had become an Impressionist. Toward the end of the decade, however, he set out "to make of Impressionism something solid and durable, like the art of the museums." What he meant by this can be seen in *Fruit Bowl, Glass, and Apples* (colorplate 24): every brush stroke is like a building block, firmly placed within the pictorial architecture, and the colors are deliberately controlled so as to produce "chords" of warm and cool tones that reverberate throughout the canvas. Not since Chardin have simple everyday objects assumed such importance in a painter's eye. We also notice another aspect of Cézanne's mature style: the forms are deliberately simplified, and outlined with dark contours; and the perspective is "incorrect" for both the fruit bowl and the horizontal surfaces, which seem to slant upward. The longer we study the picture, the more we realize the rightness of these apparently arbitary distortions. When Cézanne takes these liberties with reality, his purpose is to uncover the permanent qualities beneath the accidents of appearance (all forms in nature, he believed, are based on the cone, the sphere, and the cylinder). This order underlying the external world was the true subject of his pictures, but he had to interpret it to fit the separate, closed world of the canvas. One detail of our painting is particularly instructive in this respect—the stem of the fruit bowl is slightly off center, as if the oval shape of the bowl, in response to the pressure of the other objects, were expanding toward the left.

To apply this method to landscape became the greatest challenge of Cézanne's career. From 1882 on, he lived in isolation near his home town, exploring its environs. One motif, the distinctive shape of a mountain called Mont Sainte-Victoire, seemed almost to obsess him; its craggy profile looming against the blue Mediterranean sky appears in a long series of compositions, such as the monumental late work in figure 230. There are no hints of man's presence here—houses and roads would only disturb the lonely grandeur of this view. Above the wall of rocky cliffs that bar our way like a chain of fortifications, the mountain rises in triumphant clarity, infinitely remote yet as solid and palpable as the shapes in the foreground. For all its architectural stability, the scene is alive with movement; but the forces at work here have been brought into equilibrium, subdued by the greater power of the artist's will.

Georges Seurat shared Cézanne's aim to make Impressionism "solid and durable," but he went about it very differently. His career was as brief as that of Masaccio, and his achievement just as astonishing. Seurat devoted his main efforts to a few very large paintings, for which he made endless series of preliminary studies. This painstaking method reflects his belief that art must be based on a system; but, as with all artists of genius, Seurat's theories do not really explain his pictures—it is the pictures, rather, that explain the theories. The subject of *A Sunday Afternoon on the Grande Jatte* (colorplate 25) is of the sort that had long been popular among Impressionist painters. Impressionist, too, are the brilliant colors and the effect of intense sunlight. Otherwise, however, the picture is the very opposite of a quick "impression"; the firm, simple contours and the relaxed, immobile figures give the scene a timeless stability that recalls Piero della Francesca (see fig. 132). Even the brushwork shows Seurat's passion for order and permanence; the canvas is covered by systematic, impersonal dots of intense color which were to merge in the beholder's eye and thereby produce intermediary tints more luminous than those obtainable from pigments mixed on the palette. This procedure he called Divisionism (others spoke of Neo-Impressionism, or Pointillism). The actual result, however, did not conform to the theory. Looking at the *Grande Jatte* from a comfortable distance, we find that the mixture of the colors in the eye is still

230. PAUL CEZANNE. *Mont Sainte-Victoire Seen from Bibemus Quarry.* c.1898–1900. Canvas, 25½ x 32". The Baltimore Museum of Art (The Cone Collection)

incomplete; the dots are clearly visible, like the tesserae of a mosaic. Seurat must have liked this unexpected effect—otherwise he would have reduced the size of the dots—which gives the canvas the quality of a shimmering translucent screen.

While Cézanne and Seurat were converting Impressionism into a more severe, classical style, Vincent van Gogh pursued the opposite direction, believing that Impressionism did not provide the artist with enough freedom to express his emotions. He is sometimes called an Expressionist, but the term ought to be re-

served for certain later painters (see p. 184). Van Gogh, the first great Dutch master since the seventeenth century, did not become an artist until 1880; since he died only ten years later, his career was even briefer than Seurat's. His early interests were in literature and religion. Profoundly dissatisfied with the values of industrial society, and imbued with a strong sense of mission, he worked for a while as a lay preacher among poverty-stricken coal miners. An intense sympathy for the poor pervades his early paintings. In 1886, however, he came to Paris and met Degas, Seurat, and other leading French artists. Their effect on him was electrifying: his pictures now blazed with color, and he even tried the Divisionist technique of Seurat. Although this Impressionist phase was vitally important for Van Gogh's development, he had to integrate it with the style of his earlier years before his genius could fully unfold. Paris had opened his eyes to the sensuous beauty of the visible world and taught him the pictorial language of the color patch, but painting continued to be a vessel for his personal emotions. To investigate this spiritual reality with the new means at his command, he went to Arles, in the south of France. It was there, between 1888 and 1890, that he produced his greatest pictures. Like Cézanne, he now devoted his main energies to landscape painting, but the sun-drenched countryside evoked a very different response in him: he saw it filled with ecstatic movement, not architectural stability and permanence. In his *Wheat Field and Cypress Trees* (colorplate 26), both earth and sky show an overpowering turbulence—the wheat field resembles a stormy sea, the trees spring flamelike from the ground, and the hills and clouds heave with a similar undulant

above: 231. VINCENT VAN GOGH. *Self-Portrait.* 1889. Canvas, 22½ x 17". Collection Mr. and Mrs. John Hay Whitney, New York

right: 232. PAUL GAUGUIN. *Offerings of Gratitude.* c.1891–93. Woodcut

motion. The dynamism that is in every brush stroke makes of each one not merely a deposit of color, but an incisive graphic gesture. Yet to Van Gogh himself it was the color, not the form, that determined the expressive content of his pictures. Although his desire "to exaggerate the essential and to leave the obvious vague" makes his colors look arbitrary by Impressionist standards, he nevertheless remained deeply committed to the visible world. The colors of *Wheat Field* are stronger, simpler, and more vibrant than those in Monet's *The River* (compare colorplate 23) but in no sense "unnatural." They speak to us of that "kingdom of light" Van Gogh had found in the South, and of his mystic faith in a creative force animating all forms of life. The missionary had now become a prophet. We see him in that role in the *Self-Portrait* (fig. 231), his emaciated, luminous head with its burning eyes set off against a whirlpool of darkness. At the time of this *Self-Portrait*, he had already begun to suffer fits of mental illness that made painting increasingly difficult for him. Despairing of a cure, he committed suicide a year later, for he felt that art alone made his life worth living.

The quest for religious experience also played an important part in the work—if not in the life—of another great Post-Impressionist, Paul Gauguin. He began as a prosperous stockbroker in Paris, and an amateur painter and collector of modern art (he once owned Cézanne's *Fruit Bowl*, colorplate 24). At thirty-five, however, he became convinced that he must devote himself entirely to art: he abandoned his business career and his family, and by 1889 he was the central figure of a new movement called Symbolism. His style, though less intensely personal than Van Gogh's, was an even bolder advance beyond Impressionism. Gauguin believed that Western civilization was "out of joint," having forced men into an incomplete life dedicated to material gain while their emotions lay neglected. To rediscover for himself this hidden world of feeling, Gauguin went to live among the peasants of Brittany in western France. Here religion was still part of everyday life, and in works such as *The Yellow Christ* (colorplate 27) he attempted to depict the simple, direct faith of country people. Here at last is what no Romantic painter had achieved: a style based on pre-Renaissance sources. Modeling and perspective have given way to flat, simplified shapes outlined heavily in black, and the brilliant colors are equally "unnatural." This style, inspired by folk art and medieval stained glass, is meant to re-create

233 HENRI DE TOULOUSE-LAUTREC. *At the Moulin Rouge.* 1892. Canvas, 48⅜ x 55¼". The Art Institute of Chicago (Helen Birch Bartlett Memorial Collection)

both the imagined reality of the Crucifixion and the trancelike rapture of the peasant women. Yet we sense that Gauguin did not share this experience: he could paint pictures *about* faith, but not *from* faith.

Two years later, Gauguin's search for the unspoiled life led him even farther afield. He voyaged to Tahiti as a sort of "missionary in reverse," to learn from the natives instead of teaching them. Yet none of his South Pacific canvases are as daring as those he had painted in Brittany. His strongest works of this period are woodcuts; *Offerings of Gratitude* (fig. 232) again presents the theme of religious worship, but with the image of a local god replacing Christ. In its frankly "carved" look and its bold white-on-black pattern, we can feel the influences of the native art of the South Seas and of other non-European styles. The renewal of Western civilization, and of Western art, Gauguin believed, must come from "the Primitives"; he advised his fellow Symbolists to shun the Greeks and to turn instead to Persia, ancient Egypt, and the Far East. This idea itself was not new. It stems from the Romantic myth of the Noble Savage, and its ultimate source is the age-old dream of an earthly paradise where Man had lived—and might live again—in a state of nature and innocence. But no one before Gauguin had gone so far in putting the doctrine of primitivism into practice. His pilgrimage to the South Pacific symbolizes the end of four hundred years of colonial expansion which had brought the entire globe under Western domination. The "white man's burden," once

234. EDVARD MUNCH. *The Scream*.
1893. Canvas, 36 x 29".
National Museum, Oslo

of Gauguin. Although Toulouse-Lautrec was no Symbolist, the Moulin Rouge that he shows us here has an atmosphere so joyless and oppressive that we can only regard it as a place of evil.

Something of the same macabre quality pervades the early work of Edvard Munch, a gifted Norwegian who came to Paris in 1889 and based his starkly expressive style on Toulouse-Lautrec, Van Gogh, and Gauguin. *The Scream* (fig. 234) shows the influence of all three; it is an image of fear, the terrifying, unreasoned fear we feel in a nightmare. Munch visualizes this experience without the aid of frightening apparitions, and his achievement is the more persuasive for that very reason. The rhythm of the long, wavy lines seems to carry the echo of the scream into every corner of the picture, making earth and sky one great sounding board of terror. When the young Pablo Picasso arrived in Paris in 1900, he came under the spell of the same artistic atmosphere that had generated the style of Munch. His so-called Blue Period (referring to the prevailing color of his canvases as well as to their mood) consists almost entirely of pictures of beggars and derelicts such as *The Old Guitarist* (fig. 235)—outcasts or victims of society whose pathos reflects the artist's own sense of isolation. Yet these figures convey poetic melancholy more than outright despair. The aged musician accepts his fate with a resignation that seems almost saintly, and the attenuated grace of his limbs reminds us of El Greco (see fig. 155). *The Old Guitarist* is a strange amalgam of Mannerism and the art of Gauguin and Toulouse-Lautrec (note the smoothly curved contours) imbued with the personal gloom of a twenty-two-year-old genius.

A few years later, Picasso and his friends discovered a painter who until then had attracted no attention, although he had been exhibiting since 1886. He was Henri Rousseau, a retired customs collector who had started to paint in his middle age without training of any sort. Rousseau is that paradox, a folk artist of genius. How else could he have done a picture like *The Sleeping Gypsy* (fig. 236)? What goes on in the enchanted world of this canvas needs no explanation, because none is possible, but perhaps for that very reason its magic becomes unbelievably real to us. Here at last is that innocent directness of feeling which Gauguin thought was so necessary for the age and had traveled so far to find. Picasso and his friends were the first to recognize this quality in Rousseau's work. They revered him, justifiably, as

so cheerfully—and ruthlessly—shouldered, was becoming unbearable.

Van Gogh's and Gauguin's discontent with the spiritual ills of Western civilization was part of a sentiment widely shared at the end of the nineteenth century. A self-conscious preoccupation with decadence, evil, and darkness pervaded the artistic and literary climate. Even those who saw no escape analyzed their predicament in fascinated horror. Yet this very awareness proved to be a source of strength (the truly decadent do not realize their plight). The most remarkable instance of this strength was Henri de Toulouse-Lautrec; physically an ugly dwarf, he was an artist of superb talent who led a dissolute life in the nightspots of Paris and died of alcoholism. He was a great admirer of Degas, and his *At the Moulin Rouge* (fig. 233) recalls the zigzag composition of Degas' *The Glass of Absinthe* (see fig. 228). But this view of the well-known night club is no Impressionist "slice of life"; Toulouse-Lautrec sees through the gay surface of the scene, viewing performers and customers with a pitilessly sharp eye for their character (including his own; he is the tiny bearded man next to the very tall one in the background). The large areas of flat color and the emphatic, smoothly curving outlines reflect the influence

the godfather of much of twentieth-century painting.

Impressionism, it is often said, revitalized sculpture no less than painting. The claim is at once true and misleading. Auguste Rodin, the first sculptor of genius since Bernini, redefined sculpture during the same years that Manet and Monet redefined painting; in doing so, however, he did not follow these artists' lead. How indeed could the effect of such pictures as *The Fifer* or *The River* be reproduced in three dimensions and without color? What Rodin did accomplish is strikingly visible in *The Thinker* (fig. 237), originally conceived as part of a large unfinished project called *The Gates of Hell*. The welts and wrinkles of the vigorously creased surface produce, in polished bronze, an ever-changing pattern of reflections. But is this effect borrowed from Impressionist painting? Does Rodin dissolve three-dimensional form into flickering patches of light and dark? These fiercely exaggerated shapes pulsate with sculptural energy, and they retain this quality under whatever conditions the piece is viewed. For Rodin did not work directly in bronze; he modeled in wax or clay. How could he calculate in advance the reflections on the surfaces of the bronze casts that would be made from these models? He worked as he did, we must assume,

235. PABLO PICASSO. *The Old Guitarist*. 1903. Panel, 47¾ x 32½″. The Art Institute of Chicago (Helen Birch Bartlett Memorial Collection)

236. HENRI ROUSSEAU. *The Sleeping Gypsy*. 1897. Canvas, 51 x 79″. The Museum of Modern Art, New York

237. AUGUSTE RODIN. *The Thinker*. 1879–89.
Bronze, height 27½". The Metropolitan Museum of Art,
New York (Gift of Thomas F. Ryan, 1910)

238. AUGUSTE RODIN. *Balzac* (portion). 1892–97.
Plaster, entire height 9' 10". Rodin Museum, Paris

for an entirely different reason: not to capture elusive optical effects, but to make emphatic the process of "growth"—the miracle of dead matter coming to life in the artist's hands. As the color patch, for Manet and Monet, is the primary reality, so are the malleable lumps from which Rodin builds his forms. By insisting on this "unfinishedness," he rescued sculpture from mechanical verisimilitude just as Manet had rescued painting from photographic realism.

Who is *The Thinker*? Partly Adam, no doubt, partly Prometheus, and partly the brute imprisoned by the passions of the flesh. Rodin wisely refrained from giving him a specific name, for the statue fits no preconceived identity. In *The Thinker*, as in Michelangelo's superhuman bodies whose action-in-repose he shares, form and meaning are one. But, despite his tremendous admiration for Michelangelo, Rodin was a modeler, not a carver. His works reveal their full strength only when we see them in plaster casts made directly from the clay originals, rather than in bronze. The *Balzac Monument* (fig. 238), his most daring creation, remained in plaster for many years, rejected by the committee that had ordered it. The figure is larger than life, physically and spiritually; it has the overpowering presence of a specter. Like a huge monolith, the man of genius towers above the crowd—he shares the "sublime egotism of the gods" (as the Romantics put it). Rodin has minimized the articulation of the body so that from a distance we see only its great bulk. As we approach, we become aware that Balzac is wrapped in a long, shroudlike cloak. From this mass the head thrusts upward with elemental force. When we are close enough to make out the features clearly, we sense beneath the disdain an inner agony that stamps *Balzac* as the kin of *The Thinker*.

3. THE TWENTIETH CENTURY

In our account of modern art we have already discussed a succession of "isms": Neoclassicism, Romanticism, Realism, Impressionism, Post-Impressionism, Divisionism, Symbolism. There are many more to be found in twentieth-century art—so many, in fact, that nobody has made an exact count. These "isms" can form a serious obstacle to understanding; they make us feel that we cannot hope to comprehend the art of our time unless we immerse ourselves in a welter of esoteric doctrines. Actually, we can disregard all but the most important "isms"; like the names for the styles of earlier periods, they are merely labels to help us put things in their proper place. If an "ism" fails the test of usefulness, we need not bother with it. This is true of many "isms" in contemporary art; the movements they designate either cannot be seen clearly as separate entities or have so little importance that they interest only the specialist. It has always been easier to invent a new label than to create a new movement that truly deserves one.

Still, we cannot do without "isms" altogether. Among the international trends of twentieth-century art, we find three main currents, each comprising a number of "isms," that began with the Post-Impressionists and have developed greatly since then: Expression, Abstraction, and Fantasy. The first stresses the artist's emotional attitude toward himself and the world; the second, the formal structure of the work of art; and the third explores the realm of the imagination, especially its spontaneous and irrational qualities. But we must not forget that feeling, order, and imagination are all present in *every* work of art: without imagination, it would be deadly dull; without some degree of order, it would be chaotic; without feeling, it would leave us unmoved. These currents, therefore, are not mutually exclusive. We shall find them interrelated in many ways, and the work of one artist may belong to more than one current. Moreover, each current embraces a wide range of approaches, from the realistic to the completely nonrepresentational (or nonobjective). Thus these three currents do not correspond to specific styles, but to general attitudes. The primary concern of the Expressionist is the human community; of the Abstractionist, the structure of reality; and of the artist of Fantasy, the labyrinth of the individual human mind.

The twentieth century may be said, so far as painting is concerned, to have begun five years late. Between 1901 and 1906, several comprehensive exhibitions of the work of Van Gogh, Gauguin, and Cézanne were held in Paris. The young painters who had grown up in the "decadent," morbid mood of the 1890s were profoundly impressed, and some of them developed a radical new style, full of violent color and bold distortions. On their first public appearance, in 1905, they so shocked the critics that they were dubbed the *Fauves* (wild beasts), a label they wore with pride. Actually, it was not a common program that brought them together, but their shared sense of liberation and experiment. Thus Fauvism comprised

a number of loosely related individual styles, and the group dissolved after a few years. Its leading member was Henri Matisse, the oldest of the founding fathers of twentieth-century painting. *Harmony in Red* (colorplate 28) shows what made him so revolutionary an artist: his radical simplicity, his "genius of omission." Everything that possibly can be, has been left out or stated by implication only, yet the scene retains the essentials of plastic form and spatial depth. Painting, Matisse seems to say, is the rhythmic arrangement of line and color on a flat plane, but it is not *only* that; how far can the image of nature be pared down without reducing it to mere surface ornament? Thus he spreads the same blue-on-red pattern on the tablecloth and on the wall, yet he distinguishes the horizontal from the vertical planes with complete assurance. Cézanne had pioneered this integration of the "2-D" and "3-D" aspects of painting (see colorplate 24), but Matisse carries it a great deal further. Equally bold—but perfectly readable—is the view of a garden with flowering trees, seen through the window; the house in the distance is painted

239. GEORGES ROUAULT. *Head of Christ*. 1905. Oil on paper, 45 x 31″. Walter Chrysler Museum, Provincetown

240. CHAIM SOUTINE. *Dead Fowl*. c.1926.
Canvas, 38½ x 24½". The Art Institute of Chicago
(Joseph Winterbotham Collection)

the same bright pink as the interior, and is thereby brought into relation with the rest of the picture. Likewise the blue of the sky, the greens of the foliage, and the bright yellow spots all recur in the foreground. Here, too, Matisse's "genius of omission" is at work: by reducing the number of tints to a minimum, he makes of color an independent structural element. It has such importance that *Harmony in Red* would be meaningless in a black-and-white reproduction.

"What I am after, above all," Matisse once explained, "is expression. . . . [But] expression does not consist of the passion mirrored upon a human face. . . . The whole arrangement of my picture is expressive." Another member of the *Fauves* group, Georges Rouault, would have disagreed. For him, expression still included, as it had in the past, "the passion mirrored upon a human face"; we need only look at his *Head of Christ* (fig. 239). But the expressiveness does not reside only in the "image quality" of this face. The savage, slashing strokes of the brush speak even more elo-

quently of the artist's range and compassion. (If we cover up the upper third of the picture, it is no longer a recognizable image, yet the expressive effect is hardly diminished.) Rouault is the true heir of Van Gogh's and Gauguin's concern for the corrupt state of the world. He, however, hoped for spiritual renewal through a revitalized Catholic faith. His pictures, whatever their subject, are ardent statements of that hope.

Rouault's Expressionism was unique among French painters. The only artist in Paris to follow his lead was Chaim Soutine, an immigrant from Eastern Europe. The tempestuous, violent brushwork in *The Dead Fowl* (fig. 240) clearly reflects the influence of the older master. Although the picture belongs conventionally to the class of still life, the dead bird is a terrifying symbol of death. As we look at the plucked, creamy-white body, we realize with sudden horror its close resemblance to a human shape. It evokes the earthward plunge of Icarus, or it is, perhaps, a cruelly direct image of Plato's definition of Man as a "featherless biped." For his power to transmute sheer anguish into visual form, Soutine has no equal among modern artists.

It was in Germany that Fauvism had its most enduring impact, especially among the members of a society called *Die Brücke* (the bridge), a group of like-minded painters who lived in Dresden in 1905. One *Brücke* artist, Emil Nolde, stands somewhat apart; older than the rest, he shared Rouault's predilection for religious themes, although he was a far less articulate painter. The thickly encrusted surfaces and the deliberately clumsy draftsmanship of his *Last Supper* (fig. 241) make it clear that Nolde rejected all pictorial refinement in favor

241. EMIL NOLDE. *The Last Supper*. 1909.
Canvas, 32½ x 41¾". Stiftung Seebüll Ada und
Emil Nolde, Neukirchen, Germany

of a primeval, direct expression inspired by Gauguin. Another artist of highly individual talent, related to the *Brücke* although not a member of it, is the Austrian painter Oskar Kokoschka. His outstanding works are his portraits painted before World War I, such as his splendid *Self-Portrait* (fig. 242). Like Van Gogh, Kokoschka sees himself as a visionary, a witness to the truth and reality of his inner experiences (see fig. 231); the hypersensitive features seem lacerated by a great ordeal of the imagination. It may not be fanciful to find in this tortured psyche an echo of the cultural climate that also produced Sigmund Freud. A more robust descendant of the *Brücke* artists was Max Beckmann, who did not become an Expressionist until after he had experienced the First World War, which left him with a deep despair at the state of modern civilization. The wings of his triptych, *Departure* (fig. 243), completed when, under Nazi pressure, he was on the point of leaving his homeland, are a nightmarish world crammed with puppet-like figures, as disquieting as Bosch's *Hell* (see fig. 122). Their symbolism, however, is even more difficult to interpret, since it is necessarily subjective, though no one would deny its evocative power. In the hindsight of today, the topsy-turvy quality of these two scenes, full of mutilations and meaningless rituals, seems to

242. OSKAR KOKOSCHKA. *Self-Portrait*. 1913. Canvas, 32 x 19½". The Museum of Modern Art, New York

243. MAX BECKMANN. *Departure*. 1932–35. Canvas; center panel 84¾ x 45⅜", side panels each 84¾ x 39¼". The Museum of Modern Art, New York (Anonymous gift, by exchange)

have the force of prophecy. The stable design of the center panel, in contrast, with its expanse of sea and its sunlit brightness, conveys the hopeful spirit of an escape to distant shores. After living through the Second World War in occupied Holland, under the most trying conditions, Beckmann spent the final three years of his career in America.

But the most daring and original step beyond Fauvism was taken in Germany by a Russian, Wassily Kandinsky, the leading member of a group of artists in Munich called *Der Blaue Reiter* (the blue horseman). After 1910, Kandinsky abandoned representation altogether. Using the rainbow colors and the free, dynamic brushwork of the Paris *Fauves*, he created a completely nonobjective style. These works have titles as abstract as their forms: our example, one of the most striking, is called *Sketch I for "Composition VII"* (colorplate 29). Perhaps we should avoid the term "abstract," which is often taken to mean that the artist has analyzed and simplified the shapes of visible reality (note Cézanne's dictum that all natural forms are based on the cone, the sphere, and the cylinder). This was not the method of Kandinsky. Whatever traces of representation his work contains are quite involuntary—his aim was to charge form and color with a purely spiritual meaning (as he put it) by eliminating all resemblance to the physical world (see p. 283). Whistler, too, had spoken of "divesting his picture from any outside sort of interest"; he even anticipated Kandinsky's use of "musical" titles. But it was the liberating influence of the *Fauves* that permitted Kandinsky to put this theory into practice. The possibility was implicit in Fauvism from the start, as shown in our experiment with Rouault's *Head of Christ*: when the upper third of the picture is covered, the rest becomes a nonobjective composition strangely similar to Kandinsky's. How valid is the analogy between painting and music? When Kandinsky carries it through so strictly, does he really lift his art to another plane of freedom? Or could it be that his declared independence from representation now forces him instead to "represent music," which limits him even more severely? Kandinsky's advocates like to point out that representational painting has a "literary" content, and to deplore such dependence on another art. But why should the "musical" content of nonobjective painting be more desirable? Is painting less alien to music than to literature? The case is difficult to argue, nor does it matter whether this theory is right or wrong; the proof of the pudding is in the eating, not the recipe. Kandinsky's—or any other artist's—ideas are important to us only if we are convinced of the importance of his pictures. Did he create a viable style? Admittedly, his work demands an intuitive response that may be hard for some of us, yet the painting here reproduced has density and vitality, and a radiant freshness of feeling that impresses us even though we are uncertain what exactly the artist has expressed.

The second of our main currents is the one we called Abstraction. Literally, to abstract means to draw away from, to separate. If we have ten apples, and then separate the ten from the apples, we get an "abstract number," a number that no longer refers to particular things. But "apples," too, is an abstraction, since it places ten apples in one class, without regard for their individual qualities. The artist who sets out to paint ten apples will find no two of them alike, yet he cannot possibly take account of all their differences: even the most painstaking portrayal of these particular pieces of fruit is bound to be some sort of an abstraction. Abstraction, then, goes into the making of *any* work of art, whether the artist knows it or not. The process was not conscious and controlled, however, until the Renaissance, when artists first analyzed the shapes of nature in terms of mathematical bodies (see p. 105). Cézanne and Seurat revitalized this approach and explored it further; they are the direct ancestors of the abstract movement in twentieth-century art. Its real creator, however, was Pablo Picasso.

About 1905, stimulated both by the *Fauves* and by the great Post-Impressionists, Picasso gradually abandoned the melancholy lyricism of his Blue Period for a more robust style. He shared Matisse's enthusiasm for Gauguin and Cézanne, but he viewed these masters very differently; in 1906–7, he produced a monumental canvas (fig. 244) so challenging that it outraged even Matisse. The title, *Les Demoiselles d'Avignon* ("The Girls of Avignon"), refers not to the town of that name but to Avignon Street in a notorious section of Barcelona; when Picasso started the picture, it was to be a temptation scene, but he ended up with a composition of five nudes and a still life. But what nudes! The three on the left are angular distortions of classical figures, while the violently dislocated features and bodies of the other two have all the barbaric qualities of primitive art (see figs. 6, 7). Following Gauguin, the *Fauves* had discovered the aesthetic appeal of African and Oceanic sculpture, yet it was Picasso, rather than they, who used primitive art

Colorplate 24. PAUL CEZANNE. *Fruit Bowl, Glass, and Apples.* 1879–82. Canvas, 18 x 21½".
Collection Mr. and Mrs. René Lecomte, Paris

Colorplate 25. GEORGES SEURAT. *A Sunday Afternoon on the Grande Jatte.* 1884–86. Canvas, 6′ 9″ x 10′.
The Art Institute of Chicago (Helen Birch Bartlett Memorial Collection)

Colorplate 26. VINCENT VAN GOGH. *Wheat Field and Cypress Trees*. 1889. Canvas, 28½ x 36″.
The National Gallery, London (reproduced by courtesy of the Trustees)

Colorplate 27. PAUL GAUGUIN. *The Yellow Christ*. 1889.
Canvas, 36⅜ x 28¾". Albright-Knox Art Gallery, Buffalo, New York

Colorplate 28. HENRI MATISSE. *Harmony in Red (Red Room).* 1908–9.
Canvas, 71¼ x 96⅞″. The Hermitage Museum, Leningrad

Colorplate 29. WASSILY KANDINSKY. *Sketch I for "Composition VII."*
1913. Canvas, 30¾ x 39⅜". Collection Felix Klee, Bern

Colorplate 30. PIET MONDRIAN. *Composition with Red, Blue, and Yellow*. 1930.
Canvas, 20 x 20″. Collection Mr. and Mrs. Armand P. Bartos, New York

Colorplate 31. JACKSON POLLOCK. Detail of *One* (*#31, 1950*). 1950. Canvas.
The Museum of Modern Art, New York (Gift of Sidney Janis)

244. PABLO PICASSO. *Les Demoiselles d'Avignon*. 1906–7.
Canvas, 96 x 92″. The Museum of Modern Art, New York
(Acquired through the Lillie P. Bliss Bequest)

245. PABLO PICASSO. *Ambroise Vollard*.
1909–10. Canvas, 36 x 25½″.
Pushkin Museum, Moscow

as a battering ram against the classical conception of beauty (see also p. 284). Not only the
proportions, but the organic integrity and continuity of the human body are denied here, so
that the canvas (in the apt words of one critic)
"resembles a field of broken glass." Picasso,
then, has destroyed a great deal; what has he
gained in the process? Once we recover from
the initial shock, we begin to see that the destruction is quite methodical: everything—the
figures as well as their setting—is broken up
into angular facets. These, we will note, are not
flat, but shaded in a way that gives them a certain three-dimensionality. We cannot always be
sure whether they are concave or convex; some
look like chunks of solidified space, others like
fragments of translucent bodies. They constitute a unique kind of matter, which imposes a
new kind of integrity and continuity on the entire canvas. Unlike Matisse's *Harmony in Red*,
the *Demoiselles* can no longer be read as an
image of the external world; its world is its
own, analogous to nature but built along different principles. Picasso's revolutionary "building material," compounded of voids and solids,
is hard to describe. The early critics, who saw
only the prevalence of sharp edges and angles,
dubbed the new style Cubism.

That the *Demoiselles* owes anything to Cézanne may seem hard to believe. Nevertheless,
Picasso had studied Cézanne's late work with

care (see fig. 230), finding in its abstract treatment of volume and space the translucent
structural units from which he derived the facets of Cubism. The link is clearer in Picasso's
portrait of Ambroise Vollard (fig. 245),
painted four years later: the facets are now
small and precise, more like prisms, and the
canvas has the balance and refinement of a
fully mature style. Contrasts of color and texture are reduced to a minimum, so as not to
compete with the design. And the structure has
become so intricate a web that it would seem
wholly cerebral if the "imprismed" sitter's face
did not emerge with such dramatic force. Cubism here has become an abstract style within
the purely Western sense, as against the "barbaric" distortions of the *Demoiselles*. But its
distance from observed reality has not significantly increased—Picasso may be playing an
elaborate game of hide-and-seek with nature,
but he still needs it to challenge his creative
powers. The nonobjective realm held no appeal
for him, then or later.

By 1910, Cubism was well established as an
alternative to Fauvism, and Picasso had been
joined by other artists, notably Georges
Braque, with whom he collaborated so intimately that their work at that time is hard to
tell apart. Both of them initiated the next phase
of Cubism, which was even bolder than the
first, as evidenced by Braque's *Le Courrier* of

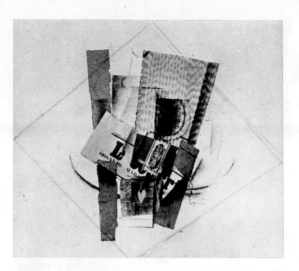

246. GEORGES BRAQUE. *Le Courrier*. 1913. Collage, 20 x 22½". Philadelphia Museum of Art (Gallatin Collection)

1913 (fig. 246). It is composed almost entirely of cut-and-pasted scraps of material, with only a few lines added to complete the design; we recognize strips of imitation wood graining, part of a tobacco wrapper with a contrasting stamp, half the masthead of a newspaper, and a bit of newsprint made into a playing card (the ace of hearts). This technique came to be known as *collage* (French for "paste-up"). Why did Picasso and Braque suddenly prefer the contents of the wastepaper basket to brush and paint? Because they had come to think of the picture surface as a sort of tray on which to "serve" the still life to the beholder, and they found the best way to explore this new concept was to put real things on the tray. The ingredients of a collage actually play a double role; they have been shaped and combined, then drawn or painted upon so as to give them a representational meaning, but they retain their original identity as scraps of material. Thus their function is both to *represent* (to be part of an image) and to *present* (to be themselves). In the latter role, they endow a collage with a self-sufficiency that no facet-Cubist picture could have. A tray, after all, is a self-contained area, detached from the rest of the physical world; unlike a painting, it cannot show more than is actually on it. The difference between the two phases of Cubism may also be defined in terms of picture space: facet Cubism retains a certain kind of depth, the painted surface acts as a window through which we still perceive remnants of the familiar perspective space of the Renaissance. This space lies behind the picture plane and has no visible limits; it may contain objects that are hidden from our view. In collage Cubism, on the contrary, the picture space lies in front of the plane of the "tray"; space is created not by illusionistic devices, such as modeling or foreshortening, but by the actual overlapping of layers of pasted materials. Collage Cubism, then, offers a basically new space concept, the first since Masaccio: it is a true landmark in the history of painting.

By now, Picasso was internationally famous. Cubism had spread throughout the Western world: it influenced not only painters, but sculptors and even architects. Picasso himself, however, was already striking out in a new direction. By 1920, he was working simultaneously in two separate styles: collage Cubism and a Neoclassic style of strongly modeled, heavy-bodied figures such as his *Mother and Child* (fig. 247). To many, this seemed a kind of betrayal, but in retrospect the cause of Picasso's double-track performance is evident: chafing under the limitations of collage Cubism, he needed to resume contact with the classical tradition, the "art of the museums." The figures in *Mother and Child* have a mock-monumental quality that suggests colossal statues rather than flesh-and-blood human beings, yet the theme is

247. PABLO PICASSO. *Mother and Child*. 1921–22. Canvas, 38 x 28". Collection the Alex L. Hillman Corp.

treated with surprising tenderness. The forms, however, are carefully dovetailed within the frame, not unlike the way a collage is put together. A few years later the two tracks of Picasso's style began to converge, making an extraordinary synthesis that has been the basis of his art ever since. The *Three Dancers* of 1925 (fig. 248) shows how he managed this seemingly impossible feat. Structurally, the picture is pure collage Cubism, even though, instead of cutting and pasting, the artist has imitated the appearance of collage with his brush; the canvas even shows painted imitations of specific materials—patterned wallpaper, and samples of various fabrics cut out with pinking shears. But the figures, a wildly fantastic version of a classical dance, are an even more violent assault on convention than the *Demoiselles d'Avignon* (fig. 244). Human anatomy is here simply the raw material for Picasso's incredibly fertile inventiveness; limbs, breasts, and faces are handled with the same sovereign freedom as the fragments of external reality in Braque's *Le Courrier*. Their original identity no longer matters—breasts may turn into eyes, profiles merge with frontal views, shadows become substance, and vice versa, in an endless flow of transformations. They are "visual puns," offering wholly unexpected possibilities of expression—humorous, grotesque, macabre, even tragic.

As originally conceived by Picasso and Braque, Cubism offered a formal discipline of subtle balance, used for traditional subjects—still life, portraiture, the nude. Other painters, however, saw in the new style a special affinity with the geometric precision of engineering that made it uniquely attuned to the dynamism of modern times. The short-lived Futurist movement in Italy exemplifies this attitude; in 1910 its founders issued a manifesto violently rejecting the past and exalting the beauty of the machine. Their output was more original in sculpture than in painting (see fig. 262). Strong echoes of Futurism appear in *Brooklyn Bridge* (fig. 249), by the Italo-American Joseph Stella; with its maze of luminescent cables, vigorous diagonal thrusts, and crystalline "cells" of space, it conjures up a vision of mechanized utopia. The most radical extension of Cubism, however, may be found in the work of a Dutch painter nine years older than Picasso, Piet Mondrian. He came to Paris in 1912 as a mature Expressionist in the tradition of Van Gogh and the *Fauves*. Under the impact of Cubism, his ideas underwent a complete change, and within the following decade he developed a

248. PABLO PICASSO. *Three Dancers*. 1925. Canvas, 84½ x 56½". Collection the Artist

249. JOSEPH STELLA. *Brooklyn Bridge*. 1917. Canvas, 84 x 76". Yale University Art Gallery, New Haven (Collection of the Société Anonyme)

totally nonobjective style that he called Neo-Plasticism. *Composition with Red, Blue, and Yellow* (colorplate 30) shows Mondrian's style at its most severe: he restricts his design to horizontals and verticals and his colors to the three primary hues, plus black and white, thus eliminating every possibility of representation. Yet Mondrian sometimes gave his works such titles as *Trafalgar Square* or *Broadway Boogie-Woogie*, which hint at some degree of relationship with observed reality. Unlike Kandinsky, Mondrian did not strive for pure, lyrical emotion; his goal, he asserted, was "pure reality," and he defined this as equilibrium "through the balance of unequal but equivalent oppositions." Perhaps we can best understand what he meant if we think of his work as "abstract collage" that uses black bands and colored rectangles, instead of recognizable fragments of everyday materials. He was interested only in relationships, and wanted no distracting elements or fortuitous associations. But, by establishing the "right" relationship among his bands and rectangles, he transforms them as thoroughly as Braque transformed the snippets of pasted paper in *Le Courrier* (fig. 246). How did he go about discovering the "right" relationship? And how did he determine the shape and number of the bands and rectangles? In *Le Courrier*, the ingredients are to some extent "given" by chance; Mondrian, apart from his self-imposed rules, constantly faced the dilemma of unlimited possibilities. He could not change the relationship of the bands to the rectangles without changing the bands and rectangles themselves. When we consider his task, we begin to realize its infinite complexity. If we measure the various units in *Composition with Red, Blue, and Yellow*, we find that only the proportions of the canvas itself are truly rational, an exact square; Mondrian arrived at all the rest "by feel," and must have undergone agonies of trial and error. Strange as it may seem, Mondrian's exquisite sense of nonsymmetrical balance is so specific that critics well acquainted with his work have no difficulty telling fakes from genuine pictures. Designers who work with nonfigurative shapes, such as architects and typographers, are most likely to be sensitive to this quality, and Mondrian has had a greater influence among them than among painters (see figs. 270–72).

The third current, which we termed Fantasy, follows a course less clear-cut than the other two, since it depends on a state of mind more than on any particular style. The one thing all painters of fantasy have in common is the belief that imagination is more important than the outside world. And since every artist's imagination is his own private domain, the images it provides for him are likely to be equally private, unless he subjects them to a deliberate process of selection. But how can such "uncontrolled" images have meaning to the beholder, whose own inner world is not the same as the artist's? Psychoanalysis has taught us that we are not so different from each other in this respect as we like to think. Our minds are all built on the same basic pattern, and the same is true of our imagination and memory. They belong to the unconscious part of the mind where experiences are stored, whether we want to remember them or not. At night, or whenever conscious thought relaxes its vigilance, our experiences come back to us and we seem to live through them again. However, the unconscious mind does not usually reproduce our experiences as they actually happened. They will often be admitted into the conscious part of the mind in the guise of "dream images"—in this form they seem less vivid, and we can live with our memories more easily. This digesting of experience is surprisingly alike in all of us, although the process works better with some individuals than with others.

250. GIORGIO DE CHIRICO. *Mystery and Melancholy of a Street*. 1914. Canvas, 34¼ x 28⅛".
Collection Mr. and Mrs. Stanley R. Resor, New Canaan

Hence we are always interested in imaginary things, provided they are presented to us in such a way that they seem real. What happens in a fairy tale, for example, would be very dull in the matter-of-fact language of a news report, but when it is told to us as it should be told, we are enchanted. The same is true of paintings—we recall *The Sleeping Gypsy* by Henri Rousseau (fig. 236). But why does private fantasy loom so large in present-day art? There seem to be several interlocking causes: first, the cleavage that developed between reason and imagination in the wake of rationalism, which tended to dissolve the heritage of myth and legend that had been the common channel of private fantasy in earlier times; second, the artist's greater freedom—and insecurity—within the social fabric, giving him a sense of isolation and favoring an introspective attitude; and, finally, the Romantic cult of emotion that prompted the artist to seek out subjective experience, and to accept its validity. In nineteenth-century art, private fantasy was still a minor current. After 1900, it became a major one.

The heritage of Romanticism can be seen most clearly in the astonishing pictures painted in Paris just before World War I by Giorgio de Chirico, such as *Mystery and Melancholy of a Street* (fig. 250). This large and deserted square with its endless receding arcades, illuminated by the cold light of the full moon, has all the poetry of Romantic reverie. But it has also a strangely sinister air; it is "ominous" in the full sense of that term—everything suggests an omen, a portent of unknown and disquieting significance. De Chirico himself could not explain the incongruities in these paintings—the empty furniture van, the girl with the hoop—that trouble and fascinate us. Later on he adopted a conservative style and repudiated his early work, as if he were embarrassed at having put his dream world on public display. The power of nostalgia, so evident in *Mystery and Melancholy of a Street*, also dominates the fantasies of Marc Chagall, a Russian Jew who came to Paris in 1910. *I and the Village* (fig. 251) is a Cubist fairy tale that weaves dreamlike memories of Russian folk tales, Jewish proverbs, and the Russian countryside into one glowing vision. Here, as in many later works, Chagall relives the experiences of his childhood; they were so important to him that his imagination shaped and reshaped them for years without diminishing their persistence.

The "fairy tales" of the German-Swiss painter Paul Klee are more purposeful and controlled than Chagall's, although at first they

251. MARC CHAGALL. *I and the Village.* 1911. Canvas, 75½ x 59½". The Museum of Modern Art, New York (Mrs. Simon Guggenheim Fund)

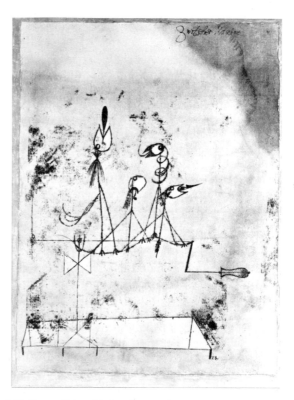

252. PAUL KLEE. *Twittering Machine.* 1922. Watercolor, ink, 16¼ x 12". The Museum of Modern Art, New York

253. MARCEL DUCHAMP. *The Bride*. 1912.
Canvas, 34¾ x 21½″. The Philadelphia Museum of Art
(Louise and Walter Arensberg Collection)

254. MAX ERNST. *1 Copper Plate 1 Zinc Plate 1 Rubber
Cloth 2 Calipers 1 Drainpipe Telescope, 1 Piping Man*.
1920. Collage, 12 x 9″. Succession Arp, Meudon, France

may strike us as more childlike. Klee, too, had
been influenced by Cubism; but primitive art,
and the drawings of small children, held an
equally vital interest for him. During the First
World War, he molded from these disparate
elements a pictorial language of his own, marvelously economical and precise. *Twittering
Machine* (fig. 252), a delicate pen drawing
tinted with water color, demonstrates the
unique flavor of Klee's art; with a few simple
lines, he has created a ghostly mechanism that
imitates the sound of birds, mocking our faith
in the miracles of the machine age as well as
our sentimental appreciation of bird song. The
little contraption (which is not without its sinister aspect—the heads of the four sham birds
look like fishermen's lures, as if they might en-
trap real birds) thus condenses into one striking invention a complex of ideas about present-
day civilization. The title has an indispensable
role; it is characteristic of the way Klee works
that the picture itself, however visually appealing, does not reveal its full evocative quality unless the artist tells us what it means.
The title, in turn, needs the picture—the witty

concept of a twittering machine does not kindle
our imagination until we are shown such a
thing. This interdependence is familiar to us
from cartoons. Klee lifts it to the level of high
art, yet retains the playful character of these
visual-verbal puns. To him art was a "language
of signs," of shapes that are images of ideas as
the shape of a letter is the image of a specific
sound, or an arrow the image of the command,
"This way only." But conventional signs are no
more than "triggers"; the instant we perceive
them, we automatically invest them with their
meaning, without stopping to ponder their
shape. Klee wanted *his* signs to impinge upon
our awareness as visual facts, yet also to share
the quality of "triggers."

In Paris, on the eve of World War I, we encounter still another painter of fantasy, the
Frenchman Marcel Duchamp. After basing
his early style on Cézanne, he had initiated a
dynamic version of facet Cubism, similar to
Futurism, by superimposing successive phases
of movement on each other, as in multiple-ex-
posure photography. Almost immediately,
however, Duchamp's art took a far more dis-

turbing turn. In *The Bride* (fig. 253) we will look in vain for any resemblance to the human form; what we see is a mechanism—part motor, part distilling apparatus; the antithesis of Klee's twittering machine, it is beautifully engineered to serve no purpose whatever. Its title causes us real perplexity (Duchamp has emphasized its importance by lettering it right onto the canvas). Did he intend to satirize the scientific view of man, by "analyzing" the bride until she is reduced to a complicated piece of plumbing? If so, the picture may be the negative counterpart of that glorification of the machine so stridently proclaimed by the Futurists.

It is hardly surprising that the organized mass killing during World War I should have driven Duchamp to despair. With a number of others who shared his attitude, he launched in protest a movement called Dada (or Dadaism). The term, French for "hobbyhorse," was reportedly picked at random from a dictionary, but as an infantile "all-purpose word" it perfectly fitted the spirit of the movement. Dada has often been called nihilistic, and its declared purpose was indeed to make clear to the public that all established values, moral or aesthetic, had been rendered meaningless by the catastrophe of World War I. During its short life from 1916 to 1922, Dada preached non-sense and anti-art with a vengeance. Duchamp put his signature, and a provocative title, on ready-made objects such as bottle racks and snow shovels, exhibiting them as works of art. Not even modern art was safe from the Dadaists' assaults; one of them exhibited a toy monkey inside a frame, entitled *Portrait of Cézanne*. On the other hand, they adopted the technique of collage Cubism for their own purposes: figure 254, by the German Dadaist Max Ernst, an associate of Duchamp, is largely composed of cuttings from illustrations of machinery. The caption pretends to enumerate these ingredients, which include "1 piping man." Actually there are two figures made of piping, who stare at us blindly through their goggles, the one on the left a postwar version of Duchamp's *Bride*.

Yet Dada was not completely negative. In its calculated irrationality there was also liberation, a voyage to unknown provinces of the creative mind. The only law respected by the Dadaists was that of chance, and the only reality that of their own imaginations. This is the message of Duchamp's Ready-Mades, which the artist created simply by shifting their context from the utilitarian to the aesthetic. Certainly they are extreme demonstrations of a

principle. But the very principle—that artistic creation does not depend on manual craftsmanship—is an important discovery. Duchamp himself, having made this point, soon withdrew from artistic activity altogether; some of his fellow "chance-takers" founded, in 1924, Dada's successor, Surrealism. They defined their aim as "pure psychic automatism . . . intended to express . . . the true process of thought . . . free from the exercise of reason and from any aesthetic or moral purpose." Surrealist theory is heavily larded with concepts borrowed from psychoanalysis, and its overwrought rhetoric is not always to be taken seriously. The notion that a dream can be transposed directly from the unconscious mind to the canvas, bypassing the conscious awareness of the artist, did not work out in practice; some degree of control was simply unavoidable. Nevertheless, Surrealism stimulated several novel techniques for soliciting and exploiting chance effects. Max Ernst, the most inventive member of the group, often combined collage with "frottage" (rubbings from pieces of wood, pressed flowers, etc. —the process we all know from the children's pastime of rubbing with a pencil on a piece of paper covering a coin). In *Totem and Taboo* (fig. 255) he has obtained fascinating shapes and textures by "decalcomania" (the transfer, by pressure, of wet paint to the canvas from some other surface). This procedure is in essence akin to those recommended by Cozens and Leonardo (see p. 166), and Ernst has certainly found and elaborated upon an extraordinary wealth of images among his stains. The end result does have some of the qualities of a

255. MAX ERNST. *Totem and Taboo*. 1941. Canvas, 28 x 36". Collection William N. Copley, New York

dream, but it is a dream born of a strikingly Romantic imagination.

Surrealism, however, has a more vigorously imaginative branch: such works by Picasso as the *Three Dancers* (fig. 248) have affinities with it, and its greatest exponent is another Spaniard, Joan Miró, who painted the striking *Composition* (fig. 256). His style has been labeled "biomorphic abstraction," since his designs are fluid and curvilinear rather than geometric. "Biomorphic concretion" might be a more suitable name, for the shapes in Miró's pictures have their own vigorous life. They seem to change before our eyes, expanding and contracting like amoebas until they approach human individuality closely enough to please the artist. Their spontaneous "becoming" is the very opposite of abstraction, although Miró's formal discipline is no less rigorous than that of Cubism (he began as a Cubist).

Equally misleading is the term Abstract Expressionism, often applied to the style of painting that was dominant on both sides of the Atlantic during the 1950s. One of its originators, the American Jackson Pollock, did the huge picture entitled *One* (fig. 257) mainly by

pouring and spattering his colors instead of applying them with the brush. The result, especially when viewed at close range (colorplate 31), suggests both Kandinsky and Max Ernst. Kandinsky's nonobjective Expressionism, and the Surrealists' exploitation of chance effects, are indeed the main sources of Pollock's work, but they do not sufficiently account for his revolutionary technique and the emotional appeal of his art. Why did Pollock "fling a pot of paint in the public's face" (as Ruskin accused Whistler of doing)? Not, surely, to be more abstract than his predecessors, for the strict control implied by abstraction is just what Pollock gave up when he began to dribble and spatter. A more plausible explanation is that he came to regard paint itself not as a passive substance to be manipulated at will but as a storehouse of pent-up forces for him to release. The actual shapes visible in our colorplate are largely determined by the internal dynamics of his material and his process: the viscosity of the paint, the speed and direction of its impact upon the canvas, its interaction with other layers of pigment. The result is a surface so alive, so sensuously rich, that all earlier painting looks pallid by comparison. But when he releases the forces within the paint by giving it a momentum of its own—or, if you will, by "aiming" it at the canvas instead of "carrying" it on the tip of his brush—Pollock does not simply "let go" and leave the rest to chance. He is himself the ultimate source of energy for these forces, and he "rides" them as a cowboy might ride a wild horse, in a frenzy of psychophysical action. He does not always stay in the saddle, yet the exhilaration of this contest, which strains every fiber of his being, is well worth the risk. Our simile, though crude, points up the main difference between Pollock and his predecessors: his total commitment to the *act* of painting. Hence

above: 256. JOAN MIRO.
Composition. 1933. Canvas,
51¼ x 63½ ". Wadsworth Atheneum,
Hartford

right: 257. JACKSON POLLOCK.
One (#*31, 1950*). 1950. Canvas,
8' 10" x 17' 5½"
(see detail, colorplate 31).
The Museum of Modern Art,
New York (Gift of Sidney Janis)

258. ROY LICHTENSTEIN.
Girl at Piano. 1963. Canvas, 68 x 48″.
Private collection, New York

his preference for huge canvases that provide a "field of combat" large enough for him to paint not merely with his arms but with the motion of his whole body. "Action Painting," the term coined some years ago for this style, conveys its essence far better than does Abstract Expressionism.

If Pollock represents the avant-garde of the 1950s, that of the 1960s is a movement called "Pop Art." The term, coined in analogy to "pop music" (popular music as against highbrow music), also suggests the "pop" in popgun. It reminds us of "dada," and thus provides a clue to our understanding of the nature of the movement, for Pop Art has borrowed many of the "outrageous" tricks of Dadaism. It, too, is "anti-art," if by art we understand Abstraction and Expression, but the savage satire of Dada is missing in Pop. Rather, Pop Art is an attempt to rehabilitate representation; what might be called lowbrow art—photography, magazine illustrations, advertisements, comic strips, picture postcards—had of course remained strictly representational all along, unaffected by the "Manet Revolution" and its consequences. For the Pop artist, this meant that representation was the very essence of art,

that to eliminate it might lead to the death of art by starvation. The Abstractionist, to them, was like the man who said he had been teaching his horse not to eat, and just as he was on the point of success, the fool creature died. But the Pop artists were sophisticated enough to realize that the "how" of representation no longer could be a challenge to anybody; its problems had all been solved long ago. What fascinated them were the purposes of representation, and how representation was determined both by its "message" and by the reproduction techniques that fed the insatiable image-hunger of the man in the street. Figure 258, by Roy Lichtenstein, shows one frame from a comic strip, painstakingly reproduced by hand on a huge scale, including every single dot of the screen pattern in which colors are printed by newspaper presses. Here is a painting that claims importance by its large size and yet makes it impossible for us to analyze it in terms of any of those values of form and color which the "Manet Revolution" has trained us to expect. At the same time—and this is perhaps its greatest challenge—it absolutely resists reproduction, and thereby proclaims its uniqueness. Unlike all the other illustrations in this book, Lichtenstein's work when reproduced on a book page simply reverts to being a comic strip frame, and thus gives us no clue to what the artist has actually done to his model. Paradoxes of this kind abound in Pop Art, implying basic questions not only about the nature of art but about the nature of thought. Whatever the ultimate results of the movement, they are likely to have a profound effect upon the future course of art.

The three currents we have traced in painting may be found also in sculpture. The parallelism, however, should not be overstressed. While painting has been the richer and more adventurous of the two arts, its leadership has not remained unchallenged, and sculpture has often followed its own path. Tendencies equivalent to Post-Impressionism do not appear in sculpture until about 1900. Sculptors of a younger generation had by then been trained under the dominant influence of Rodin, and were ready to strike out for themselves. The finest of these, Aristide Maillol, began as a Symbolist painter, although he did not share Gauguin's anti-Greek attitude. Maillol might be called a "classic primitivist"; admiring the simplified strength of early Greek sculpture, he rejected its later phases. The *Seated Woman* (fig. 259) evokes memories of the Archaic style (see figs.

259. ARISTIDE MAILLOL. *Seated Woman (Méditerranée)*. c.1901. Marble, height 41″. Collection Dr. Oskar Reinhart, Winterthur, Switzerland

24, 26) rather than of Phidias and Praxiteles. The clearly defined volumes also recall Cézanne's statement that all natural forms are based on the cone, the sphere, and the cylinder. But the most notable quality of the figure is its harmonious, self-contained repose. A statue, Maillol thought, must above all be "static," structurally balanced like a piece of

architecture; it must represent a state of being that is detached from the stress of circumstance, with none of the restless, thrusting energy of Rodin's work. In this respect, the *Seated Woman* is the exact opposite of *The Thinker* (see fig. 237). Maillol later called it *Méditerranée*—the Mediterranean—to suggest the source from which he drew the timeless serenity of the figure.

Expressionism was a far less important current in sculpture than in painting—rather surprisingly, since the rediscovery of primitive sculpture by the *Fauves* might have been expected to evoke a strong response among sculptors. Only one important sculptor shared in this rediscovery: Constantin Brancusi, a Rumanian who came to Paris in 1904. But he was more interested in the formal simplicity and coherence of primitive carvings than in their savage expressiveness. This is evident in *The Kiss*, executed in 1908 as a funerary monument for Montparnasse Cemetery in Paris (figure 260 is a small version of the work). The compactness and self-sufficiency of this group is a radical step beyond Maillol's *Seated Woman*, to which it is related much as are the *Fauves* to Post-Impressionism. Brancusi has a "genius of omission" not unlike Matisse's; to

right:
260. CONSTANTIN BRANCUSI.
The Kiss. 1908. Stone,
height 22¾″.
The Philadelphia Museum of Art
(Louise and Walter
Arensberg Collection)

far right:
261. CONSTANTIN BRANCUSI.
Bird in Space. 1919. Bronze,
height 54″. The Museum
of Modern Art,
New York (Anonymous gift)

262. UMBERTO BOCCIONI. *Unique Forms of Continuity in Space*. 1913. Bronze, height 43½". The Museum of Modern Art, New York (Lillie P. Bliss Bequest)

him, a monument is an upright slab, symmetrical and immobile, and he disturbs this basic shape as little as possible. The embracing lovers are differentiated just enough to be separately identifiable; they seem more primeval than primitive, a timeless symbol of generation, innocent and anonymous.

About 1910, Brancusi began to produce nonrepresentational pieces in marble or metal, reserving his "primeval style" for wood and stone. The former fall into two groups: variations on the egg shape, with such titles as *The Beginning of the World*; and soaring vertical "bird" motifs (*Bird in Space*, figure 261, is an example). Because he concentrated on two forms that have such uncompromising simplicity, Brancusi has at times been called the Mondrian of sculpture; the comparison is misleading, however, for Brancusi strove for essences, not relationships. He was fascinated by the antithesis of life as potential and as kinetic energy—the self-contained perfection of the egg, which hides the mystery of all creation, and the pure dynamics of the creature released from this shell. *Bird in Space* is not the abstract image of a bird; rather, it is flight itself, made visible and concrete. Its disembodied quality is emphasized by the high polish that gives the surface the transparency of a mirror and thus establishes a new continuity between the molded space

within and the free space without. Other sculptors at that time were tackling the problem of body-space relationships with the formal tools of Cubism. The running figure entitled *Unique Forms of Continuity in Space* (fig. 262), by the Futurist Umberto Boccioni, is as breath-taking in its complexity as *Bird in Space* is simple. Boccioni has tried to represent not the human form itself but the imprint of its motion upon the medium in which it moves; the figure remains concealed behind its "garment" of aerial turbulence. The statue recalls the famous Futurist statement that "the automobile at full speed is more beautiful than the Winged Victory," although it obviously owes more to the Winged Victory (fig. 35) than to the design of motor cars (in 1913, streamlining was still to come). Raymond Duchamp-Villon, an elder brother of Marcel Duchamp, achieved a bolder solution in *The Great Horse* (fig. 263). He began with abstract studies of the animal, but his final version is an image of "horsepower," where the body has become a coiled spring and the legs resemble piston rods. Because of their very remoteness from their anatomical model, these quasi-mechanical shapes have a dynamism that is more persuasive—if less picturesque—than that of Boccioni's figure.

Dada uncompromisingly rejected formal discipline in sculpture, as it did in the other arts

263. RAYMOND DUCHAMP-VILLON. *The Great Horse*. 1914. Bronze, height 39⅜". The Art Institute of Chicago (Gift of Miss Margaret Fisher)

—perhaps even more, since only objects in three dimensions could become Ready-Mades, the sculpture of Dada. Duchamp's examples consist in part of combinations of found objects; these "assisted" Ready-Mades approach the status of constructions, or three-dimensional collage. This technique, recently baptized "assemblage," has proved to have unlimited possibilities. It was taken up by Picasso, whose *Bull's Head* (fig. 264) is made up of the seat and handlebars of a bicycle; and numerous younger sculptors have explored it since World War II, especially in junk-ridden America. The Surrealist contribution to sculpture is harder to define: it was difficult to apply the theory of "pure psychic automatism" to painting, but still harder to live up to it in sculpture. How indeed could solid, durable materials be given shape without the sculptor being consciously aware of the process? Thus, apart from the devotees of the Ready-Made, few sculptors were associated with the movement. One of these was Alberto Giacometti, a Swiss sculptor and painter working in Paris. *The Palace at 4 A.M.* (fig. 265), an airy cage made of wood, glass, wire, and string, is the three-dimensional equivalent of a Surrealist picture; unlike earlier pieces of sculpture, it creates its own spatial environment that clings to it as though this eerie miniature world were protected from everyday reality by an invisible glass bell. The space thus trapped is mysterious and corrosive; it gnaws away at the forms until only their skeletons are left. Even they, we feel, will disappear before long. Surrealism may also have contributed to the astonishing sculptural imagination of Julio Gonzalez,

a wrought-iron craftsman from Catalonia who had come to Paris in 1900. Although he was a friend of Brancusi and Picasso, he produced no work of any consequence until the 1930s, when his creative energies suddenly came into focus. It was he who established wrought iron as an important medium for sculpture, taking advantage of the very difficulties that had discouraged its use before. The *Head* (fig. 266) combines extreme economy of form with an aggressive reinterpretation of anatomy that is derived from Picasso (see fig. 248, especially the head of the dancer on the left): the mouth is an oval cavity with spikelike teeth, the eyes two rods that converge upon an "optic nerve" linking them to the tangled mass of the "brain." Similar gruesomely expressive metaphors have since been created by a whole generation of younger sculptors, in wrought iron and welded steel, as if the violence of their working process mirrored the violence of modern life.

The early 1930s, which brought Giacometti and Gonzalez to the fore, produced another important development, the mobile sculpture —mobiles, for short—of the American Alexander Calder. These are delicately balanced constructions of metal wire, hinged together and weighted so as to move with the slightest breath of air. They may be of any size, from tiny tabletop models to the huge *Lobster Trap and Fish Tail* (fig. 267). At first, Calder had made motor-driven mobiles. It was his contact with Surrealism that made him realize the poetic possibilities of "natural" as against fully controlled movement; he borrowed biomorphic

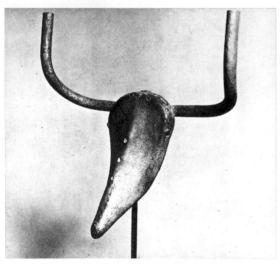

264. PABLO PICASSO. *Bull's Head.* 1943.
Handlebars and seat of a bicycle, height 16⅛".
Galerie Louise Leiris, Paris

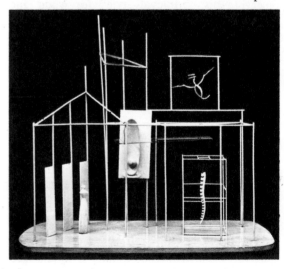

265. ALBERTO GIACOMETTI. *The Palace at 4 A.M.*
1932–33. Wood, wire, glass, and string, height 25".
The Museum of Modern Art, New York (Purchase)

266. JULIO GONZALEZ. *Head.*
c.1935. Wrought iron, height 17¾".
The Museum of Modern Art (Purchase)

267. ALEXANDER CALDER. *Lobster Trap and Fish Tail*
1939. Wire and aluminum, c. 8½ x 9½'. The Museum
of Modern Art, New York (Gift of Advisory Committee)

shapes from Miró, and began to think of mobiles as similes of organic structures—flowers on swaying stems, foliage quivering in the breeze, marine animals floating in the sea. Such mobiles are infinitely responsive to their environment. Unpredictable and ever-changing, they incorporate the fourth dimension, time, as an essential element of their structure. Within their limited sphere, they are more truly alive than any other man-made thing.

For more than a century, from the mid-eighteenth to the late nineteenth, architecture had been dominated by a succession of "revival styles" (see p. 162). The use of this term, we will recall, does not imply that earlier forms were slavishly copied; the best work of the time has both individuality and high distinction. Yet the architectural wisdom of the past, however freely interpreted, proved in the long run to be inadequate for the needs of the present. The authority of historical modes had to be broken if the industrial era was to produce a truly contemporary style. The search for such a style—the analogue of Manet's achievement in painting—began in earnest about 1880. It demanded more than a reform of architectural grammar and vocabulary: to take full advantage of the expressive—not merely the utilitarian—qualities of the new building techniques and materials that the engineer had placed at

his disposal, the architect needed a new philosophy. He had to redefine the traditional concepts regarding form and function, as well as the broader role of architecture in society. The leaders of modern architecture have characteristically been vigorous and articulate thinkers, in whose minds architectural theory is closely linked with ideas of social reform. It is equally significant that the movement began in commercial architecture (stores, offices, apartments), outside the range of traditional building types; that its symbol was the skyscraper; and that its birthplace was Chicago, then a burgeoning metropolis not yet encumbered by any firm allegiance to the styles of the past.

Chicago was the home of Louis Sullivan, the first indisputably modern architect. His achievements are summed up in the department store of Carson Pirie Scott & Company (fig. 268), which he designed shortly before the turn of the century. If it is not a skyscraper by present-day standards, it is at least a potential one, for its structural skeleton, a steel frame, embodies the same principle on which the much taller skyscrapers of today are built. The Carson Pirie Scott store also illustrates Sullivan's dictum that "form follows function." The external walls do not pretend to support anything, since they no longer do; they have been reduced to a "skin" or sheathing over the steel beams, with most of the surface given

268. LOUIS SULLIVAN. Carson Pirie Scott & Company, Department Store. 1899–1904. Chicago

over to huge windows. Yet Sullivan's dictum meant not rigid dependence but a flexible relationship capable of a wide variety of expressive effects. Here the white terracotta sheathing emphasizes the horizontal continuity of the flanks as well as the vertical accent at the corner by subtle differences in spacing and detail.

If Sullivan represents, as it were, the Post-Impressionist stage of modern architecture, his great disciple, Frank Lloyd Wright, represents its Cubist phase. This is certainly true of his brilliant early style, between 1900 and 1910, which had vast international influence. (His late work, beginning with the 1930s, will be omitted from this account.) During that first decade, Wright's main activity was the design of suburban houses in the Chicago area; these were known as "Prairie Houses," because their low, horizontal lines were meant to blend with the flat landscape around them. The last, and most accomplished, example is the Robie House (fig. 269). Its "Cubism" is not merely a matter of the clean-cut rectangular elements composing the structure, but of Wright's handling of space. It is designed as a number of "space blocks" grouped around a central core, the chimney; some of the blocks are closed and others are open, yet all are defined with equal precision. Thus the space that has been architecturally shaped includes the balconies, terrace, court, and garden, as well as the house itself: voids and solids are seen to be equivalent, analogous in their way to facet Cubism in painting, and the entire complex enters into active and dramatic relationship with its surroundings. Wright did not aim simply to design a house, but to create a complete environment. He even took command of the details of the interior, designing fabrics and furniture for it. The controlling factor here was not so much the individual client and his special wishes as Wright's conviction that buildings profoundly influence the people who live, work, or worship in them, so that the architect is really a molder of men, whether or not he consciously assumes this responsibility.

Among the first Europeans to recognize Wright's importance were some Dutch architects who, at the end of World War I, joined forces with Mondrian. They found his principle of "the balance of unequal but equivalent oppositions" fully compatible with Wright's architecture. Their influence was so pervasive that the movement they represented soon became international. The largest and most complex example of this "International Style of the 1920s" is the group of buildings created in 1925–26 by the German architect Walter Gropius for the Bauhaus at Dessau (fig. 270), a

269. FRANK LLOYD WRIGHT.
Robie House. 1909.
Chicago

270. WALTER GROPIUS.
Shop Block, the Bauhaus.
1925–26. Dessau

271. LE CORBUSIER.
Savoye House. 1929–30.
Poissy-sur-Seine

272. LUDWIG MIES VAN DER ROHE
and PHILIP JOHNSON.
Seagram Building. 1958. New York

famous art school whose curriculum embraced all the visual arts, linked by the root concept of "structure," *Bau*. The most dramatic is the shop block, a four-story box with walls that are a continuous surface of glass. This radical step had been possible ever since the introduction of the structural steel skeleton; Sullivan had approached it, but he could not yet free himself from the old notion of the window as a "hole in the wall." Gropius frankly acknowledged, at last, that in modern architecture the wall is no more than a curtain or climate barrier, which may consist entirely of glass if maximum daylight is desired. A quarter-century later, the same principle was used on a much larger scale for the two main faces of the great slab that houses the Secretariat of the United Nations in New York.

In France, the most distinguished representative of the "International Style" during the 1920s was Le Corbusier. At that time he built only private houses—from necessity, not choice —but these are as important as Wright's

"Prairie Houses." Le Corbusier called them *machines à habiter* (machines to be lived in), a term meant to suggest his admiration for the clean, precise shapes of machinery, not a desire for "mechanized living." Perhaps he also wanted to convey that his houses were so different from conventional ones as to constitute a new species. Such is indeed our impression as we approach the most famous of them, the Savoye House at Poissy-sur-Seine (fig. 271); it resembles a low, square box resting on stilts— pillars of reinforced concrete that form part of the structural skeleton and reappear to divide the "ribbon windows" running along each side of the box. The flat, smooth surfaces stress Le Corbusier's preoccupation with abstract "space blocks." To find out how the box is subdivided, we must enter it; we then realize that this simple "package" contains living spaces that are open as well as closed, separated by glass walls. Indoors, we are still in communication with the outside world (views of the sky and of the surrounding terrain are everywhere to be seen),

above: 273. LE CORBUSIER. Notre-Dame-du-Haut,
view from southeast. 1950–55. Ronchamp

right: 274. LE CORBUSIER. Interior, South Wall,
Notre-Dame-du-Haut

yet we enjoy complete privacy, since an observer on the ground cannot see us unless we
stand next to a window. The functionalism of
the Savoye House, then, is governed by a "design for living," not by mechanical efficiency.

America, despite its position of leadership at
first, lagged behind in the 1920s. Not until the
very end of the decade did the impact of the
"International Style" begin to be felt on this
side of the Atlantic. A few years later, the best
German architects, whose work Hitler condemned as "un-German," came to this country
and greatly stimulated the development of
American architecture. Gropius, appointed
chairman of the architecture department at
Harvard University, had an important educa-
tional influence; Ludwig Mies van der Rohe,
his former colleague at Dessau, settled in Chicago as a practicing architect. His severely elegant Seagram Building in New York (fig. 272)
exemplifies his dictum that "less is more." Mies
van der Rohe is the great spiritual heir of
Mondrian among present-day designers, possessed of the same "absolute pitch" in determining proportions and spatial relationships.

Le Corbusier, in contrast to Mies van der
Rohe, abandoned the geometric purism of the
"International Style" in his later years. Instead,
he showed a growing preoccupation with sculptural, even anthropomorphic effects. His
church of Notre-Dame-du-Haut at Ronchamp
in southeastern France is the most revolutionary building of the mid-twentieth century. Rising like a medieval fortress from the crest of a
mountain (fig. 273), it has a design so irrational that it defies analysis. The massive walls
seem to obey an unseen force that makes them
slant and curl like paper; and the overhanging
roof suggests the brim of a huge hat, or the
bottom of a ship split lengthwise by the sharp-
edged buttress from which it is suspended.
There is a conscious evocation of the dim, prehistoric past here; asked to create a sanctuary
on a mountain top, Le Corbusier must have felt
that this was the primeval task of architecture,
placing him in a direct line of succession with
the men who had built Stonehenge, the ziggurats of Mesopotamia, and the Greek temples.
Hence, he also avoids any correlation between
exterior and interior. The doors are concealed:
we must seek them out like clefts in a moun-
tainside, and to pass through them is much like
entering a secret—and sacred—cave. Only inside do we sense the specifically Christian aspect of Ronchamp. The light, channeled
through windows so tiny that they seem hardly
more than slits or pinpricks on the exterior,
cuts widening paths through the thickness of
the wall, and thus becomes once more what it
had been in medieval architecture—the visible
counterpart of the Light Divine (fig. 274).
There is true magic in the interior of Ronchamp, but also a strangely disquieting quality,
a nostalgia for the certainties of a faith that is
no longer unquestioned. Ronchamp thus mirrors the spiritual condition of Modern Man—
which is a measure of its greatness as a work
of art.

BOOK TWO
MUSIC

❧ ❧ ❧

by Joseph Kerman

PART ONE

MUSIC IN THE ANCIENT WORLD

Architecture, sculpture, and painting are the most permanent of the arts. Music and dance are the most perishable. Cave paintings and pyramids survive, but the music and dance of the ancient world are lost completely. Even with the music of much later times, where we have a great deal of material, we "have" it in a strikingly incomplete way. People think they know how a Beethoven sonata should sound, and they may indulge in fine points of criticism of someone's performance of it—but when we stop to think, we should ask: How did it actually sound to Beethoven? How do we know? It will be well to take up some of these questions at the outset of our study of music history, in order to understand some of its problems and peculiarities.

Only very recently have recordings (for music) and movies (for the dance) made it possible to preserve the actual artistic phenomena, as primary source material analogous to existing art objects. Thanks to the technical advances of the last few decades, this preservation can now be carried out with amazing fidelity; the recorded examples accompanying this book give as good "reproductions" of music as do our colorplates of the visual artifacts themselves. Twentieth-century music will be a relatively simple matter for historians of the future to study. But the music of earlier centuries cannot be known to us in the way it actually sounded to its composers and their audiences. It can be known only approximately, through *notation* and *tradition* and through reconstructions based upon these means. Is it surprising that the study of music history is a late and a speculative development—that, indeed, the history of music has never made as strong an impression on musicians as history has done in such fields as poetry and sculpture?

Tradition can be helpful, so long as it is interpreted with great care. If we want to find out how Beethoven might have expected his sonatas to sound, we can listen to performances of them by students of Paderewski, who was a student of a student of Beethoven; but the

dangers in this approach are obvious. Tradition may count for more in certain other situations, such as religious music handed down from one generation to another by communities of monks, or folk music preserved in relatively isolated regions. Not many years ago, scholars who ventured off the beaten track in the Appalachian Mountains could still hear folk songs in a fairly unspoiled tradition extending back for centuries. But in general, musical scholars have to rely on secondary sources—written or physical sources, not "sounding" ones—and they have had to develop sophisticated techniques of interpretation. Among these sources are ancient instruments in various states of preservation, treatises about music, accounts of performances, and of course items in actual musical notation: musical scores and separate vocal and instrumental parts.

Even these latter items count as secondary sources, in a very real sense; for a notated score falls far short of being a work of art. The score of a medieval Mass, of which the actual sound has vanished, may be compared to the architectural plan of a medieval monastery that has long since been destroyed (such as that of St. Gall; fig. 68). Neither of these documents means anything to a non-expert; to yield up the work of art, they have to be reconstructed by the application of imaginative scholarship. One of the most important branches of musicology—perhaps the most important of all, and certainly one of the most difficult and controversial—is that concerned with translating written scores into sound. There are various avenues of assistance in this matter, such as the examination of ancient instruments themselves (and, with the dance, the examination of "still" pictures and statues of dancers: see figs. 17, 111, colorplate 14). With a little luck, musical instruments can be as permanent as pyramids—but one still has to learn to play them.

The further back in history we go, the less we know of the actual sound of music, and the more we have to rely on all forms of secondary information. When we get back to the ancient world of Mesopotamia, Egypt, Palestine, and early Greece, there is simply no musical notation to reconstruct from. These civilizations left fragments of instruments, as well as representations of them in art (see the Sumerian harp inlaid with musical scenes illustrated in fig. 17). They also left documentary information about music, as witness the numerous references to music in the Old Testament: Gideon foxes the Midianite army with the help of three hundred trumpets (Judges 7); the victorious David is feted "with tabrets, with joy, and with instruments of musick" (I Samuel 18:6); long lists of names are given for temple singers, players of harps, lyres, and brass cymbals, as well as their directors (I Chronicles 15:16–28). From all this evidence, scholars have managed to piece together an account of music history in ancient times. Their work has been aided by anthropological studies, for in certain carefully delimited areas, analogies can be drawn between ancient cultures and ones that still exist. Until recently, there were Jewish tribes living in the Yemen desert under isolated conditions little changed from those of Biblical times.

The fact remains that most of the music itself cannot be pieced together—and so a very natural question arises as to the real value that is to be derived from music history of this sort. The reader whose main interest is in musical enjoyment can hardly be blamed for finding it bloodless. However, to expand and refine musical enjoyment is just one good reason to study music history, not the only one. Music history is a part of history at large; even when we cannot hear the music of a certain people, knowledge of their attitudes toward it and the role it plays in their life helps to complete our picture of the culture as a whole. Furthermore, we may need to understand music history at one period in order to understand another period in which music may be better preserved or may command more intrinsic interest. History is a continuous thread, even if sometimes it is sadly frayed.

These are reasons why it is important to study the music of ancient Greece—the earliest music that will be treated in this book. The course of Western music history in the Early Christian era, the Middle Ages, the Renaissance, and even later, cannot be understood properly without reference to Greek music, or at least to Greek ideas about music. We shall see, in fact, that the heritage of ancient Greece is as impressive in music as it is in the arts and in the other fields of human endeavor. This is true in spite of the extremely tenuous state of

tradition and notation: a remarkable situation, and a remarkable tribute to the seminal force of Greek civilization.

1. GREEK MUSIC

Ancient Greece, it should be remembered, flourished for the better part of a millennium, and during this time an entire musical culture evolved from primitive beginnings, flowered, and decayed. In the early period, the age of Homer, the history of music (like everything else) merges imperceptibly with myth. The importance of music is sufficiently indicated by the fact that the god of music was Apollo, the god of light and order. Apollo practiced and patronized the disciplined music of the kithara and the smaller lyre (harplike instruments: a Greek kithara of the fifth century B.C. is shown in colorplate 2). But there was also another, unrestrained kind of music, that of Dionysus, the god of orgies and wine, associated with the strident aulos or reed pipe (a sort of double oboe). And already in pre-Classic times, music was the subject of highly interesting formal speculation. The Greeks were to become great theorizers and writers about music, as about all other subjects.

Music appears to have reached a high stage of sophistication during the Classic Period of Athens (c. 500–350 B.C.), the era of Phidias and the architects of the Parthenon, of the great historians, orators, and dramatists, and of the philosophers Socrates and Plato. But since musical notation was not yet in use, we cannot know the music of this period or of earlier ones —neither the music of the bards who chanted Homer's *Iliad,* nor of the lyric poets Sappho and Pindar when singing their odes and dithyrambs, nor that of the Athenian citizen-choruses declaiming Greek tragedy. Notation was developed later, during the Hellenistic period. From this period on, upwards of a dozen pieces and fragments have been preserved, extending all the way to a Christian hymn of the third century A.D. In a thousand years, that is the extent of the Greek repertory remaining to us.

We shall speak of these fragments in a moment; but a conscientious analysis of them would be somewhat beside the point, paradoxical as this may appear. They have little to do with the powerful influence exerted by ancient Greece on music at the time of the Early Christian period, the Middle Ages, the Renaissance, and at points beyond—they were not even known before the Renaissance. It was not the actual music of the Greeks that was so influential, but their ideas and ideals of music, drawn from their theoretical and other writings. "Heard melodies are sweet, but those unheard/ Are sweeter;" according to John Keats in his *Ode on a Grecian Urn,* and Keats spoke truer than he knew. There is an important lesson contained in this strange historical phenomenon. What people mean by music differs vastly between one age or culture and another, as the reader will admit if he tries to compare Western music with Japanese music, or any sophisticated music with that of aboriginal tribes, or symphonic music with rock-and-roll. So also it is the case that at certain times in certain places, ideas of music are almost as important as "sounding" music itself. To limit the study of music history to music as we would define it according to our familiar listening habits would be to limit it to the span of a very few centuries in a very few lands.

The most striking Greek notion about music was developed by the pre-Socratic philosopher and mathematician Pythagoras, popularly known for his theorem about the right-angled triangle. Pythagoras was the first to think seriously about the musical notes produced by strings of various lengths. A taut string, when plucked, gives out a certain pitch or note, called the fundamental note. Then if the same string is caught exactly in the middle, so that it divides in the proportion 1:1, the note produced by plucking it (on either side) will be exactly an octave higher than the fundamental note, and the two notes seem to blend perfectly. The two notes are said to be consonant, or to make a consonance or concord. If the string is caught at a point so that it divides in the proportion 1:2, the note produced by plucking it on one side will be a fifth higher than the fundamental,* on the other side an octave and a fifth higher—and again there is an excellent blend, though not quite a perfect one. If the string is caught at a different point so that it divides in the proportion 1:3, the note produced by plucking it on one side will be a fourth higher than the fundamental, and on the other side, two octaves higher. And so on, all the way up through the proportions, making an elaborate and, in a sense, an almost magical numerical system.

Magical—that is the way it really seemed to

---

* The term "fifth" is used in music to refer to the "interval," or difference in sound, between a note and the one that is five notes (inclusive) higher or lower. If the fundamental note is C, a fifth higher is G. A "fourth" (see next sentence, above) is the interval between C and F.

Pythagoras, who was the inventor of a number theory and inclined to mystical notions about numbers (i.e., thirteen is unlucky, the trinity is perfect). For it appeared that the tuning of strings, which could be checked by the senses, was related to simple numbers, which could be checked by the mind. Thus the phenomenon of musical consonance was evidence of a rhyme and reason within the physical world. Pythagoras had no way of knowing that falling bodies, light waves, planets in their orbits, and so on, all obey mathematical laws too; but with a bold leap of the imagination, he conjectured something of the kind. Encouraged by his experimental observations of strings, he claimed that the universe was governed by number. The planets, he said, moved on the surface of huge spheres whose sizes were determined by the same perfectly blended proportions as those of the strings. This he called "music of the spheres" or "the harmony of the universe" (the Greek word *harmonia* meant a "tuning"). Taken literally, the theory seems preposterous to us, but reduced to its barest essentials— mathematics makes order out of the physical world—it is not strange at all.

Pythagoras also claimed that numbers controlled human psychology (a claim that may yet be borne out, in a sense, by modern research into the physical bases of brain processes). The consonant blendings of string sounds, matched to simple numerical proportions, served as a model for the balanced human personality. Thus for Pythagoras, music and number lay at the heart of a comprehensive philosophical scheme embracing mind, matter, and the universe. Of course, we would not call this music, but number mysticism, or at best the physics of sound; but the Greeks made no distinction.

Nor did thinkers of the Middle Ages, in their own brand of Pythagoreanism. We may look ahead briefly to this. The Middle Ages conceived of music in three strictly analogous categories: *musica mundana, musica humana,* and *musica instrumentalis*—by which they meant the divine order of the heavens, the harmony of the human soul, and actual "sounding" music (both vocal and instrumental). Each category was supposed to obey the same numerical laws, which could be tested in the case of the third category. But given the medieval system of values, with things of the world placed below things of God, *musica instrumentalis* was considered the least important or "real." The reader will now see the point of our lengthy discussion of acoustically oriented philosophy.

What the medieval system did was to put all "sounding" music into a decidedly inferior position.

Conversely, *musica mundana* and *musica humana* were considerably respected. In medieval universities one could study for degrees in music, which was never the case with painting. The curriculum was not concerned with composition, performance, or aesthetic matters— still less with music history or "appreciation" —but rather with studying mathematical proportions, a laborious branch of arithmetic that is now obsolete, though memorialized in such terms as "harmonic mean" and "harmonic progression." The connection between music and mathematics, which goes back to Pythagoras, persists today in a common superstition about an affinity between musical and mathematical talents.

Pythagorean ideas persisted until late in the Renaissance. The last scene of Shakespeare's *The Merchant of Venice,* we may recall, takes place away from that discordant, unruly, passionate city; it is removed to an idyllic, perfectly harmonious island where Portia makes her home. In a famous passage, the two lovers, having eloped there, contemplate the planet-studded heavens on a beautiful evening while they hear sweet music. When Lorenzo says

The man that hath no music in himself,
Nor is not mov'd with concord of sweet sounds,
Is fit for treasons, stratagems, and spoils, . . .

he actually means it literally. His reference is to *musica humana*: the man whose soul is not "tuned" to the proper numerical proportions, those of the music they are hearing, will make an ugly discord in his whole soul. He will probably commit treason, which might be called an "untuning" of the state. This beautiful scene brings together all the elements of Pythagorean doctrine: the celestial music of the stars in their spheres, and the harmony of the well-tuned soul and of the state, all symbolized by actual sounding music played by musicians on stage. That this world view did not altogether satisfy Shakespeare is suggested by his complex characterization of "the man that hath no music," namely Shylock—but that is another story.

To return to ancient Greece: a background of Pythagoreanism helps explain the great importance attached to music by Plato in such deeply influential books as *The Republic* and the *Timæus*. To us, it must surely seem an exaggerated importance. But when Plato insisted that music must be primary in the education of the young—like the three R's today—he did so not because it might be nice for young men to enjoy playing or listening to music, or to gain dexterity, a rhythmic sense, or a social attribute. He did so for the practical reason (as he saw it) that music tunes the soul correctly. Plato was also an impressive witness for the deep conviction among the Greeks that music possessed near-magical healing powers, could sway the emotions, and could inspire men to heroic or vile actions. (No doubt there were awesome deeds done in the trancelike states induced by music at the dance rites of Dionysus.) This conviction was expressed in Greek mythology, where the feat of going down to Hades and rescuing a dead spirit was credited to only two persons: the great hero Herakles (Hercules), who was half divine anyway, and the great musician Orpheus, a mortal whose singing first charmed stones and wild animals and finally prevailed upon the King of the Dead himself. Most Greek writers repeat a number of supposedly historical facts demonstrating the great power of music. This so concerned Plato that in *The Republic* he specifically banned certain varieties of music, associated with certain Greek races, as detrimental to the common good.

At several critical junctures in the history of Western music, the reputed emotional power of Greek music provided composers with practical inspiration. In Shakespeare's time, Italian musicians in search of a more passionate means of expression wrote a new kind of play, treating the subject of Orpheus in a musical style vaguely modeled on what they knew of Greek music. The result was the foundation of opera. In the nineteenth century, the idea of Greek drama—a sort of intense civic ritual, half spoken, half sung—greatly appealed to the very influential composer Richard Wagner. And modern dictatorships such as Nazi Germany and Soviet Russia have also banned certain varieties of music, sometimes along racial lines —though it would probably be unfair to lay this at Plato's door.

Two final points should be made about Greek music, points about "sounding" music, at last, rather than about philosophies. What can we tell from the surviving Greek fragments? They confirm, first of all, the high position that all the writers granted to music with words—for all the fragments are vocal pieces. Purely instrumental music was considered a lower form, unfit for the best musicians. The ideal was music sung with the kithara to lyric or dramatic poetry, and indeed, one of the fragments consists of six lines from a tragedy by Euripides (*Orestes*—the music was written later than the play). The rhythm of this vocal music follows the poetic meter slavishly, and indeed helps to bring out the intricate metrical schemes in which Greek poetry was so rich. As for the kithara or the lyre, we have no independent parts for them. Instruments simply played along with the voice, for the Greeks never developed polyphony or harmony (in the modern sense) to vie with the main interest of the sung part. The technique of Greek music would certainly strike us as elementary, in spite of the enormous power and prestige attributed to it.

The other point is that it was the Greeks who fixed the scale employed by Western music up to the present day. We may be inclined to take the notes on the piano keyboard for granted, but a few minutes with Japanese or aboriginal music will remind us that out of the continuum of pitch frequencies a great many different selections can be made for different bodies of music. The selections made by the Greeks are carefully recorded by writers on the theory of music—who had the method to specify pitches in their well-developed study of string lengths. They tell us that in Plato's time, several scales existed: one called the diatonic scale, roughly equivalent to the series of white notes on the modern piano (C, D, E, F, G, A, B), and some others, much more Oriental-sounding. But the third-century Christian hymn which is among the Greek remains uses the diatonic scale, and we gather that by then all the others had become obsolete. With some modifications (see p. 254), this is the scale that is still in use. So in a very basic sense the language of Western music can be said to be Greek.

2. EARLY CHRISTIAN MUSIC

The music of Christianity during its first few hundred years is no better preserved than Greek music itself, as may well be supposed. However, an appreciable body of information gleaned from secondary sources points to the high prestige of music and its important place in Early Christian services. The Fathers of the Church took it for granted that music, in the form of singing holy texts, worked powerfully to turn man's feelings toward worship. This was part of their Greek heritage; in their influential writings from 200–400 A.D., they naturally encouraged the singing of Psalms, hymns, and other sacred songs. Just as emphatically, they discouraged instrumental music, ev-

idently because of its associations with pagan rites, the sensualities of dancing, and the obscenities of the stage. It might be said that Christianity converted the music of Apollo, god of light, reason, and order, into the music of Christ. The music of Dionysus, god of wine and orgies, was very deeply buried—or consigned to hell, if we can believe the vivid painting by Jerome Bosch more than a thousand years later (fig. 122). And it was many more centuries before the orgiastic, primitive, sensual element would reassert itself powerfully in Western music.

Apart from psychological reasons, the Fathers of the Church had also practical ones to encourage singing. Basic to the idea of communal worship is the repetition of devotional texts—not silent repetition (few could read) but *sounded* repetition, through which the holy words could be heard, mouthed, and absorbed by all. And for such "sounded repetition," singing has always seemed more natural than speaking. Not to mention the tediousness of communal speech, the rhythm of song (even when it is comparatively free) keeps everyone together and allows for audibility, and the melody of song helps one remember the words. By means of greater or less elaboration in the style of singing, furthermore, certain parts of the services could be made to seem more important than others. Besides contributing to clarity and memory (and keeping awake), music also provided a strong means to decorate and shape the services.

Thus began an alliance that was to be basic to the Early Christian era and far beyond: the alliance between music and Christian liturgy. As the Early Christian sects developed intricate systems of services, they developed associated musical repertories that were equally rich and intricate. Some elements from ancient Jewish services seem to have been taken over, and modified according to the standards of the Greek culture which dominated the Mediterranean basin and the Near East. The Syrian, Armenian, Coptic, and Ethiopian Christian churches all had their own bodies of music, though we know less about them than about the longer-lasting Byzantine and Western ones. Once again music history has to rely largely on secondary sources—in this case, on sources illustrating the histories of the various liturgies, with which music was so closely associated.

In 323 A.D., Constantine removed the capital of the Roman Empire to Byzantium (renamed Constantinople) in the East. This action was as important for the history of music as for the history of art, for the ensuing split between the Eastern and Western churches inevitably led to a major split in Christian music. As the liturgies drew apart, the Byzantine branch developed its own musical traditions, which influenced the West only slightly. Like Byzantine art, Byzantine music grew static, even stagnant. An important contributing factor was the prejudice against instruments held by the Fathers of the Church, which was extended to a complete ban on instrumental participation in Eastern services. There were no church organs, for example, such as existed in the West from early times. Although the role of the organ and other instruments in early Western church music cannot be traced at all precisely, it seems clear that without instruments to help the singers along, polyphony and harmony would never have evolved according to the lines that we shall trace in the next chapter.

In the Western orbit there were in fact several distinct church-music repertories, of which the Roman proved to be the most important. St. Gregory the Great (Pope from 590–604) is credited with gathering and codifying the Roman chant; hence the term "Gregorian chant." Certainly this was firmly enough established by the year 800 so that Charlemagne, in consolidating the Roman Church in northern Europe, made a point of suppressing other repertories and prescribing the Roman as the official church music of the Holy Roman Empire. It was nurtured particularly in the monasteries, which had become more and more important after the time of St. Benedict (died c. 547). For many centuries, monasteries were to be the great centers of artistic cultivation and learning; they were also centers of musical composition and theoretical writing about music.

These activities took place much later than the time of the actual composition of Gregorian chant, or at least, later than the time we believe its composition began. In any case, the term Gregorian chant is a misnomer—on two counts—and the alternative term, "plainsong," is only slightly better. As we have just seen, Gregory was a late figure in the development. Furthermore, the music includes not only "chant"—recitation on a repeated monotone with only slightly complicated beginning, ending, and punctuating formulas—but also "song" which rises to amazing flights of rhapsodic elaboration that can scarcely be called "plain."

We must approach the plainsong repertory through the liturgy it served. The monastic life involved a heavy, carefully prescribed schedule of daily services, all of them sung in part. The most important was the Mass, which centers on the communion of the celebrants at a symbolic enactment of the Last Supper. More than twenty items have to be sung or chanted at Mass, some of them remaining the same every day (called the "ordinary" items) and some varying from day to day ("proper" items) in order to tie the service in with the time of year or the feast of a particular saint (Christmas, St. Stephen, Whitsun). One or more Masses were celebrated daily—and in addition, no fewer than eight other services called the Canonical Hours, or Office Services. These center around the chanting of Psalms, a feature taken over from ancient Jewish services. In principle, the entire Psalter of 150 Psalms is to be sung through every week. The best-known Office Service is the evening Vespers and the largest is the midnight Matins, which besides "ordinary" Psalms includes up to twelve "proper" Lessons with elaborate musical numbers following them called responsories. In the Anglican and Episcopal liturgies, Vespers survives as Evensong, and Matins—combined with elements from the Mass—as the Morning Service.

What determined the musical style of a particular plainsong was not the wish of the composer or the meaning of the words, but the position it was to occupy in the service. Song tended to be used for the climactic and "proper" parts of more important services, chant for the routine and "ordinary" parts of less important ones. There is even a slight but clear distinction made between the kind of chanting used for, say, the reading of the Gospel at Mass and the recitation of the numerous Office Psalms. In the category of "song," there are much greater differences, such as that between the very simple pieces called antiphons sung at the Office with each of the Psalms, and the lengthy Matins responsories.

The most elaborate songs of all come at the high point of Mass, in pieces called graduals and alleluias. Our first example (RECORDED EXAMPLE 1) is one continuous segment from the third (and main) Mass for Christmas Day. It includes the alleluia *Dies sanctificatus* (*The consecrated day*), sung by the choir and a solo singer; a brief dialogue between the priest and the choir; and then the start of the Gospel reading for the day (St. John 1: "In the beginning was the Word, . . ."), which is *chanted* by the priest. Whereas any priest could learn to chant the Gospel in this simple manner, the alleluia required monks with musical training to lead it and to take over the particularly complex middle section. Like Greek music, Gregorian chant consists of a single voice-line with no accompaniment or harmony; but unlike Greek music, it is completely free in rhythm, and does not follow the accent of the words. Indeed, most of the words of the alleluia *Dies sanctificatus* are obscured by coloratura passages—many notes to a syllable, involving extended runs, turns, and other products of a rich virtuoso singers' tradition. The lack of harmony and clear rhythm is likely to puzzle us at first; the coloratura, too, reminds us (correctly) of rhapsodic Oriental or Near Eastern singing, rather than of the more restrained Western music with which we are familiar. But once we have got over the strangeness, we can begin to appreciate the melody itself, the long, wonderfully controlled train of notes which seems to trace endlessly complex intertwining patterns. The melodic "line"—a moving line —may mount up, or swoop quietly down, or wind its delicate and intricate arabesque around certain central foci. In terms of purely melodic subtlety, highly developed Gregorian chant as represented by graduals and alleluias goes far beyond most later music.

Notice that the choir of monks sings the same section of music both before and after the soloist's section in the middle of the alleluia. Such an arrangement, or "form," is usually designated by the diagram A B A—and a very satisfactory form it is, too, to judge from its employment all through the history of music, albeit with many modifications (see pp. 247, 264, 269). Musicians speak of a balance between sections of time almost as though in physical terms, just as artists speak of balance between areas of space. It is of course a well-developed memory that allows us to perceive such balances, and then respond to them aesthetically. The most important aspect of an "ear for music," in fact, is memory.

Recalling that there were at least nine distinct services daily, that each one changes a little from one day of the year to the next, and that there are even some differences year by year (if Christmas Eve falls on a Sunday, for instance)—recalling all this, we can appreciate the extent, complexity, and refinement of the plainsong repertory. Different musical material is provided for every occasion, according to the detailed requirements of the services. In fact, plainsong came to form an impressive, characteristically medieval system, with everything precisely distinguished and categorized, and arranged in a hierarchy according to the services and the church year—all pointing, ultimately, to God, recipient of the devotions.

It is also characteristic that the *type* of plainsong assumes almost more importance than the individual piece. Thus the simple Office antiphons fall into a number of recognizable types, each type containing melodic formulas that are repeated from one antiphon to the next. The process of composition was less a matter of free invention than rearrangement of cell-ideas and variation upon standard types.

Charlemagne, as we have already seen, prescribed the Roman plainsong as the official church music for the Holy Roman Empire. What is most impressive is the fact that this repertory has remained stable throughout the centuries, surviving additions, corruptions, and "reforms," as the official music of the Catholic Church until the present day. Hence the basic importance of plainsong to the history of later music. At least until 1520, and much later in some countries, almost all musicians grew up in the Church as choirboys and then spent their lives working for the Church. Gregory's music was in their ears day in and day out, year in and year out; consciously or unconsciously, they adopted its accents into their own music. And for centuries, as we shall see, plainsong formed the underpinning for church music.

SUGGESTIONS FOR LISTENING

Third Mass for Christmas Day (*Tertia missa in Nativitate*)
DGG-ARCHIVE

Second Vespers, Christmas Day
DGG-ARCHIVE

PART TWO

MUSIC IN THE MIDDLE AGES

1. EARLY MEDIEVAL MUSIC

In discussing the music of the Early Christian era, we have made the point that Gregorian chant was and is the official music of the Church to the present day. But this is not to say that it has always been the only music sung at services; people would never have stood for that. The Catholic Church in all ages has tolerated and even encouraged other kinds of music, as we quickly discover on entering any American Catholic church at Mass time. A spirit of flexibility was already abroad in the Carolingian era, as Christianity turned its face increasingly away from the Near East and toward the North. Charlemagne had established the Roman chant in the Holy Roman Empire, but we may suppose that this essentially Mediterranean repertory presented real difficulties to the Germanic and Celtic peoples. They needed another kind of music, and the energies of the age found an outlet in a great new wave of musical composition.

After about 800 A.D., the plainsongs composed by Frankish monks differed from strictly Gregorian plainsongs in important ways. A first difference was in function. Generally speaking, one could not tamper with the services, which by then were codified for all time, and one could not compose substitutes for the Gregorian chant. However, a rich outlet for religious fervor—and with it, for artistic activities—lay in the simple expedient of adding to the official services. We would consider that nine a day was already exhausting enough, but the age had a passion for extending them with commentaries, interpolations, insertions, appendages, and incrustations of text and music. To be sure, this elaboration was regarded as unofficial. It was subject to change and, indeed, to censorship, for authorities periodically felt it wise to "purify" the services by banning additions. But also the process of addition allowed for some individuality—if not personal individuality, at least that of a particular church, monastery, or monastic order. In this spirit, an enormous body of new plainsongs, in a confusing array of types and categories, was composed over a period of several centuries. A parallel with the visual arts suggests itself: while the medieval miniature painter decorated the Bible, the medieval musician decorated the services.

One new plainsong type was the trope, a piece which hooks directly onto (or into) an established plainsong such as a responsory or a Mass section. A trope may have six hundred new notes for the sixty of the original plainsong, and new words to match: a case of the tail wagging the dog. The *conductus,* another type, was designed to accompany the colorful processions which enlivened many medieval services. Perhaps the most fascinating type of all was the liturgical drama. This started out as a modest plainsong treating a small Biblical scene (say, the three Marys at the Tomb, as an addition to an Easter service), with one or two singers assuming different roles. Later liturgical dramas have half a dozen characters, and last a full hour. Somewhere along the line, they have obviously broken free of an actual service; they would now have been sung in the churchyard with dramatic action of some sort, and very likely with the participation of instruments. These are the actual beginnings of European drama. The liturgical plays *Daniel* and *Herod* (c. 1150) have been revived recently, with great success.

A second difference in the new plainsongs concerns their texts. No longer bound to the words of the Bible and the Church Fathers, the texts are commentaries on those time-honored words. And whereas the old Gregorian texts were in prose, the new ones came ultimately to be written in (Latin) poetry—whence the name of another musical type, the *versus.* These centuries saw the evolution of the kind of verse familiar to us, verse with rhymes, simple stanzas, and clear rhythmic scansion based on strong and weak accents. These characteristics are not found in classical Greek or Latin poetry, and they have an important bearing on the new musical style; musical rhythms and phrases began to run parallel to the new poetic ones. Incidentally, poets sometimes took it on themselves to add words to the long coloratura passages of Gregorian music, a process known as "texting." Texting of alleluias led to a very popular musical type called the *sequentia,* or sequence, which found a regular place in the Mass.

The new musical style brought the art of melody much closer to what we now understand by the term. This strikes us at once if, directly after listening to the Gregorian alleluia, we listen to the famous Whitsun sequence *Veni Sancte Spiritus* (*Come Holy Spirit,* RECORDED EXAMPLE 2: this adheres to the general features of Carolingian style even though it was probably composed much later). Instead of rhapsodic coloratura swamping the few words, there is now usually but one note to a syllable, so that the text—the poetry—is clear. Heavy musical stops bring out the rhyming words at the end of every third line. Corresponding to the lines of poetry, vigorous musical phrases are neatly separated from one another, and neatly balanced. Since the melody itself has a lively sense of "up" and "down," it has a sense of shape or form: see especially the second stanza. Phrases of melody are often repeated —a welcome feature for the ear to catch hold of, after the leisurely and rather unpredictable rambling of Gregorian chant. The piece consists of five well-balanced little tunes, one after another, each sung twice before the next tune is used. One could quickly learn these tunes and enjoy singing them much in the spirit of a modern hymn, in spite of (or perhaps because of) their elementary rhythmic shape. In all this, we can detect Mediterranean and Near Eastern musical features giving way to what was native in the music of the Franks—the ancestors of the French and Germans who have contributed so much to modern music.

Some Frankish plainsongs have survived to the present day even without the protection of the Catholic Church. Another famous Whitsun piece, the hymn *Veni creator Spiritus,* has shown such a timeless attraction that Martin Luther—no friend of the Catholic liturgy!— appropriated it for a Lutheran hymn (*Komm Gott Schöpfer*), and the Episcopalians have kept it in their current hymnal (*Come, Holy Ghost, our souls inspire*).

In one respect, however, the new plainsongs seem to modern ears just as remote as the old: in a peculiar vagueness that has to do especially with the endings (cadences) of the pieces or the sections of pieces. We feel something arbitrary, something unsatisfactory and flabby about the points of stopping. Almost every one of the forty-odd lines of *Veni Sancte Spiritus* has this character. So does a great deal of later medieval music. What is it that is actually troubling us?

This can be explained if the reader has access to a piano and can pick out a simple tune like *Yankee Doodle* (start from C). This tune has all the firmness and clarity that plainsong lacks—in particular, it concludes with a very satisfying ending formula, or cadence: the note B progressing to the note C (B → C). This is called a semitone cadence, a semitone being the (equal) distance between any note on the piano and the very next one, up or down, black or white. Now perform the experiment of playing *Yankee Doodle* starting from G, *using only white notes.* The final cadence (F → G) sounds flabby because it consists of two semitones, not one. (F → G amounts to F → F-sharp, plus F-sharp → G. F-sharp → G would sound fine.)

In the real version of *Yankee Doodle,* the note C sounds very central. C begins the piece, ends it, and occurs throughout more often than any other note. On the other hand, the note B sounds definitely subsidiary. B has the "function" of strengthening C by means of the cadence B → C; in fact, each note of the scale has its special character or "function" in relation to that central-sounding C. The trouble with *Yankee Doodle* starting on G is that the note F does not support G, that F strikes us as somehow too independent.

Medieval composers used only the diatonic, or white-note, scale (plus B-flat under certain conditions), and they built plainsongs around D, E, F, and G only. With melodies built around D, E, and G, there is no possibility of having the semitone cadence—and in any case this seems to have been disliked, for even with melodies built around F, the progression of notes E → F was carefully avoided as a cadence. Both the alleluia *Dies sanctificatus* and the sequence *Veni Sancte Spiritus* (RECORDED EXAMPLES 1 and 2) are built around D. Perhaps these plainsongs can be *seen* to gravitate around a central note, but they cannot easily be *heard* to do so, because the critical semitone cadence is not available, and because, in a more general sense, the notes do not relate functionally to the central note. Melodies built in this way are called modal; many folk songs are modal (and very old). Melodies built like *Yankee Doodle* are called tonal.

But musical centrality and function, both

later expressed in the so-called tonal system of modern times, is one of the most sophisticated of musical concepts, and one of the last to evolve from that remote ancestor of modern music, the service music of the medieval monasteries. The tonal system slowly asserts itself after 1500; after 1700, it dominates and determines music; and it fades away in advanced music after 1900. We shall have more to say about this matter as we approach each of these dates.

SUGGESTIONS FOR LISTENING

Plainsong hymns

Sequence *Dies irae,* from the Mass for the Dead

DGG; LONDON

The Play of Daniel

DECCA

2. ROMANESQUE AND GOTHIC MUSIC

The year 1000 A.D. is a convenient one from which to date the serious development of polyphony—that is, music consisting of two or more simultaneous voice-lines rationally ordered together. Or more correctly, this is the date at which polyphony begins to be written down in sources that have been preserved and can be deciphered. The importance of this development for the history of Western music hardly needs to be stressed for the modern reader; the existence of two simultaneous notes means harmony, and harmony is what we now expect of music. We may also be struck by a close chronological parallel with the evolution of Romanesque art and architecture, which has been discussed on pages 57–67. This is one case, however, in which it is hard to draw any meaningful analogy between the two major movements in art and music, beyond a general great quickening of activity and broadening of artistic horizons.

Even before 1000—indeed, long before—it appears that singers in some areas used to improvise extra polyphonic voice-lines to go along with the standard plainsongs. (English monks were still doing this late in the Middle Ages, using "faburden," a special process which fortunately left clearer traces than most early medieval music.) This improvisation was similar in spirit to singing in thirds today, as in barbershop harmony. But we are very incompletely informed about the practice. Musicians of early medieval times saw little need to write down even Gregorian chant; by the same token, they were in no hurry to write down something that was easily improvised on the basis of chant (and that was "unofficial," besides). About 900, one or two authors give rules for such improvisation: it was a simple business, the plainsong and the added voice moving together note by note in "parallel motion." The practice surely did not stop about 1000, when a more sophisticated form of polyphony first makes its appearance in a few scattered manuscripts.

It is well to make a clear distinction between composed polyphony of this kind and the older improvised kind, although at the time both manners went under the name of *organum* (plural: *organa*), the Latin word for organ. Are we to understand that this music was performed with the help of the organ? We do not know, but that is what we would be inclined to guess, for organum became so complex over the years that it is hard to think of singers managing it unaided. We do know that organs were in use in the Western church; since organs are large and expensive items, people tend to keep careful records about them, and some of these early records are preserved. In 956 at Winchester, England, we read of an instrument with 400 pipes and 26 bellows.

Great advances were made by composed polyphony during the first two hundred years of its existence (c. 1000–1200). What might be called its first stage still consists mostly of note-against-note writing, one note of the new voice to each note of the plainsong. But there is a good deal of "contrary motion" (one voice going up when the other goes down, and vice versa); as a result, the new voice takes on genuine independence and interest, and some ingenuity is required to adjust it smoothly to the plainsong, which it no longer follows slavishly. In general, composers tried to arrange things so that the notes that sounded simultaneously were consonant (see p. 215).

A second stage can be discerned after 1100, represented by a few manuscripts stemming from the pilgrimage center of Santiago de Compostela in northern Spain and from St. Martial at Limoges, along the famous pilgrimage route through France. (We have mentioned the role of this pilgrimage route in the development of Romanesque sculpture, page 63.) Each plainsong note in the organum is now often fitted with more than one note in the new voice. An interesting process of abstraction may be said to have set in, for in order to accommodate the new voice, the plainsong may actually slow down to a succession of drones, like bagpipe drones, which can scarcely be grasped as a melody at all. Once again, the tail is beginning to wag the dog.

The new voice was still in the free rhythm of plainsong. But in a highly important third stage after 1160, emanating from the Church (later the Cathedral) of Notre-Dame in Paris, fixed rhythm at last entered Western music. (Or was fixed rhythm already being used for plainsong, without its being indicated in the manuscripts, at least in any obvious way? This is a difficult and much-debated problem.) At first the fixed rhythms of polyphony were very simple: only a few different note-lengths arranged in regular patterns, such as ♩ ♩♩ ♩ ♩ ♩. It was not even necessary to make up a notation for rhythm (such as half-notes, quarters, sixteenths); the composer simply indicated which of the few standard patterns were to be applied. Rhythm of this sort is called modal rhythm, the patterns rhythmic modes.

The function that music of the Notre-Dame School filled was one of building up or interlarding the official service-music. This function complements that of the "new plainsong" development which, it is important to stress, continued to flourish alongside of polyphony. Certain selected plainsongs were elaborated by the addition of polyphony—a sort of vertical extension comparable to the horizontal extension accomplished by tropes (see p. 220). It is no accident that a trope book, the so-called Winchester Troper, should also be one of the main sources of early polyphony; tropes and organa were two sides of the same coin. But in addition to organa, independent pieces were written to be inserted into the services—the polyphonic *conductus,* typically (but not always) intended for processions.

Which plainsongs were selected to be turned into organa? It is obvious that composed polyphony, as against improvised, depended on trained singers who could read music and hold to their part while the next man was singing something else. Therefore composed polyphony dealt with those parts of the service traditionally reserved for trained singers; Notre-Dame organa were restricted to the rich plainsongs we have spoken of above—the graduals and alleluias of Mass and the responsories of Matins, and indeed, only to the solo parts of these plainsongs. The choir of monks would continue to sing in just one line until the point where the solo singer would formerly have come in, who was now replaced by two soloists singing in polyphony.

The time and place of origin of the Notre-Dame School coincide with those of Gothic architecture, and in this case there are meaningful analogies to be drawn between the two major movements in art and music. (This is not to say that Gothic music can be ranked with Gothic art in aesthetic terms.) In both art and music, a very coherent repertory established itself at Paris and then spread like wildfire over all of Europe. The Notre-Dame repertory itself dominated the musical scene for more than a century, and its outgrowths, which we may regard as the later phases of Gothic music, lasted until 1400 or, depending on the location, as late as 1550. A strongly constructive quality was evident from the first, and this soon turned to technical virtuosity and elegance as phases of development followed one another in a markedly logical sequence.

Master Léonin of Paris (c. 1160) is the first composer in the history of Western music whom we know by name. In Léonin's hands, the older dronelike organum was drawn out with more notes than ever for each plainsong note. (These long drones seem tailor-made for performance on the organ.) Léonin also practiced a more modern kind of organum: here the plainsong moves in a definite rhythm that is only slightly slower than that of the added voice. He thus seems to be the first composer to face the problem of combining two different rhythms, as well as two different melodies. His successor, Master Pérotin "the Great," sometimes added a third voice—which more than tripled the technical problem. Pérotin even experimented with some four-voiced compositions, which astounded his contemporaries and remained unmatched for over a century. One of these, dated 1199, adorned the gradual for the Mass for St. Stephen's Day (December

26), *Sederunt principes* (*The princes sat in council*). This famous organum draws out the two-minute original plainsong to fifteen minutes. In our recorded section, which comprises only the very end of it (RECORDED EXAMPLE 3), the plainsong can first be heard moving in regular notes while the three added voices twine around it more rapidly, in modal rhythm. Then the plainsong slows down. Then it freezes into a series of solemn drones. Then the choir takes over to conclude in ordinary Gregorian fashion. If we imagine this music in its original setting, sonorously echoing throughout the choir of Notre-Dame Cathedral (the section beyond the transept; see fig. 89), we will perhaps detect features analogous to Gothic architecture: a "weightless" quality and an effect of powerfully ordered intricacy, all achieved by an increasingly impressive technical command.

An interesting development at this time consisted of building polyphony on sections of plainsong arbitrarily repeated several times. Again we can speak of a process of abstraction, for Pérotin was getting farther away from the plainsong as actually sung. He was interested in giving himself the framework for longer pieces; he was also interested in seeing what would happen when the plainsong was put in a different rhythm the second time, and adjusted differently to the upper voice (or two upper voices, as was now usual). Besides this expansion in the technical range of polyphony, there was also a widening of the text repertory. A process of "texting" took place, comparable to that mentioned in reference to the Carolingian sequence (p. 221); modal rhythms fitted well with Latin poetry, and sections of organa were fitted with new poems commenting on the words of the underlying service piece. Such pieces were called motets, from the French *mot* (word). Motets became very popular, and were soon being composed freely—that is, poems were set in organum style directly, without being adapted to actual already-existing organa.

After about 1250, motets were the main type of music being cultivated, and we find them with rhythms that are significantly more complex than modal rhythms, and sometimes with French texts instead of Latin ones. The first of these characteristics was reflected in the gradual working-out of a real notation for rhythm. This had never been necessary for plainsong, nor for modal rhythms, but from now on rhythm and its notation become more and more of a preoccupation with medieval musicians and theorists. As for the existence of mo-

tets with French words, this has a significance that is radical indeed. For it tells us that polyphonic music, in the form of the motet, had found its way out of the Church and into the court.

The step was not unexpected, given the steady expansion over these centuries of the range of artistic activities of every kind. Each new century saw the growth of great new monastic orders, but after 1000 A.D. urban life grew more vigorous, too, and the courts of kings and great barons began to develop the arts with some regularity. The Age of Faith was also the Age of Chivalry, and this expressed itself in a rich tradition of courtly songs long before the appearance of polyphonic motets in court circles. This was the tradition of the troubadours in southern France (Provence) around 1050–1200, the trouvères in northern France around 1150–1300, and the minnesingers in Germany around 1150–1400.

These noble poet-composers wrote works praising their ladies' beauty, or lamenting their coldness, or debating fine points of chivalrous behavior, or narrating the knight's encounter with a shepherdess—and there were a number of other standard subjects. Included among the ladies and their suitors were some of the greatest names of Europe: Eleanor of Aquitaine, the crusader-king Richard the Lion-Hearted of England, and Thibault, King of Navarre. So far as we know, they wrote both the words and music of their songs, though perhaps for the latter they may have accepted some anonymous help from their jongleurs—the court musicians who performed these songs. The verse forms of troubadour and trouvère poetry formed the basis of later European lyric poetry, and with it, of later secular song. As for the music, it was not polyphonic; it consisted simply of tunes—admirable tunes, some of them, with modal rhythms (as in Notre-Dame organa) and with orderly, well-balanced phrases (as in organum, once again, and in the new plainsong—for example, the *versus*). It is striking to see, in the period after 1250, fragments of trouvère tunes finding their way quite openly into polyphonic motets. Clearly Gothic polyphony was now directed to the court as much as to the Church, and was crossed with an older tradition of courtly music.

We can speak now of a final phase of Gothic music, after around 1300. This resembles the latest style of Gothic architecture in such tendencies as exaggeration and virtuosity, in such characteristics as fantastic lacework and a feeling of unsubstantiality, and even in the geographical fact of diffusion away from the original center at Paris. To be sure, this phase was sharply marked off from the past by musicians of the time, who proudly contrasted their *ars nova* (new art) with the *ars antiqua* (old art) of the 1250s. Music historians have generally tended to agree with them. However, as compared to the situation after 1400, which those musicians could not foresee, the undeniable novelties in music around 1300 seem less significant than its strong ties to the past.

This is particularly true if attention is focused on the important matter of texture, a term used by musicians to refer to the "weave" of polyphonic music—to the relationship among the simultaneous voices (or "threads") and the way they are combined. In most medieval polyphony, the weave can be described as loose and heterogeneous, with the various voices being kept essentially distinct from one another. Naturally, the voices were made to fit together, at least on the main beats, where consonance (see p. 215) was the rule; but the resulting sonority—the sensuous quality of the combined sound of the voices at any instant—was a secondary consideration. Individuality of the voices was the keynote. And individuality was still the keynote after 1300; indeed, it was carried to the extreme. When after 1400 a reaction set in at last in the direction of a more homogeneous, sonorous texture, a fundamental step had been taken toward the Renaissance and the modern conception of music.

We shall attempt to clarify musical textures by means of line-diagrams. An early Notre-Dame organum or motet might be represented like this:

DIAGRAM ONE

added voices

tenor (plainsong)

The plainsong and the two added voices are indicated by lines in a steady pattern, because the modal rhythms are absolutely steady. But each line has a different pattern to show that the rhythms are different. It will be recalled, furthermore, that the voices are quite different also in their melodic character: the plainsong is in the rhapsodic coloratura style of the Gregorian alleluias, while the added voices are in a neat, Frankish style close to that of the sequences and other "new plainsongs." Utter individuality of the voices appeared so natural to medieval motet composers that they did something that seems very peculiar to us: they used different poems (sometimes even in different languages!) simultaneously in the two added voices. Like sonority, comprehensibility of the words was now secondary to the separateness of the various voices.

In the *ars nova* music after 1300—indeed, the process started earlier—the voices became more and more differentiated in rhythm, melody, and range. Musical texture now looks like this:

DIAGRAM TWO

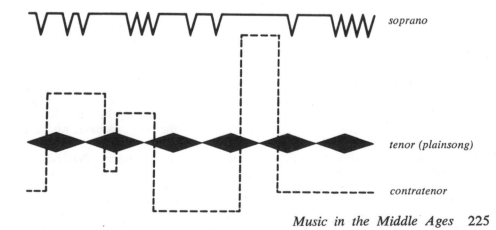

soprano

tenor (plainsong)

contratenor

Music in the Middle Ages 225

The added voices are no longer regular in rhythm, and the plainsong goes much more slowly. Whereas in earlier polyphony the voices occupied the same range and often crossed one another (thus the lines in diagram 1 are placed right next to one another), now each voice tends to gravitate to a distinct section of the vocal range. This explains how the word "tenor," originally applied to the plainsong when it held (Latin: *tenere*) drone notes in organum, came to refer to a particular voice-range. As for the dotted line in diagram 2, that represents a special new type of voice-line called the contratenor, whose special destiny was to hop around between the tenor and the other voices, or below the tenor. The presence of the contratenor shows that the medieval composer was concerned with sonority at least to the extent of filling in spaces. But its awkward and subsidiary quality also shows that this concern remained an afterthought.

A little polyphonic song by Guillaume de Machaut (c.1300–c.1377), *Je puis trop bien* (*I can right well*, RECORDED EXAMPLE 4), illustrates this texture. Appropriately enough, the performance involves different kinds of sound in the different voice-lines: the top line or soprano is sung or occasionally played by a recorder, the tenor is played on a medieval fiddle (forerunner of the violin), and the contratenor is played on a lute (a widely used guitarlike instrument). The tenor does not carry a Gregorian chant, but it treats its original material in the slow, stiff way that had been developed for chant. The rhythm is intricate, the melody angular, the harmonies pungent. The poem develops a favorite trouvère theme—the coldness of the singer's lady—but the actual sound of the words interested Machaut so little that he often put lengthy coloratura passages on unimportant syllables. The quality of the texture is reminiscent of Late Gothic art, perhaps: vivid, nervous, elegant, rather spiky, and often curiously perforated.

About 1500—to look ahead for a moment (turn to diagram 3 on page 234)—the characteristic texture of music involved voices all of the same smooth rhythmic and melodic nature. The tenor is just another voice along with equal partners, weaving in and out of one another in a beautifully balanced way. We shall return to this texture in discussing the music of the Renaissance.

What was chiefly new in the Gothic *ars nova* after 1300 was refinement of rhythm, a refinement that made the distinction in the role of the voices so sharp. It is literally true that around 1390 music was being written with a rhythmic virtuosity that was not matched until the 1950s. The great development of rhythm led to a remarkable compositional principle known as isorhythm ("same-rhythm"). Large-scale motets were composed in several distinct sections or blocks of, say, twenty measures; these are different as to their actual notes, but identical or almost identical in over-all rhythm. In some voices, the over-all rhythmic plan of the sections can be a fantastically complex pattern involving up to seventy-five notes: the basic rhythm returns again and again, embodied in completely other notes. Meanwhile, the tenor slowly repeats its piece of plainsong (or other melody) according to the scheme laid down by Pérotin.

In view of the increasingly rarefied and complex tendencies in musical composition, it is perhaps not surprising that in 1324 the new polyphony was banned by papal edict from actual church services. (Pope John XXII was only too familiar with advanced French music: driven out of Rome in 1309, the popes had set up a brilliant and somewhat secular court at Avignon in the south of France.) Motets in the new polyphonic style tended to be used only on special festive occasions, such as the dedication of a new cathedral, or the signing of a peace treaty. For such occasions, there was no harm in excess brilliance, and isorhythm was the rule. The courtly French love song, or chanson, was the other main form of the time. Descended from the trouvère song and the *ars antiqua* motet, the *ars nova* chanson developed into a polyphonic composition of considerable complexity, as we have seen in Machaut's *Je puis trop bien*. Words and music were thought of together, and it is worth noting that Machaut, the greatest composer of the century, was also the leading poet of France, an honored contemporary of Chaucer and Petrarch.

In Italy, meanwhile, a fine local variety of this late Gothic music flourished, melodically more ingratiating and less learned than the French. The foremost composer was the blind organist of Florence, named Francesco Landini (1325–97). This was the great age of Italian poetry, and music was closely bound up with it; although no original music has survived for the sonnets and other lyrics written by Dante about 1300 (which he himself traced back to those of the troubadours), we have, about 1350–75, one or two musical settings of poems by his great successors, Petrarch and Boccaccio. Besides the inevitable love songs, an interesting minor type was the *caccia* in Italian, *chace* in

French. This was devoted to descriptions of the hunt—a "chase" which probably had erotic overtones. The voices were made to echo a great profusion of hunting cries, birdcalls, etc. —a sudden flash of the vivid naturalism we know from late International Gothic painting (see p. 87).

That instruments participated in secular motets and chansons is quite clear. Either instrumentalists took over some of the voice-lines entirely, as in our Machaut example, or else they played along with the singers. This we can tell (even though the composers say nothing whatsoever about it) because the manuscripts have pointedly left out the words for certain voice-lines, especially the highly unsingable tenors and contratenors, and because musical scenes in paintings often show singers together with players. Significantly, it is usually a mixed group that is shown: in the *Ghent Altarpiece* by the Van Eycks, for example (fig. 114), singers are on one side panel, and on the other a small pipe organ, a harp, and a viol (a descendant of the medieval fiddle, and another forerunner of the violin). Each polyphonic thread, we believe, gets its own individual instrument, without any thought of blending. This corresponds with—and exaggerates—the independence of the threads which we have traced on purely stylistic grounds.

But in the music of this time, particular instruments were never specified. Composers seem to have been content to hear their pieces performed sometimes by one group of voices and instruments, sometimes by another. They also gave only scant indication of a very significant practice that is described by theorists of the time under the name of *musica ficta* ("false music"—notice the tone of apology or downright disapproval). Singers and players were directed under certain conditions to supply sharps that were not noted in the manuscripts, so as to produce the "smooth-sounding" semitone cadence. As we have seen (p. 221), this type of cadence gives music a clearer sense of centrality; the practice of *musica ficta* was not only a concession to sonority but also a first step in the direction of the tonal system of later music. But the casualness of medieval musicians in writing down details in this area, while at the same time they were developing the art of rhythmic notation to a dizzy state of complication, reminds us that their interest was not centered on the sensuous quality of sound.

At the center of their interest—men of the Middle Ages were always being told—was God, and their entire way of life was directed *de contemptu mundi,* toward disdain for this world. Earthly sights and sounds were transitory phenomena, if not dangerous temptations, on the road to the afterlife in Christ. It is not easy for us to grasp this fundamental frame of mind, which in some ways is closer to the Orient than it is to the Western world since the Renaissance, but we must reckon with it in trying to understand medieval music. To be sure, music was no mortal sin; doubtless Machaut and Landini, and the jongleurs and fiddle players, all took honest pleasure in their music, just as we do in ours. But like pop musicians of today, perhaps, they labored (however cheerfully) under a certain blanket of disapproval. There were always authorities to remind them of the Pythagorean doctrine (see discussion, pp. 215–16), a doctrine that amounted to disdain for the music of this world. "Sounding" music justified itself by leading man first to the harmony of the soul, and secondly to the music of the spheres, God's order in the universe.

SUGGESTIONS FOR LISTENING

Léonin, Organum *Judaea et Jerusalem*
Pérotin, Organum *Sederunt principes*
Troubadour and trouvère songs and motets of the 13th century
ON SAME RECORD: DGG-ARCHIVE

Guillaume de Machaut, Chansons and Notre-Dame Mass
DGG-ARCHIVE

Francesco Landini and others, Caccie and other works
DGG-ARCHIVE

And all through the Middle Ages, music sounded hourly to the glory of God in monasteries and cathedrals. In innumerable Masses and Office services, Gregorian chants and Frankish sequences were sung, sometimes decorated by sophisticated forms of polyphony, and more often decorated by primitive—even improvised—forms that in some cases had been invented hundreds of years before. Most often, they were sung alone, without any polyphonic decoration at all. This was the essential music of the Middle Ages: essential, because the chant was supposed to have come from St. Gregory, who was supposed to have had it from the Holy Spirit (medieval miniatures show the saint receiving a music scroll from the Dove). Since our eye ranges restlessly toward the future rather than the past, we cannot help concentrating on the advanced secular developments of later medieval music, on polyphonic chansons and large isorhythmic motets composed for festive occasions. It is from these that the lineage can be traced, ultimately, to the music of the modern world. But in looking at medieval music in this way, we expose the gap that separates our attitude from that held in the Middle Ages. This gap opened up in the era of the Renaissance.

PART THREE

MUSIC IN THE ERA OF THE RENAISSANCE

Perhaps no period of cultural history has stimulated historians to more brilliant and diverse thought than the era of the Renaissance. One reason for this is simply that it has been studied for so long; as we observed on page 88, the Renaissance was the first period to think of itself as a historical entity, and therefore to speculate about itself in what we now call historical terms. Then, much later, the most signal and influential monuments of art scholarship in the last century were concerned with the Renaissance, rather than with the Middle Ages or later times. The same held true in the nineteenth century for music history, a much newer field which in many ways followed the lead of art history. But of course the longevity of Renaissance studies is only one reason for their luxuriant development. The other reason is the seemingly endless fascination we find in the story of the birth of modern man—his institutions, his attitudes and frame of reference, his art and music.

In music, for a variety of reasons, Renaissance ideas at first made their way slowly. In the fourteenth century the striking individualism of Petrarch—so characteristic for the early direction of the Renaissance—found little echo in his esteemed contemporary Guillaume de Machaut. Only after several generations of humanist thought did this begin to affect the actual composition and performance of music. But once planted, the seeds grew rapidly enough. By 1500 the music of Pérotin and Machaut had been forgotten, and the next century saw a transformation in every aspect of medieval music: sound, texture, form, style, concept. By 1750—if we include the Baroque within the broad "era of the Renaissance"—we are faced with a revolution in music no less decisive than that in the visual arts, and in literature, philosophy, science, manners, and every

other aspect of life. The distance from Machaut to Haydn and Mozart is certainly as great as that from Giotto and Duccio to J. L. David and Goya.

In tracing the course of this revolution over the following pages, we shall attempt to show how some of the same guiding ideas were reflected in music and in the visual arts. We must not expect, however, to find meaningful analogies in painting and architecture for every important composer and musical phenomenon. This is simply not in the nature of things, in the Renaissance or at any other time. There are physical and geographical conditions, among other factors, that are unique to the evolution of any art, and these conditions may cause such serious differences that they outweigh the influence of a common climate of ideas. To speak only of music in the early Renaissance, two such factors deserve special mention.

One is the state of classical remains—or rather, the absence of classical remains. The admiration for, and revival of, Graeco-Roman ideals and achievements was a major feature of the Renaissance; we have seen its far-reaching effects in architecture, sculpture, and painting. But whereas the literary humanists could read ancient plays and works of moral philosophy, and the artists could gaze upon statues and friezes and ruined buildings, the musicians could only puzzle over tantalizing reports *about* Greek music. Greek music itself had not survived. Much ingenious work, against great odds, was devoted to interpreting these reports in the light of Renaissance musical realities—until finally, around 1600, a group of humanists made an impressive attempt to create a modern parallel to Greek dramatic recitation or singing. The result was the invention of opera. But when some nineteenth-century music historians hailed this as the Renaissance in music—two hundred years after the advent of the Renaissance in art!—they were drawing an analogy with little meaning.

Then there is a question of geography, the conflicting claims of North and South. Renaissance—*rinascità*—was originally an Italian concept; the Italian Renaissance flowered in the fifteenth century. In music, however, Italy did not grow prominent on the European scene until about 1530, a date well after the periods referred to as the Early and High Renaissance in the visual arts. Back in the fifteenth century, Italian music had actually lost ground, for the promising development begun by Landini and his predecessors (see p. 226) found no native continuation. A strange phenomenon: the Italians did not suddenly turn unmusical, but they were content to import their principal musicians from the North, in great numbers. Italians greatly admired Northern painting, too, but not to the same extent. When Renaissance Florence dedicated Brunelleschi's great cathedral dome in 1436 (fig. 95), the music for the occasion was written not by a Florentine but by the most celebrated Northern composer of the time, Guillaume Dufay, who was then serving in the Papal Chapel at Rome.

The lack of genuine, local Italian music during the fifteenth century has never been adequately explained. (In fact, the problem has never been adequately studied.) A contributing factor may be found in the literary situation. After the glorious century of Dante, Petrarch, and Boccaccio—from around 1300 to 1400—nearly another century elapsed before poets of comparable rank emerged again in Italy. Perhaps the music of Landini fell out of fashion along with the poetry it accompanied, and in the absence of vital new schools of poetry, there was no impetus for new schools of music. To the Italian Renaissance mind, as we shall see, music and the words to which it was set were bound together very closely.

However this may be, it is to the North that we must continue to look for the central currents in music, and for evidences of "the discovery of the world and of man," in the famous phrase by the historian Jakob Burckhardt. In the rapidly crowding canvas of music history from 1400 to 1600, we shall trace—among other things—a new attitude toward the traditional plainsong; a growing respect for the individual act of musical composition; an increasing interest in the literary quality and the meaning of texts set to music; and most fundamental of all, a radical change in musical texture, that is, in the sensuous quality of musical sound. In all of these features we can detect the spirit of the Renaissance at work.

1. THE FIFTEENTH CENTURY

In the older histories of music, the fifteenth century used to be divided up into several "Netherlands Schools" of composers. Strictly speaking, however, most of the famous musicians of the time came not from the present Netherlands (Holland) but from Flanders (now called Belgium) and the northern part of France. The Cathedral of Cambrai, just below the Franco-Flemish border, was an important musical center; so was the court of Burgundy, which, under the powerful dukes Philip the Good and Charles the Bold, controlled much of this territory. These centers supplied all Europe with singers and composers.

It was a Flemish composer and musical theorist, Johannes Tinctoris, who declared roundly in 1477 that "although it seems beyond belief," the only music worth listening to had been written in the last forty years. His date of 1437 is not far from the beginning of the significant activity of the first Renaissance artists: Campin, the Van Eycks, Donatello, Brunelleschi, and Masaccio. In his sharp awareness of the novelty of the music of his own time and his contempt for the Middle Ages, Tinctoris sounds very much like the contemporary Italian humanist. But it is very striking that he gave credit for the revival of music not to Italy in the south, but to a land at the perimeter of northern Europe, England.

This brings us, in fact, to the one point in history at which England exerted a serious influence on the course of European music. Just as the architects of the cathedrals of Salisbury and Gloucester (see figs. 92, 93) had made individual interpretations of Continental Gothic architecture, so English composers developed their own distinct dialect of Gothic music. They were also able to offer the Continent something in return. As a result of an insular style of improvised polyphony called faburden (see p. 222), unusually rich and sonorous accents found their way into written English music, such as that by the composer-mathematician-astrologer John Dunstable (c.1370–1453), which in turn made its mark upon his French contemporaries. Many opportunities arose for the exchange of ideas, because the English were then spending much time in France waging the Hundred Years' War, generally in league with the Burgundians. Dunstable was in the service of the Duke of Bedford, brother of

Henry V and, after Henry's death, regent and chief prosecutor of the war. (It was under Bedford's rule that Joan of Arc was burned.)

Partly as a result of this influence from England, the chansons composed by French musicians after 1400 were much simpler in rhythm than those of Machaut and Landini, and markedly more sonorous in texture. Also, great care was now devoted to the molding of long plastic melodies. The chanson developed into a very sophisticated and delicate art form, well matched to the elegance of art, costume, and manners for which the Burgundian court was renowned all over Europe. Perhaps it is no accident that we find Burgundian chansons collected in richly illuminated manuscripts patterned after the private prayer books called "books of hours" that were fashionable at the time (compare fig. 112).

In addition to chansons, composers also began producing small-scale sacred motets in chanson style—for in the wake of the new modesty of musical idiom, music increasingly found its way back into the Church (modern polyphonic music, that is; plainsong had never left the Church). They dedicated motets particularly to the Virgin Mary (Marian motets); Mary, who was thought of as the very human agent who could intercede for mankind with Christ her Son, enjoyed great popularity in the religious life of the period. Whole repertories of Latin poetry grew up in her honor, and with them, incidentally, some new plainsongs, composed late in the Middle Ages. We have already observed the effects of the cult of Mary in the numerous Annunciations, Nativities, Pietàs, and Madonnas of the fourteenth and fifteenth centuries (figs. 102, 104, 105, 110, 113; colorplates 10, 11).

In Dunstable's intimate Marian motet *Speciosa facta es* (*Fair hast Thou been made*, RECORDED EXAMPLE 5), it may not be fanciful to feel some of the same tenderness that is evoked by an Annunciation such as that of the *Merode Altarpiece* (colorplate 11). Attention centers on the soprano melody, a fascinating combination of innocence, intricacy, and limpid grace. Though the polyphonic texture still holds to the heterogeneous type illustrated in diagram 2 (p. 225), a clear intention to balance the sound can be detected; notice the almost chordal passage around the words *"filiae Sion."* This resembles English faburden. Composers were still not specifying instruments, but since the sonority as a whole is much more ingratiating than in the little Machaut chanson (RECORDED EXAMPLE 4), the performance can appropri-

ately employ more blending instruments: the tenor and contratenor are each played on medieval fiddles, while the sung soprano is doubled by a fiddle. Dunstable did not pay much more attention to the words than did Machaut, however. The text in praise of Mary is often swamped by graceful vocal decorations.

The main composer of the early and middle fifteenth century was Guillaume Dufay of Cambrai (c.1400–74). Dufay learned something about texture from Dunstable and the English, and he learned something about melody from the Italians, among whom he worked for a number of years. We have a greater amount and variety of music by him than by any earlier composer. Among his compositions is a touching Marian motet written toward the end of his life, *Ave Regina coelorum* (*Hail, Queen of heaven*), in which Mary is asked to intercede on behalf of "Thy dying supplicant, Guillaume Dufay." By medieval standards, this humble act was also an arrogant one: Dufay not only signed his composition, he included himself in it. This bespeaks a new self-awareness of his role as a composer, and a growing respect for the calling in the world at large. Around this time, we begin to find elaborate musical elegies composed to commemorate the deaths of famous composers. Not unnaturally, Dufay's little personal prayer set the words in a very clear fashion, so that the Virgin (or his fellow singers at Cambrai?) would be sure to get the message.

This motet incorporates a Gregorian plainsong, following the regular procedure in sacred music since the beginnings of polyphony. Unlike Pérotin and Machaut, however, Dufay placed the plainsong in the soprano voice, not in the tenor, and he decorated it with extra notes, runs, turns, and rhythmic displacements in much the same way that a jazz musician decorates the notes of a melody on which he is improvising. This kind of plainsong treatment, called "paraphrase," is highly significant for the frame of mind at the time of the dawning Renaissance. For the plainsong was now being thought of as a thing of beauty, rather than as a structural or doctrinal element; it was placed where it would be clearly heard, and modernized to fit in with the polyphonic piece as a whole. The desire for modernity grew so strong that ultimately a Renaissance pope authorized a new edition of the complete Gregorian plainsong repertory, purified of its medieval "barbarities" and revised according to current canons of melodic beauty. The Renaissance did not abandon plainsong, then; plainsong remained the essential music of the Church, and the Renaissance, for all its pagan interests, remained an essentially Christian movement, not a neo-pagan one. But the Renaissance did view plainsong in a significantly new light.

Dufay's principal successors were Johannes Ockeghem (c.1420–95) in Antwerp and Tours; Jakob Obrecht (c.1430–1505) in Cambrai, Bruges, and Ferrara; Josquin Desprez (c.1440–1521) in various Flemish, north French, and Italian towns; and Heinrich Isaac (c.1450–1517) in Brabant, Florence, Constance, and Vienna. The international range of their activity should be noted. These composers carried forward the work of Dunstable and Dufay in the area of intimate chansons and motets, and also in another area initiated by the older masters, that of large-scale compositions belonging to a markedly constructional type. Here the principal new form was the polyphonic Mass.

As explained on page 218, the liturgy of the Mass, the most important of the daily services, contains many items sung in plainsong or chanted. Some of these are "ordinary" (the same every day) and others "proper" (varying from day to day). Composers at this time began to make polyphonic settings of the five main ordinary sections of the Mass: the Kyrie, Gloria, Credo, Sanctus, and Agnus Dei. This was certainly a reasonable idea, in that such settings could be used again and again. But when, in addition, composers began to unify all five sections by musical means, this was a very unreasonable idea, at least from the liturgical point of view—for the sections do not follow one another in the service, they do not fulfill the same religious function at all, and they differ in length, form, and even language (the Kyrie is in Greek). The concept was a purely technical one, and would never have occurred to men of the early Middle Ages, with their deep concern for liturgical propriety. Nevertheless it has held good through the centuries: Palestrina, Monteverdi, Bach, Beethoven, Liszt, and Stravinsky have all composed five-section Masses which are unified works in one sense or another.

At first, the favorite means of musical unification was the use of a single slow melody in the tenor voice as the structural basis for each of the five sections. Hence the terms "tenor Mass" or "cantus-firmus (fixed-song) Mass." For the tenor melody, either a secular song or a plainsong drawn from another service was selected—it is hard to guess which would have astonished the early Middle Ages more, the use of secular songs in the Mass or the mixing up of the Mass with other services. When we ob-serve more than twenty composers basing Masses on one and the same melody, the famous *L'Homme armé (The Man of Arms,* a satirical song about the marauding armies of the Hundred Years' War), we gather that a technical, individualistic, competitive spirit was definitely in the air. By comparing the various *L'Homme armé* Masses, music historians can make fine discriminations of style, just as art historians can by comparing successive treatments of the same subject (see figs. 124, 142, 169).

Composers developed highly ingenious devices in composing Masses, as though trying to outdo one another in technical prowess. They could turn the basic melody upside down, speed it up, slow it down, or present it in canon—that is, one voice would start the tune and then another would sing it simultaneously but staggered, starting a few beats later and perhaps also a few notes higher or lower. A round such as *Three Blind Mice* is a simple sort of canon. They were not above devising riddles to tell the singers how to perform these technical feats ("canon" means a rule or direction). In Josquin Desprez's *L'Homme armé* Mass, one of his most brilliant, he directs the singers with a mild canon using the words *"Sancta Trinitas, salve me"* (Holy Trinity, save me) to perform a certain section as a three-voiced canon—but they will also have to figure out for themselves that each one must sing in a different time-signature before the day may be called "saved." Furthermore, Josquin's tenor voice sometimes presents the melody of *L'Homme armé* backward, and he starts it on different notes of the scale in each of the five sections. (This is like playing *Yankee Doodle*—another satirical song about soldiers—starting first from C on the piano, its proper place, and then from D, E, F, and G without using any sharps or flats.) Something of the same mentality can be observed here that led to the esoteric symbolism that characterizes Flemish painting from Campin and the Van Eycks to Bosch.

The polyphonic Mass, with its five great sections all unified according to some musical scheme, constituted the most impressive form of sustained musical thought that had yet been produced. For us, unfortunately, it is less easy to appreciate the beauty of this music than to observe its preoccupation with technique and construction—the necessary underpinning for beauty. This preoccupation persisted in the old complex ways of the fourteenth century, which Dunstable and Dufay were deserting in other aspects of their music. As late as around 1450, old-fashioned isorhythmic motets were still in demand for special festive occasions (such as, in Dufay's case, the dedication of the dome of Florence Cathedral), and Dunstable and Dufay could turn them out with the best. The difference is that the music of the later fifteenth century cultivated complexity of combination, rather than complexity of rhythmic differentiation, as in the fourteenth century. The musical texture was growing constantly smoother and more sonorous. The device of canon, as the reader may have realized already, links voices in the polyphony so that they cannot be distinguished in quality. This marks an important step toward a genuinely homogeneous musical texture.

However, the Italians of the sixteenth century found nothing but scorn for these Northern technical devices, which they cheerfully confounded with Gothic elements in art and music. To men steeped in Cicero's Latin prose and Petrarch's Tuscan poetry, the very names Ockeghem and Obrecht were an object of fun, and seemed to sum up a crabbed, unmelodious concept of the art of music. In actual fact, the Italians had profited deeply from these technical advances. And as the sixteenth century progressed, Italy—which we tend to think of as the "land of song"—assumed the dominant position in Western music, for the first time. Henceforth it was here rather than to Flanders that Europe turned for singers, composers, and new ideas about music. Italy was to keep this position for two hundred years or more.

2. THE SIXTEENTH CENTURY

The musical Renaissance in Italy began, paradoxically enough, with those Flemings and Frenchmen who in the late fifteenth century overran the Papal Chapel and the brilliant courts of the Medici, the Este, and the Sforza. As Northern musicians came in contact with Italian humanistic ideas and Italian popular music, a distinctive new musical style which may be called the "High Renaissance" style came to fruition simultaneously in the North and in the South. It will be simplest first to describe and illustrate this important style, and then to trace aspects of it that show the influence of Italy.

The main distinguishing feature—the main stylistic change from the Middle Ages—is a matter of musical texture. In discussing medieval polyphony on pages 225–26, we pointed out that the fundamental concept involved highly individualized voice-lines, analogous to multicolored threads in a heterogeneous weave. Now, however, the voice-lines grew to resemble one another so closely that the whole texture became essentially homogeneous.

The change-over can be traced step by step in the music of the late fifteenth century. The slow tenors started to move faster—even in the tenor Masses—and in order to match them, the intricate, wide-ranging sopranos proceeded in a slower, more stately way. As composers developed in technical skill, contratenors were made to fill in the gaps without awkwardness and to move as smoothly as the other voices. Indeed, the function of the contratenor as a filler disappeared, and the contratenor was itself replaced by two voices, in the middle (alto) and low (bass) ranges. The standard medieval grouping of three voice-lines was felt to be too thin; composers preferred four voice-lines, each occupying its own particular segment of the available sound range.

And since the voice-lines were now very similar in melodic and rhythmic quality, their actual sonorous quality was required to be similar also. The colorful mixed vocal-plus-instrumental ensembles of the Middle Ages no longer suited the balanced, relatively bland musical texture. Typically, the voice-lines were all sung; the standard choral grouping of today—soprano, alto, tenor, bass—finds its origin in the High Renaissance style. Or else the voice-lines were all played on instruments of the same family—that is, on a group of recorders, viols, or trombones. The angels in Matthias Grünewald's *Isenheim Altarpiece,* dated c. 1510–15, are all playing on viols of different sizes (albeit fantastic viols—see colorplate 16).

The voice-lines also came to employ the same melodic material. It was no longer the case that one of them carried the most interesting melody, and the second an altogether different plainsong melody, while the third served merely as an unmelodious filler. Even in the tenor Masses, as time went on, portions of the basic tenor tune began to be echoed by the other voices. Finally, about 1500, composers standardized the technique of fugal imitation (often called simply "imitation"), in which a small melodic fragment was introduced in one voice (it did not matter which, for all were similar) and then passed systematically through the others. The writing of canons—in tenor Masses, once again—had prepared the way for this technique. But whereas the whole idea of canon is to keep going rigorously throughout a long melody, fugal imitation was applied freely to small fragments of melody only. A sixteenth-century Mass, motet, or chanson would consist of a whole series of different small sections in imitative style ("points of imitation").

The new texture can be expressed by a line-diagram as follows (compare diagrams 1 and 2, p. 225):

DIAGRAM THREE

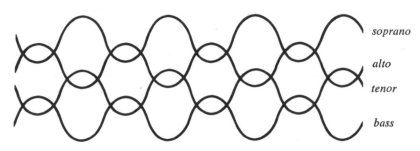

soprano

alto

tenor

bass

Fugal imitation was the great technical invention of Renaissance music. It can probably be singled out as the earliest compositional device that has enjoyed uninterrupted vigorous life from early times right down to the present day. The name reminds us that fugal imitation led to the fugue of later centuries (see p. 250), but it should be understood that a Josquin motet has numerous separate small fragments of melody treated successively in imitation, whereas a Bach fugue typically has only one, which is extended at considerable length throughout the entire work.

A further characteristic of the imitative style has to do with the treatment of words. In medieval polyphonic compositions, the text generally comes in a single voice—or else several texts go on at once, voice by voice. In Renaissance compositions, each voice has the entire words; each point of imitation has its own small portion of the total text and passes this through all the voices. Thus homogeneous texture implies homogeneous setting of the words. Since the voices are staggered, often enough the words in the soprano are obscured by what the alto, tenor, or bass are singing. Still, if the lis-tener misses the words the first time, at least he has several more opportunities to catch them in another voice; and each verbal phrase has its own melody which comes again and again and so characterizes it distinctly. In comprehensibility of the text, this marks a decided advance over the Middle Ages.

Our illustration of the new style is a segment of a late work—probably c.1515–20—by Josquin Desprez, the *Pange lingua* (*Let the tongue record*) Mass (RECORDED EXAMPLE 6). The five sections of this Mass are unified by the use of a single tune, the plainsong hymn *Pange lingua* (a fine tune of Carolingian origin, to which words were later added by St. Thomas Aquinas in building his service of Corpus Christi. Josquin's Mass would therefore be especially appropriate to this Feast). But the tune does not go into a structural tenor voice, as in an isorhythmic motet by Dufay or in Josquin's earlier *L'Homme armé* Mass, mentioned above. Instead, lines of the hymn are paraphrased (see p. 231) so as to provide fragments of melody to start up successive points of imitation. Hence the term "paraphrase Mass." But even this relatively loose connection with the plainsong is often broken; Josquin felt quite free to drop it for long periods, composing as his fancy directed him. In our recorded segment, only the musical phrases with the words "*Et incarnatus est . . .*" and "*Crucifixus etiam pro nobis*" refer to the melody of the hymn, in each case to its first line. There are about a dozen points of imitation (which do not, however, necessarily run through all four voices; this segment is from one of the more wordy sections of the Mass, the Credo, and composers tended to hurry through it). Fugal imitation is perhaps easiest to hear at the words "*Crucifixus*," "*et resurrexit*," "*et ascendit*," and "*vivos et mortuos.*"

Very different from this, and very striking indeed, is the treatment of the opening phrase of our segment, "*Et incarnatus est . . . .*" This is harmonic setting of a self-conscious simplicity, all four voices singing together to form block chords, and all speaking the words at exactly the same time—that is, as clearly as possible. Evidently Josquin intended to give special tender emphasis to these words, dealing once again with Mary's role: "And He was incarnate by the Holy Ghost of the Virgin Mary: and was made man." Surely he also intended to bring out the meaning of the text by means of his relatively harsh, angular music for the word "*Crucifixus*" (He was crucified) and his joyful upward line for the words "*et ascendit in caelum*" (and He ascended into heaven). The recorded performance is by an unaccompanied choir, a very suitable arrangement given the style, although in Josquin's time some instruments might well have played along with the singers.

In what features of this High Renaissance style can we trace an Italian influence? On the simplest level, first of all, in the musical style exemplified by Josquin's *Et incarnatus est*. Harmonic setting in block chords is derived directly from a contemporary Italian practice. During the 1480s, an unassuming popular or semipopular musical style grew up for settings of equally unassuming Italian poems; two forms were the *lauda* (praise), a popular religious song, and the secular *frottola,* which means something like potpourri. Trivial in themselves, these pieces seem to have fascinated Northern musicians by their straightforward harmonic texture. Josquin, who wrote one or two frottole himself, developed the technique in a more sophisticated context. This is the first time in the history of music that we can speak of "chords" or a real "chordal conception" of music.

Secondly, the whole concept of homogeneous musical texture, with its qualities of rational order, evenness, and balance, owes a great deal to the classicism of Italian humanist thought. The perfect division of the sound range and the even distribution of labor among the voices; their beautifully calculated interrelation and counterpoise; the general calm, smooth momentum without any abrupt surprises to attract undue attention—all this recalls the earlier Renaissance ideal in the visual arts. Even in what may strike us as a negative aspect of this music, its lack of interest in brilliance and color, it reminds us of the "harmonious grandeur" of Bramante's architecture or the restraint of Raphael's early paintings (figs. 147, 150). The crucial step, before this ideal could be realized, was that of cutting down the tenor voice. It could no longer enjoy the primacy and the authority granted it by the composers of tenor Masses in a direct line from the composers of isorhythmic motets and organa. Josquin's evolution from the *L'Homme armé* Mass to the *Pange lingua* Mass is typical: from a type of construction in which the basic melody is isolated in the tenor (tenor Mass) to one in which the melody is evenly distributed throughout a homogeneous texture (paraphrase Mass).

Thirdly, there is the matter of the treatment of words in relation to musical expressiveness, which we have already touched on in reference to Josquin and will see growing more and more important in the later Renaissance. This was the favorite subject of the humanists who restudied Classic writings about music. What struck them particularly were reports of the expressive nature of Greek music and its extraordinary power in moving men's emotions (see pp. 215–16). Why should not music of their own time do the same? Politian, the great humanist at the court of Lorenzo de' Medici, wrote a celebrated play on the subject of Orpheus, the mythological figure who more than any other symbolizes the power of music. (The play was accompanied by music that unfortunately is lost, though a stage design for it by Leonardo da Vinci has been preserved.) As more and more Greek documents yielded to humanistic scholarship, the burden of advanced thought pressed upon musicians to recapture an expressiveness similar to that reported of the Classic golden age.

The only apparent way to do this was with the help of words. Greek theory stressed the intimate association of music and words; this seemed only natural to the humanists, who were above all literary men. First of all, it was necessary—as it never had been in the Middle Ages—to *hear* the words when they were sung, to have them declaimed correctly (i.e., to adjust rhythms and pitches to the various syllables in a way that corresponds to normal speech). Beyond that, words could be *illustrated* by musical means. Certain melodies, rhythms, or combinations could sound tender, harsh, or joyful; and gradually composers such as Josquin learned to match the words that they were treating to music of an appropriate sentiment. Previously word-illustration of this sort had been employed only tentatively. Later it was greatly refined and indeed exaggerated, as we shall see, in the development of the Italian madrigal.

Like all the most far-reaching human discoveries, the significance of this one took some time to sink in, from its first intimations to its universal acceptance. But a discovery it was— for in fact Greek music had not achieved its expressiveness in this way at all. Only the animating idea was Greek, filtered through the minds of the humanists. The particular implementation could only have occurred at this particular stage of musical evolution, with Josquin and his generation. If, as we have said, fugal imitation counts as the great technical invention of the Renaissance composers, then word-illustration may be judged their great expressive discovery.

Josquin himself was considered pre-eminent by his contemporaries—the notion of artistic genius was just developing (see p. 110)—and also by musicians for many years after his death. This was an unusual tribute; remember Tinctoris' opinion of all music composed forty years before the time he was writing. What contemporaries admired especially was Josquin's range and intensity of expression, though they also appreciated his technical virtuosity and his unprecedented boldness. They pointed to specific pieces of his that seemed to them majestic, violent, passionate, gentle, and humorous. Modern criticism would confirm contemporary opinion in this case. Josquin seems to us perhaps the first composer in the history of music having the comprehensive mastery shown by a Bach or a Beethoven in later times.

We are also in a position to see how over his career Josquin grew less interested in the Mass, with its fixed liturgical text, and more interested in the motet, where he could choose the words himself and set them in an appropriately expressive manner. In choosing texts to set to music (or "subjects" to treat), composers found a real outlet for the individuality that is so charactertistic of the Renaissance frame of mind. The range of the Latin motet spread to include humanistic poems, fragments of Vergil and Horace, and certain highly emotional sections of the Bible that have no liturgical position whatsoever in the services. There was a corresponding expansion of range in Italian texts. Whereas the medieval composer was by and large confined to certain parts of the liturgy and to secular poems of stereotyped form and content, the Renaissance composer had, as it were, discovered the whole world.

Modern attitudes began to emerge—with Josquin, even in respect to "artistic temperament." He would appear to have caused his princely patrons almost as much trouble as did his younger contemporary, Michelangelo. There exists a letter in which an Italian recruiting agent advises his master to hire Heinrich Isaac, even though Josquin is admittedly the best composer available, because Josquin has the reputation of being difficult, composes only when he feels like it, and commands an appreciably higher salary. But this advice was not followed; Josquin occupied positions all over Italy, including almost a decade at Rome in the Sistine Chapel (during the time the building was being decorated by Botticelli, Ghirlandaio, and Perugino). In this important musical establishment, heavily supported by such art-loving Renaissance popes as Sixtus IV, Julius II, and Leo X, his music and that of his countrymen made a lasting impression.

The High Renaissance style proved to be so fruitful that for several generations composers of sacred music could occupy themselves by exploiting it and refining it. The harmonic style became smoother, the fugal imitations were made to sound regular and effortless. As more and more facility was developed, the number of voices was increased from four to five or six as the norm, with a resulting increase in richness of texture. Indeed, things began to run in a pattern and by 1550, motets and Masses had become rather predictable entities, whether they were composed in Italy or in the North.

The celebrated Roman composer Giovanni Pierluigi da Palestrina (c.1525–94) standardized the style to such a degree that his music lived on as a model for the study of counterpoint, which is the technique of combining polyphonic voice-lines. Students labor over "counterpoint in the Palestrina style" even today. This gave Palestrina an exaggerated reputation in later centuries, as did also his well-publicized role in the Counter Reformation as a result of some edicts of the Council of Trent (1545–63). Called to rally and reform the Catholic Church after the staggering blows it had received from the Reformation, the Council decided among other things to "purify" Church music: most Carolingian sequences (see p. 221) were now ejected, polyphonic Masses based on secular tunes such as *L'Homme armé* were condemned, and simplicity and comprehensibility of the words were demanded above all. Palestrina's best-known composition, the Pope Marcellus Mass—Marcellus II was Pope briefly in 1555—was an effort to fall in with these demands.

While we may admire the limpid perfection of Palestrina's technique and the purity of his melodic invention, we may also regret a certain repetitiousness in the hundred-odd Masses that he composed, and miss the force and variety of the previous generation. Nor is it pleasant to read his public recantations of his youthful secular compositions (madrigals). Especially in Rome, the Counter Reformation exerted an inhibiting force on music as on the visual arts.

SUGGESTIONS FOR LISTENING

JOSQUIN DESPREZ, *Pange lingua* Mass
DGG; DECCA; MUSIC LIBRARY

JOSQUIN DESPREZ, Motet *Tribulatio et angustia*
HISTORY OF MUSIC IN SOUND

GIOVANNI PIERLUIGI DA PALESTRINA, Pope Marcellus Mass

WILLIAM BYRD, Mass for Five Voices

WILLIAM BYRD, Motets
LYRICHORD

THE MADRIGAL. More vital developments occurred outside Church music. The most forward-looking music was Italian, for after the time of Josquin, the French chanson assumed a relatively bland and stereotyped form. Around 1530, a genre called the madrigal sprang up in Northern Italy. Humble in its beginnings, it spread all over Europe as the most important and characteristic musical form of the late Renaissance.

The early madrigal was closely tied to a resurgence of Italian poetry. The sonnets of Petrarch, the great humanist and poet who had prefigured the Renaissance in the fourteenth century, now—some two centuries later—enjoyed a remarkable revival and produced many imitators. Important new figures emerged, including Ariosto and Tasso, whom the Italians rank with Dante and Petrarch as the four members of their poetic Parnassus. From the beginning, the madrigal movement was as much a literary phenomenon as a musical one, and it owed much of its impetus to literary societies with a humanistic orientation, called academies (for art academies, see p. 149). Academies commissioned books of madrigals, debated fine points of musico-literary relationship in them, and sometimes even engaged staff composers.

In musical style, the madrigal stemmed from the High Renaissance motet, with a passing reference to the simple-minded frottola of the 1480s. A madrigal was a moderately short piece for four voices (and later, for five or six) consisting of sections in fugal imitation and sections of harmonic setting. However, as compared to the sacred music, the techniques were applied in a lighter, more informal way, and much more attention was paid to the words. This was the key feature. If Josquin's generation had learned to declaim the words of Latin motets correctly, the madrigalists strove to declaim Italian verse beautifully, subtly, or dramatically. But over and above this, the main point of madrigal composition was not simply declamation but expressive illustration of the words. In this, the madrigal realized the aspirations of the humanists better than any other music of the time.

Innumerable rhythmic, melodic, and harmonic devices were developed to mirror the meaning of individual words and phrases. Some of these devices strike us as farfetched: using only two voices when the word "two" appears; using the notes G–A (sol-la) when the word *"sola"* (alone) appears. Others have a psychological aptness that has kept them in service to the present day: using repeated upward melodic movement for the expression of joy or excitement; using shifting harmonies for the expression of trouble or uncertainty. Some of the poems that inspired madrigals were playful, others were intense, passionate, meditative, religious—the entire spectrum of lyric poetry lay at the composer's disposal. The academies that sponsored madrigals encouraged composers to set the same famous sonnets of Petrarch in a quite frankly competitive spirit. In the *L'Homme armé* competition, the Flemish composers had tried to outdo one another in technical ingenuity, but the madrigalists now tried to excel in imaginative expressive effects.

In the early decades of the madrigal development, after 1530, Northern composers dominated the field (still!), but later in the century Italians took it over. The most famous of them, Luca Marenzio (1553–99), wrote twenty-three books of madrigals (with about twenty madrigals per book) which went into numerous editions all over Europe, including some with English and German translations. Marenzio was a composer of the greatest sensitivity, even hypersensitivity—a sixteenth-century counterpart to Chopin in the nineteenth century or Debussy in the twentieth.

Since madrigals depend so much on the relation between words and music, the best example for our purposes will be one with English words—not by Marenzio, but by one of his English admirers, Thomas Morley (1557–1603), a member of Queen Elizabeth's Chapel Royal. In the madrigal *Stay, heart, run not so fast* (RECORDED EXAMPLE 7), Morley projects the words with a nice sense of their natural speech quality throughout. Furthermore, the music is constantly bringing out sentiments latent in the text—halting at the words "stay, heart"; lighthearted at "then let her go"; hurried at "and after her I run"; pathetic or mock-pathetic at "Flora, farewell!"; and ironic, perhaps, at "I care not." When the second speaker in the poem scolds the first, notice how a sudden change of harmony mirrors the sudden change of attitude (on the word "O" in "O vile wretch"). The words "sharp disdain" give rise to the note G-sharp, incidentally—a musical pun. The six-voice texture, typical of the late madrigal, with its half-harmonic and half-imitative style, is handled so skillfully that it all sounds quite airy, swift, and delicate—as is appropriate to the amorous fripperies of the poem.

Many madrigals by Marenzio, set to less trivial verses, aim at more serious effects than this. Intensely emotional effects were a specialty with Prince Carlo Gesualdo of Venosa (c.1560–1613), who made a sensation of one sort by murdering his wife and her lover in bed, and of another sort by daring to use the most astonishingly modern-sounding chords in his madrigals. Contemporary critics were astonished, but they did not go out of their way to criticize the Prince. Late madrigal poetry is full of complex, contrived "conceits"; the music relies also on exaggeration and distortion of normal musical procedures—normal according to the standards of the High Renaissance style. As musical contrast was pushed to extremes in order to match the eccentric poems, formidable technical skill was developed to make the contrasts hold together. All this suggests Mannerism in the visual arts, and the mood of certain Mannerist artists finds parallels in Marenzio's mercurial, nervous elegance and in Gesualdo's barely controlled hysteria.

At the opposite extreme, many subclasses of light, short madrigals grew up, often with parodistic or erotic texts. These pieces naturally inclined toward simple harmonic setting, rather than intricate fugal imitation. The best-known of these subclasses is the ballett, or fa-la, so called because it was intended to accompany or suggest dancing and because it involved refrains set to nonsense-syllables such as "fa la la la la." Such balletts as Morley's *Now is the month of Maying* and *My bonny lass she smileth* are still popular today, and may give the false impression that all madrigal music is light and dancelike. But Marenzio, Gesualdo, and their contemporaries in Italy and England also wrote serious madrigals of great expressive power and psychological penetration. The madrigal owes its position as the most impressive musical form of the sixteenth century to its great range of style, scope, and sentiment.

A tendency toward harmonic setting can also be observed in another important development of the late sixteenth century, that of Venetian music. Its special feature was the manipulation of grand "stereophonic" effects for two or more choirs; and for this, once again, harmonic setting was more suitable than fugal imitation. Music of this kind sounded especially splendid in the Basilica of St. Mark, with its two widely separated choir lofts. As a musical center, Venice came to the fore as the century progressed, until the positions of chapelmaster and organist at St. Mark's were regarded as the most prestigious in Europe. The most famous of the organists were the Gabrielis: an uncle, Andrea (1510–86), who also played a key role in the madrigal development, and a nephew, Giovanni (1557–1612), who experimented with brilliant vocal-instrumental combinations. The line of chapelmasters culminated in Claudio Monteverdi, the foremost figure of the early Baroque period (see p. 245).

In general, Venice, home of the most notable colorists in painting of the time, also pioneered in musical effects that we call "colorful": mass effects, instrumental sounds, solo and choral combinations, as well as the double-choir style itself. At last we have come to a point in the history of music at which particular instruments began to be specified with some regularity. For one of his celebrated motets or *sinfoniae sacrae* (sacred symphonies), Giovanni Gabrieli called for a chorus of ten voice-lines, four trombones, bassoon, organ, and two *cornetti* (not cornets, but obsolete instruments something like curved recorders with trumpet mouthpieces).

Many currents, in addition to the madrigal and the Venetian double-choir style, were leading toward a more purely harmonic concept of music in the late sixteenth century. The demand of the Counter Reformation for comprehensible words led to simple harmonic setting in Masses and motets; meanwhile the French chanson evolved in the direction of a plain tune with chordal accompaniment on the lute or guitar. This emphasis on harmony, rather than on the polyphonic or "linear" aspects of music, caps the Renaissance tendency toward a sensuous, pleasurable quality of musical sound, and it marks an important step toward the modern world. What was sixteenth-century harmony like?

Listening to the Morley madrigal *Stay, heart* (RECORDED EXAMPLE 7), we will doubtless agree that the harmony sounds more familiar than that of any earlier music—and yet it is still not quite "right" to our ears. The familiar sound results from the fact that most of the chords are in the form of the triad (sometimes called "the common chord"). A triad consists of a note, the next note but one, and then again the next note but one: C E G or D F A, etc.— and the notes can be duplicated at will in other octaves (can and must, if six voices are involved, as in Morley's madrigal). These chords came up in medieval polyphony, but it was the sixteenth century that made them into the basis of harmony, a position they continued to occupy up to the beginning of the twentieth century. The most influential musical theorist of the time, Gioseffe Zarlino, chapelmaster at St. Mark's from 1565–90, made a special point of the full, rich sonority of the triad.

What had not yet evolved was a concept of "functional harmony," an ordering of the triads so that each has its particular role or "function" in reference to the centrality of one chief triad, the tonic triad. Plenty of semitone cadences (see p. 221) occur and make for a satisfactory sound on the momentary level; composers regularly used sharps and flats for this very purpose (though *musica ficta*—see p. 227 —was still left largely to the singer). But the triads do not seem to support a central one, nor to gain meaning themselves from their position in reference to a center. Each triad tends to sound too independent. The main feature of the modern tonal system, the feeling of centrality, is not yet present, and for this reason Morley's madrigal still has a vague, unsettled sound to our ears, in spite of its liveliness. Just as we refer to plainsongs and some old folk songs as modal melodies, we refer to sixteenth-century harmony as modal harmony.

Our discussion of Renaissance music has been restricted essentially to vocal music, music with words. That accords with the humanistic bias of the time; the humanists shared the Greek prejudice against instrumental music, and the main composers were interested first and foremost in the relation of words and music. Nevertheless, music for instruments made signal advances during the sixteenth century. In this area foundations were laid for later developments that were to be of the greatest importance for the history of modern music.

Instruments could always play polyphonic vocal pieces, of course, and frequently did. Benvenuto Cellini mentions in his autobiography an occasion when he and some friends played motets for Pope Clement VII on an ensemble of wind instruments; in England books of madrigals were often advertised as being "apt to voices and viols." However, a need was felt for something more idiomatic—that is, something designed to fit the peculiarities of the various instruments and to show off their capabilities. Composers began to write special pieces both for chamber-music ensembles, as we would call them today, and also for certain favorite solo instruments.

The chief of these, the lute, was a widespread, all-purpose instrument as popular as the piano in later times. A guitarlike instrument of Islamic origin, it may have come to Europe in early medieval times (Renaissance lutes are shown in figs. 122, 162). Castiglione's *The Courtier,* a famous etiquette book of 1514, recommends that gentlemen learn to sing to their own accompaniment on the lute; in Elizabethan times barbershops furnished their customers with a cheap variety of lute, a cittern (see colorplate 20), to keep them occupied while waiting their turn. Great lute virtuosos came to the fore, and with them, lute music of considerable subtlety and intricacy. Idiomatic music also was written for the keyboard instruments: for the organ (here the leading role was played by the Venetians mentioned above, such as the Gabrielis); for the quiet clavichord, a small instrument which hits its strings with little levers; and for the brittle-sounding harpsichord, which plucks its strings with sharp quills (a harpsichord can be heard in RECORDED EXAMPLE 12). Neither of these two forerunners of the modern piano had much range in volume of sound—and therefore that new instrument of the eighteenth century would be christened pianoforte, or "soft-loud."

Lutes, harpsichords, viols, and other instruments were perfected in the sixteenth century, especially in Italy. The same is true of the members of the violin family—violin, viola, cello—although their greatest period came later. Instrument making was a minor art, sometimes practiced by painters and other artists, who on occasion decorated instruments lavishly with paintings on the wood, wood inlay, or metal etching. That so many Renaissance pictures have instruments in them can be explained partly by the fact that Renaissance instruments were such beautiful objects.

The central language of Renaissance music— the High Renaissance style of Josquin and his contemporaries, the later Italian madrigal, and the idioms of instrumental music—spread very effectively throughout Europe. Music printing flourished after its introduction at Venice about 1500; music circulated freely; musicians could travel from post to post more easily than in earlier times. Each country developed its own "dialect" of the central language. A composer such as Roland de Lassus (1532–94), who was a Fleming, could grow very skillful in all the dialects, issuing quantities of French chansons, German polyphonic songs, Italian madrigals, Venetian dialogues, Latin Masses and motets, and even one French Protestant Psalm setting. The Italians, in fact, insisted on claiming him as "Orlando di Lasso," for he was probably the most impressive and productive composer of the time, as well as the most international. Born not far from Cambrai, the nerve-center of Flemish music for a hundred years, he was thrice kidnaped as a child on account of his beautiful voice and taken to Italy. After spending time also in London and Antwerp, he settled down in Munich as the honored director of the palace chapel of the dukes of Bavaria.

In northern Europe, the Reformation naturally had a serious effect on the art of music, so closely bound to the Catholic liturgy. Depending on their individual orientations, the various Protestant churches jettisoned most or all of the Catholic services, and with them almost every note of the Gregorian chant—to say nothing of standard polyphonic church music such as the Masses and Marian motets of Josquin and his contemporaries. In place of all this, the new churches fostered congregational singing of simple devotional songs in the language of the people, not in Latin. This meant that church music really touched the people; but it also meant that there was need for quantitatively less music, for less complex music, and fewer musicians. In some denominations, musicians were able to recoup some of their losses, but only at the price of considerable caution in musical style.

The devotional songs were of two types, hymns and metrical Psalms. The Lutherans in Germany and Scandinavia opted for hymns, or chorales (the German word *Choral* means hymn); these were newly written religious poems, set to tunes assembled by Luther's musical advisers from a variety of sources. Besides items composed on the spot, older semi-popular religious songs were pressed into service, along with some secular songs and even some pieces filched from Catholic plainsong (see p. 221). Luther himself, as a former monk, believed firmly in the importance of music and was a special admirer of Josquin Desprez (who was still alive in 1517 when Luther's ninety-five theses were nailed onto the church door at Wittenberg). By temperament he was inclined to encourage polyphonic settings of the chorales. Thus the old musical traditions of tenor construction and paraphrase technique gained a new stay of life under Lutheran auspices. We shall see the effects of this, two centuries later, in the work of the greatest Lutheran composer, Johann Sebastian Bach.

The Calvinists of France, Switzerland, and the Low Countries were stricter. They objected to freely invented poems (hymns), insisting on the Word of God, namely Psalms, which however they did not mind rewriting as wretched rhyming jingles. Calvin took pains to establish a regular series of tunes to which the metrical Psalms should always be sung, in the famous

French Psalter of 1564; but he did not encourage rich polyphonic settings of these tunes. Nonetheless, some were written.

In England, characteristically, the Anglicans took a position somewhere between the Catholic and Protestant extremes. Besides hymns and Psalms, polyphonic services and anthems were allowed, analogous to polyphonic Masses and motets but composed in a very much simpler style. However, the English Puritans held Calvinist views, and so the only music on board the *Mayflower* was a book of Psalms with their tunes: the *Ainsworth Psalter,* named after the divine who had retranslated and re-rhymed the texts. And the first book printed in the Colonies was the *Bay Psalm Book* of 1640. This contained only the words of the Psalms, without music, since evidently one or two well-known tunes sufficed for Puritan services and it would not have been worth while to print them. The colonists had other things on their minds besides music.

Many present-day hymns preserve original Lutheran and Calvinist melodies, as is shown by the little annotations provided in all modern hymnbooks. *All people that on earth do dwell* is from Calvin's *French Psalter,* a tune once sung with Psalm 100 ("Old Hundredth"). *A mighty fortress is our God* is the famous chorale written (and composed, it is said) by Luther himself. Tunes such as these have been sung and loved from one generation to the next; they have supported four centuries of Protestant worship, and have become deeply imbedded in the musical consciousness of many nations.

It must be remembered that France and half of Germany remained Catholic, so that many French and German composers of this and later centuries continued to produce music for the Catholic rite. Even in England, Catholic church music was written in a defiant spirit after the Reformation by the greatest composer of the Elizabethan period, William Byrd (1543–1623). Byrd's three surreptitiously published Masses are perhaps the most beautiful examples of the later Renaissance style that can still be heard with some frequency today.

Of the various Northern "dialects" of music, it is likely that the English will interest us the most, although it probably does not really stand out over the others. The Golden Age of Queen Elizabeth, Sir Philip Sidney, Shakespeare, and Sir Francis Drake was also a golden age of music, secular as well as sacred. References to music in Shakespeare's plays—we discussed one at the beginning of this study, page 216—are frequent and often highly technical, which seems to confirm that the general level of musical sophistication in those days was high. Playwrights employed songs and instrumental pieces with an excellent sense of their dramatic effect. As we noted in reference to RECORDED EXAMPLE 7, there was a lively English madrigal school founded by Thomas Morley on the Italian model; there was also an attractive repertory of relatively simple songs with lute accompaniment, on the French model. Among the composers of these lute airs, the Irishman John Dowland (1562–1626) excelled also as a lute virtuoso in great demand abroad, and the physician Thomas Campion (1567–1620) was well known also as a literary figure, writing polished verses for his own and other people's songs. Instrumental music reached a very high level, especially music for harpsichord, the main variety of which was called (for some obscure reason) the virginal.

SUGGESTIONS FOR LISTENING

LUCA MARENZIO AND GESUALDO DA VENOSA, Madrigals

DGG-ARCHIVE

"Elizabethan and Jacobean Ayres, Madrigals, and Dances"

DECCA

GIOVANNI GABRIELI, Sinfoniae sacrae

VOX

3. *THE BAROQUE*

One of the marked changes in musical taste over the last few decades has been a general growth in interest in Baroque music, music from the period c.1600–1750. Works of J. S. Bach, the greatest of Baroque composers, are now widely performed in church and concert hall; record listeners have established a vogue for such lesser lights as Vivaldi and Telemann;

and even Baroque operas—once considered "impossible" for modern audiences—have recently been revived at important festivals. Amateur chamber-music players, too, turn more and more to the music of this period. Characteristic Baroque instruments such as the recorder and the harpsichord are enjoying a new wave of popularity—one can even buy a do-it-yourself harpsichord-building kit.

All this has made the term "Baroque music" a familiar one, though the adjective was borrowed from art history only in fairly recent times. The borrowing has occasioned a good deal of debate among music historians. Is it really wise to hitch the star of music so firmly to the fine arts, even if parallels between music and art seem to be especially impressive in this period? Indeed, are we really dealing with a single unified period of music history? How should we balance in our minds (and in our terminology) those stable features that distinguish the music of this hundred-and-fifty-year span from that of earlier and later times, as against the features that change and develop —and do so more seriously in the music than in the fine arts of this period? And if the period should indeed be thought of as unified, is it best thought of as the end of "the era of the Renaissance" or as the beginning of "the modern world"?

On the side of modernity, we meet the slogan "new music" as soon as we start to study music around 1600. (We have met it once before, with the Gothic *ars nova* after 1300.) It was coined by a member of a group of self-conscious innovators who stimulated one of the most interesting movements in the entire history of music. They called themselves the "Camerata," because they met "in camera" (behind closed doors) at the palace of Count Giovanni Bardi of Florence. Indeed, the membership included several wealthy dilettantes as well as poets, humanist scholars, theorists, and singers—but, perhaps significantly, no composers of the first rank. (One of the best of them was a peppery composer-theorist named Vincenzo Galilei, whose son was the astronomer Galileo Galilei.) The Camerata worked out musical experiments together, put on theatrical performances, and infiltrated various influential musical positions. We know about them because they were natural publicists, issuing numerous treatises, tracts, prefaces, and gossipy public letters to explain and promote their ideas.

How different this sort of activity is from the slow, obscure maturing of a new style in the hands of professional church musicians such as Dufay or Josquin! Music history was certainly happening in a new way; but when we examine the actual program of the Camerata, our first impression is of its deep roots in Renaissance musical thinking. For their essential goal was far from novel: it was simply to recapture the emotional power that music and words had achieved together in classical Greece. The Camerata was in fact another humanistic society, or academy, of a kind that had figured all through the later sixteenth century in connection with the madrigal development. Though the Camerata turned sharply against the madrigal, we shall not be wrong to regard their activity as part of a long Renaissance tradition.

Indeed, they must be accorded the credit for bringing this tradition to a rousing climax, for in one respect they were really prepared to go all the way with Greek music. Its power, they felt, could only be regained if modern music restored the Greek condition of individuality, one singer expressing himself to the accompaniment of the lyre or its equivalent. This was musical humanism with a difference, a humanism that formed its musical ideal on a single free agent rather than on the anonymous "harmonious" cooperation of a vocal or instrumental ensemble. Polyphony—the condition of that cooperation, and the very condition of musical development for five hundred years—struck the Camerata as impersonal and artificial (and, of course, un-Greek). The madrigalists' devices to reflect the meaning of words and phrases struck them as childish and unemotional. Seeking a new way of matching music to the words, as the Greeks had insisted, they proposed to stress the natural declaiming of words, if necessary sacrificing other musical elements.

This far earlier composers had not been prepared to go. We have seen that Josquin learned to declaim words consistently—his generation was the first to do so—and that Marenzio and Morley labored to declaim them more and more subtly; but these composers always fitted the words to recognizable fragments of melody, which typically served for fugal imitation. The Camerata scorned melody as such, to say nothing of fugal imitation. Their ideal was to imitate the accents of passionate speech, the kind of excited sing-song which a great orator or actor begins to use at moments of highest intensity. Even the name for this style, recitative, comes from the word "recite." Everything depends on the words, so much so that while motets or even madrigals can be played with good effect on a group of instruments, recitatives make no sense at all without the words that generate them. The recitatives at the end of our RECORDED EXAMPLES 8, 9, and 14—however different they are in other respects, as we shall see in due course—are all equally incomprehensible (and boring) if we do not follow the words or at least an English translation along with the music.

The emphasis on individuality—one singer —led naturally toward the stage. The new style was called the *stile rappresentativo,* or theatrical style. While the Camerata never meant to revive Greek drama as such, they acknowledged its inspiration and they did indeed mean to imitate the musical style of the Greek theater. They started out composing short dramatic monologues, such as laments, and soon moved on to real theater pieces—plays set to music all the way through; predictably, the first ones were based on Greek myths (Daphne, Orpheus, Cephalus, Ariadne). The original names *dramma per musica* and *opera in musica* (drama for—or through—music, work in music) were ultimately shortened to plain "opera." Opera was the great invention and fascination of the Baroque period and its main musical form, comparable in importance to the motet, Mass, and madrigal in earlier times, and to the symphony later.

Before speaking of the actual development of opera, we need to discuss the change in musical texture that prepared the way for it. The "theatrical style" demanded a completely new musical texture. With all attention focused on the individual singer, everything else had to be minimized; in the interests of expressivity, the singer had to be given great latitude in such matters as slowing down and speeding up, and also in using notes quite unrestrainedly, without worrying about clashes with other polyphonic lines. So a flexible new texture was developed, which was essentially harmonic in orientation. It consisted of the main line, sung in recitative; a strictly subsidiary bass line acting as a prop for it below; and, between them, background harmonies filled in by a chord instrument such as a lute or a harpsichord. The chords did not need to be specified exactly; they could be improvised by the player, keeping one eye on the singer and the other eye on the bass line of the score. To help him, the bass line was furnished with figures that indicated the correct harmonies in a generalized shorthand way. Hence the term "figured bass," the usual English equivalent for the term *basso continuo* (continuous bass. The English translation was "thorough bass," "thorough" being

an old form of "through" or "throughout").

Continuo texture constituted the main feature common to Baroque music over its whole span of a hundred and fifty years, a span during which other features changed very considerably. (The Baroque period in music used to be called simply—and quite reasonably—the "*basso continuo* period.") The texture was harmonic in orientation, as we have said, and certainly new; yet we also remember that many currents of Renaissance music had been leading in this same direction. As the voice-lines in a polyphonic piece increased from a normal number of three (Dufay) to four (Josquin), to five or six (Marenzio), and to even more (Gabrieli), they tended to coagulate, as it were, into a harmonic mass. Sections of block-chord writing were familiar in Masses and motets. Songs with a simple chordal accompaniment for lute had been known for decades. What the *continuo* idea did was to systematize all these harmonic tendencies, and provide a very convenient technique for composers and performers in the figuring of basses and the improvising of chords with the help of these figures.

From opera and other "theatrical" music, the *basso continuo* spread rapidly to madrigals, church music (where the chord instrument was the organ), and instrumental music. The favorite instrumental texture involved not one but two main lines above the *basso continuo* and the fill-in chords. This "trio texture" is represented by diagram 4 on the following page. The two main lines (most frequently played on violins) are identical in nature. They occupy the same range in the treble, share the same musical material, and often work in fugal imitation or in parallel motion. Acting as a support, the *basso continuo* (a cello) tends to differ from them in quality; typically it moves at a steady pace, thus setting up a rhythmic framework analogous to the harmonic framework derived from the figures. (In some styles, however, the *basso continuo* does sometimes share the material of the main lines.) The harpsichord, lute, or organ fills in the gaping space between the treble and the bass—as is indicated on the diagram by shading. In both RECORDED EXAMPLES 8 and 9, the brief sections played by the violins employ a simple form of this trio texture.

Some analogies may be suggested between Baroque musical texture and the treatment of light and space in Baroque art. Whereas in the High Renaissance, fugal imitation kept all the voice-lines in perfect balance, in the Baroque, one or two lines were strongly highlighted and

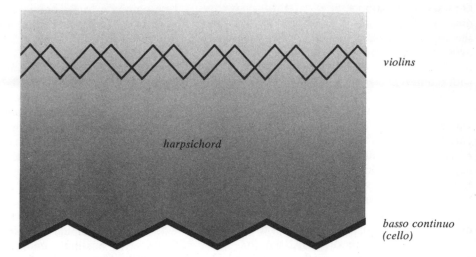

violins

harpsichord

basso continuo (cello)

others placed in the shade; we can think of the "theatrical" lighting of Caravaggio's *The Calling of St. Matthew* (fig. 167) as contrasted to the even illumination of Early Renaissance painting. We can also think of the *basso continuo* as generating a sort of harmonic "space" (or "space-time") within which the singers or the solo instruments could trace patterns that were increasingly brilliant and elaborate, now that they had been freed from the responsibility of keeping in line with other polyphonic strands. In a fully developed Baroque piece, the "space" could be crowded with a complex array of musical lines and colors, superimposed one on the other from the lowest depths to the dizziest heights—for the chords could be extended through all the octaves, to the limits of hearing.

DIAGRAM FIVE

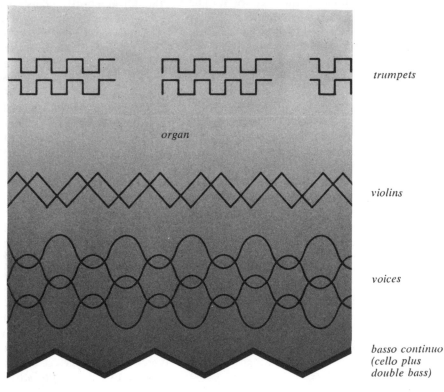

trumpets

organ

violins

voices

basso continuo (cello plus double bass)

The most magnificent example of this is the Sanctus section (1724) of the famous Mass in B minor by Johann Sebastian Bach (the beginning is heard in RECORDED EXAMPLE 10).* As the voices and instruments pursue their multiple lines—some of them rhapsodic, others emphatic, but all intricately bound together—the space almost seems to sway with the change of the framework harmonies determined by the *basso continuo.* We can well imagine numberless angels singing praises to God ("Holy, holy, holy, Lord God of Hosts!") as they swirl around the clouds and drapery on a great Baroque ceiling—under which, indeed, this music would have been performed. Diagram 4 can be filled up as in diagram 5 (see preceding page).

Notice that in spite of the classicizing theories of the Camerata, polyphony still played a key role in fully developed Baroque music (and even in the trio texture, with its tendency toward fugal imitation in the two main lines). We cannot draw any simple distinction between Renaissance and Baroque music on the basis of polyphonic versus harmonic style, for both styles were prominent in both periods. The difference lies in the fact that Baroque polyphony works against a background of chords predetermined by the *basso continuo.* Whereas in the Middle Ages and the Renaissance, harmony came about as the result of the combination of polyphonic lines, in the Baroque, harmony was a primary element providing the channels in which the polyphonic lines could be traced.

Thus a figure such as Bach owes his outstanding position among late Baroque composers both to his profound sense of harmony, and also his unparalleled mastery of polyphony, in the fugue. Indeed, all Baroque music can be said to occupy a range between two diametrically opposed musical forms, recitative and fugue. Recitative within a harmonic texture was the new unrestrained, highly individual way of expressing emotion; fugue was the powerful new constructive principle, the new way

of ordering polyphonic lines. Taking a cue from the Camerata, we may perhaps see a renewal of Greek "archetypes" here: the music of Dionysus, god of wine and orgies, opposed to the music of Apollo, god of light and order.

The leading figure of the early Baroque was Claudio Monteverdi (1567–1643), who has been called "the last great madrigalist and the first great opera composer"—a neat epithet which reminds us that Baroque opera came as a culmination of the expressive tendencies of Renaissance music, notably in the madrigal. Monteverdi started composing in the chief musical form of the time, the madrigal. In about a dozen books of madrigals and related forms, published between 1583 and 1638, we can trace the gradual transformation of the old style into the new, as he imported recitative, the *basso continuo,* trio texture, and much else into the pieces until they were madrigals in name only. In 1600, a notorious attack was leveled against Monteverdi's license with respect to counterpoint in the Palestrina tradition (see p. 236), in a book with the amusingly stuffy title *On the Imperfections of Modern Music.* Attacks of this sort, which are not uncommon in the annals of music history, and which tell us how extreme and unsettling the innovations seemed to the conservative older generation, rarely hurt the innovators. Monteverdi, who was as skillful as the Camerata members in propaganda, replied that since he and others were composing an altogether new type of music with expressiveness as its one goal, the traditional restraints simply did not apply.

As a madrigalist, Monteverdi surpassed even Marenzio and Gesualdo in expressive power, boldness, and flair. And his first opera, *La Favola d'Orfeo* (*The Fable of Orpheus,* 1607), written in his fortieth year, showed what a composer of genius and experience could do with a form invented just a few years earlier by the intellectual dilettantes of the Camerata.

Besides writing recitative that is infinitely more moving, Monteverdi enriched opera by drawing on the full range of the music of his time. This appears in a short continuous excerpt that comes near the dramatic climax of *Orfeo* (RECORDED EXAMPLE 8). The passage opens with a brief madrigal-like chorus (the inhabitants of Hades, speaking like a Greek chorus, remark that Pity and Love have triumphed). It proceeds to a brief recitative (a Spirit announces that "the gentle singer" is leading his wife back to the upper world). Then, as the long journey begins, Orpheus

* For late Baroque composers, the Mass still consisted of the same five "ordinary" sections as it did for Dufay, Josquin, and Palestrina (see p. 232). But these sections were now subdivided into arias—a reflection of the Baroque fascination with opera—and choruses of various kinds. As for the qualification "in B minor," this is a way of referring to pieces and distinguishing them from others that came into use with the development of the tonal system (see p. 255). The Bach Mass begins on the note B and on the B-minor triad, and uses the minor scale (however, the Sanctus section, an interior section, is in the tonality of D major).

sings a regular song, or aria, in praise of the power of his lyre; this aria is a sprightly tune enlivened by instrumental interludes. He breaks off dramatically at the end, wondering whether perhaps the Spirits mean to trick him; overcome by anxiety and desire, he decides to look back at Eurydice in spite of Pluto's injunction not to do so until they are out of Hades. This section is handled in flexible recitative, a fine example of this style in its early period, from the pen of its greatest master.

Neither the *basso continuo* line, consisting of long drawn-out notes, nor the chords filled in by the harpsichord above it, has any character worth mentioning. All interest focuses on Orpheus' reciting line. Sometimes he speaks in a great emotional rush, at other times he pauses tenderly on certain key words— "*ohime*," "*amata*," "*luci*," "*io pur*" (alas; beloved; eyes; I now). Large and small melodic intervals, and consonance or lack of it with respect to the accompanying harmony, are handled with great awareness of their affective power. The result is an astonishingly lifelike portrayal of an impetuous and passionate personality; we feel a sense of tragic inevitability when Orpheus yields to his feelings, and looks back. At the point of crisis, the chord instrument changes from the bright harpsichord to the somber organ—an early instance of the use of orchestration for dramatic effect. In fact, the harpsichord has been used throughout the opera as the instrument of the upper world, the organ as the instrument of Hades. Notice also the harmonic wrench at the very end of the excerpt as Orpheus actually looks back, and is horrified to see Eurydice enveloped in a cloud and taken from him ("*Ma quel ecclisi . . .*"). The sequence of chords resembles one that comes at a semidramatic place we have mentioned in Morley's madrigal *Stay, heart* (p. 238), but Monteverdi's effect is much more excruciating, and he uses technical means of the very sort that laid him open to conservative attacks. But as he himself would have said, the extreme means seem perfectly justified by the expressive end.

As for the little aria *Qual onor,* that is clearly set off from the surrounding recitative by its tuneful nature, its coherent bass line, its punctuating instrumental sections (in trio texture), and by the fact that it is made up of three poetic stanzas with parallel music. In these, the *basso continuo* (in a characteristic steady motion) and the chords are identical each time, but the vocal melody changes somewhat. This is a simple example of an important musical technique known as variation, whereby a single element—a tune, or, as here, a bass—is repeated a number of times with some changes that modify its nature in interesting ways without entirely obscuring it. This technique, too, had been pioneered in the sixteenth century; fine sets of variations for virginals were written by the Elizabethan composers. After Monteverdi, variation technique was little used for opera arias, but it grew more and more important in the instrumental music of the Baroque and later periods.

The earliest operas were private court entertainments. The wedding of Marie de' Medici, which we have seen celebrated in Rubens' series of paintings glorifying her life (fig. 177), was also celebrated in an opera promoted by the Camerata at the Florentine court. All through the Baroque period, opera performances were considered obligatory for royal weddings, birthdays, and coronations, and to this day opera carries overtones of "high society." But a crucial step was taken in 1637 with the opening of public opera houses in Venice. Opera became the rage not only with the aristocracy but also the middle classes and, it is said, the gondoliers. Monteverdi, who at the age of seventy was still very much in evidence as chapelmaster of St. Mark's Cathedral, contributed several excellent new operas; many more were written by composers of a new generation. Later in the century, Venice with its population of nearly 140,000 could support seven opera houses, an example followed only a little less enthusiastically by musical centers all over Italy.

These figures would be about right for movie theaters in a modern city; and some instructive parallels can be drawn between Baroque opera and the movies of today, even though the conjunction may seem surprising. Both opera and the movies were and are deeply popular arts, responsive to the wishes of the public and the pressures of the box office in a way that church music, for example, is not. The public demanded fresh entertainment all the time; opera houses did not generally present last year's operas, any more than movie theaters generally run last year's movies (though today, opera houses seem to be repositories of the past). Most operas were hastily put together out of a stock of facile formulas, routines, and clichés, both musical and dramatic. Like the movies, opera depended critically on stars. The domination of great virtuoso singers, which followed naturally from the emphasis on individuality in the original thinking of the Camerata, came to be a characteristic (or a curse) of opera up to the present day. And in the same way that movie directors take second place to the actors, opera composers often took second place to the singers, the authors of the words (librettists, after the Italian *libretto,* little book), and especially the stage designers. For seventeenth-century opera developed fantastically in the direction of scenic effects of a highly spectacular sort, using moving scenery and stage machinery of the most ingenious manufacture. Monteverdi's Eurydice was doubtless whisked away from Orpheus in an elaborate machine; gods and goddesses descended from the heavens on illusionistic moving platforms—complete with sunburst, as in figure 172. In this spectacular tendency, again, Baroque opera was not so far from the movies.

It also approached the visual arts of the time in an unusually close way. For at the same time that opera was bringing Baroque music into the theater, Baroque art was also looking in that direction. Quite apart from the frankly theatrical conception found in Bernini's *Ecstasy of St. Theresa* (see p. 137 and fig. 170), there is something distinctly stagy about such paintings as Poussin's *Rape of the Sabine Women* (fig. 186), with its self-conscious choreography and its posed attitudes of anguish, or Rubens' *Marie de' Medici* (fig. 177), with its exaggerated gesturings—note the figures on the far right—and its histrionic timing (clearly Marie has just made a dramatic entrance). A number of important artists and architects, including Bernini himself, collaborated in operatic productions. The ambitious blending of the arts—movable architecture, scene painting, vocal and instrumental music, poetry, drama, costume, the dance—realized one tendency of the Baroque even more fully than did the great ceilings, in which architecture, sculpture, decoration, and painting blend to create an illusion of constant movement. Looking at figure 176 and colorplate 17, we almost expect stage machinery to swirl the clouds, figures, and drapery up to extraordinary new spatial vistas. But stagecraft has not survived as well as ceilings have. We can only imagine it, on the basis of descriptions, and "still" pictures like figure 172.

To speak now of the music, the development of Baroque opera after the time of Monteverdi was remarkably rapid and diverse. Even historians who are most inclined to view the Baroque as a single unified period must admit that opera in 1700 wears a very different aspect from that of 1600. Besides the main Italian variety, there was a distinctive French offshoot centered at the court of Louis XIV. And if religious sculpture could become as theatrical as in Bernini's *St. Theresa,* church music could also become thoroughly operatic: we shall see two important religious offshoots of opera, the oratorios of Handel and Bach's church cantatas.

In Italy, the great change in emphasis was from recitatives to arias. After 1650, arias began to dominate at the expense of recitatives, choruses, and (for a time) even instrumental parts. Declamation, passion, and all the other ideals of the Camerata were forgotten in face of an overwhelming interest in virtuoso singing. Seventeenth-century Italian opera plots were incredibly involved, making a special point of multiple disguises and subplots; they were less like dramas than great rambling extravaganzas. But these plots did maneuver the characters into a great variety of situations allowing them to express various sentiments in arias—and it was the arias that showed off their voices to the best advantage. The lessons learned from Renaissance experimentation in musical expressiveness were standardized into a series of effective formulas by which arias could express rage, disdain, fear, tenderness, or rapture. As these musical numbers grew more elaborate and impressive, the recitatives grew simpler and more perfunctory. The result was a sharp dualism that imposed an artificial "stop-and-go" quality on the dramatic action.

Of later Italian opera composers, the most important was Alessandro Scarlatti (1659–1725) of Naples, which was a major operatic center. He wrote some 115 operas, an unusual number even in those facile times. Arias became standardized into the *da capo* ("from the beginning") form, a rigid A B A structure in which both text and music of the A-section returned verbatim after the different, contrasting text and music of the B-section—and the A-section could last as long as five minutes or more. Obviously this form, repeated twenty or thirty times in an evening, made a shambles of the dramatic illusion; a character could hardly say anything without being obliged to return to the same words a little later. But the form was admirably calculated for purely musical expansion. Furthermore, the singers developed the art of improvising vocal variations during the second A-section—roulades, trills, and coloratura passages. Thus the *da capo* aria form became another device to show off the stars.

Scarlatti's *Fugge l'aura (Fled's the breeze,* RECORDED EXAMPLE 9) is a typical small *da capo* aria—relatively short and vigorous, and accompanied only by *basso continuo* and harpsichord chords. (It should be understood that operas of the time also included much larger, slower arias, accompanied by full orchestra, and that the singers—unlike the singer on our recording—improvised vocal variations during the second A-section.) Though the melody is actually very long, it does not sound unduly complex because it is shaped into attractive and easily grasped phrases. Words are repeated as many times as necessary to allow the music to round out its fertile, expansive form; many words are lost in the fluid coloratura passages. Above all, notice how beautifully the melodic patterns have been calculated to suit and flatter the soprano voice, which seems positively to blossom in response to them. Our excerpt also includes a fragment of the decidedly routine recitative following the aria. This *secco* (dry) recitative causes an abrupt change of style as well as an abrupt lowering of musical interest.

Standardization—and a modicum of order and elegance—was also applied to the opera plots. After about 1720, an extremely influential poet-librettist, Pietro Metastasio, cut down the fantastic adventures that delighted the seventeenth century into something closer to the "classical" French drama of Racine. Metastasio's librettos, involving noble Roman types caught up in high-minded and neatly balanced conflicts between love and honor, were set again and again—some of them nearly a hundred times in all, some of them several times by the same composer. This curious phenomenon shows the extent to which the dramatic aspect of Italian opera was secondary to what someone later called "concert in costume."

Yet undoubtedly this very fact contributed to its success abroad. With the important exception of France, the other countries of Europe were entranced by Italian opera, sung in Italian by Italians. We meet the further curious phenomenon of major Italian opera theaters flourishing for years in places as remote as London, Vienna, Hamburg, and St. Petersburg. (One thinks of the vogue for foreign movies today and the subtitles, provided to help audiences follow the action; in the eighteenth century, they bought printed translations of the libretto —together with candles.) Italian opera became the common musical language of Europe, and the most impressive composer of Italian opera was a German working in England, George Frideric Handel (1685–1759).*

---

* His own spelling, after he was naturalized a British subject. The original German form was Georg Friedrich Haendel or Händel.

Handel's years of apprenticeship were passed in the opera houses of Hamburg, Florence, and Venice. In Italy he met Alessandro Scarlatti and also Alessandro's son Domenico (see p. 260). Settling in London, Handel produced about forty Italian operas there—"produced" in both senses of the word, for he acted as impresario as well as composer. After two centuries of neglect, these works are finding performances today, and they show how a great composer could overcome rigid formal conventions and the tyranny of the singers; Handel's operas are full of beautiful music and also create a powerful impression of characterization and drama. The subjects, which were typical of the times, ranged all the way from Tamerlane, Richard the Lion-Hearted, Julius Caesar, and Alexander the Great to the myth of Jupiter and Semele—his single quasi-operatic venture in English, and a very good one.

When his various opera companies at last failed, the resourceful composer concentrated on oratorio, a religious offshoot or analogue of opera, written in English and designed neither for the stage nor for actual church services but for concert presentation. Stories mostly from the Old Testament, such as those of Samson, Saul, or Jephthah, were expanded to provide extra roles, develop a love interest, and so on. The characters held forth in recitatives and arias, like opera characters. But unlike opera, oratorio found a large place for the chorus, which represented the people of Israel or their enemies, or else an anonymous commenting group. These choruses, composed by Handel with particular power and imagination, sometimes even overshadowed the dramatic action; the oratorio *Israel in Egypt* involves scarcely any arias and scarcely any story. Handel's most famous work, *Messiah*, also lacks a regular cast of characters, though it contains many beautiful and well-loved arias in addition to choruses. These two works, however, are exceptions, and they should not make us forget that oratorio in England was actually a local reflection of the universal Baroque fascination with opera.

France, as we have said, was the only nation besides Italy to translate this fascination into its own national style of opera. The founder of French opera was a Florentine dancer and violinist, Jean-Baptiste Lully (1632–87), who became an influential figure at the court of Louis XIV, along with the playwrights Molière (with whom he collaborated) and Racine, and the architects and painters of Versailles and the Louvre. More single-mindedly than elsewhere in Europe, opera in France served and celebrated the monarchy. The atmosphere that produced the "royal style" in the visual arts (see p. 148) also contributed to a particular rigidity and pomp in Lully's style. This is most familiar to us through the so-called French overture, a type of orchestral piece used to open operas and other works, consisting of a solemn, high-flown section followed by a faster, fugal one.

Basically, Lully held to the ideals of the Camerata rather than to those of his Italian contemporaries, for he would not follow these composers in sloughing off recitatives and staking everything on arias. This led to a characteristic difference in emphasis between French and Italian opera, which formed a favorite topic of smart conversation at the time, and which to some extent has held true through the centuries. In brief, while the Italians stressed arias and beautiful singing, the French stressed the ballet, choruses, and careful declamation; and the French would not tolerate the picaresque stories of seventeenth-century Italian librettos. As compared to Italian opera, French opera was more spectacular, pompous, subtle, and reasonable, but less melodious, less emotional, and much less well sung.

A miniature opera combining French and Italian characteristics, but leaning toward the French, is *Dido and Æneas* (1689) by the English composer Henry Purcell (1659–95). Though Purcell ranks as one of England's greatest composers, it cannot be said that musical standards in general were kept up to the level of the Elizabethan era. By the time Handel came to London in 1710, and for some two hundred years thereafter, the English were content to import foreign musicians, as the Italians had done during the fifteenth century.

For a variety of reasons, French opera resisted any serious innovations, once a successful standard mold had been established by Lully. His operas held the stage for an entire century—a very unusual situation at that time —and later composers felt obliged to duplicate his patterns. The best of them, Jean Philippe Rameau (1683–1764), was an organist and important musical theorist who turned to opera composition only after 1730. Rameau particularly developed orchestral and choral effects; he produced music of great beauty and distinction, comparable in quality to that of his contemporaries Handel and Bach. Nevertheless, to the advanced spirits of the day his operas seemed impossibly stilted, old-fashioned, and overloaded by heavy, unnatural ornamentation.

SUGGESTIONS FOR LISTENING

CLAUDIO MONTEVERDI, *Orfeo,* Act II
DGG-ARCHIVE

CLAUDIO MONTEVERDI, Madrigals
CAMBRIDGE RECORDS, "ARIE MUSICALI"

GEORGE FRIDERIC HANDEL, *Semele,* Act III
OISEAU-LYRE

GEORGE FRIDERIC HANDEL, *Messiah,* Part I (note French overture)

HENRY PURCELL, *Dido and Aeneas*

JEAN PHILIPPE RAMEAU, *Hippolyte et Aricie,* Act V
OISEAU-LYRE

INSTRUMENTAL MUSIC. By the time of Handel and Rameau, instrumental passages played an integral part in opera. This was a reflection of the very significant development of instrumental music in the Baroque period, the first period in music history during which purely instrumental music began to approach vocal music in quality and importance.

Monteverdi's use of brief string interludes in Orpheus' aria *Qual onor,* and Scarlatti's use of a string postlude in *Fugge l'aura,* seem simple and obvious enough. But it was quite another problem for composers to know how to make an entire instrumental piece of some sophistication stand by itself, without words. To understand the problem takes some effort, for to us nothing seems more natural than writing or listening to a piece just for instruments. To the sixteenth and seventeenth centuries, however, what was "natural" was music with words— music tied to a liturgical text from the church services, to a madrigal poem, or to a libretto. If there was no line of thought established by a verbal text, on what principle should one note or one section of music follow the next? If there were no words, how could the composer hold the listener's attention?

There were three ways of solving this problem. In essence each was well understood by the sixteenth century. Baroque instrumental music stemmed directly from the Renaissance, with no noticeable break around the year 1600.

First of all, the composer could divert or dazzle the listener by special idiomatic effects peculiar to the instrument in question. Works produced on this principle are generally called toccatas (from the Italian *toccare,* to touch). They feature rapid runs, broken chords, and perhaps bold effects of harmony and volume, all presented in a somewhat disorganized, rhapsodic way. Though these pieces may indeed seem very flamboyant and exciting—witness Bach's well-known Toccata and Fugue in D minor for organ—the genre does not allow for much development.

The second possibility issued from the dance. Simple music for dancing was of course the original and eternal province of instruments —and the original source of the antipathy toward instruments on the part of the Fathers of the Church. No longer disturbed by this antipathy, Renaissance composers began to write what we may call "idealized" or "stylized" dances. These highly sophisticated pieces suggested particular dances by using their general rhythm, mood, and pattern of repeats, but they grew much too subtle to serve for actual dancing. (When a great jazz player or group gets to work on a well-known dance tune today, everybody stops dancing and listens.) The idea of "stylized" dances has a long history after the Baroque period, as we know from the minuets of Haydn, the mazurkas of Chopin, and the *Roumanian Dances* of Bartók.

In Baroque times, the actual dances suggested were of great variety. In the decades following 1600, older types such as the pavane and galliard gave way in popularity to the stately allemande (German dance), the lively courante (running dance), the slow sarabande, and the rapid gigue (jig). It became customary to compose these stylized dances in a group, called a suite. Baroque suites generally made a framework out of the four dances just named, which form a well-contrasted set, and added a few miscellaneous lighter, more modern ones. Of these, the minuet enjoyed special popularity (and we shall see that the minuet also played a unique role in music after c.1750). The first minuet is said to have been danced by Louis XIV to music composed by Lully; however this may be, it was probably French in origin, for the French were the ballet masters of Europe, dominating the European dance scene until the rise of Russian ballet in the nineteenth century. The writing of suites, both for harpsichord and for orchestra, became a specialty with French composers, of whom the most famous were an uncle and nephew, Louis (c.1626–61) and Francois Couperin (1668–1733).

The third possibility lay in instrumental music's copying vocal music. This amounted to adapting the style of fugal imitation which dominated all vocal music of the time. Even without words, the interplay of instrumental parts carrying the same melodic fragments gave the listener something to follow, and gave the composer something that might be described as a principle of purely musical organization. However, there was no longer any reason to keep changing the melodic fragments, a process that arose in vocal compositions in order to differentiate successive portions of the text being set to music. In instrumental music, then, fugal imitation was typically limited to a single melodic fragment, called the fugue subject, that was handled in various ways throughout the whole extent of a relatively long polyphonic piece. In this way, the Renaissance Mass and motet led ultimately to the fugue, one of the most characteristic and important forms of Baroque music.

A fugue for organ by Bach, the so-called Cathedral Fugue in E minor, is our RECORDED EXAMPLE 11 (without the short toccata, called "prelude," that was composed to go with it. A toccata plus a fugue made a well-contrasted combination). This is an early Bach fugue (before 1708), concise and relatively simple. The short, forthright fugue subject stands out clearly at each of its dozen-odd appearances in the course of the work, which simulates the standard Renaissance texture of four "voices." We follow it with considerable interest, waiting to hear just how, when, with what accompaniments, and in which part of the range the subject will return—perhaps in the "soprano" (the top of the keyboard), perhaps in the "bass" (the pedals). Fugues sometimes have the reputation of being dry and mathematical, but in fact they convey as wide an expressive range as any other Baroque music, along with a greater sense of tightness, workmanship, and intellectual fascination. The Fugue in E minor sounds sturdy and responsible; other fugues sound brilliant, powerful, solemn, or deeply serene.

Keyboard instruments, and idiomatic music written for them, flourished in the Baroque period. The clavichord and the harpsichord (see p. 240) were much cultivated; the harpsichord served very widely as a chord-filling instrument, and its crisp, acerbic accents form an essential component of the typical "Baroque sound." Solo harpsichord music took over some of the characteristics of lute music, as the lute declined sharply in popularity from its high position in the sixteenth century. The organ, the oldest Western instrument still in use (it is documented in Roman and Carolingian times: see p. 222) as well as the most grandiose, reached its peak of development during the Baroque period, notably in Germany. Some organs were small and even portable, containing only one set of pipes (for an early example, see fig. 114). But wealthy churches ordered instruments with several dozen different sets of pipes; these provided a great variety of timbres and different volume levels, and could be played in all groupings or combinations derived from up to three separate keyboards plus a pedalboard (a keyboard for the feet). A number of Baroque organs are still in working condition; our recording employs one originally built for Hamburg in 1695. Many organ firms nowadays are building instruments on the Baroque model, and as compared to usual church organs, these certainly produce better results with Baroque organ music, both for clarity of polyphonic texture in the fugues and for brilliance in the toccatas.

The important orchestral and chamber-music instruments were flutes, recorders, oboes, bassoons, horns, trumpets, and especially members of the violin family. A large orchestra of the late Baroque period, such as that required for Bach's Mass (RECORDED EXAMPLE 10), might employ in the upper range violins and violas, three flutes, three oboes, and three trumpets, and on the *basso continuo* cellos, double basses, and bassoons; the organ further reinforces the bass and fills in chords above it. And the more powerful rhythms are underlined by timpani (kettledrums).

This was the great age of the violin, the age of the masterly, still-unequaled violin maker Antonio Stradivari or Stradivarius (1644–1737) of Cremona. The favorite chamber-music combination of the time grouped two violins, cello, and harpsichord, which we recognize as the characteristic trio texture (see p. 243); pieces written for this combination were called trio sonatas ("sonata" from the Italian *suonare*, to sound, and "trio" from the fact that there were three main lines, although four instruments were required in all). One type of sonata was equivalent to a dance suite; another type consisted of a rather loose number of miscellaneous musical sections, called "movements," some of them always in fugal style. For orchestra, the main form was the *concerto grosso*. Here the orchestra alternated and contrasted with a smaller group of soloists—a principle which may seem simple enough, but which has proved to be endlessly fertile, both during and after the Baroque period. There was also the solo concerto, a solo violin holding its own against the orchestra; and the "solo" sonata, a single violin supported by cello and harpsichord. A major role in establishing the Baroque sonata and the *concerto grosso* was played in one generation by the great Roman violinist Arcangelo Corelli (1653–1713), and in the next by the Venetian Antonio Vivaldi (c.1675–1741).

The fully developed *concerto grosso* is doubtless the most impressive instrumental form of the Baroque period. It shows more clearly than any other how far purely instrumental music had advanced in little more than a hundred years. The reader should hear one of these works all the way through; a good choice would be one of the famous set of six Brandenburg Concertos by Bach (dated 1721; dedicated to the Margrave of Brandenburg). Whereas Corelli and the Italians preferred to make their solo group out of the standard trio-sonata combination—two violins, cello, and harpsichord)—Bach seems to have had the idea of demonstrating the whole spectrum of instrumental possibilities in his set. Each Brandenburg Concerto features a different and very original combination. (A somewhat encyclopedic turn of mind is characteristic of Bach, as we shall see, and also of the Baroque period in general.) Less variety is shown in the number and order of movements, which, after Vivaldi, had become almost standardized to three: fast, slow, and faster. Almost, but not quite:

Brandenburg Concerto No. 3, in G major, for nine string instruments, contains only two movements, both of them fast. Perhaps Bach expected a slow movement to be inserted or even improvised in the middle.

No. 1, in F major, for a special type of high violin (now obsolete), three oboes, bassoon, and two horns plus string orchestra, has a couple of minuets and other dances tacked onto the end of the regular three movements, like movements of a suite.

No. 2, in F major, is the most brilliant and famous of the set, with its fascinating combination of high trumpet, recorder, violin, and oboe plus string orchestra. In the first movement, the two forces alternate in a fairly regular way; indeed, each tends to play its own separate musical material. The loud, rousing orchestral music at the beginning—very typical of the *concerto grosso* as a genre—returns with a solid effect to "wrap up" the end of the movement. However, in the third movement—a brisk, triumphant fugue played all the way through by the solo group—the orchestra has a much less functional role, and it does not play at all during the second.

The second movement amounts to a piece of expressive chamber music in a fugal style for three of the soloists plus *basso continuo* and harpsichord—a "quartet-sonata" movement for violin, recorder, and oboe (the noisy trumpet takes a rest, along with the orchestra). As is often the case, the *basso continuo* provides the upper instruments with an absolutely regular rhythmic framework, as well as a harmonic one; it never shares their melodic material. The upper instruments do share material, quite systematically. Typically Baroque is the nobility of feeling—whether sorrowful, as here, or joyful, as in the other movements—and also the steady, thorough, almost relentless way in which the feeling is projected.

No. 4, in G major, has a solo group consisting of two flutes and a violin; but with considerable subtlety, Bach sometimes employs the flutes as part of the orchestra, rather than as solo instruments. In the second movement, the frequent solemn alternation between solo and orchestral forces comes as near to the older style of Corelli as any music in the Brandenburg Concertos. The third movement is a fine spirited fugue, once again.

No. 5, in D major, for flute, violin, and harpsichord plus string orchestra, has a strong tendency to lapse into a solo concerto for harpsichord, a form that Bach was one of the first to employ. The first movement includes a long toccatalike cadenza, or free improvisatory passage, for the harpsichord, while all the other instruments stand by. In the slow movement, another dignified chamber-music piece with the orchestra silent, a trio texture is created not from the usual two violins and cello, but from flute, violin, and the left hand of the harpsichord—the right hand of the harpsichord filling in chords as needed.

No. 6, in B-flat major, has a curiously "dark" solo group consisting of two violas, cello, and two viola da gambas (forerunners of the cello, which were then still current in conservative circles). Nothing could contrast more sharply with the brightness of Brandenburg Concerto No. 2. As usual, the second movement is a fugal chamber-music piece, a serious trio-sonata movement for two violas, *basso continuo,* and harpsichord. The last movement has the lilt of a gigue, the customary last movement of a suite; however, it does not follow the customary form of the gigue but instead is a literal A B A form. This is another example of instrumental music copying vocal music, for in the Baroque period, A B A form meant the *da capo* aria form of Italian opera.

SUGGESTIONS FOR LISTENING

ARCANGELO CORELLI, Christmas Concerto

JOHANN SEBASTIAN BACH, Toccata and Fugue in D minor for organ

JOHANN SEBASTIAN BACH, Six Brandenburg Concertos
TELEFUNKEN (esp. Concerto No. 2)

FRANÇOIS COUPERIN, Suites for harpsichord
MACE; MUSIC LIBRARY

HENRY PURCELL, Fantasias for strings
VANGUARD

ANTONIO VIVALDI, Trio sonatas
BACH GUILD; TURNABOUT

The name of Johann Sebastian Bach (1685–1750) has already figured largely in our discussion of Baroque music. That it should have done so is inevitable, for Bach, like Josquin Desprez, seems to sum up his entire era. Indeed, his work not only helps to clarify all of Baroque music, but even casts new light on some aspects of sixteenth-century music as well.

Bach's career was as humdrum and provincial as that of his great contemporary Handel was glamorous and cosmopolitan. His years of apprenticeship were passed as church organist in sleepy towns and villages in central Germany, and as musician at minor courts. He settled in Leipzig as cantor of St. Thomas' Church —a high position in the Lutheran world, analogous to chapelmaster of St. Mark's, Venice, in the Catholic world a hundred years earlier. Bach raised an enormous family; four of his sons grew up to be composers, as many of Bach's ancestors had also been. He rarely traveled except to consult on the purchase of new organs, a service for which he was sometimes paid with a cord of wood or a barrel of wine. Between him and the Leipzig bureaucrats there was little love lost, and he would doubtless have preferred a great court position.

The chief music that Bach was employed to provide for the Lutheran services was the Sunday cantata. Now, cantata was originally an Italian term (meaning "sung") for a brief chamber-music piece for voice and instruments —a few arias linked in a semidramatic way by recitatives, like a fragmentary opera. Scarlatti, Handel, and most other opera composers wrote dozens of cantatas. Around 1700, the prestige of Italian opera was such that some Lutheran pastors imported the cantata form boldly and frankly into the church service. Occasionally cantata librettos had symbolic figures, such as Hope and Fear, converse with one another, or the voice of Jesus answer inquiries from a repentant sinner. Generally, though, unspecified Christians meditated or theologized in the recitatives and agonized or affirmed their faith in the arias. To this operatic framework, choruses were often (not always) added, representing the Christian world at large rather than any individual communicants.

We can see that in externals a Lutheran cantata resembled a short Handel oratorio. Both were operatic analogues. But whereas the oratorio was an informal religious presentation in concert, the cantata was liturgical. It filled exactly the same spot in the Lutheran Sunday service that the Gregorian alleluia did in the Catholic Mass (see p. 218). Like the alleluia, furthermore, the cantata was "proper," referring in its text to the feast or the church season and perhaps quoting the particular Gospel reading of the day. Since the Lutheran Church had a long tradition of proper hymns, or chorales, which Luther himself had said might well be incorporated into full-scale musical pieces (see p. 240), composers naturally liked to incorporate chorales into their cantatas. Cantatas by Bach generally end with a simple harmonic setting of some appropriate chorale—simple so that the congregation could either sing along, or at least feel that they had a part in summarizing the little drama they had just witnessed.

A chorale could also be incorporated in a much more subtle way; it could be fitted into a highly complex chorus at the beginning of a cantata, or even into an aria. Composers learned to enrich the hymn tunes with their own musical comments, while the congregation found their religious experience enriched by a reference to a familiar tune and a well-remembered pious thought. Indeed, the tunes were familiar enough to make an effect even without the words, in compositions for organ called chorale-preludes (because originally they were played just before the singing of the chorales). As the greatest composer of Lutheran church music, Bach composed many magnificent organ chorale-preludes as well as five different complete cycles of cantatas for all the Sundays and feasts of the year. So at least we are told; only about two hundred Bach cantatas have survived, together with two Passions—settings of passages from the Gospels telling the complete story of the last days of Jesus. In the Catholic Church, these passages were sung during Holy Week to a Gregorian chant-formula. For the Lutheran Church, the Biblical text was troped (see p. 220) with plenty of chorales, recitatives, and arias, while one singer presented the words of the Evangelist in recitative and others took the roles of Jesus, Peter, and Pilate. Bach's highly dramatic and moving *Passion According to St. Matthew* lasts three and a half hours, forming only a fraction of a Good Friday service that counted as long even in those pious days.

Notwithstanding Bach's impressive achievement in church music, recent research has suggested that this was not at the heart of his interest. Concentrating for his last twenty years on purely instrumental music, he issued one great collection after another in which he seemed to treat a certain kind of music in an exhaustive, definitive way. Sometimes described as "didactic" compositions, these were intended less as teaching material for the young than as encyclopedic examples for the learned and—one rather feels—as monuments for eternity. The best known is *The Well-tempered Clavier,* forty-eight preludes and fugues for harpsichord (alternatively, clavichord), two in each of the existing major and minor tonalities. The preludes are generally toccatalike; the fugues were composed with masterly care and with an astonishing expressive range. This famous work also demonstrated the feasibility of a new tuning system closely resembling our modern equal temperament (see p. 255). In a four-volume serial publication of *Clavierübung* (*The Use of the Keyboard*),* Bach spoke his last word on the harpsichord suite, the organ chorale-prelude, the organ fugue (the *St. Anne Fugue*), and the variation set (the *Goldberg Variations*). At his death in 1750, he had almost completed *The Art of Fugue*, a series of nearly twenty different canons and fugues all based on some variant of a single eight-note subject. In spite of containing some of his greatest music, *The Art of Fugue* was rejected by the generation after Bach, and did not come into its own until the twentieth century.

In the didactic works, Bach summed up the forms of Baroque music in an almost self-conscious way. In *The Art of Fugue,* he seems also to have reached back to the spirit of Flemish polyphony of the early Renaissance; we are hardly surprised to read that he made a "modern" transcription of a Mass by Palestrina a century and a half after it was written. At the other, diametrically opposed pole of Baroque music, Bach was the most powerful writer of emotional recitatives since Monteverdi, and he understood better than any other composer how to manipulate the new principles of "functional harmony." Bach did not introduce functional harmony—it had grown up slowly, and Scarlatti was already fully conversant with it—but he exploited its possibilities so profoundly that his work remains a model in this respect to the present day. Music students are taught to emulate the harmonic settings of chorales at the end of Bach cantatas, just as they learn to write "counterpoint in the Palestrina style."

It is important for us to end our study of Baroque music with a brief discussion of functional harmony, for this technical matter was

perhaps as crucial for the future development of music as was a technique such as perspective for the development of painting (see p. 100). The reader will do well to review our discussions of modal melodies in the Middle Ages (pp. 221–22) and modal harmony in the Renaissance (p. 239). We have seen that the Renaissance had established harmony based on triads, the chords that remain the basis of Baroque music, but had not treated them in what we describe as a "functional" way. The notes and chords were not all related to one another in such a way that each had its particular function in a total system and contributed in its own fashion to a feeling of centrality for one triad. It was this that the Baroque period, with its strong systematic tendencies, developed into a beautifully elaborate system known as the tonal system. The triads had been there all along, but now composers developed a new way of looking at them—or, rather, a new way of hearing them, and a new way of juxtaposing them to encourage this kind of "relational" hearing.

The comparison between the tonal system and perspective has some validity in terms of technique and aesthetic principle, even though it has little or none in historical terms. (The tonal system evolved several hundred years after perspective; however, both were abandoned about the same time.) We may say that the tonal system provided the Baroque composers with a method of ordering "soundspace" by setting up a "vanishing point"—the tonic triad—against which every aspect of the composition was reckoned. Here at last was a rationale that could serve purely instrumental music, that could substitute for the old reliance on words to provide the essential line of thought. Like perspective, the tonal system proved to be a rich, flexible means of organizing works of art during a long period of history.

How exactly were the triads related to the "vanishing point" and to one another? This can be explained in general terms if the reader has an approximate idea of musical notation. Line (a) of diagram 6 shows the C-major scale, which is simply the diatonic or white-note scale (see p. 217) with the note C singled out as the tonic, and accordingly numbered "1." The point in singling out C, rather than some other note as in medieval music, is that a semitone cadence between the notes marked 7 and 8 supports the tonic (see p. 221). It was only during the Baroque period that the major scale (and the minor scale, oriented around A) finally replaced the medieval modes as the basis of all music.

---

* Engraved on copper; Bach, a craftsman in everything, did some of his own engraving, in a very beautiful hand. Note that the process (see Synopsis of Terms) involved tracing the music backward.

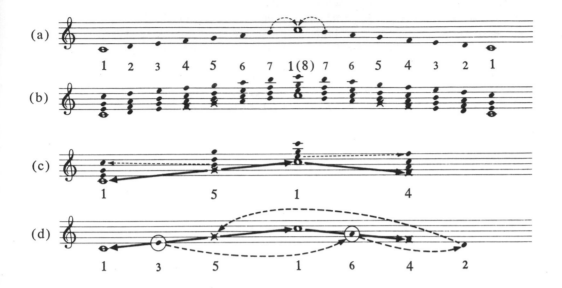

Line (b) shows the C-major scale again, with the triads built on each note. A special mark (x) has been added to the notes and triads that came to be seen as next in importance to the tonic: G (5) and F (4).

Line (c) shows the two basic "relationships" of tonality. The function of the 5-triad is to lead strongly to the tonic triad (the 1-triad); every time 5 is played it seems to lead or pull toward 1. The "natural" basis for this leading quality is a large question, but it has something to do with the semitone cadence between certain notes of the triads (B → C, indicated by a dotted line on the diagram). Furthermore, the relationship between 1 and 4 is equivalent to that between 5 and 1, because in each case the triads are a fifth apart. Therefore 1 has a tendency to pull toward 4, or conversely, 4 has the solid quality of underpinning 1. For this reason, a particularly conclusive, satisfactory cadence can be made out of the triads 4, 5, and 1.

We have allowed line (d) to become rather complex, in order to suggest some of the complexities that come up as soon as we get past the fundamentals. The triads 3 and 6 act as way stations between 5 and 1, and 1 and 4, respectively; but between themselves they exhibit a two-way "leading-and-underpinning" relationship. Again, the triad 2 underpins 6, and also—more importantly—leads to 5 and thence indirectly to the tonic.

By exploiting these subtle relationships, and many more, composers developed a powerful tool for relating not only one chord to the next, but also one part of a movement to another, and indeed, even one whole movement to another movement. Thus the tonal system became a guiding principle of composition. Also, once a clear sense of centrality was established, it became a matter of some interest to see the consequences of deliberately shifting the centrality from one tonic to another, as though changing the location of the vanishing point. When this occurs, there is said to be a change of tonality (or key)—that is, a change from the galaxy of relationships around one tonic (a set of lines converging toward one vanishing point) to another such galaxy.

Composers investigated this process not only with respect to the seven notes of the diatonic scale, but also the five sharps and flats. They ran into difficulties, because the tuning that was in use for the notes of the scale, being designed for the diatonic notes only, left the sharps and flats badly out of tune with one another. To make the entire space negotiable, as it were, the octave had to be divided up absolutely evenly between the twelve notes C, C-sharp, D, D-sharp, E, etc. This is in fact how the modern piano keyboard is tuned (but Renaissance harpsichords were not so tuned). Our "diatonic scale" starting from C is slightly off tune, from Pythagoras' standpoint; however, our piano allows us to build exactly similar (and, again, only slightly off tune) scales on B, C-sharp, and all the rest. The point is not so much to be able to write a Mass in B minor or in some other unusual tonality, as to be able to change tonalities within the course of a single work. The tuning system that provided for this is called equal temperament, and its first thorough demonstration came in J. S. Bach's *Well-tempered Clavier*.

Referring to the establishment of the diatonic scale in ancient times, on page 217, we remarked that the basic language of Western music can be said to be Greek. Perhaps this statement should now be qualified to say that after the late Baroque period, the language was Greek with a modern accent. For the modification of the diatonic scale into equal temperament had far-reaching implications, both theoretical and practical. Only this modification made possible the most impressive landmarks of music in the modern world: the symphonies of Beethoven, the operas of Wagner, and the twelve-tone compositions of Schoenberg.

SUGGESTIONS FOR LISTENING

JOHANN SEBASTIAN BACH, Cantata No. 140, *Wachet auf (Sleepers, awake)*

JOHANN SEBASTIAN BACH, Chorale-preludes for organ: *Wachet auf, Kommst du nun, Jesu,* etc.
DGG-ARCHIVE

JOHANN SEBASTIAN BACH, *Passion According to St. Matthew,* Part I

JOHANN SEBASTIAN BACH, *The Well-tempered Clavier* (on harpsichord or clavichord)

JOHANN SEBASTIAN BACH, *The Art of Fugue,* contrapunctus 4, 5, and 7
BACH GUILD

PART FOUR

MUSIC IN THE MODERN WORLD

1. ENLIGHTENMENT AND REVOLUTION

In the 1750s Bach, Handel, and Rameau all came to the end of their long careers. They might well have looked back over the musical scene with astonishment as well as nostalgia, for after 1730 music had begun to take new paths. In music, as in art, the Enlightenment caused a reaction against the aristocratic Baroque style, and during the last decades of the activity of these composers, when they were bringing Baroque music to a brilliant summation, critics already regarded their work as old-fashioned and out of sympathy with the times. After Bach's death, his music went underground, as it were, for nearly a century until it was rediscovered by musicians of the Romantic era.

The positive program of the Enlightenment called for the rule of reason, nature, and the common good in place of tradition, artifice, and established authority. This "revolution of the mind," as we have called it (p. 156), was the intellectual precursor of the industrial revolution and the great political revolutions in America and France, the effects of which still define and control the modern world. Modern music, too, began with a rapid reversal of taste and style—a "revolution" comparable to the one that we have seen in the visual arts. Comparable—but more drastic in the case of music, and, initially at least, more fruitful. Whereas in art the reaction led to a fairly lengthy period of diffusion and uncertainty, in music it led as early as the final third of the eighteenth century to a powerful new synthesis. This was the so-called Viennese Classic style, whose great practitioners were Haydn, Mozart, and Beethoven.

The new style was to crystallize in Austria. Indeed, during the eighteenth century a shift can be discerned in the geographical center of musical thought and activity. In the Middle Ages, it will be recalled, the center was France. For a time, Flanders took the lead, and then,

from about 1550 to 1750, Italy. Now Italy yielded to Austria and Germany, partly as a result of yielding intellectual leadership too; for the Enlightenment took its roots from empirical philosophy in England, flowered in France with Voltaire, Rousseau, and the Encyclopedists, and came to fruition with an impressive group of German thinkers. These included Winckelmann, who "discovered" Greek antiquities (see p. 157); Herder, who developed a new interest in folk culture; the dramatist and aesthetician Lessing; the great philosopher Kant; and the poets Goethe and Schiller. For the history of music, Herder's emphasis on the natural—and to the period, therefore admirable—quality of folksong was especially important. And Lessing deserves mention in a book of this sort because he was the first to think of the arts in the way we do today—that is, to think of music, painting, architecture, and poetry as parallel manifestations of a single basic artistic impulse.

It was during the eighteenth century, too, that the German-speaking countries grew important in the political sense. The groundwork for a united northern Germany was laid by Frederick the Great of Prussia, a model of an "enlightened" ruler, while the Austrian Empire reached its peak under the somewhat less enlightened Maria Theresa. We may regard it as symptomatic that Frederick himself not only patronized music generously, as did a great many German princes, but also played the flute and even composed tolerably well.

The Viennese style that grew out of the Enlightenment is called "Classic," a term that we shall continue to use, even though admittedly it confuses as many issues as it clarifies. There can be no analogy here to Neoclassicism (see p. 157), for composers, unlike the artists of the time, were not evoking or reinterpreting any earlier style. They were developing an entirely fresh one, and they did indeed pay much attention to form and structure—more attention, certainly, than did the Romantics, who were the first to apply the term "Classic" to the Viennese composers. They worked for precision and clarity, and they greatly refined such matters as musical articulation, symmetry, and balance. In this, the Romantics sensed a spiritual affinity with the ideals of the ancients as newly expounded by Winckelmann and Goethe. The analogy was irresistible, but, like much Romantic thought, more suggestive than precise.

There is a not uncommon misconception that an emphasis on form, precision, and clarity must stem from intellectuality and the absence of emotion. The Romantics, who prided themselves on their emotionality above all, may have meant to suggest this when they contrasted themselves with the earlier generation. But on the contrary, the manipulation of form is one of the chief means by which emotion in the arts is created. When and how a theme comes back in a Mozart symphony—a matter of form, or structure—is a real part of the feeling of the work, like the grouping of figures and distribution of planes in a well-structured painting. (The dichotomy that is sometimes referred to between "form" and "content" in the arts is a false one, for all the arts obtain "content" through the construction of "forms," whether they be in space or time: form *is* content.) At all events, and whatever the Romantics may have thought, no musician today thinks that music such as Mozart's is any less emotional for being perfectly constructed. In fact, it often seems to embody feeling more genuinely than some music that parades its passions in a more obvious way.

A new mood in eighteenth-century music first became evident in Italian comic opera, or *opera buffa* (the French term is *opéra comique*; the German, *Singspiel*). Comic opera around 1730 resembled "grand opera" much less than it resembled modern musical comedy. The tone was light, the appeal definitely lowbrow. The plots often amounted to little more than expanded vaudeville acts, involving horseplay, wisecracks, facile but vivid characterization, and a more or less "natural" pace for the action. The musical numbers were short and unassuming; composers concentrated on catchy tunes, and amused their audiences with a new style of casual patter singing, designed principally for a distinctive type of blustering bass-voice character, the "*buffo* bass." The performers thought of themselves primarily as actors and comics, secondarily as singers. Obviously, this kind of opera could flourish only at a time when the dignity and heavy elaboration of the Baroque was being replaced by a new simplicity, even to the point of frivolity.

In the early history of *opera buffa*, Giovanni Battista Pergolesi's *La Serva padrona* (*The Maid Made Mistress*, 1733) stands out as the most famous work, partly because of the sensation it made when it played in 1752 to audiences in Paris. (A short piece well suited to opera workshop productions, *La Serva padrona* is the earliest opera that can still be seen with some regularity today.) With their instinct for formulating what the rest of Europe was just coming to realize, the French proclaimed a new ideal for music: simplicity, naturalness, and unaffected feeling (their ideal in every area of life at this time). They contrasted the vivid simplicities of Pergolesi with the pompous artificialities of Rameau, then the leader of French opera (see p. 249). Rameau immediately stepped into a lively journalistic controversy with the influential philosopher and writer Jean-Jacques Rousseau, among others. Rousseau actually composed an *opéra comique* himself in the same year, *Le Devin du village* (*The Village Soothsayer*). From the point of view of the learned, sixty-seven-year-old Rameau, the piece was scandalously naïve; but that was just the point. *Le Devin du village* stayed in the French opera repertory for seventy-five years.

The difference between serious Italian opera of Metastasio's kind (see p. 248)—now called *opera seria*—with its earnest Roman heroes speaking in rhetorical figures, and *opera buffa*, with its impudent servant types speaking the dialect of Naples or the Veneto, marks the difference of attitude very clearly. Complexity was to give way to directness, artifice to nature, solemnity to amusement. Art was asked to appear sophisticated rather than elevated; artists should "please"—a favorite slogan of the time —rather than impress or instruct. Another catchword of the time was "good taste," which meant moderation in all things—except, perhaps, in the incessantly brittle and lighthearted tone. Above all, people would no longer tolerate a heavy self-serious pose, and that is what they thought they saw in the Baroque.

Translated into technical terms, this attitude led to a reaction against polyphony, or counterpoint. Difficult, contrived, learned—counterpoint was in *very* bad taste. Not all Baroque music depends so heavily on counterpoint as a Bach fugue (RECORDED EXAMPLE 11) or the Sanctus of his Mass in B minor (RECORDED EXAMPLE 10; also see diagram 5, p. 244); but it all includes a certain number of separate melodic lines in combination. The omnipresent trio texture (see diagram 4, p. 244) has three, and even a so-called solo sonata has the violin line on top worked in with the *basso continuo* line on the bottom. Even this much polyphony was resented by the mid-eighteenth century. In place of a real melodic line on the bottom, a so-called harmonic bass was now used merely as an underpinning for the succession of chords that provided harmony for the top melody. Not since the contratenors of the Middle Ages (see p. 226) had there existed anything so lifeless in music.

DIAGRAM SEVEN

melody

harmonic bass

The dots on this diagram are meant to suggest chords having no real "linear" connection. And if the dots appear to occupy only a few different levels, that is because few different chords were used, in comparison with the Baroque.

It is surely no accident that this was the first age to produce a coherent "science" of harmony based on the concept of actual chords, rather than on the vertical results of the combination of several horizontal voice-lines. In this connection, a pioneering role must be credited to the Renaissance theorist Zarlino (see p. 239). But the man who instituted the real study of harmony, in several important treatises written around 1730, was Rameau. The Encyclopedists, committed to a scientific inquiry into all phenomena, debated Rameau's theories with great thoroughness and interest.

Simplification of harmony and texture led to impoverishment, and a great deal of very trivial music was listened to in those days. However, some compensations began to appear. Once the harmonic style was made so simple, composers found it easy enough to replace the improvised filling-in of chords at the harpsichord or organ (see p. 243) by the specific allocation to a particular instrument of each note in each chord. In short, the *basso continuo* texture—the basis of music for a hundred and fifty years—was now abandoned. Undoubtedly the sound-quality of Baroque music had tended toward thickness, and, from the new point of view, untidiness. Things now became much more lucid, precise, and crystalline.

As a result of the abandonment of the *basso continuo,* the make-up of the orchestra changed very considerably (see diagram 8, p. 263). Instead of the polarity of Baroque texture—all tops and bottoms, with chords filled in—a more even sound was cultivated. The violas found a respectable role in the middle, in the space between the violins on top and the cellos (with double basses) on the bottom. A four-part "choir" consisting of violins, divided into two groups, violas, and cellos (with double basses) became the standard framework of Classic orchestration. As the term "choir" suggests, there is an analogy here with the evenly distributed vocal texture—soprano, alto, tenor, bass—established in the Renaissance.

With strings as a framework, woodwind instruments were added on the outside, generally in the highest range. More or less in the spirit of decorative frosting, pairs of flutes, oboes, bassoons, and (later) clarinets served to provide variety in certain melodic passages, as well as strengthening the string sounds in loud passages. And brass instruments were added on the inside, as it were, in a middle range. Pairs of horns and trumpets served as solid support for the main harmonies, limiting their activity to occasions when the harmonies needed to be made especially clear. This worked only because harmonies were now simple; eighteenth-century brass instruments could not play many different notes, since the finger keys that later enlarged their range had not yet been invented. The trumpet could manage only the fanfare notes available to the bugle then and now, and the horn was similarly restricted. The assignment of the brass to a supportive role in Classic orchestration, then, is an elegant case of making a virtue out of a necessity.

From the above discussion, it is clear why the string quartet (violin, violin, viola, cello: see diagram 8, p. 263) developed into the main chamber-music combination of the time. This combination is a miniature version of the basic framework of the Classic orchestra. The string quartet is obviously a much more intimate medium than the full orchestra, and in the hands of the Viennese composers it proved to be extraordinarily flexible and expressive.

There was another compensation for the simplification that took place in harmony and in musical texture. Now that the harmonic style was so simple (not to say bland), even slightly unusual chords could produce unusual effects by contrast with their surroundings. Indeed, musical contrast of every kind was pursued eagerly—in rhythm, melody, and texture as well as in harmony—in order to obtain that "pleasing variety" demanded by the taste of the time. (It was thought inexpressibly dull for anything to go on for very long in the same vein.) Composers developed new skill in manipulating sharp contrasts, at first for contrast's sake, but later for the purpose of developing new expressive resources. We shall see this tendency culminate in the sonata-allegro form (pp. 263-65).

By 1750 all these stylistic features were eating away at music of every variety. From the *opera buffa* they spread to the *opera seria* itself, which, it must be said, seemed more incongruous than ever, with its noble Romans now expressing themselves in a new language of elegance and insipidity. *Opera seria* nevertheless managed to stay alive until the time of the French Revolution, along with the aristocratic society it served and celebrated. Sonatas, concertos, and *concerti grossi* became progressively lighter in tone with each successive generation. Fugues, needless to say, were taboo. The French overture (see p. 249), with its strong feeling of aristocratic pomp and circumstance, went out of fashion as a beginning number for operas and other large works, and was replaced by the Italian *sinfonia,* a new kind of piece with no pretensions other than that of making a bright, forceful noise. From this developed the symphony as we know it.

To speak of individual composers: one of the most accomplished was Domenico Scarlatti (1685–1757), an older man—he was actually a close contemporary of Bach and Handel—who did not work at the centers of musical activity. His harpsichord sonatas, which he wrote in great numbers, have a deftness, humor, and polish perfectly attuned to the ideals of the time, and a sophisticated structure well in advance of them. Brilliantly written for the most brilliant-sounding of musical instruments, the harpsichord, these small works often seem to incorporate echoes of Pergolesi and the other tunesmiths of the *opera buffa.* But since he worked in Lisbon and Madrid, Domenico (who was the son of the *opera seria* composer Alessandro Scarlatti) achieved less European fame than two of Bach's sons, who became leading composers in their own right when their father had been forgotten.

Johann Christian Bach (1735–82) developed the light style to an extremely graceful but ultimately vapid stage (the term Rococo is sometimes applied to music in this style, with some show of reason). Johann Christian moved to London in the 1760s, succeeded Handel in one of his court positions (as though to symbolize the change in taste), and organized some of the first European public concerts—an activity with some prophetic significance, as we shall see. His older brother, Carl Philip Emmanuel Bach (1714–88), was a more substantial and imaginative composer. Especially noted as a composer for keyboard instruments, he did not favor the harpsichord as much as the expressive clavichord and the new pianoforte—an instrument that was even more expressive, with its range of loud and soft. For these instruments, Carl Philip developed an emotional if somewhat disorganized style of writing, sometimes tender, sometimes stormy, which should have made good sense to Rousseau, with his call for unaffected feeling. Active in northern Germany, where he spent many years in the service of Frederick the Great, Carl Philip was also a major influence on the constellation of great composers centered at Vienna in the south, especially on Haydn and Beethoven.

An unusual Double Concerto for Harpsichord, Pianoforte, and Orchestra by C. P. E. Bach displays with special clarity the difference in tone quality between the harpsichord and the early piano, which sounded rather thin and hollow before technical improvements were made during Beethoven's lifetime. Bach's Concerto was written close to the very end of his career; in the last movement, of which the beginning is heard in RECORDED EXAMPLE 12, we can discern the reverse influence of Haydn in the humorous orchestral tune and in the repeated use of short musical motifs throughout.

More typical of mid-eighteenth-century style are the solo piano and harpsichord sections (which come in that order). They sound graceful, lucid, and neat in the extreme; played after our Baroque RECORDED EXAMPLES 9–11, they seem almost dangerously fragile.

SUGGESTIONS FOR LISTENING

GIOVANNI BATTISTA PERGOLESI, *La Serva padrona*
DGG-ARCHIVE; VOX; NONESUCH

DOMENICO SCARLATTI, Sonatas (on harpsichord)

FREDERICK THE GREAT, Symphony in D major
DGG-ARCHIVE

JOHANN CHRISTIAN BACH, Concerto in B-flat major for bassoon and orchestra
DGG-ARCHIVE

CARL PHILIP EMMANUEL BACH, Concerto in F major for two harpsichords and orchestra
HARMONIA MUNDI

VIENNA. With pardonable pride, musicians can point to the flowering of Viennese music from about 1760 to 1825 and compare it to the extraordinary achievements of literature and art in Athens under Pericles, or to those in Florence under the Medici. Geography plays a part in these phenomena; Vienna is a cosmopolitan center near the hub of Austria, Bohemia (Czechoslovakia), Hungary, and Italy. (Bohemia, Hungary, and parts of northern Italy were within the Austrian Empire, of which Vienna was the capital.) The North Germans and the highly musical Bohemians contributed a flair for instrumental music. The Italians contributed a flair for opera; as the southernmost German-speaking large city, Vienna has always had a special fondness for opera. For half of the eighteenth century, the Austrian court poet —a poet writing for a German-speaking court in Italian!—was Metastasio, the influential librettist of *opera seria*.

It was in the field of serious opera, indeed, that Viennese music made its first important strides, but not in any kind of opera that Metastasio could take comfort from. Christoph Willibald von Gluck (1714–88) set out very consciously to accomplish an anti-Metastasian operatic reform. This composer was born in central Germany and traveled extensively, but he always seemed to gravitate back to Vienna, where in the 1760s he produced the famous reform operas *Orfeo ed Euridice* and *Alceste*. These are very serious works, written—by a German, for Germans—in Italian. In their own way they represent as sharp a reaction against traditional *opera seria* as those of the *opera buffa* composers had done—even sharper, perhaps, in that they challenged *opera seria* on its own ground. The challenge was issued under the familiar banner of simplicity, naturalness, and unaffected feeling.

With the assistance of an excellent librettist, Gluck turned away from the intrigue-ridden Roman plots of Metastasio to austere subjects taken from Greek mythology. Thus his *Alceste* comes from the ancient Greek play by Euripides, and *Orfeo ed Euridice* treats the same beautiful legend that attracted Monteverdi and the inventors of opera, around 1600. Naturalness was served by Gluck's boldest reform of all, the ruthless limitation of the singers' role. He cut out coloratura passages and replaced the elaborate, stilted *da capo* aria form by plain songlike structures. Nothing was allowed to interfere with the stately progress of the drama; Gluck was as much a dramatist as a musician. As for unaffected feeling, only Gluck's wonderful talent for noble directness of expression made his whole enterprise possible. By means of Gluck's music, Orpheus lamenting the loss of his wife and Alcestis resolving to die for her husband become characters as moving and real as any in the whole range of opera.

Other reforming features are all related to the single great appeal to "a beautiful simplicity," as Gluck put it in a telling manifesto, his Preface to *Alceste,* 1767. Thus the chorus assumes a large and impressive role, something new for Italian opera (though not at all new for Rameau in France). Gluck took the decisive step of eliminating *secco* recitative (see p. 248) so that the orchestra plays throughout the opera. This went far to minimize the artificial "stop-and-go" quality of *opera seria,* and placed all the action in the same musical framework—a decided gain in naturalism. A powerful composer for the orchestra, Gluck proposed to use instrumental effects only for dramatic purposes, never for mere decoration; he also had the idea of making the overture anticipate the mood (and some of the tunes) of the opera to come. At a time when Johann Christian Bach was weaving endless pretty nothings out of the orchestra, Gluck's music was always unpretty, austere, and strong. Small wonder, perhaps, that after listening and applauding, the Viennese found Gluck too demanding and gratefully returned to Italian *opera buffa.*

He achieved more lasting success in Paris, a city which at this time was a great consumer of German music. There in the 1770s he rewrote *Orfeo* and *Alceste* in French versions, to the great approval of such veteran opera enthusiasts as Rousseau, and he produced new operas, even more flexible in style, on the Greek subjects of *Iphigenia in Aulis* and *Iphigenia in Tauris.* Incidentally, the latter story—again from Euripides—also formed the subject of a celebrated play by Goethe, the leader of literary classicism. Indeed, Gluck's operas provide the one strong link between Classic music and contemporary Neoclassicism. *Alceste* was produced when Winckelmann's writings about ancient Greek art were enjoying their greatest influence, and later the Paris of J. L. David, Ingres, and Napoleon proved hospitable to classic evocations of every sort (see pp. 157–59). But Gluck's own combination of musical and literary classicism—like David's variety —had congealed into academicism with the next generation. This is indicated with deadpan accuracy by Ingres' portrait of the Italian-born, but French-domiciled, opera composer Luigi Cherubini (1760–1842: see fig. 205); in this extraordinary (and unconscious?) piece of music criticism, Gluck's follower seems utterly crushed by frigid tradition as imparted by his Muse.

To return to Vienna: the 1760s also saw the first compositions of a young musician from the neighboring region, Franz Joseph Haydn (1732–1809). Most of Haydn's life was spent in the service of a court forty miles to the south of Vienna, service which often brought him in to the metropolis; and after he was pensioned, he retired in Vienna. Haydn's earliest instrumental music is already more purposeful than that of Johann Christian Bach and more tightly controlled than that of Carl Philip; by the 1770s, he had far surpassed the one in polish and the other in emotional power. Over the span of his career Haydn produced—besides great quantities of other music—over a hundred symphonies and over eighty string quartets, almost all of them masterpieces, at least those written from the 1770s on. With this enormously impressive repertory Haydn played the major part in establishing the Viennese Classic style.

The symphony as Haydn standardized it was a substantial work consisting of four more or less independent movements. The first is typically lively and forceful; in this it may be contrasted with a typical Baroque piece, which likes to put its best foot forward with something solemn, such as a French overture. The second movement of a symphony is slow and lyric. The third is a minuet—the one stylized dance that remains as a relic of the many different items in the old dance suite. The fourth is again fast and lively, faster and lighter than the opening movement. To us, the minuet carries suggestions of Rococo elegance and exaggerated formality, but it is fascinating to watch Haydn play with this dance—he wrote hundreds—and make it sometimes witty, sometimes earthy, sometimes raucous. Sometimes it ends up not far from a Viennese waltz. In the next generation, Beethoven could easily transform the minuet into a rough, very fast dance-like composition to which he gave the name *scherzo* (jest).

This particular plan of four movements was used not only for symphonies, written for full orchestra, but also for sonatas and for the various chamber-music combinations that became established in this period. (See diagram 8. The term "sonata" was henceforth restricted to pieces written for one or two instruments. The terms "trio," "quartet," and on up to "octet" may refer to the combination of instruments, or to the group of players, or to the piece of music written for them.) The same basic movement plan, minus the minuet, was used for the Classic concerto. Here the Baroque scheme of orchestra plus a small group of soloists was standardized into the Classic orchestra plus a single soloist; the favorite solo instrument soon came to be the piano, the favorite new instrument of the day. It should be understood that in spite of the similarity of names, the Classic sonata and concerto departed from the Baroque sonata and *concerto grosso* in form (as we have just indicated), style, and practically every other respect.

DIAGRAM EIGHT

The Main Instrumental Combinations of Classic Music
(The most important combinations are in SMALL CAPITALS.
All forms normally have four movements, unless otherwise indicated.)

PIANO SONATA [2–4 movements]

Sonata for Violin (or Cello) and Piano [2–4 movements]

Piano Trio		*violin,*		*cello,*	*piano*	String Trio		*violin, viola, cello*	
Piano Quartet		*violin,*	*viola,*	*cello,*	*piano*	STRING QUARTET	*violin, violin, viola, cello*		
Piano Quintet	*violin,*	*violin,*	*viola,*	*cello,*	*piano*	String Quintet	*violin, violin, viola, cello, cello*		
						or:	*violin, violin, viola, viola, cello*		

Woodwind Quintet *flute, oboe, clarinet, horn, bassoon*

(Numerous less frequently used combinations, from two to nine instruments, often combining wind instruments with strings and piano)

SYMPHONY	*the Classic orchestra:*
string choir:	*violins 1 and 2, violas, cellos, double basses*
woodwind choir:	*2 flutes, 2 oboes, 2 clarinets, 2 bassoons*
brass choir:	*2 horns, 2 trumpets*
percussion:	*2 kettledrums*

CONCERTO FOR PIANO (OR VIOLIN) [3 movements]
  the Classic orchestra (as above) plus the solo instrument

Not because they are very significant, but because they are very typical of the spirit of the time, mention should be made of the serenade and the *divertimento* (entertainment-piece). These are lighter forms than those listed above; their "pleasing variety" comes through the use of smaller, less taxing movements and more of them. A *divertimento* has two fast movements, two minuets, and two contrasted slow movements. A serenade, being outdoor music, as its name implies, has a march at the beginning and at the end, and sometimes a whole little concerto in the middle.

On the level of individual movements, one particular ground plan or form looms very large in the late eighteenth century, larger than any such form in the music of any other period,

perhaps. It is called the sonata-allegro form, or sonata form, because of its regular employment in the lively (Italian: *allegro*) opening movements of sonatas, symphonies, and quartets. This is the form that exploits and systematizes the new interest in manipulating contrasts of all kinds. In particular, the sonata-allegro form exploits contrast of thematic material and contrast of tonality (see p. 254 for a definition of tonality).

It is not hard to see what is meant by contrast of thematic material. A composer might start a piece with a "theme" consisting of nothing more than a few memorable rhythms, and directly afterwards go into a long suave tune —another "theme"; simply by the juxtaposition he will get an effect of contrast. Contrast of tonality, however, is a more difficult concept. If the reader will go back and pick out *Yankee Doodle* on the piano, first using white notes starting from C and then using black notes starting from F-sharp, he will satisfy himself that a single tune can indeed be played in different tonalities—which sound different, in some sense. But contrast means more than mere difference: it implies a feeling of active opposition between the two tonalities. How does a composer obtain such a feeling, and use it for aesthetic purposes?

A movement in sonata-allegro form begins with a large section of music that is called the exposition. In the first tonality (which is that of the piece as a whole: in Mozart's Symphony in G minor, the first tonality is G minor) a main theme is presented. As we have said, it may be a regular tune, or a group of small phrases that sound as though they want to grow into a tune, or even less extended material—small "motifs" of a memorable rhythmic character. Soon after the main theme is well established, there comes a change in tonality, technically known as a modulation. The composer tries to make the change not too smooth, so that there will be some tension in the way the new themes, now to be introduced, "set" in the new tonality. To this end, the new themes usually contrast with the main theme in melody and rhythm, as well as in tonality. The end of the exposition section is marked by an emphatic series of repeated closes or cadences ("presenting arms," this was called by unfriendly critics in the nineteenth century).

The following section is called the development. This tends to work with or "develop" fragments of earlier themes and motifs, which are shown in unexpected and often exciting new contexts and combinations. In the matter of tonality, the development section moves around restlessly; there is constant modulation, constant change of tonality. We have the feeling of a purposeful search for the proper position for the music.

After a time—usually after the tension has built up considerably—the last modulation in the development section leads back to the first tonality. With a real sense of relief or resolution, we hear the themes of the exposition come back in their original order, or at least in something recognizably like their original order. Hence the name for this third section: the recapitulation. But there is an important difference: everything now remains in the same tonality (the first tonality). Stability of tonality is very welcome after the instability in the de-

velopment section; and what is more, the old material now has a slightly new look. Thus the strong feeling of balance between the exposition and the recapitulation (A B A) is a weighted balance, for the second A-section has now achieved a new solidity. If even more solidity seems to be needed, another section will be added at the end, as though delivering concluding remarks on the subject matter of the movement. This coda (tailpiece) is generally subsidiary and quite brief, at least during the eighteenth century.

Perhaps it is no accident that the terminology of the sonata-allegro form—exposition, development, recapitulation—resembles the terminology of the drama. It has been well observed that Classic music has a "dramatic" quality, as compared to the "architectural" quality of Baroque music. In a complex Classic piece, we almost feel that the themes are like people to whom things are happening. They seem to change, grow, have adventures, and to react in relation to other themes.

A simple example of a movement in sonata-allegro form—simple because of the kind of music it is, an outdoor serenade—is the first movement of Mozart's well-known *Eine kleine Nachtmusik* (*A Little Night-Music*), K. 525.* This crystalline little piece seems to sum up all the charm, intelligence, and good taste that eighteenth-century musicians worked for. Everything is easy to listen to, nothing goes on for too long, and the tunes tickle the ear with a grace unknown to music before or after. Studied simplicity is Mozart's aim, in texture, harmony, and melodic structure. The first theme at the start of the exposition section, for instance, amounts to no more than an elegant fanfare.

But this fanfare stands in distinct contrast to the themes introduced after the modulation: two suave little tunes, one of which may be de-

---

* "K" numbers, placed next to Mozart works only, are numbers assigned in a chronological catalogue compiled by the musicologist Ludwig von Köchel. With composers who publish most or much of their output while they are alive, works with similar or identical titles (Symphonies in D major, for example) are distinguished by "opus" numbers assigned at the time of publication; such numbers form a rough—but by no means infallible—guide to the chronology of composition. (Opus—Latin for "work"—is abbreviated "Op."; for a use of this abbreviation, see p. 269.) But with Mozart, who was able to publish very little, musicological scholarship was faced with the task of assembling his 600-odd pieces from scattered manuscripts, sorting out the genuine ones from the fakes, and determining their chronology.

scribed as having a sly lilt about it, the other as having a rather high-strung tic. They make an intriguing set of protagonists for the action that is to come. The development section opens with the fanfare theme, but, since this is the development section, the end of the fanfare modulates to another tonality. There follows the theme with the tic, which also modulates several times, thereby changing its mood considerably before preparing the recapitulation. This section duplicates the exposition measure by measure, except of course for the fact that everything remains in the first tonality, the tonality of the beginning of the piece. As a coda at the very end, however, a delicious sliding figure which has not been heard before converts what might have been a mechanical A B A balance between exposition and recapitulation into a vital and delightful relationship.

Late Classic symphonies and quartets yield up much more complex sonata-allegro forms than do modest serenades. In the last movement of Haydn's String Quartet in G minor, Op. 74, No. 3 (RECORDED EXAMPLE 13), the themes contrast still more sharply than in *Eine kleine Nachtmusik,* and the contrast of tonality strikes the ear more decisively. The driving, irascible first theme (someone nicknamed this quartet *The Horseman*) almost seems to be mocked by the debonair theme in the second tonality; yet there is an element of subtle wit in the fact that both themes include some of the same rhythmic motifs. We will find the most striking difference between this movement and the Mozart in their development sections. In the quartet, all themes and motifs are given an exhaustive workout, running through various tonalities, stopping, backtracking, breaking apart, shooting off in fresh directions, and so on and so on. Then the recapitulation section —which begins with an interesting rhythmic surprise—follows the course of the exposition section only rather freely. The A B A balance is looser in this piece than in *Eine kleine Nachtmusik.* Finally, the coda here assumes real importance, expanding upon a three-note up-the-scale motif that was first "developed" in the development section. In fact, the coda seems to balance the development. The whole structure is thoroughly rich and intricate.

The listener may be interested to find the point in the exposition section from which the three-note up-the-scale motif is derived, and see whether his pleasure in the piece increases with the discovery.

Obviously, this is no longer simple entertainment music, no mere "*divertimento*." There is too much for the mind. Observe the greater sensitivity and responsiveness of the quartet texture, as opposed to that of Mozart's string orchestra. Furthermore, there is an element in the quartet—especially in the development section—that was scarcely present in *Eine kleine Nachtmusik*: counterpoint. What has happened to the eighteenth-century distaste for this technique? The answer is that Haydn found it necessary to restore vigorous contrapuntal action in order to obtain the effects of subtlety that he saw the new style could provide. But it is a wonderfully light, delicate counterpoint, with nothing ostentatious or heavy about it.

And comparing the Mozart and Haydn examples, we should be satisfied that Classic form is not a rigid mold into which the composer may dutifully pour ready-made themes. The ground plan of sonata-allegro form is sufficiently generalized to accommodate all kinds of ideas—light, intellectual, pathetic, tragic. It no more represses an artist's imagination than does the prescription that a play should have a beginning, a middle, and an end, or the tradition that the plan of a church should incorporate the shape of a cross (a requirement that would seem to have left architects plenty of leeway—compare figs. 72, 148, and 173). As a result of its sturdy flexibility, sonata-allegro form served music for nearly two hundred years.

In the eighteenth century, it spread to every conceivable kind of composition. If a label has to be found for the music of this period, the term "Classic period" is really less apropos than "sonata period" or "period of the sonata style" would be. Sonata-allegro form occurs in most opening movements and many slow movements and last movements of Classic symphonies and quartets, and even in some minuets. Clear traces of it are to be found in church music, and—especially with Mozart— in the various musical numbers of both serious and comic opera.

Wolfgang Amadeus Mozart (1756–91) wrote most of his important music after coming to Vienna, in the decade of the 1780s. Taken all over Europe as a child prodigy, he soaked up impressions of the entire range of contemporary music; for a time the graceful works of Johann Christian Bach seem to have struck him particularly. Afterwards he attempted to settle down in his home town of Salzburg, a hundred miles west of Vienna. But rankling under court service, he determined to strike out for himself as an independent musician in the capital. Ten years later, Beethoven would be successful at this, but Mozart had an extremely difficult time of it.

Mozart and Haydn knew each other well enough to play in an amateur string quartet together, and they influenced each other's music to a significant extent. Haydn showed Mozart something about the power of thematic manipulation, while Mozart showed Haydn something about lyricism, grace, and delicacy of harmonic effect. Among Mozart's best instrumental music is a set of six string quartets issued with a moving public dedication to his older friend; Haydn on his part remarked quite simply that Mozart was the greatest composer he had ever met. Seventeen magnificent piano concertos were composed by Mozart in Vienna, mostly for his own use as a piano virtuoso. He wrote fewer symphonies, since he received no commissions for them, but his last three—the Symphonies in G minor and E-flat major and the so-called *Jupiter* Symphony—are very famous. In the first movement of the *Jupiter,* an unusually dignified first theme is followed by an unusually jaunty *opera buffa* tune borrowed from an actual *opera buffa.* This is an extreme example of the Classic composers' interest in the lightest sort of musical material, of their preoccupation with contrast, and of their ability to make even the most sharply contrasted material hold together through the skillful manipulation of musical form.

As an opera composer, Mozart did not try to follow Gluck's lead. By nature he was not a reformer of the music of his time but a quiet perfecter of it. He worked in the currently popular types of comic opera, the Italian *opera buffa* and the German *Singspiel* (for Vienna was bilingual, operatically speaking, and so was Mozart). On commission, he even wrote an *opera seria* on a libretto by Metastasio—in 1791, a real dinosaur (*La Clemenza di Tito*).

In some ways, *opera buffa* had not changed too much in the fifty years since Pergolesi. Some sentimental subjects were treated—they satisfied much the same taste as did the paintings of Greuze (see fig. 201)—but in general the plots were still farcical and undistinguished. Most of the action took place in *secco* recitative, which gave the actor-singers plenty of scope for comic acting business; alternating with this, they sang simple tuneful arias or, in the sentimental scenes, more elaborate ones. In addition to the aria, there was another kind of musical number, the ensemble, that alternated with the recitative. The ensemble included two, three, or more characters simultaneously; therefore it took account of their interaction,

and often incorporated some dramatic action too. Especially in Mozart's hands, the ensemble came to be an extremely subtle form. Using all the resources of the sonata-allegro form, so well calculated for the manipulation of contrasts, he was able to depict conflicting emotions felt by different characters at the same time, and to set them in vivid relief. Within a single ensemble, furthermore, he could depict changes in people's attitudes as a result of unexpected dramatic events. Mozart had a unique talent for delineating character through music, building dramatic structure, and casting an aura of intelligence and humanity over all his operatic figures.

As an example of an *opera buffa* ensemble in which characters are drawn and contrasted, and in which dramatic action takes place (and farcical action, at that), we may take a tiny duet from Mozart's opera *The Marriage of Figaro,* "*Aprite presto, aprite*" ("Quick, open up now, open," RECORDED EXAMPLE 14). Cherubino, a page boy about fourteen—his voice has not changed—is in a state of puppy love with all women but especially with the beautiful Countess. He has somehow got himself locked into her dressing room; the Count, having heard him through the door, has grimly left the scene just long enough to fetch a crowbar and his sword. Susanna, the Countess' maid, lets Cherubino out, and the two of them scurry around frantically looking for a way out of the Countess' suite. The repetition of a very small, rapid orchestral motif all through the number catches the sense of desperate hurry, while the breathless patter singing of the two characters depicts their confusion in a most amusing way. As they search for exits, the music modulates constantly, very much in the manner of a development section in sonata-allegro form. Out the window is the only way; Susanna is terrified, Cherubino quite resolved—a young hero in embryo ("*lasciami! lasciami!*"—"let me go," back in the first tonality, like a recapitulation section). He will brave all perils, even a leap down into the geranium bed, for the sake of his lady—and just before jumping, he snatches a kiss from the completely flustered Susanna.

Our recorded excerpt includes a few measures of the *secco* recitative which follows, to show how ensemble and recitative alternate in this kind of opera. Naturally, not all ensembles are as minuscule as this one, which is a special *tour de force* matched to the dramatic situation. Matching the music to the situation, however, is what Mozart was always able to do brilliantly.

His operas are always amusing, then, but they are not all for fun. In their urbane way, they make serious points about human conduct. We can think of them in a category of "high comedy," along with the contemporary plays of Richard Brinsley Sheridan (*The Rivals, The School for Scandal*). Mozart's *Così fan tutte* (freely paraphrased as *Females Are Fickle*: an Italian *opera buffa*) makes something very touching out of a refined and witty little play about high society. On the other hand, *Die Zauberflöte* (*The Magic Flute*: a German *Singspiel*) makes something very moving out of a theatrical hodgepodge including such low-comedy features as animal acts and audience-participation gags, as well as religious scenes of an austerity that Gluck might have envied—all in the service of a parable about young people growing up. Most impressive of all, perhaps, is *Don Giovanni,* an Italian *opera buffa* with a difference, based on the old legend of Don Juan. The career of the compulsive seducer of "a thousand and three" women carries with it an inevitable aura of obscene farce, and Mozart does not gloss over this. Included are crude slapstick scenes which look back to Pergolesi in concept, if not in musical style. But there is also an aspect of grandeur to the outcome, a gripping scene in which Don Juan is dragged down to hell rather than repenting and so denying his authentic commitment to the life of the senses. Or so at least Mozart's music makes us feel.

The Mozart operas occupy a high place in the current estimation of opera and music in general. For our purposes, we might notice not only their intrinsic quality but also the artistic principle they illustrate: the idealization of a simple and rather low style, at the hands of a great composer, into something highly artistic. Haydn (and Mozart, too) had done much the same thing with eighteenth-century instrumental music.

After Mozart, it must be confessed, *opera buffa* reverted to its old farcical and rather brainless ways. This becomes clear if we compare two famous operas based on stage plays having the same cast of characters: Mozart's *The Marriage of Figaro* (1786) and *The Barber of Seville* (1816) by Giacomo Rossini, the chief opera composer of a later generation. The comparison is not altogether fair to Rossini, since the original play that he used is much less fine, but it is not altogether unfair, either. Rossini's heroine is a brittle, shallow creature in comparison with Mozart's memorable Countess. His *buffo* bass (see p. 258) bullies and fumes and gets his comeuppance, whereas Mozart's also reveals a warm sympathetic streak. And Rossini's Figaro—the familiar Figaro of "*Largo al factotum*"—seems like only a boisterous chatterer next to Mozart's very human figure with his good and bad points, his strong feelings, and his really vivid sense of fun.

Rossini captivated all Europe from about 1815 to 1830 (when to everyone's astonishment he gave up composing operas and lived on his fortune for his nearly forty remaining years). The sparkle—the chatter—of his music is hard to resist, even today. Vienna succumbed to it, too, and Beethoven complained about the low taste of his city's music lovers.

SUGGESTIONS FOR LISTENING

CHRISTOPH WILLIBALD VON GLUCK, *Orfeo ed Euridice,* Act II

FRANZ JOSEPH HAYDN, String Quartet in G minor, Op. 74, No. 3
DGG; VANGUARD

FRANZ JOSEPH HAYDN, Symphony No. 104 in D major, *London*

WOLFGANG AMADEUS MOZART, *Eine kleine Nachtmusik,* K.525

WOLFGANG AMADEUS MOZART, Concerto in C minor for piano and orchestra, K.491

WOLFGANG AMADEUS MOZART, Symphony No. 41 in C major, K.551, *Jupiter*

WOLFGANG AMADEUS MOZART, *The Marriage of Figaro,* Act II

BEETHOVEN. From Bonn, a town far to the west of Germany, Ludwig van Beethoven (1770–1827) came to Vienna in 1792 because Vienna was where an ambitious young musician simply had to go. After studying briefly (and not very hard) with Haydn, Beethoven became more and more of an original, both as an artist and as a person, until after 1800 he produced a series of works that may fairly be said to have transformed the art of music. With Haydn and Mozart, one can speak of evolution of the Classic style, but with Beethoven, one can hardly use any other term than revolution.

In a word, the revolution consisted of a radically new seriousness. Beethoven saw in the Classic style not a means of creating high comedy, whether operatic or symphonic, but an astonishing instrument for the expression of tragedy, heroism, ecstasy, momentousness, and power.

As the reader will see, the wheel has turned full circle from the point early in the eighteenth century where this chapter began. The premium on simplicity, charm, and "pleasing variety," the dislike of earnestness, of taking oneself seriously, and any kind of excess—all this has disappeared. One should not be too quick in attributing the cause of this change to the French Revolution, which after all was as much a symptom of new attitudes as a source of them. Might it not be just as correct to say that new attitudes such as Beethoven's caused the French Revolution? Nonetheless, that devastating political and moral upheaval certainly left a profound impression on him. When the Bastille was stormed by the citizens of Paris in 1789, Beethoven was eighteen years old, just beginning his career, and living not so very far from the French border. (At that time Haydn, fifty-seven, was no longer very impressionable, and Mozart, thirty-three, was preoccupied with his losing battle for survival in Vienna.) The coach taking Beethoven to Vienna had to dodge invading French troops; they actually occupied the city on two later occasions, much to his discomfort. In a famous and characteristic gesture, Beethoven dedicated a symphony to Napoleon, the liberator of mankind, only to tear up the dedication in a rage when the liberator turned out to be a tyrant. Beethoven was an outspoken democrat all his life.

That symphony, his third, was in fact Beethoven's most revolutionary composition. Characteristically, again, he wrote it as a result of a spiritual crisis (as the nineteenth century would call it; today we might rather say a breakdown) and gave it the name *Sinfonia Eroica*

(*Heroic* Symphony, 1803). This title—his own, not nicknamed by somebody else, as in the case of Haydn's symphonies and quartets —seems to refer more to the composer's self-image than to his idea of Napoleon. In forcefulness, emotion, and sheer length and loudness, it was unlike any symphony known at the time. During the next decade Beethoven followed up the *Eroica* with a series of symphonies, concertos, chamber-music works, and piano sonatas that firmly established the new aesthetic position.

The reader should listen several times to one of these compositions. In all of them, Beethoven worked within the spirit of Classic form —and he still found the sonata-allegro form to be the best tool for him, as it had been for Haydn and Mozart. But Beethoven expanded it, or reinterpreted it in some other imaginative way. The contrasts between themes (and between tonalities) are usually sharper than in the work of the earlier composers. The balance between large sections is more monumental. The process that Haydn had worked out for development sections becomes especially exciting in Beethoven's hands; he modulates farther, breaks the themes down in more radical ways, and finds more dramatic contexts and combinations in which to present them. Themes and motifs are not merely "developed": they seem to be transformed, transfigured, revolutionized. In this, Beethoven provided a point of departure for Richard Wagner, the leading musical figure of the mid-nineteenth century.

All of these extensions of Classic form, as we have said, served a new expressive vision, one that was more serious and intense than anything Haydn or Mozart would have wanted. Some suggested examples for listening:

In the first movement of the *Eroica* Symphony, the scope of the sonata-allegro form is greatly expanded (and the other movements of the symphony are stretched to match). The first movement lasts for fifteen minutes, twice as long as an average Haydn symphony movement and four times as long as our example from *Eine kleine Nachtmusik*. All the sections are expanded, but especially the development section. If we spoke of an exhaustive workout in a Haydn development section, we should have to speak of a definite struggle in this one. Indeed, things come so close to breaking down completely, in a passage of apocalyptic sound —almost noise—without any themes at all, that Beethoven felt the need to introduce a very striking new melody, the most lyric melody in the entire piece. Within the middle of a development section, this was a great novelty.

Then, after suspense has been built up to an unprecedented level, the recapitulation begins, with a melodramatic stroke that amazed Beethoven's contemporaries. As is frequently the case with this composer, an extensive coda (see p. 263) serves to balance the long development section. (The striking new melody from the development probably required another niche in the form, and the coda provided that niche.) One feature that helps to hold this lengthy movement together is the treatment of the first theme. This theme always starts out with determined energy, but after a few moments it seems to hit some kind of obstacle. In the coda, however, the obstacle is finally overcome, and the theme blares out as a triumphant—indeed, a "heroic"—fanfare on the brass instruments. The struggle has not been in vain.

The Fifth Symphony shows that Beethoven soon grasped the possibility of getting powerful results out of sonata-allegro form by compression, as well as by expansion. The famous theme at the beginning of the first movement amounts to little more than a rhythmic motif; Beethoven might have learned from Haydn and Mozart to use such material, but the vision of tragic energy in it was strictly his own. "Here Fate knocks at the door!"—the phrase may be hackneyed, but according to reports Beethoven actually said it. Some of the fateful quality comes from the urgent rhythm of the motif and the uninhibited force with which it is first played (though hardly from its melody as such: Beethoven could be as strong and unpretty as Gluck). But the quality comes more from a prime feature of formal manipulation, namely, the saturation of the entire movement by the motif. It appears everywhere, sometimes blustering, sometimes murmuring in the background, sometimes held to its original shape, but more often "developed" in apparently inexhaustible new ways. It is not surprising that people began comparing compositions like this to living organisms, as though such works had grown like plants from a single seed.

The third movement of the Fifth Symphony, an inspired *scherzo* (see p. 262), treats another Classic form in a new way. Classic minuet movements all follow a balanced A B A plan: first minuet; second minuet, contrasted; exact repetition of the first minuet. Beethoven starts from this model, but he presents the second "A" in a ghostly new orchestration which completely changes, though it certainly does not destroy, the balance. Then, after an even more mysterious-sounding passage, a fourth and last movement emerges having the character of a triumphant military march. We now realize that all the other movements have been leading up to this as a consummation. The impression is confirmed when we hear the theme of the third movement actually return at the end of the development section of the fourth, with a highly dramatic effect. Carrying over themes from one movement to another was to become typical of Romantic symphonies, but in Beethoven's time it was a great novelty.

With the so-called *Appassionata* (*Impassioned*) Sonata in F minor, Op. 57, one gets the distinct impression that Beethoven was trying to turn the piano sonata into an orchestral symphony. Already in the first few measures, the range of sound quality and contrast seems to strain past the frail bounds of the piano, especially the somewhat primitive piano of the early 1800s. The brooding, mysterious first theme itself; the sinister rhythmic motif that recalls the Fifth Symphony; and the loud chords that smash into the main theme at its second playing—this is contrast with a vengeance and without any regard for the Classic canons of good taste. (Haydn never quite approved of Beethoven.) The exciting modification of the loud chords in the recapitulation section—to mention only one detail out of many—illustrates how Beethoven could manipulate Classic form in order to provide variety within the ordinary A B A balance. In the development section, the brooding first theme is forced to modulate wildly, but in the recapitulation section it returns to its original mood. A free variant recurs at the conclusion of the long, eventful coda. At this point, perhaps, it sounds gloomier than ever, as though it has really earned its gloom.

In the *Leonore* Overture No. 3, we can observe Beethoven taking a cue from Gluck in making the overture look forward to the opera itself. This was his only opera, *Fidelio* (1805; it was originally called *Leonore*). Beethoven wrote several different overtures for various revivals of the work, hence "No. 3"). The story of *Fidelio* brings together two of Beethoven's favorite ideas, personal heroism and political freedom. Set in some unspecified revolutionary atmosphere, it tells of a heroic wife rescuing her husband from an *oubliette,* or dungeon, for political prisoners.

Slow music, modulating for an impression

of gloom and duress, then yields to a fast movement in sonata-allegro form. The first theme, an irresistible avalanche of sound, already bodes well for the outcome of the drama. The development section, however, suggests a death struggle between antagonists, an effect that results naturally from an intensification of the regular technique for such sections. Just as this is reaching a climax, there is a sudden surprising halt for a trumpet call, offstage. In the opera itself, this constitutes the signal for the rescue —the good Minister is arriving, and the villain must rush off leaving his nefarious deeds undone. But even without this advance information, the overture sounds excellently dramatic: a prayerful passage follows the trumpet, the trumpet sounds once again, closer this time, and so on. After the recapitulation section, a dazzling coda depicts the rejoicing of all the characters (and the composer) at the outcome of the drama—the freeing of a whole chorus of political prisoners.

As a matter of fact, this fine piece of music turned out to be a revealing failure as an opera overture, for it is so intensely dramatic that it spoils the opera to come. Beethoven realized this, and replaced it by a more modest piece, known as the *Fidelio* Overture.

These comments, dealing with some of Beethoven's most characteristic works from 1800 to 1810, may give the impression that his music invariably summons up tragic, heroic, or titanic emotions. This is not the case. Beethoven is al-

ways strong, but he also has his gentle, contemplative, and mystical moods, as is shown by many compositions written in the same decade: the Fourth Piano Concerto, in G major, the Sixth (*Pastoral*) Symphony, the *Archduke* Trio, and other less famous works. Such moods occur frequently in his later music, which becomes more introspective and visionary in character. It is well known that Beethoven's hearing failed progressively after about 1800, and while this certainly did not inhibit his composing—there was nothing wrong with his "inner ear"—it certainly did cause him as a personality to turn inward upon himself. He never married, and became a noted Vienna eccentric, emanating an almost Michelangelesque *terribilità*. Though not always well understood at the time, Beethoven's late music is now regarded as his greatest. Mention should be made of the Mass in D major, known as the *Missa solemnis,* for solo singers, chorus, and orchestra; the Ninth Symphony; the last five piano sonatas; and, greatest of all, the last five string quartets, written in 1824–26.

In summary: the golden age of Viennese music—the "Classic period" or the "period of the sonata style"—was the age of Gluck in the 1760s, Haydn in the 1770s, Haydn and Mozart in the 1780s, Haydn again in the 1790s, and Beethoven from 1800 to 1827. If now we also add the name of Franz Schubert, a real Viennese (by birth, not just by adoption), we find ourselves at the brink of Romanticism. Indeed, we find ourselves belatedly well into the tide.

SUGGESTIONS FOR LISTENING

LUDWIG VAN BEETHOVEN, Symphony No. 3 in E-flat major, Op. 55, *Eroica*

LUDWIG VAN BEETHOVEN, Symphony No. 5 in C minor, Op. 67

LUDWIG VAN BEETHOVEN, Sonata in F minor for piano, Op. 57, *Appassionata*

LUDWIG VAN BEETHOVEN, *Leonore* Overture No. 3, Op. 72a

LUDWIG VAN BEETHOVEN, String Quartet No. 16 in F major, Op. 135

2. *ROMANTICISM AND AFTER*

That a special affinity exists between Romanticism and music was an article of faith with the Romantics themselves. All the arts, they believed, have one essential function: not the praise of God, or the imitation of the external world, or the gratification of the senses—as might have been claimed at earlier times—but the expression of human feeling and inner experience. And of all the arts, music was the one that could fulfill this function most deeply and freely. Deeply, because music is closest of all to the subjective, instinctive springs of emotion, what we now call the unconscious; freely, because the musician's imagination is not tied down to matter-of-fact words and statements, like the poet's, or to the representation of things, like the painter's. Music seemed to be the perfect outlet for an age that insisted on the high value of individual emotional expression.

This general view was widely shared and widely expressed, by musicians as well as other artists and thinkers. It found a definitive formulation in the works of Arthur Schopenhauer, a much-read German philosopher who influenced the composer Richard Wagner at a critical period of his life. Wagner's opera *Tristan und Isolde,* a key work in the history of Romanticism, practically spells out Schopenhauer's philosophy, as we shall see. Music gained enormous prestige and status ("All art aspires to the condition of music," wrote a famous later nineteenth-century critic, Walter Pater). Indeed, music was taken more seriously in the nineteenth century than in any other period since the Middle Ages. But whereas music then had commanded respect as a manifestation of the divine order of things, now it was revered as the most effective and thrilling language of man's innermost emotional life.

Thus Romanticism hastened the long historical process whereby instrumental music, music without words, became self-sufficient in artistic terms. As we have seen, only in the late Renaissance did idiomatic music for instruments arise beside the predominantly vocal music of the time. It gained in significance during the Baroque period, until finally, in the age of the Viennese Classics, sonatas and symphonies—not songs or operas—stood out as the main works of composers such as Haydn and Beethoven. The Romantics felt that symphonies could express the noblest feelings and truths in a direct, instinctual way that did not require any verbal explanation of what was being expressed. Beethoven was their shining example. Yet the century also witnessed a great upsurge of song and opera composition, and an amazing proliferation of literary associations with music of all sorts. Like painters of the time, composers were inspired by and attracted to literary "subject matter"; many of them fancied themselves as writers, too. Emotion was sought on every side, and if poetic associations could deepen the emotional effect of a piece of music, so much the better.

The glorification of personal feeling naturally entailed new prestige for the artist himself. Performers and composers no longer regarded themselves—and no longer allowed themselves to be regarded—as servants or craftsmen serving society, but rather as free spirits expressing their own souls with a genius not granted to the common run of mankind. "My nobility is *here*," Beethoven is supposed to have said, pointing to his heart. The pianist-composer Franz Liszt started his career playing in drawing rooms where a silk cord separated him from the noble listeners, but he lived to be sought out by those same people on terms of equality. Liszt's well-publicized liaisons with several high-born ladies may be regarded as a symbol of the change.

The artist came to be a sort of hero in the vanguard of spiritual movements, often flouting society by his actions and attitudes (and dress). Freedom, progress, and revolution in the arts were now considered to mirror these qualities in the wider human sphere. Some leading composers took part in revolutionary movements with democratic or nationalistic aims. Richard Wagner delivered speeches from the barricades during the Dresden uprising of 1849, and was exiled for his pains. Giuseppe Verdi allowed—and to some extent, planned—his operas to be used as propaganda in the struggle for Italian liberation. For his efforts he became a national hero and an honorary deputy in the first Italian parliament.

Nationalism in the nineteenth century encouraged a widespread interest in folk music, and folk music in turn proved to be a useful adjunct to nationalistic ideology. As we have observed (p. 257), enthusiasm for folk culture had arisen in the Enlightenment as part of the new emphasis on "nature"; but since the natural man sang with the accent of his particular country, his folk songs could foster nationalism as well as naturalism. Many composers built their styles to a considerable degree on the use, imitation, or evocation of folk songs and on the rhythms of national dances. Another important Romantic current, the new interest in the past, affected music appreciably though not to the extent that it affected art (see p. 157). Medieval subjects were chosen for operas and songs, old music was revived, and stylistic elements of Palestrina and Bach were echoed in not a few Romantic compositions. However, these were not so many that we are impelled to speak of "revival styles" in music, as we do in art.

Since the Romantics set such high store by individuality, we shall take them at their word and survey the period man by man—a procedure that might not be so suitable in other periods. For all their individuality, however, these composers shared some concerns. In their common search for momentary sensation and expressiveness, all of them tended to make striking innovations in the quality of musical sound, notably in the areas of harmony and instrumental color.

Fascinating untried chords and sequences of chords were explored, less for their "functional" quality in the scheme of tonality (compare the discussion on pp. 254–55) than for the sake of their momentary effect. Harmony could contribute potently to those mysterious, ethereal, rapturous, or sultry moods that were so greatly enjoyed at the time. Indeed, much of the individuality of the Romantic composers can be laid to their personalized harmonic usages (and, as we shall see, the exhaustion of harmonic exploration led to a veritable crisis at the beginning of the twentieth century). In respect to pure sonority, too, the Romantics stepped out onto new territory. They invented new instruments, coaxed new sounds out of old instruments, and combined sounds in unprecedented ways. For the first time in Western music, the sensuous quality of sound may be said to have assumed major artistic importance, on a level with melody, rhythm, and form. Bach and Beethoven wrote carefully for the various instruments, of course, but in one sense they seem to have applied their instrumental "colors" as a last touch, over and above the real foundation of notes and structure. This is generally not so with the Romantics. For Chopin or Berlioz, piano sound or orchestral sound is primary. Their music can no longer be thought of in abstract terms apart from the particular sonorities.

This cultivation of sound quality was often gained at the expense of logical continuity; or to put it another way, structural perfection was neither the main interest nor the main strength of many Romantic composers. This did not prevent them from planning bigger and bigger symphonies, cantatas, and operas, highly emphatic works in which the continuity was hopefully aided by literary factors, the listener being impressed by a combination of great thoughts, opulent sounds, and grandiose emotions. These works always run the danger of seeming windy. It must be remembered that form in the arts need not be a dry, mathematical exercise but may offer the means for power and coherence. When the Romantics neglected (or even ignored) structure in favor of momentary sensa-

tion, they sometimes lost control over the very expressiveness that they were pursuing so strenuously.

At the other extreme, Romanticism lent new dignity to very small compositions of an intimate nature, in particular short piano pieces and songs. Song composers found ample inspiration in folk song on the one hand, and in the great outpouring of lyric poetry during this period on the other. Since piano pieces had not the advantage of literary associations, they were often furnished with evocative titles, either of a general nature (*Songs without Words, Nocturnes, Woodland Sketches*) or else more specific (*Dream of Love, The Poet Speaks, Rustle of Spring*). We say that such music follows a "program" set forth by the verbal title; the concept of program music was enormously popular in the Romantic period and was by no means restricted to small compositions. For the present, let us make the point that in mapping out their compositions, the Romantics showed two rather strikingly opposed tendencies—one impressive, emphatic, and grandiose, and the other private, miniature, and intimate.

Was Beethoven a Romantic? Definitely not, in his commitment to Classic structural principles and the small attention he paid to novel harmonies or instrumental effects. But definitely yes, in the shattering emotional effect of his pieces, in his bold exploration of musical horizons, and in the almost mythical circumstances of his life: his eccentricity, his democratic stance, deafness, isolation, and inner suffering. On these grounds the Romantics could fairly claim him as one of their own, and in any case, his influence lasted long into the nineteenth century. Beethoven even provided a precedent in the matter of grandiose and miniature compositions. Though in most of his late music he still held to Classic proportions, he produced one enormous symphony—the Ninth and last, 1824 —introducing solo singers and a full chorus (they thunder out a hymn which is both revolutionary in sentiment and folklike in tone). At the same time he was writing intimate piano pieces he called *Bagatelles* (*Trifles*—one of them is only twelve measures long).

Beethoven's younger contemporary and neighbor in Vienna, Franz Schubert (1797–1828), should also be thought of as a transitional figure. He composed numerous short piano pieces with characteristically Romantic names, such as *Impromptu* (*Improvisation*) and *Moment Musical*, and an even greater number of songs with piano accompaniment—

more than six hundred, half of them written during his teens. They range from simple but unforgettable folklike evocations (such as *Hedge-Rose* and *The Linden Tree*) to powerful dramatic or psychological studies (*Erlking, Margaret at the Spinning Wheel, The Phantom Double*). Later he wrote some songs in sets, or song cycles, twenty-odd pieces linked together by means of a vague narrative thread—a loose form of literary continuity which, once again, is characteristically Romantic. Schubert was a superb melodist, and the greatest of all song writers, but like Beethoven, he too held to Classic principles of harmony, instrumentation, and form (with some qualifications). And it is a mistake to categorize Schubert solely as a miniaturist. Dying in 1828 at the very early age of thirty-one, he nonetheless left a dozen large instrumental works—symphonies, sonatas, and chamber-music works, composed, roughly

speaking, in Beethoven's manner—that are among the most impressive in the literature.

Romantic music had its first great flowering shortly afterwards, around 1830, at the hands of a generation liberally endowed with genius, though not liberally endowed with long life (see diagram 9). Vienna was replaced as the center of musical activity by Germany and Paris, the Paris of Delacroix (see p. 168). If any doubts lingered as to the direction being taken by the young, the composer Robert Schumann helped dispel them by editing a magazine devoted to propaganda for the "new music." In writing fancifully about a "League of David" doing battle against the musical "Philistines," Schumann described a significant new polarity in musical life. The gap between "avant-garde" musical composition and conservative taste widened during the nineteenth century, and is a real breach in the twentieth.

DIAGRAM NINE

Time Chart of the Romantic Composers

with some Earlier and Later Nineteenth-Century Figures

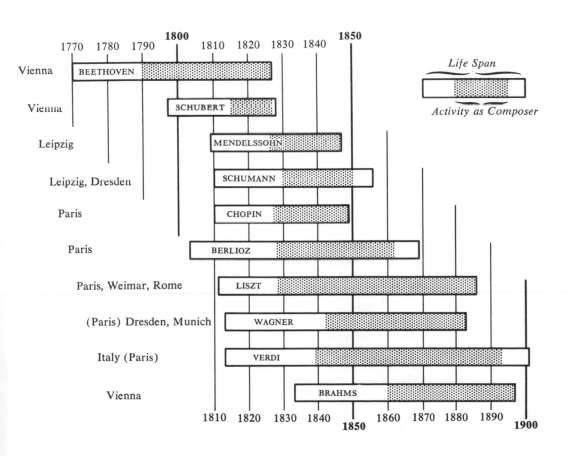

The most refined of the Romantic composers, Frédéric Chopin (1810–49: see fig. 221), was also the most limited in certain obvious ways. Writing almost exclusively for the piano, he concentrated on small pieces: *Nocturnes* (*Night Pieces*), *Ballades,* and various "stylized" dances, notably mazurkas—a Polish folk dance. Chopin was a Pole who made his home in Paris; his use of this dance reflects the Romantic nationalism of the time, but more significantly, it also reveals Chopin's interest in piquant rhythms and harmonies that could be derived from Slavic folk music. In conveying delicate sentiments—melancholy, languorous, spirited, hectic—Chopin is unmatched; there is an altogether new quality of intimacy and (as the nineteenth century would say) "poetry" in his music. To achieve this, he had to transform the sheer sound of the piano—that is, he had to revolutionize the technique of playing it. Chopin's fundamental concern with this problem is shown by his famous *Études* (*Studies*) which create exquisite mood-pictures even as they train the pianist's fingers.

Robert Schumann (1810–56) was another very original composer for the piano. His piano pieces are a little heavier than Chopin's, and often even more introspective (or "inward," "*innig,*" as he himself liked to put it). They generally come in large sets loosely grouped together according to some literary thread or program, such as the masked ball which is supposedly documented by the 22 pieces of his *Carnaval* (1835). Included are musical portraits of Chopin, of the famous violin virtuoso Paganini, of Pantaloon and Columbine, of two women friends plus "Coquette," of the League of David, and of Florestan and Eusebius—the composer's private names for the two sides of his personality, what would now be called his id and his superego. This kind of grouping recalls that of the song-cycle; Schumann was also a prolific writer of songs. In these, the piano becomes a sensitive partner for the singer, a peer rather than merely an accompanist, so that it sometimes wanders off by itself into long expressive passages of a meditative nature.

This happens at the end of *Am leuchtenden Sommermorgen* (*A lustrous summer morning,* RECORDED EXAMPLE 15), a song from Schumann's song-cycle *Dichterliebe* (*Poet's Love*). Notable here—in addition to the poem, by the important German poet Heinrich Heine—is the characteristically free broken-chord style of piano writing, which sounds as though the player were making it up out of his fantasy as he goes along. The voice line is cunningly contrived to sound like a simple folk song, but its simplicity is belied by the magical chords introduced to set the mood at the beginning and to illuminate the words "*sprechen die Blumen*" (the flowers speak) and "*blasser*" (paler—recall Keats's "palely loitering"). Features such as these can be multiplied in Romantic songs and piano pieces; some the reader will doubtless know, and his pianist friends will be only too pleased to play others for him.

Unlike Chopin, Schumann devoted a good deal of attention to symphonies, fugues, chamber-music pieces, and other large works. In these, he frequently carried themes over from one movement to another, a practice that was to become increasingly common and important. (Again, Beethoven provided some precedents, in the Fifth Symphony and elsewhere, and Berlioz had systematized the practice in a literary context, as we shall see.) By this means, composers hoped to make large works in several sections more "organic"—a favorite concept a little later, in the age of Darwin. We may say that they were seeking cohesiveness of a different sort from that provided by Classic structural principles, such as those underlying the sonata-allegro form. In Schumann's output, there are interesting cases in his well-known Piano Concerto, in his First, Second, and Fourth Symphonies, and elsewhere (the piano passage concluding *Am leuchtenden Sommermorgen* also returns later in the cycle, like a meditative recollection of the earlier song). Felix Mendelssohn (1809–47), Schumann's friend and a paler personality, though a very attractive one, experimented more cautiously along similar lines.

Chopin, Schumann, and Mendelssohn were happiest when composing in the intimate vein. The grandiose side of Romantic music found its impetus in Paris—partly, perhaps, in response to the bloated and very successful French operas of Jacob Meyerbeer, themselves a reflection of the garish, luxurious quality of Parisian bourgeois life. (Another reflection was the Opera House built for those very operas: see fig. 210.) The better composers despised Meyerbeer, but something of his ostentatiousness (as well as some of his impressive orchestral tricks) left a mark on them.

Hector Berlioz, who lived from 1803 to 1869 but wrote his most influential music before 1850, began his career with two sensational program symphonies, large works built upon a loose literary continuity. The *Fantastic Symphony* (1830) purports to depict the experiences on an opium "trip," and *Harold in*

Italy (1834) traces the adventures of one of the gloomy heroes so beloved of Romantic writers, in this case Byron's Childe Harold. Here is how one of Berlioz' own programs reads:

PROGRAMME OF THE SYMPHONY. *A young musician of morbid sensibility and ardent imagination is in love, and has poisoned himself with opium in a fit of desperation. Not having taken a lethal dose, he falls into a long sleep in which he has the strangest dreams, wherein his feelings, sentiments, and memories are translated by his sick brain into musical ideas and figures. The beloved herself has become a melody which he finds and hears everywhere as an* idée fixe. *First movement: "Reveries. Passions." First he remembers the uneasiness of mind, his aimless passions, the baseless depression and elation which he felt before he saw the object of his adoration, then the volcanic love which she instantly inspired in him, his delirious agonies, his jealous rages, his recovered love, his consolations of religion. . . .*

—and so on through a total of five full-length symphony movements. Soon Berlioz felt the need for even greater scope, and produced lengthy symphony-cantata-oratorios on such tried-and-true Romantic subjects as *Romeo and Juliet* and *The Damnation of Faust.**

None of these works makes much sense as a total musical structure, even when a single tune runs through the various movements as an "*idée fixe*" (fixed idea) standing for some person—Childe Harold, or the opium-eater's fickle beloved. But Berlioz' works do contain one marvelous idea after another, and one vivid surprise after another, all presented in a breath-taking new orchestral sound. What Chopin did for the piano, Berlioz did for the orchestra: he transformed it into a powerful medium for the expression of Romantic emotion. And as Chopin felt compelled to compose *Études* for piano, so Berlioz wrote a revolutionary treatise on orchestration. New instruments were added to the Classic orchestra (compare diagram 8, p. 263; in fact, they had been quietly working their way in for years): trombones, tubas, harps, many kinds of percussion; also different sizes of the standard instruments: an E-flat clarinet (small clarinet), bass clarinet (large one), piccolo (small flute), English horn* (large oboe), and double bassoon or contrabassoon (large bassoon). And as the technical manufacture of all wind instruments improved, brass instruments were fitted with finger valves that at last enabled them to play all the notes of the scale (compare p. 259). Even more important, Berlioz studied the particular quality of each instrument with enormous care, note by note, and produced novel solo effects and fresh composite sounds. After this, the strings were no longer invariably the basis of orchestral sound. The woodwinds and brasses assumed richer, more flexible roles.

The Paris of Chopin and Berlioz made a very deep impression on the young Hungarian piano-virtuoso and composer Franz Liszt (1811–86: he was also active in Germany). His exuberant, highly imaginative talent, as well as a lifelong instinct for the limelight, made Liszt a force in nineteenth-century music, despite a streak of vulgarity in his musical personality that offended many musicians—and still does. (His familiar *Rákoczi March,* a work with Hungarian nationalist inspiration, is a case in point.) In his harmony and piano style, Liszt exaggerated all of Chopin's innovations and added several of his own. His highly charged orchestral writing borrowed much from Berlioz. He carried forward Berlioz' ideas by composing symphonic poems—orchestral pieces again loosely organized around literary programs, but generally cast in one long continuous movement. To run through the names of the poets who inspired Liszt's symphonic poems in the 1850s is to draw up a typical Romantic reading list: Dante, Tasso, Shakespeare, Herder, Goethe, Schiller, Byron, Hugo, Lamartine.

In the symphonic poem, said Liszt, the composer "reproduces his impressions and the adventures of his soul in order to communicate them." To narrate these soul adventures, he developed an important technique of transforming a small number of musical themes in various ways—a technique with roots in thematic practices of Beethoven, Schumann, and especially Berlioz' *idée fixe*. A serene theme, for example, might be made to sound restless by having its rhythm stiffened and its harmonies changed a little; such a thematic transformation could obviously mirror some aspect of the program. The last important composer of

---

* Goethe's *Faust* also inspired important pieces by Schumann, Liszt, and Wagner. Incidentally, Berlioz and Liszt sometimes changed literary programs for their pieces, or supplied them after composition, rather as Turner occasionally did for his paintings.

---

* The name of this instrument represents utter confusion; it is neither English nor a horn.

symphonic poems recalling those of Liszt was Richard Strauss, at the end of the nineteenth century (see p. 282). But by that time, taste was turning away from so literary a conception of musical continuity, and Strauss abandoned the genre quite early in his career.

And indeed, the fulfillment of the grandiose tendencies of Romantic music was not in the program symphonies of Berlioz or the symphonic poems of Liszt, but in the operas of a man who had learned much from both genres: Richard Wagner (1813–83). In a remarkable way, Wagner's life and works summed up the artistic intentions of the Romantic era.

SUGGESTIONS FOR LISTENING

FRANZ SCHUBERT, *Winterreise* (song-cycle), Op. 89

FRANZ SCHUBERT, String Quintet in C major, Op. 163

FRÉDÉRIC CHOPIN, Mazurkas, Nocturnes (piano)

ROBERT SCHUMANN, *Carnaval,* Op. 9

ROBERT SCHUMANN, Concerto in A minor for piano and orchestra, Op. 54

HECTOR BERLIOZ, Symphony *Harold in Italy* for viola and orchestra, Op. 16

FRANZ LISZT, *Faust* Symphony

As the reader may well suppose, opera composers had a field-day in the early nineteenth century. Tales of cliff-hanging rescues, star-crossed young lovers, and knightly derring-do were enthusiastically taken up and proved wildly popular. In general, all these subjects were compressed into the standard operatic framework of recitatives, arias, and ensembles, though to be sure, operatic structure was becoming more flexible as a result of the examples of Gluck and Mozart. But the "tyranny of the prima donna" continued; however much the style of singing had changed, displays of virtuoso singing still remained to plague the dramatic continuity, just as in the days of Baroque *opera seria.* Composers now invented all kinds of melodramatic musical effects, forerunners of those used in this century as background music for silent movies and television shows. Jacob Meyerbeer (1791–1864) was by no means the first to cultivate flashy orchestral tricks for theatrical purposes. In this area the tradition goes back to the 1790s and includes several important operas by Karl Maria von Weber (1786–1826). *Der Freischütz* (1821; freely rendered as *The Magic Bullet*), with its sensational scene of devilish conjuration in the ghostly "Wolf's Glen," and *Euryanthe* (1823), a garbled tale of chivalry and true love, made an impression on all German musicians, as they did on Berlioz in Paris. All the composers mentioned in the previous section (except Chopin) tried their hand at opera, but without much success.

Wagner's successful operatic formula—successful, however, only after a long, tenacious struggle—was worked out by him in a long series of books and essays. (Of the many literary-minded Romantic composers, he was the most prolific—and pretentious—writer.) With some justice, he castigated the popular French and Italian opera of the time as artificial, undramatic, and artistically shabby. The breakdown of the dramatic action into recitative and aria was stiff and childish; the stories could not be taken seriously; emphasis on virtuoso singing turned the whole enterprise into a "concert in costume." As a true Romantic, Wagner thought it outrageous for music to be used for mere "trivial entertainment" when it could be expressing the noblest aspirations of mankind. Instead he conceived of a highly serious dramatic art-form integrating vocal and instrumental music, poetry, drama, philosophy, and stagecraft—what he called a *Gesamtkunstwerk* (combined-art-work).

The dramatic continuity, Wagner proclaimed, should be unbroken, like life itself, not broken into arbitrary numbers such as arias and ensembles. The words (which he himself wrote, in addition to the music) should be decidedly "literary" in tone, and set to music with enormous care for correct declamation. The stories should narrate myths, because myths embody the most profound human truths in symbolic form—and the myths should be German for good measure: then the *Gesamtkunstwerk* would express the very spirit of the German folk (another emphatic reflection of Romantic nationalism). Back of all this lay a vague but potent Romantic conception of Greek drama. Greek plays had been sung, it will be remembered, and therefore Wagner could recklessly compare them to operas. They enacted myths as a kind of Athenian folk ritual. They were serious, passionate, high-minded, and noble.

The idea of the *Gesamtkunstwerk* found a sympathetic echo in the Romantic imagination. Was not every song or program symphony a combined-art-work in embryo? The grandiose instincts of the age rallied to the notion that the greatest art would be produced by the greatest number of components.

The role of music in all this was to express the emotions of the participants—the highest role, according to Romantic doctrine. So with more regard for consistency than for the patience of his audiences, Wagner cut down the dramatic stage business as far as possible, in order to concentrate on emotion. In his most intensely emotional scenes, little happens on the stage, however much happens in the souls of his actors—and especially in the orchestra. Wagner was a magnificent orchestrator, and incidentally the inventor of several new instruments as well as one of the best conductors of his time; it is the orchestra that really carries his operas along, not the singers. (The Italians never forgave Wagner for this.) He took plenty of time with his orchestral music, developing a distinctive manner of continuously surging up and up and apparently never stopping, piling one gorgeous harmony and instrumental sound upon another. This can become boring—it was criticized as "endless melody"—but at its best it can create an overpowering impression of churning emotions.

Wagner's most famous innovation was the leitmotif (*Leitmotiv*, leading motif), a small orchestral fragment that recurs over and over again in an opera, and is associated with some object, person, or idea—or, better, associated with the *emotion* that adheres to that object, person, or idea. The leitmotif differs from the Berlioz *idée fixe* in its brevity and flexibility, in the almost infinite number of times it is used, and in Wagner's superior skill and imagination with the technique. A leitmotif could be transformed in Liszt's manner to reflect a major turn in the drama, or it could be altered very slightly to reflect a subtle one. It could sound in the orchestra to suggest a character's unconscious thought without his even mentioning it. Besides "telling a story" in the orchestra, these motifs provided the necessary material for

Wagner's typical surging passages. Dense "symphonic" development of leitmotifs, in the manner of a Beethoven development section, is Wagner's basic technique and the one that gives his operas their peculiarly supercharged atmosphere.

Of all composers, Wagner is the least susceptible to illustration through small excerpts. However, a passage from near the end of his last opera, *Parsifal* (1882), can give some idea of his methods and also of his characteristic tone (RECORDED EXAMPLE 16). The story of this opera, from the so-called Grail cycle, which is related to the Celtic medieval legends of King Arthur and the Round Table, is now recognized as a version of the universal fertility myth of the Fisher King. The priest-king of the Knights of the Holy Grail, Amfortas, has sinned carnally and been wounded; hovering in agony between life and death, he cannot perform the rites of the Grail. The entire community languishes, awaiting the fulfillment of the prophecy that says he can be cured by a touch of the selfsame spear that wounded him, wielded by a knight of perfect innocence and purity. In our recorded excerpt, Parsifal (Sir Percival) performs this healing—or, better, universal redeeming—act and assumes the priestly office as Amfortas' successor.

The listener must try to imagine that the associations of all of the leitmotifs have been drummed into his ear during the four hours of the opera that have already passed. Thus at the opening of the excerpt, the somewhat sanctimonious leitmotif played by the brass instruments inevitably makes one think of the Grail itself. An expressive descending leitmotif that has been associated throughout with Amfortas' suffering now appears before the words "*Sei heil*" (be cured) and then four times more—modulating each time—during the next lines. But it appears transformed into a serene new version; Amfortas suffers no more. As Parsifal speaks of "compassionate power" and the "timid Fool," an important leitmotif used in relating the prophecy surges up in the orchestra, until there is a burst of knightly music characterizing Parsifal. In this way the orchestra finally reveals or confirms that the innocent knight of the prophecy is Parsifal himself. More leitmotifs follow, including an agonized one associated with the spear itself (four ascending notes, just before "*Der deine Wunde*," "*ihm seh' ich*," and "*in Sehnsucht*").

As far as method is concerned, it will be noted that the essential continuity is provided by the orchestra, not the voice. The passage is quite unlike a traditional opera aria, for what Parsifal sings is often less important than the leitmotifs that sound simultaneously in the orchestra. In tone, the brassy music associated with Parsifal is no less characteristic than the spear leitmotif, with its rich, sultry harmonies, continuous modulation, and relentless forward drive; Wagner's music can sometimes be blatant as well as powerfully sensual. Characteristic, too, is the sheer variety and opulence of orchestral sound, qualities cultivated by the Romantic composers for half a century. Finally, we must not neglect the "message"—even though nowadays we may find it hard to take —for this was central to Wagner's conception. *Parsifal* seems to present a cloudy allegory of the corruption of modern life and its need for renewal through a sort of hero-religion which, though Christian in name, is vaguely pagan in locale and disturbingly so in emotional quality.

Each Wagner opera was a major undertaking, and in his fully mature period he wrote no more than four of them—or seven, depending on how they are counted. *The Ring of the Nibelung* (1853–74), a work lasting four long evenings, surely marks the climax of the grandiose tradition. Wagner conceived it as a trilogy with an introduction, after the model of Greek drama; the same characters and leitmotifs run through all four operas, which require an unprecedented force of performers: a cast of 35, an orchestra of 105. He incorporated plenty of the apparatus found in his literary source, a famous Germanic saga (or, as he saw it, national myth): gods and goddesses, magic swords plunged in trees, dragons guarding treasures, dwarfs turned into toads, love potions, blood, walls of fire, scenes at the bottom of the Rhine. The work ends with the chief warrior-maiden riding her steed onto a funeral pyre as the whole world collapses.

On the other hand, in *Tristan und Isolde* (1859) Wagner compressed saga material that was equally diffuse into an intense, single-minded, slow-motion vision of the triumph of human passion. Taking a medieval tale of love and adultery and plunging it into music, Wagner compels us to see individual emotion as more important or "real" than worldly convention, reason, the flesh, and finally life itself. This was carrying Schopenhauer's almost mystical glorification of emotion and music (see p. 271) to its logical conclusion; *Tristan* is the ultimate statement of the Romantic creed. *The Mastersingers of Nuremberg* (1867), a realistic comedy full of local color and German history, seems uncharacteristic at first glance.

But below the surface it is another turgid allegory, this time about Romantic music and its Philistine enemies—and another celebration of the German artist-hero.

Wagner's identification with his own heroes grew almost ominous as the years went on. As ruthless in self-interest as his own Nordic supermen, he was able to exert influence over the slightly deranged King Ludwig II of Bavaria, dabble in statecraft, make off with other men's wives, and promote a monument to the arts that probably counts as the most astonishing ever erected. This was a special opera house in the tiny town of Bayreuth, in central Germany, designed exclusively for Wagner festivals (the rest of the time the theater was dark). For his last festival, the composer produced his semiritual opera *Parsifal*. When he died soon afterwards, in 1883, Bayreuth was beginning to take on the aspect of a temple devoted to a new Wagnerian religion.

The operas are perhaps easy to laugh at today, with their constant heroics and endless emoting and strained stage effects. But this is true, to some extent, of most great Romantic art. One side of Romanticism deals with our private emotional fantasy world, and this may look a little ludicrous in the cold light of day. If, however, one begins to submit to Wagner's illusion—not in the cold light of day, but in the mysterious depths of the Bayreuth Theater— one is likely to be swept away by the hypnotic power of his "combined-art-work," and one can take it all very seriously indeed. While some of his contemporaries laughed, many others submitted; no musician or artist has ever had such an impact upon artists and thinkers in every area. Probably the most graphic evidence of this is that Friedrich Nietzsche, one of the most influential philosophers of the century, wrote his first book as a kind of glorification of Wagner—and then, after a great change of heart, felt impelled to write two tracts denouncing him as a symbol of all that was corrupt in nineteenth-century culture. This seems like a strong line to take, but there are grounds for it. Nietzsche, who was steeped in the Greek classics, certainly remembered Plato's warnings that some varieties of music are profoundly destructive of the common good.

The lengthening shadow of Wagner fell over all aspects of musical life in the later nineteenth century. His personality was so forceful, and his musical stance so uncompromising, that people found themselves almost driven to take strong positions for or against him. And since

Wagner insisted on identifying his work as "the Music of the Future," a new split became evident between freshly composed "avant-garde" music and the established "classics." This split, forecast in the journalism of Schumann, is now a disturbing feature of today's musical scene.

There are other important respects in which musical life of today was prefigured by the later nineteenth century. One is simply the growing prominence of old music. Whereas previously all the music that was performed was more or less contemporary, and the "classics" were not widely known even in the classroom, the nineteenth century grew increasingly interested in masterpieces from earlier times. Mendelssohn created a sensation when he "discovered" Bach's *Passion According to St. Matthew*; Wagner revived Palestrina and Gluck; Brahms helped make scholarly editions of the complete works of Handel, Mozart, and C. P. E. Bach. This state of affairs arose partly in order to meet the demand for new emotional experiences, which has a parallel in the numerous revival styles in the visual arts of those same years. It was also part of the Romantic worship of the artist-hero: Palestrina was hailed as "the savior of Church music," Bach as "the first great German master." In the wake of this interest, incidentally, the history of music was for the first time seriously studied by analogy to literary history, which had existed from time immemorial, and to art history, which had existed ever since the Renaissance. Music had lost its place in the medieval universities as a mathematical or speculative discipline (see p. 227), but now it found its way back as a humanistic one.

Still another feature we have inherited from the last century is the use of concerts as the main show-places for music. As the support essential for musical performances moved away from the aristocracy to the newly powerful middle classes, paid public concerts replaced the private court performances of earlier times. We have mentioned that Johann Christian Bach organized concerts in eighteenth-century London, an example that was soon followed in all the main cities of Europe and America. It seems to be a fact that whereas the taste of the aristocracy tends to be capricious, ranging from reactionary to adventurous, the taste of the middle classes tends to be broadly conformist and cautious. As a consequence, concert life fell right in with the interest in older, firmly established music. Yesterday's concert life was already conservative.

Most people know a good amount of late nineteenth-century music. In fact, music of this period probably occupies a larger place in people's consciousness than is warranted by its historical importance or actual aesthetic worth. This has something to do with the conservatism of *today's* concert life. The post-Wagner period in music was actually a relatively stagnant one, as compared with the immediately preceding and succeeding periods. With the benefit of hindsight, we can see that Wagner had carried music about as far as it could go in a certain direction—and that for a time composers hesitated to go over the cliff. Some composers followed the beaten paths of the first part of the century, without finding much that was new or recapturing the fine flush of the early Romantic spirits. Others shrank from the naïve, heady expansiveness of the early time and returned to even older musical principles.

The most impressive of these composers, at all events in terms of craft—he was one of the greatest musical craftsmen of all time—went so far as to sign a foolish manifesto condemning the avant-garde music of Liszt and Wagner. Though Johannes Brahms (1833–97) composed many superbly fashioned songs and small piano pieces, according to the Romantic fashion, instrumental music on the model of Beethoven was his ideal. Significantly, Brahms is not notable for his instrumental sound, and the closest he ever came to a literary program in his many fine orchestral and chamber-music compositions was the single word "tragic" in the title of his *Tragic Overture*. Rarely did he engage in the Romantic practice of carrying themes over from one movement to another, even though this had been pioneered by his older friend and mentor, Schumann. When Brahms's First Symphony was hailed as "Beethoven's Tenth," the judgment spoke worlds for the attitudes of the 1870s. That a composer should seek, even if unconsciously, to match another composer sixty years his senior; that he should actually be praised for the effort; that an artist-hero like Beethoven should loom as a sort of timeless standard—all of this would have been unthinkable in an earlier period.

Brahms's music has a nostalgic quality comparable to that of another master craftsman of Victorian times, the poet Tennyson. Brahms's is a distinguished voice, however, alongside those of Grieg, Dvořák, Tchaikovsky, Rimsky-Korsakov, Franck, MacDowell, Rachmaninoff, Sibelius, Strauss, Bruckner, Mahler—the list is a long one, and familiar to those who know older symphony programs and courses in music appreciation. Each of these late Romantic composers explored his own channel of emotionalism; although their individual voices are often attractive, they are never very sturdy. Sometimes they are empty, sentimental, or frantic. Of the names on the above list, only Gustav Mahler (1860–1911), composer of the most grandiose symphonies ever, exerted a lasting influence on the course of music history.

Often folk material formed the basis of large compositions. The Russians were perhaps most successful in this vein, though all countries produced nationalist composers. An impressively "authentic" opera on a Russian historical subject, *Boris Godunov* by Modest Mussorgsky (1869), is so stark and primitive in quality that until recently it was always performed in a watered-down version. Indeed, the use of folk material was not always a strictly nationalistic phenomenon: Frenchmen set their operas in Spain, Russians recorded their impressions of Italy, and Czechs wrote "New World" Symphonies (Georges Bizet's *Carmen,* Peter Ilyitch Tchaikovsky's *Capriccio italien,* Antonin Dvořák's Fifth Symphony). These pieces reflect the same taste that travelogues do, perhaps. But the nationalist movement in music played an appreciable role as a springboard for twentieth-century developments that we shall see.

A composer of the middle and late nineteenth century who has risen sharply in critical estimation is Giuseppe Verdi (1813–1901). We have not discussed him in what might seem to be his proper chronological position; some justification for this may be found in the isolation of his nation, Italy, from the central musical developments of France and Germany. In some ways Italy held itself even more aloof than places with weaker musical traditions, such as Russia and England. The reason for this was not so much provincialism as a very decided national taste. In the early eighteenth century, Italy led the world both in instrumental music and in opera, but by the early nineteenth century, Italians cared only for opera, and only for opera strictly in the service of virtuoso singing. There was simply no interest in Romantic piano pieces or program symphonies, and the Wagnerian "Music of the Future" left the Italians cold. Verdi composed thirty operas, a few thoroughly operatic works for the Church, and very little else.

His career began as early as 1840, at a time when the leaders of Italian opera deserved much of the scorn that Wagner was beginning to heap upon them. (But they did write some wonderful melodies.) From the start, Verdi showed a liking for musical excitement—even violence—and a special talent for drama and characterization. Both of these qualities he refined by slow, steady steps over more than five decades. During much of this time, it would have been fair to judge him a less original composer than Wagner, less skillful than Brahms, and less "poetic" than the early Romantics. And so he was judged in northern Europe, which, however, took a certain guilty pleasure in his magnificent opera melodies. But in his last operas—*Aïda* (1871), *Otello* (1887), and *Falstaff* (1893)—Verdi demonstrated as much originality, craftsmanship, and finesse as any of his contemporaries, and a dramatic sense that surpassed them all. The last two operas in particular, which are expertly derived from Shakespeare, rank with the best ever written.

The "tyranny of the prima donna," against which Wagner raged, did not seem to bother Verdi. Always working through, not in spite of, virtuoso singing, he invariably brought his operatic characters to life, even when they are boxed in by silly melodramatic situations, as is often the case in his earlier, cruder operas. They are people, not abstractions in a philosophical system, as Wagner's characters sometimes seem to be. Though they are less intellectual than Wagner's characters, their emotional responses to the various crises in which they find themselves are admirably intense and pure. In Italy as elsewhere in Europe, the age demanded integrity of individual feeling. No composer of the century responded to this demand more truly than Verdi.

It has been said that after Wagner, all opera was more or less Wagnerian, and while this statement does not hold true for the mood, the subjects treated, and the *Gesamtkunstwerk* aspect, there is undoubtedly some truth to it in a technical sense. Thus operas by Verdi and by everybody else grew more and more continuous over the years, and less sharply divided into numbers; the orchestra was used more and more integrally; and increasing attention was paid to serious drama (though not "serious" in Wagner's sense, certainly). It remained for Giacomo Puccini (1858–1924), whose most popular operas (*La Bohème, Tosca, Madam Butterfly*) date from around 1900, to exploit leitmotifs in Italian opera. But Puccini employed them much less wholeheartedly than Wagner, never allowing them to steal interest from the voice, and never making them into an intellectual superstructure. It is a tribute to Wagner's greatness that his ideas could be used —one is inclined to say, *had* to be used—not only by his disciples, but even by musicians of utterly different talent and temperament.

RICHARD WAGNER, *Tristan und Isolde*: Prelude, Act I; Love-duet, Act II

RICHARD WAGNER, *Parsifal*: Prelude, Act III; selections, Act III

JOHANNES BRAHMS, Symphony No. 4 in E minor, Op. 98

MODESTE MUSSORGSKY, *Boris Godunov,* "Inn" scene, Act I

PETER ILYITCH TCHAIKOVSKY, *Capriccio italien,* Op. 45

GIUSEPPE VERDI, *Rigoletto,* Act IV

GIUSEPPE VERDI, *Otello,* Act II

3. *THE TWENTIETH CENTURY*

In discussing the course of modern painting (see page 174)we spoke of Manet's "revolution of the color patch" and his proclamation of an "internal logic" in painting that is distinct from the logic of familiar reality. The painter's first loyalty is to his canvas, not to the outside world; he is not to be bound by the rules of representation. From Manet to the Impressionists, and on to the Post-Impressionists, Cubists, Abstract Expressionists, and Pop and Op artists, successive generations of painters have searched for new kinds of purely pictorial logic, which ultimately became divorced from the world of appearances. Many people saw (and continue to see) this development merely as a revolt against tradition—as though revolts are staged for their own sake. The fact is that tradition has repeatedly failed to provide answers to the insistent questions raised by modern life, whether in painting, music, or indeed in any other area. Almost the first condition of modern life is the breakdown of received tradition; almost the first clue to its quality is the enormously inventive and constantly changing response to this breakdown.

Musicians have turned away from the past just as drastically as the painters, and just as imaginatively. We can see, indeed, that the development of twentieth-century music has proceeded along lines broadly comparable to those followed by painting. Although music never enjoyed (or suffered) a link to the outside world comparable to representation in the visual arts, in the eighteenth and nineteenth centuries it did have a stable, universally accepted set of principles which served as a comparable point of departure or revolt. We may speak of a traditional "internal logic" made up of certain basic elements that have come up many times

in our previous discussion: tune, motif, functional harmony, and the tonal system. Not only was the music of Bach, Beethoven, and Brahms based on this, but so was the entire stream of European folk songs, popular songs, dances, military marches, and the rest—was, and still is. Music of the twentieth century has moved away from this traditional "internal logic." Like nonobjective painting, music has worked out new principles on the basis of the material of the art itself; and this process has extended to a complete divorce from the "familiar reality" of song and dance music.

Unquestionably this divorce has made difficulties in the way of a general understanding of twentieth-century music (comparable to the situation in painting as a result of the divorce from representation). Some of the new kinds of "internal logic" make little sense to many listeners and, incidentally, also puzzle not a few trained musicians and music historians. This is an important problem, and we shall return to it later. What is much more important, however, is that composers have felt for many years that traditional principles have been more or less exhausted. They simply find no further possibilities for action in terms of the old "internal logic"; both in technique and expression, Wagner and Brahms had carried this to its limits. Its subsequent abandonment led to a feeling of exhilaration at the expansion of musical horizons, a feeling that to a remarkable extent persists after seventy years of the most varied experimentation.

For music historians, the music of our century poses historical problems in the keenest form. With such deep-rooted changes taking place, it is becoming increasingly clear that music is entering into a new period that should be differentiated from the past—as sharply, in all probability, as the Middle Ages from the

Renaissance and the Era of the Renaissance from the Modern World. But the new period has yet to be named, and indeed conflicting hypotheses are advanced about it. We are still in considerable confusion as to the meaning or destination of twentieth-century developments. The fact is worth stating, not by way of apology—why should music or art historians be expected to understand these difficult times: who does?—but by way of providing a stimulus or even a challenge to the student. For it is his generation that will be able to cut through the confusions and the "isms" and discriminate among the manifold efforts toward a new "interior logic" for music. It is always difficult to form a fully coherent impression of the contemporary arts while being still fully bound up with them.

In order to examine the main lines of twentieth-century musical development, it will be well to recall the basic elements of the traditional "internal logic"—tune, motif, functional harmony, and the tonal system. Everyone knows fairly well what "tune" means. As for motif, that can be thought of simply enough as a condensation of tune, or a memorable fragment of tune. Any tune has repeated melodic figures or fragments within it, or at least repeated rhythms; these are the motifs. The tonal system defines the "set" of the tune or the extended piece; functional harmony, as we have tried to explain, is the plan worked out by the Baroque period for clarifying and supporting the sense of centrality (see pp. 254–55). The tonal system also served as an important ground plan for composing. With the sonata-allegro form, for example, one knew that the music would return to the original tonality toward the end and would seem to "set" there.

In the long-term historical process that led to the replacement of this entire system by others, it was functional harmony and the tonal system that gave way first, while for a time tune and motif were still preserved. (In a similar way, Manet's subjects continue to be recognizable, but they have a new "set" with respect to the picture frame.) Indeed, the Viennese composers were already shaking up the tonal system in every development section of every piece in their beloved sonata-allegro form. They did so, of course, in order to strengthen, by contrast, the main tonality when it sails back triumphantly in the recapitulation section. But could not the modulatory motif technique of development sections be used without recapitulations? Wagner did exactly this.

As early as 1859, in *Tristan und Isolde,* Wagner was writing extended passages in which the feeling of centrality was seriously eroded or in doubt. He used more and more extreme chord forms, and he used more of them. Each chord had its own emotional quality, while its function or supporting quality was willingly abandoned to the quality of moment-by-moment surging. In particular, Wagner used the full set of twelve notes (C, C-sharp, D, D-sharp, E, etc.) so freely that the seven notes of the ordinary scale were no longer recognizable as such—and therefore did not give the impression of a tonality. This expanded use of all the notes is called chromaticism. Chromaticism was closely involved with the emotionalism of late nineteenth-century music and also with the continuing erosion of the tonal system.

Listeners at the time experienced great trouble with Wagner's chromaticism, which reached its extreme point in the Prelude to Act III of *Parsifal* (1882), his last opera. This astonishing, almost "atonal" (i.e., not tonal-sounding) piece presented composers with a fascinating challenge that was not really met for a quarter of a century. *Parsifal* still contained real tunes—and Manet's last paintings at exactly the same time still contained representations of the outer world. But Wagner's surging music was not held together by tunes so much as by short motifs, the famous leitmotifs. Significantly, these tended to become more distorted and chromatic with time.

Later composers whittled away steadily at tune, motif, functional harmony, and the tonal system, in search of new kinds of "internal logic" for music. The years after 1900 witnessed intense experimentation and saw the emergence of important new talents. This was as brilliant an era in music as in the visual arts, and for many members of the public an equally shocking one.

Richard Strauss (1864–1949) was mentioned above in connection with one of the most Romantic of musical forms, the symphonic poem developed by Liszt. Strauss also fostered the ideas of Richard Wagner in the field of German opera. His allegiance to leitmotifs, brilliant orchestral continuity, and increasingly involved chromaticism earned him the title of "Richard II." But in place of the hearty Romanticism of *Tristan* and the decadent, "end-of-the-century" atmosphere of *Parsifal*, Strauss's *Salome* (1905), using a play by Oscar Wilde, and *Elektra* (1909), a reworking of the tragedy by Sophocles, were violent shockers. Romanticism had started out to depict individual emotions, but new ones proved hard to find as time wore on, unless extreme mental states were explored such as blood lust and necrophilism. Shocking, too, were some of Strauss's extreme new chord forms.

Arnold Schoenberg (1874–1951) also began his career with a symphonic poem of sorts, *Verklärte Nacht* (*Transfigured Night,* 1899). In a series of extraordinary works of about 1910, Schoenberg relinquished the tonal system entirely—an action with evident analogies to the adoption of nonobjective painting by Schoenberg's friend Kandinsky at exactly this time (see p. 186). Relinquishing the tonal system meant pushing chord forms or note combinations to an unheard-of level of complexity. Chords were now so chromatic and so far from simple triads that no sense of tonality came through even on a fleeting level, as had always been the case with Wagner and even Strauss. Like these composers, Schoenberg held his music together with motifs; indeed, it was contrapuntal motif work that generated his complex harmonic style. Tunes in the ordinary sense no longer occurred. And Schoenberg's ear grew so subtle that it is often hard for us to perceive his motifs as motifs, though they can certainly be seen to "exist" in his scores. The feeling of public resentment at Schoenberg's "chaotic" experiments seems to have exceeded even that occasioned by the Fauves and the early Cubists.

It is perhaps not surprising that the first success of Schoenberg's new style was in connection with texts depicting extreme states of mind. Indeed, we are entitled to ask whether the egg came before the chicken, in view of Schoenberg's unusually close association with the Expressionist movement. He himself painted (and exhibited) a number of Expressionist paintings, and the texts he chose for his music reflected the literary tastes of German Expressionist circles. Such are his near-psychotic "monodrama" *Erwartung* (*Anticipation,* 1909) and his nightmarish chamber-music song cycle *Pierrot lunaire* (1912), the masterpiece of Schoenberg's early style. One work of this general type has achieved real popularity: the opera *Wozzeck* composed between 1917 and 1921 by Alban Berg, Schoenberg's pupil. It tells of a more or less deranged army private who is starved, tormented, beaten, and deceived to the point where he breaks down and kills first his unfaithful mistress and then himself. Our excerpt (RECORDED EXAMPLE 19) is the beginning of a scene in which a mad Doctor, who has put Wozzeck on a grotesque diet of beans for experimental purposes, is ordering him around. The quality of this scene reminds us of Expressionist pictures such as Edvard Munch's *The Scream* (fig. 234).

The other great composer of the generation of Strauss and Schoenberg, though somewhat older, was a Frenchman, Claude Debussy (1862–1918). He too began his career (and in many ways ended it) in the Romantic tradition, as an exquisite writer of songs and of piano pieces with evocative titles, an inventor of chord forms of new delicate beauty, and a miraculous orchestrator. He wrote a series of fine symphonic poems (though not so named), from *Prélude à L'après-midi d'un faune* (1894) through *Nuages, Fêtes, La Mer,* and *Iberia,* to the ballet *Jeux* (1912). (These titles mean *Prelude to "The Afternoon of a Faun"*—the title of a famous Symbolist poem by Stéphane Mallarmé—*Clouds, Festivals, The Sea, Spain,* and *Play.*) Debussy's music is often referred to as Impressionistic, because its technique bears some analogies to the slightly earlier art movement in its avoidance of clear musical "line," and its splotches of tone "color." There is an affinity with the Impressionist painters in mood, too—the reader may sense this by comparing Debussy's *La Mer* (RECORDED EXAMPLE 17) with Monet's *The River* (colorplate 23)—and also with the ultrarefined poets of the French Symbolist school, who supplied him with many of his texts.

Debussy reacted strongly against Wagner, on both personal and nationalistic grounds. Wagner had aggressively identified himself with the expansionist Germany that had humiliated France in 1870, and that was to lock her in a terrible siege of bloodletting in 1914. But as often happens with self-conscious reactions, there was also an element of attraction. Thus Debussy focused his energy on opera, like the older composer; the one opera he completed, *Pelléas et Mélisande* (1902; libretto by the Belgian Symbolist Maurice Maeterlinck), probably counts as his most important work. As in Wagner's operas, orchestral mood is of the utmost importance, leitmotifs are prominent, and the characters are symbols in the service of a larger philosophic vision. Even the story—a fateful tale of adultery in an archaic kingdom—recalls *Tristan und Isolde.* But the quality of the mood, motifs, and personalities differ so utterly between the two composers that the similarities in basic idea can easily be overlooked. Here again we have an instance of Wagner's influence even upon his enemies.

Most important, Debussy was too serious an

artist not to face up to Wagner's challenge in the matter of musical technique. Motif interested him less, at least in his earlier years; the leitmotifs in *Pelléas* are not developed rigorously in the "Germanic" manner (as Debussy himself might have put it). Rather he concentrated on harmony. His great insight was that modern harmony could be dissociated from the tonal system—that harmony could be made "nonfunctional." Perhaps this was already glimpsed by the first Romantic composer who used a gorgeous chord for its own sake, without worrying about its function—that is, about what was being supported. But Debussy took the principle much further. He ran long strings of unrelated chords together, reveling in their purely sonorous qualities. The characteristic shimmering quality of his harmony, which has since been imitated in both "serious" and popular music, resulted from a new way of looking at a chord as a thing in itself.

Debussy found no need to use especially complicated chord forms. Indeed, he shrank from the extreme, disturbed emotional states that contemporary Germans were investigating by means of such chords. In mood, his music is delicate and subtle, and extreme only in its utter refinement. So while Schoenberg was using very complex note combinations in a functional way, Debussy was using relatively simple ones in a nonfunctional way. His way of weakening the tonal system was by resurrecting medieval modes (see p. 221) which lacked a firm feeling of centrality, and by inventing new scales for the same purpose. One which is often mentioned, the whole-tone scale (C, D, E, F-sharp, G-sharp, A-sharp), turned out to be more intriguing than useful in the long run.

Igor Stravinsky (born 1882) added a drastic new rhythmic drive to the musical tradition. As a young Russian émigré to blasé Paris in 1910, indeed, Stravinsky would almost have been expected to provide something primitive and "Fauve" (see p. 183)—especially since he worked with the *Ballets Russes,* a celebrated organization which brought together glamorous arrays of artistic, musical, and dance talent for the presentation of exotic Russian spectacles. (These included the first Western showing of Mussorgsky's opera *Boris Godunov,* which made a great impression by its starkness.) Among those who did stage designs for the *Ballets Russes* were the young painters Matisse, Rouault, Braque, Picasso, and Chagall.

Stravinsky's earliest ballet scores, which remain his most popular works to this day, soon left behind the picture-postcard nationalism of his teacher Rimsky-Korsakov. All of them treat Russian subjects with the help of Russian folk music, but the attitude changes. While *The Firebird* (1910) still spins an exotic, half-Oriental fairy tale out of orchestral silk and damask, *Petrouchka* (1911) is urban in setting and parodistic in tone, and *Le Sacre du printemps* (*The Rite of Spring*; 1913) boldly represents the coming-of-age orgies of primitive Russian tribes. The music, too, grew correspondingly more "Fauve," to the point where the first performance of *Le Sacre* caused a famous riot, for which, however, Stravinsky's sensational music has to share some of the credit with the suggestive choreography of the famous Russian dancer Nijinsky.

RECORDED EXAMPLE 18 comprises a rapid section of this ballet ("The Play of Abduction") and the beginning of the following slow section ("Round-dances of Spring"). Included are some stunning rhythmic and orchestral effects, and a slow fragment of crude, folklike melody "worried" over and over again in Stravinsky's characteristic fashion. The cold, machinelike power of this music cut through the rather decadent chromaticism of the time like a knife cutting through marshmallow. Primal energies shook the sophisticated façade. One could almost imagine the music of Dionysus, god of orgies, bursting out in Western music after many centuries of repression.

But Stravinsky shortly began to do much as Picasso and other artists were doing around this time with the innovations of the Fauves. Tiring of rhythm merely as a brute effect, he started to mold it into the basis of a new musical logic. Combined with a highly individual harmonic style and a brilliant sense of instrumental color, Stravinsky's rhythmic writing gave his music a curiously dispassionate, flat quality, and allowed him to juxtapose level-sounding musical sections in a way that recalls Picasso in his Cubist phase.

Other analogies can be drawn between Stravinsky and his one-time collaborator Picasso, including the habit of dramatically changing styles or phases. Stravinsky went through a Neoclassic phase as surprising as that of Picasso (see p. 196), only of longer duration. From about 1920 to 1950, his music constantly makes references to various older musical styles, as well as to various specific pieces. Thus in his ballet *Apollon musagète* (*Apollo, Leader of the Muses,* 1928—an almost aggressively classical subject!), the first movement resurrects the style of the Baroque French overture while also echoing Tchaikovsky's rather hackneyed *Capriccio italien.* This aspect of Stravinsky's work caused much resentment among proponents of avant-garde music. However, it did not much surprise Stravinsky's painter friends, who understood from Manet and Cézanne—to look back no further—how an artist builds on another's work (see pp. 174, 176, and 178).

Few cared, or dared, to go as far as Stravinsky, but after World War I Neoclassicism grew important. It formed but one part of a widespread reaction against the heavy emotionalism of the late Romantic era, against Wagner and even such Romantically tainted prewar music as that of Strauss, Schoenberg, and Debussy. "Wagner is a great long funeral procession which is preventing me from crossing the street to get home," remarked Jean Cocteau, a spokesman for postwar France and another collaborator with Stravinsky (and other important composers). In the wake of a new interest in form and formalism, composers began writing fugues, and pieces in sonata-allegro form, aria form, and other old patterns. A young German composer of some importance, Paul Hindemith (1895–1963), even used medieval hymns and sequences (see p. 221) in his Symphony *Mathis der Maler* (*Matthias the Painter,* 1934, based on an opera he wrote about Matthias Grünewald; see fig. 159, colorplate 16). Significantly, this was the period that rediscovered Bach's *Art of Fugue* (see p. 254). Hindemith later wrote a set of preludes and fugues for piano in all the tonalities, much like Bach's *Well-tempered Clavier.*

Small, "cool" instrumental combinations became very fashionable. Apollo, not Dionysus, was now Leader of the Muses, and Stravinsky's score for this ballet used just a string orchestra. This constituted an ascetic reaction to the lavish post-Berlioz orchestra with its forty-odd different instruments required for his *Rite of Spring* only fifteen years earlier.

The reaction also involved a campaign for witty, offhand, light effects, oddly reminiscent of the reaction against Baroque music in the 1730s (p. 257). The *Ballets Russes* even turned to modernized versions of Pergolesi and Domenico Scarlatti (Stravinsky's *Pulcinella,* and *The Good-humored Ladies* by a certain Vincenzo Tommasini). The Dada movement (see p. 201) found a parallel in the much-respected, but not very productive, Parisian composer Erik Satie (1866–1925). Cocteau, Stravinsky, and others experimented with jazz.

Schoenberg, of course, would have none of this. All through his career he was dedicated to solving the essential "problems" of music (a favorite concept of the serious German school). But even he reacted against certain aspects of his earlier music. Instead of free-form compositions for large orchestra, he now wrote rather dry chamber-music suites on the Baroque model, and instead of the heated Expressionist poems of his youth, he now turned to the fourteenth-century poet Petrarch. Most strikingly of all, he developed a new plan to regulate the "chaotic" chromaticism of his early years. This plan, which he began to use after 1923, is Schoenberg's famous twelve-tone system,* or serial technique.

In order to discuss this important practice, let us turn back to Wozzeck and the Doctor (RECORDED EXAMPLE 19). As it happens, Alban Berg has organized their entire scene according to a Baroque scheme (another sign of the times): it is a passacaglia, or series of variations on a single short theme. This theme is repeated twenty times successively by various instruments, with changes in its speed and rhythm (but not in the actual notes themselves), while the other instruments and the voices go their own way. Presumably the repetition symbolizes the fixation that drives the Doctor to seek immortality through his grisly experiments. In our recorded excerpt, the theme occurs first in a sort of stammering fashion in the cello, the sole accompaniment to the Doctor's first words; then it occurs (well hidden by other material) in the horns; then high in the xylophone; then low in the bassoons; then hidden once again in the horns (after a noisy beginning at the words "*Nein! Ich ärgere mich nicht . . .*").

Now, in order to make the theme as grisly as possible, the composer decided to make it as atonal (untonal-sounding) as possible. Therefore he made it just twelve notes long; he composed it out of all the twelve different notes (C, C-sharp, D, D-sharp, etc.) in a carefully chosen irregular order. This, he felt, would assure a maximum of disconnectedness between the notes and therefore a maximum lack of centrality. (See line 1 of diagram 10, p. 286.)

However, the other instruments and voices do reinforce certain notes, thereby providing a slight feeling of centrality. For this reason, the music is not said to be "in twelve-tone technique," but it would be if at the same time all the other parts of the score were handled in the

---

* We are following the customary American usage of "twelve-tone," but the English usage, "twelve-note," is really a clearer translation of the original German form *Zwölfton.*

same way as the theme itself. A comprehensive structure of this sort is what Schoenberg developed soon afterward. He took all twelve notes and arranged them in an order which is called the series, or row; keeping this fixed for the work at hand, he composed by *going through the whole series without any backtracking* before starting over and over again in different rhythms. (Notes occurring in different octaves count as the same note.) Beyond this, no other material was used in the particular work or movement, which was therefore considered to display a high degree of "organic unity." And no note received undue reinforcement, prominence, or tonic-sounding centrality.

For this purpose, it obviously makes no difference which way round you go. So in order to increase the possibilities, Schoenberg sometimes used the notes in series-order 1 to 12, sometimes backwards in the order 12 to 1 (retrograde), sometimes upside down (inversion), or in retrograde inversion, as follows:

DIAGRAM TEN

The Twelve-tone Passacaglia Theme in Berg's *Wozzeck*

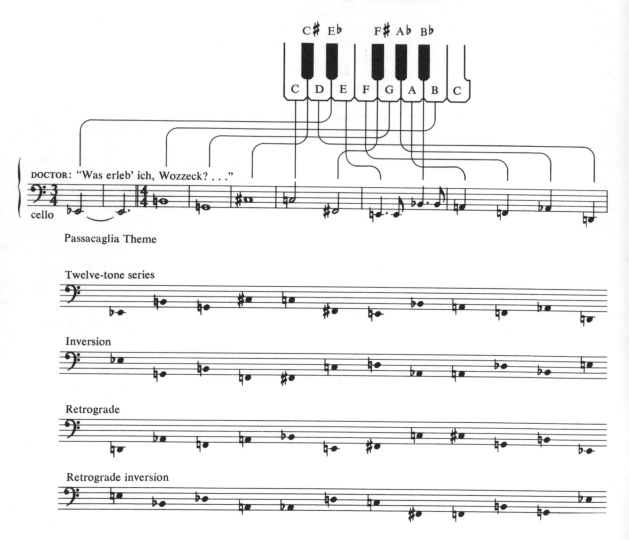

A twelve-tone series, it should be understood, is not a tune, and only rarely a regular theme. Rather it is a fund of motifs and a source of harmonies—since the notes can be presented simultaneously as well as successively. It is not a scale, but an orientation of the notes in a scale. Every twelve-tone composition can make its own vocabulary—its own "twelve-tonality"—by choosing its own series.

The series might be compared with the deal in a bridge game (the deck of cards being the scale). Once the deal is made, the players are presented with fascinating multiple possibilities. The game—and to some bridge players, the game is a highly artistic activity—can proceed according to the individuality or the fantasy of the individual player. However, the analogy breaks down in that the composer is able to deal his own hand with careful forethought, in such a way as to maximize his artistic possibilities.

But does not this strange form of "logic" actually inhibit the composer's fantasy and artistic freedom? Why use anything so artificial in the first place? Why not change series at will? How can the sequence of notes ever be heard and remembered, to say nothing of the mathematical inversions and retrogrades? Skepticism on grounds such as these was widespread in the early days of twelve-tone music, but it has abated somewhat now that most important composers have adopted twelve-tone writing to some degree. This was not the first time in history that music had come close to mathematics. We recall the isorhythmic technique in the fourteenth century and the constructive feats of the Flemish composers of tenor Masses in the fifteenth. Ultimately the twelve-tone system led to a body of mathematical writing about music that puts to shame the proportional studies of the Pythagorean doctors of music in the medieval universities.

A few of Schoenberg's students, including some very impressive composers in their own right, followed him in adopting the twelve-tone system. Although the Expressionistic element became much subdued in their music, it never disappeared altogether. The chromaticism, intensity, and complexity of their style was still reminiscent of the nineteenth-century German tradition. Indeed, two of the most famous products of the twelve-tone school were thoroughly Romantic in concept, though not in musical style. Alban Berg's Violin Concerto (1935) was written as an elegy on the death of a young girl and weaves a Bach chorale (Bach's most chromatic chorale) into the last movement. Schoenberg's great opera *Moses and Aaron* (1932, unfinished) is a grandiose Biblical epic with religious, philosophical, and political overtones.

In the 1920s, however, most composers did not want to abandon the tonal system alto-gether. Learning from the multiple innovations of Debussy, Schoenberg, Stravinsky, and others, they developed a free sort of enriched tonal music capitalizing both on a feeling of centrality, when needed, and also on the novel freedom and intensity that could be got without it. The Hungarian composer Béla Bartók (1881–1945) stood out in this group of less radical musicians. Like Stravinsky, a man of the same generation, Bartók began writing in the tradition of Romantic nationalism, with a Fauve tinge; but unlike Stravinsky he held to this style throughout his career. Almost alone among the nationalists, he succeeded in integrating folk music into a fully authentic and convincing musical style—an accomplishment that probably has to do with his being a professional folklorist as well, the author of definitive studies on Hungarian, Rumanian, and Arabic folk music.

Among Bartók's best compositions are six string quartets, written between 1908 and 1939. The fourth movement, marked *Allegretto pizzicato,* of his Quartet No. 4 (1928; RECORDED EXAMPLE 20) has the function of a short interlude between two much more intense movements. *Pizzicato* means "plucked," and Bartók has written a *tour de force* in which the strings are never played with bows, only plucked in various ways—including one way that hits against the body of the instrument with a sharp percussive knock.* The rhythm and the "worrying" of small melodic fragments often recall Stravinsky. A lot of water has gone under the bridge since Franz Joseph Haydn established the string quartet in the 1770s; nonetheless, a certain continuity can be felt in the insistent use of motifs—motif is another traditional element that Bartók did not wish to abandon—and in the use of movements of the *scherzo* type, derived ultimately from Beethoven. Although the music certainly does not sound tonal in a traditional sense, it has a free sense of centrality, achieved by modal means that owe much to Bartók's folksong investigations. The piece has the feel of an imaginative parody of a peasant dance—and there are hints of popular music in it, too. An amusing touch comes at the end, when the music seems to settle on a single central note, only to have the effect dispelled by a wild disconnected twang as the very last sound of the movement. This parodistic spirit can be traced to Cocteau and Satie and the Paris of the 1920s.

---

* There is an earlier all-*pizzicato* movement in Tchaikovsky's Symphony No. 4.

CLAUDE DEBUSSY, *Prélude à L'Après-midi d'un faune*
(many records include other orchestral works by Debussy)

ARNOLD SCHOENBERG, *Pierrot lunaire,* Op. 21
COLUMBIA; LONDON-ARGO; CONCERT-DISC

ARNOLD SCHOENBERG, Concerto for violin and orchestra, Op. 36
COLUMBIA; TURNABOUT

IGOR STRAVINSKY, *Le Sacre du printemps* (composer conducting)
COLUMBIA

IGOR STRAVINSKY, *Apollon musagète; Orpheus* (composer conducting)
COLUMBIA

ALBAN BERG, Concerto for violin and orchestra (1935)
ANGEL; COLUMBIA

BÉLA BARTÓK, String Quartet No. 4

AARON COPLAND, *Appalachian Spring* (suite)

RECENT DEVELOPMENTS. After the brilliant activity and inventiveness from 1900 to 1920, and the decade of consolidation (as it now appears) from 1920 to 1930, the years between 1930 and 1950 were relatively stagnant. Good music was written by the main composers, but there were few important advances. This was a period of economic depression and world war, and a period during which dictatorships of both the right and the left banned certain kinds of contemporary music with an efficiency that would have suited Plato. Germany's position as the leader of musical thought was destroyed overnight. Impressive Russian talents, among them Sergei Prokofiev and Dimitri Shostakovitch, were crippled. Musicians, who had in any case grown used to thinking in terms of "left" and "right"—Wagner versus Brahms, or Schumann's League of David versus the Philistines —now tended to see Schoenberg and Stravinsky as polar opposites encompassing the field of music. And many people tended to write off both radical extremes—Stravinsky because his music appeared to be increasingly derivative, and Schoenberg because the twelve-tone system appeared to be making no headway. On both counts, however, they were very badly mistaken.

Around 1950, a new wave of interest in twelve-tone music sprang up among young European composers. This music was played again after years of censorship or neglect. But perhaps the main discovery was that the technique could be used without involving Expressionistic sentiments, or even without the

modern transformation of such sentiments in Schoenberg's later music. "Schoenberg is dead!" exclaimed Pierre Boulez (born 1925), a leader of the new movement, in a celebrated magazine article. But this did not mean what it would have meant ten years earlier. Only Schoenberg's expressive vision was dead. His technical innovations proved to be very much alive, and were developed beyond his wildest imaginings.

The heir was Anton Webern (1883–1945), a Schoenberg pupil whose compositions had not made much impression previously because of their extremeness, reticence, and curious brevity (Webern's entire output has been put on four twelve-inch records). Among Schoenberg's important students, Berg (the composer of *Wozzeck*) was more Romantic, Webern more abstract, technically oriented, and visionary. His tiny compositions are models of concentration; each note is singled out and infused with remarkable energies. In Webern, furthermore, not only have tonality, harmony, and tune eroded away, but motif too. This music is "athemetic" as well as "atonal." It exists in a world of its own, entirely "nonobjective," a jewel-like study in self-defined relationships among the twelve chromatic notes.

The generation of the 1950s made another important discovery about music of the recent past. Not only could twelve-tone technique be used without Expressionist sentiments, but Debussy's innovations in the matter of pure sonority could be used without Impressionistic ones. Neither Expressionism nor Impressionism, with their echoes of the nineteenth century, seemed very useful in the age of Auschwitz and Hiroshima. So the development of the sonorous side of music, which to all intents and purposes had been halted by the Neoclassical interest in structure during the period from 1920 to 1950, proceeded in a newly imaginative way. Sounds were wrested out of individual instruments and combinations that would have astonished Debussy. The characteristic sound of the so-called post-Webern period involved a series of remarkable flickers, bloops, and explosions, in an extremely intricate rhythmic relationship. The sounds seem "far out" and utterly disso-ciated, though in fact they are often rigorously controlled by twelve-tone methods.

An astonishing event of these years was the entrance of Stravinsky into a new "phase"—a twelve-tone phase. This looked like a reversal or a conversion, but it was no hasty or irre-sponsible step. Slowly, work by work, Stravin-sky's music grew more and more chromatic, less Neoclassic, and finally "serial" in organiza-tion. This term, which means arranged in a se-ries, is now preferred to the term "twelve-tone" for the very good reason that arrangement of this sort was also observed for other elements besides pitch. The composer would make up a series of twelve different note lengths, volume levels, or instrumental sounds, and then apply them methodically note by note in the identical order (or retrograde, etc.). The complexity of managing several such serial systems simulta-neously, for pitch, rhythm, dynamics, and tim-bre, reached a dizzying stage, and left music wide open, once again, to charges of mathe-matical arbitrariness.

However, more and more composers found serial techniques valuable. Stravinsky himself was now writing impressive music by these means. In fact, there seems to have been a gen-eral falling away of the "right" and the "cen-ter" and a rather triumphant march toward the "left" or avant garde. Near the head of the col-umn was the seventy-year-old Stravinsky, but most other prewar composers continued in more conservative paths.

In search of new sounds, some composers found a powerful tool in the recently perfected tape recorder. They experimented with natural sounds such as traffic noises ("*musique con-crète,*" "concrete music"); one thinks of the Cubist collages of forty years earlier (see p. 196). More significantly, electronic generators could produce any imaginable sound—and pitch—as well as unimaginable or unimagined ones. The interesting prospect arose of compos-ing directly onto tape and thus eliminating the uncertainties of "live" performance. Such un-certainties, as may well be supposed, were reaching the danger zone, given the increasing complexity of serial music. One could even compose with computers. Indeed, serial tech-nique was getting to the point at which one could hardly compose without them.

All in all, the period from 1950 on was an-other time of great expansion of musical hori-zons, comparable only to that at the beginning of the twentieth century. The old "internal logic" of tune, motif, functional harmony, and the tonal system was really gone. People's ears had been opened to an entirely new range of experiences, and their feelings correspondingly opened to a new range of impressions. Never-theless, it does not appear that as many im-portant compositions or composers emerged as in that earlier time. An early masterpiece of contemporary music is *Gesang der Jünglinge* (*Canticle of the Hebrew Children in the Fiery Furnace,* 1956) by Karlheinz Stockhausen (born 1928). Our example includes only the ending of this striking piece (RECORDED EXAM-PLE 21), which employs sounds made by elec-tronic generators—some with exact pitches, others without—as well as a tape of a boy sing-ing which is cut up, superimposed upon itself, and treated to various other ingenious technical processes. Serial treatment is applied to pitch, length of sounds, dynamics, and aspects of the verbal text. Originally intended for five stereo-phonically placed loudspeakers, the work has been rearranged by the composer for two. Yet for all its novelty, it may remind us of certain artistic phenomena of the 1920s: the words are cut up and neutralized in an almost Cubist spirit (see p. 195), and the emotional atmos-phere is curiously reminiscent of *Wozzeck.* Ob-viously one cannot speak of tonality here, yet there is no doubt that the ending of the piece "sets" convincingly and impressively.

A striking new trend in music of the 1960s is the use of the element of chance. Composers write pieces in several sections, to be played in whatever order they happen to fall open at the piano; they put notes on music-paper according to the way an ink blob spatters (remember the ink blots of Alexander Cozens! see fig. 215). The most extreme practitioner of this, John Cage (born 1912), recalls no one so much as the Dadaists. Cage has done a piece for twelve radios picking up whatever happens to be on the air at the time, and another "piece" consisting of three minutes of silence. But be-sides much nonsense, there is an element here which perhaps the Dada movement lacked: an element of legitimate reaction against the mathematical complexity of the serial music of the 1950s, and its remoteness from ordinary aural experience. Cage asks us to listen freshly, to respect the entire range of sound (and nonsound) in whatever form life chances to present it. Perhaps chance music is another instance of the Dionysian spirit intruding upon the Apollonian, a necessary touch of irrationality in an over-structured artistic scene. However this may be, chance elements have been employed—with greater or lesser degrees of caution—by outstanding modern composers, such as Boulez and Stockhausen.

It is with mixed feelings, perhaps, that Americans can point to John Cage as the first of our nation to have made a real stir in musical circles at large. Nor can we take much comfort from the fact—though we can explain it easily enough—that America produced no composers worth mentioning all through the nineteenth century, when we had such artists as Bingham and Whistler, and such authors as Emily Dickinson and Henry James. Only after World War I did some first-rate figures emerge.

Roger Sessions (born 1896) and Aaron Copland (born 1900) provided America with examples that are roughly comparable to those of Schoenberg and Stravinsky in the wider scene. Sessions, a serious-minded and esoteric chromaticist, shows strong German sympathies, while Copland leans toward French Neoclassicism, Stravinskian rhythms, and jazz. Both were influential on young American composers, and both adopted some serial techniques in the 1950s.

The fact is that music today has been internationalized to a large extent. At international festivals of contemporary music, one can observe similar lines of experimentation issuing from American college campuses, from German electronic studios, and from Poland, behind the iron curtain—and one can hear Italian music that is no longer operatic, English music that is no longer conservative, and Japanese music that is no longer Oriental. New lines of musical logic, we have said, are replacing the old "internal logic." These new lines may be difficult to understand, but they do not appear to have any trouble in crossing the boundaries between nations.

SUGGESTIONS FOR LISTENING

ANTON WEBERN, *Six Pieces for Orchestra,* Op. 6 (1910)
IGOR STRAVINSKY, *Agon* (1957)
ON SAME RECORD: WESTMINSTER

ELLIOTT CARTER, String Quartet No. 1 (1951)
COLUMBIA

KARLHEINZ STOCKHAUSEN, *Gesang der Jünglinge* (1956)
DGG

PIERRE BOULEZ, *Le Marteau sans maître* (1954)
TURNABOUT

GYORGY LIGETI, *Atmosphères* (1961)
LARRY AUSTIN, Improvisations for orchestra and jazz soloists (1963)
MORTON FELDMAN, *Out of "Last Pieces"* (1962)
ON SAME RECORD: COLUMBIA

EPILOGUE. As for the difficulty of understanding modern music: on one level, this important fact is one that the historian of music certainly cannot ignore; and on another level, it is a source of much trouble for any person interested in participating in the art of his time. The situation is probably even more confused in music than in painting. People who claim not to understand nonobjective pictures often like to have them on their walls to look at anyhow, but people who do not understand serial music simply do not listen to it. So we are faced with the disturbing paradox that a body of music counting in some ways as the most important of our century—Schoenberg's music since the 1920s—is unknown to the musical public at large. To be sure, atonal music no longer provides the surprise or shock that it did fifty years ago, for whether we realize it or not, we have come to accept it quite naturally as background music of a particular kind for movies and television. But of course the composers have much more in mind than mere background mood-music.

In the nineteenth century, composers were probably too preoccupied with expressing their emotions for all mankind to hear. In the twentieth, they are probably too preoccupied with technique, and as a result advanced contemporary music has taken a turn toward esotericism. The best of it raises genuine difficulties of perception, to say nothing of difficulties of performance. We remarked (p. 283) that Schoenberg's ear grew so sensitive that some of the things he heard as motifs, we cannot always hear—and Schoenberg did not elect to simplify his music for our benefit. The listener who has been trying to detect the repeated twelve-tone passacaglia theme in the Doctor scene of Berg's *Wozzeck* has probably been having a hard time. Obviously repeated hearings are necessary to "educate the ear"; yet in spite of this, people tend not to listen to more contemporary music, but to concentrate more and more on old music. This tendency arose in the nineteenth century, as we have seen. For over a hundred years, the concert world has been moving toward the past—or rather, it has been standing still while the past has been receding. This amounts to a vicious circle, of course, for only frequent playings and hearings will give new music a fair chance.

And as modern music grew more esoteric, people turned to the significant stream of popular music that sprang up after around 1900, the stream including blues, jazz, swing, bop, and rock-and-roll. (This music is of course genuinely popular, enjoyed and supported by millions and tens of millions, by contrast with Pop Art, which instead evokes popular culture for the benefit of a sophisticated elite.) Jazz, the most interesting of the various forms from the purely musical point of view, is diametrically opposed in many respects to what may be called traditional music. The differences are quite thought-provoking. Jazz is American—it is our most successful indigenous art form—while traditional music is a product of the European heritage. Negro in origin, jazz nonetheless finds an instinctive response in the entire spectrum of American life (a fact of considerable sociological interest). Traditional music is middle class in orientation and is regarded as "cultural" and edifying, while jazz is low class, strictly for fun, and often

linked with dancing, courtship, and sex. Traditional music is deliberate, a composer's art preserved in a written score; jazz is spontaneous, a performer's art preserved only on records. The danger that traditional music runs is getting rarefied in the ivory tower. The danger that jazz runs is getting dirty in the market place.

Given all this, it is perhaps not surprising that jazz has been treated gingerly as an "artistic" or "scholarly" subject. But within its limits, there is no question that some forms of jazz have reached a highly sensitive artistic level. The imagination that such musicians as Louis Armstrong, Duke Ellington, Charlie Parker, and John Coltrane have shown in dealing with notes is of the same order as that of performers and composers of traditional music. The limits are quite distinct, however. In harmony, pulse, musical form, and range of expression, most persons with extensive musical experience find jazz comparatively meager, once the initial "kicks" have worn off. Attempts to expand the scope of jazz by mating it with contemporary music (or to give contemporary music a popular basis by mating it with jazz) have not succeeded noticeably. Jazz is a minor art having its own integrity and liveliness, and probably it cannot bend too far without losing many of its characteristic virtues.

As for contemporary "pop" music, which began sordidly enough with the so-called rock-and-roll of the later 1950s, interesting signs of vitality began to appear in it during the 1960s, both from the purely musical and extra-musical points of view. On the extra-musical side, pop music suddenly found itself expressing a new spirit among the youth of all nations, engaging their sympathies, and securing their participation to an unprecedented degree. The Beatles, an imaginative English group of four, were quick to catch this spirit, and also enriched the purely musical side with borrowings that surprised even the most sophisticated modern jazz musicians: unusual harmonic and rhythmic touches, Oriental instrumental sounds, electronic and chance effects. Perhaps most significant of all, a new alliance seems to have been struck up between pop music and popular poetry of some substance. This is not simply a question of content—protest songs and the like—but also of linguistic sophistication far beyond the ambitions (which is not to say the capabilities) of earlier writers of popular lyrics. The development of pop music is certainly one of the liveliest aspects of the music scene in the 1960s.

We may recall a point made in our first

pages dealing with ancient Greek music. Different people, at different times, have tended to define "music" in very different ways. Pythagoras and the medieval doctors of music meant one thing by it; modern symphony subscribers and record buyers mean something else. Perhaps today's avant-garde composers, in their restless search for a new "internal logic," have quietly worked out a new definition for music, so that this too now differs deeply—though in quite another way—from the sound-world of Bach, Beethoven, and Brahms which comes to mind whenever the word music is mentioned. Now, is the distinction between avant-garde music and traditional music any greater than the distinction between traditional music and modern pop?

The question is meant to raise implications both ways. It is an impossible question to answer, but it is a good one to ask, if it helps keep our ears and minds open to all the artistic sound-phenomena that press upon our attention. To understand the past and the future that is soon coming, we have to look, listen, and respond in ways that the immediate present has not necessarily conditioned us for. If we have learned this much from our study of Western art and music—*really* learned it, that is—we have gained one of the more important insights that history can provide.

LIST OF

RECORDED EXAMPLES

These Recorded Examples, cited throughout Book Two, have been selected by the author and may be heard on the record produced by the Deutsche Grammophon Gesellschaft to accompany this book

1. Plainsong (Gregorian chant): a continuous selection from the Third Mass for Christmas Day, comprising (*a*) alleluia *Dies sanctificatus*, (*b*) chanted responses, (*c*) beginning of the chant of the Gospel of the Day

2. Sequence for Whitsun, *Veni Sancte Spiritus* (early 13th century)

3. Pérotin (fl. 1200): ending section of the organum *Sederunt principes*

4. Guillaume de Machaut (c.1300–77): chanson *Je puis trop bien*

5. John Dunstable (c.1370–1453): Marian motet *Speciosa facta es*

6. Josquin Desprez (c.1440–1521): part of the Credo section of the *Pange lingua* Mass

7. Thomas Morley (1557–1603): madrigal *Stay, heart, run not so fast*

8. Claudio Monteverdi (1567–1643): section of the opera *La Favola d'Orfeo*, Act IV

9. Alessandro Scarlatti (1659–1725): aria *"Fugge l'aura,"* followed by a portion of *secco* recitative, from *Il Giardino d'Amore*, Act I

10. Johann Sebastian Bach (1685–1750): beginning of the Sanctus section of the Mass in B minor

11. Johann Sebastian Bach (1685–1750): Fugue in E minor ("Cathedral Fugue") for Organ

12. Carl Philip Emmanuel Bach (1714–88): beginning of the last movement of the Double Concerto for Harpsichord, Pianoforte, and Orchestra

13. Franz Joseph Haydn (1732–1809): last movement of the String Quartet in G minor, Op. 74, No. 3

14. Wolfgang Amadeus Mozart (1756–91): duet *"Aprite presto, aprite,"* followed by a portion of *secco* recitative, from *The Marriage of Figaro*, Act II

15. Robert Schumann (1810–56): song *Am leuchtenden Sommermorgen*, from the song-cycle *Dichterliebe*

16. Richard Wagner (1813–83): Parsifal's monologue from the opera *Parsifal*, Act III

17. Claude Debussy (1862–1918): *"Jeu des Vagues,"* section from *La Mer*, Part 2

18. Igor Stravinsky (born 1882): excerpts from *"Jeu du rapt"* and *"Rondes printanières,"* from the ballet *Le Sacre du printemps*

19. Alban Berg (1885–1935): section from the opera *Wozzeck*, Act I, Scene IV

20. Béla Bartók (1881–1945): fourth movement (allegretto pizzicato) from String Quartet No. 4

21. Karlheinz Stockhausen (born 1928): ending section of *Gesang der Jünglinge*

ATLANTIC OCEAN

NORTH SEA

BALTI

MEDITERRAN

ADRIATIC SEA

Oseberg

Lindisfarne

Durham

Gloucester
Winchester
Canterbury
Salisbury

Cambrai
Liège
Aachen
Cologne
Bonn

Hildesheim

Naumburg

St. Denis
Rouen
Caen
Bayeux
Chartres
Paris
Reims

Prague

RHINE RIVER

RHINE

DANUBE

Willendorf

RIVER

Bourges
Autun
Lindau
St. Gall

Klosterneuburg

Poitiers
St. Savin-sur-Gartempe
Limoges

RHONE RIVER

Santander
Moissac
Toulouse
Avignon

Santiago de Compostela

Ravenna
Padua
Prato
Pisa
Florence
Siena
Orvieto
Rome

Split

Pompeii
Paestum

CITIES AND SITES
BEFORE 1400

MILES

0 100 200 300 400

● Music   ■ Art   ▣ Art and Music

CASPIAN
SEA

BLACK SEA

DANUBE

RIVER

■ Constantinople
(Byzantium)

Samothrace

■ Troy

Olympia
Delphi
Daphnē
Athens
Samos
Miletus
AEGEAN
■ Tralles

Sparta
Mycenae
SEA
■ Halicarnassus

■ Rhodes

■ Knossos

N   SEA

■ Antioch

■ Nineveh

Assur ■
■ Tell Asmar

EUPHRATES

TIGRIS RIVER

RIVER

Babylon ■
▣ Ur

■ Jerusalem

Alexandria ■
Giza ■
Saqqara ■

Faiyum ■

NILE RIVER

Hierakonpolis ■

■ Oslo

■ St. Petersburg

BALTIC SEA

● Hamburg

● Berlin

■ Dessau

Würzburg   Leipzig ●   ● Dresden

Bayreuth
●

Nuremberg

● Augsburg

Munich ■   ■ Vienna

● Salzburg

● Budapest

Verona Vicenza Venice

Mantua

● Ferrara

Urbino
Arezzo
Volterra

■ Rome

● Naples

CITIES AND TOWNS
AFTER 1400

MILES

0   100   200   300   400

● Music   ■ Art   ■ Art and Music

BLACK
SEA

ADRIATIC SEA

AEGEAN SEA

EAN SEA

CHRONOLOGY

● *Artists, sculptors, architects*
■ *Composers, musicians, instrument makers*
*Names in italics are those of historical persons
mentioned in the text.*

c.3100–1000 B.C.

Narmer (c.3100)
Zoser (c.2650)
● Imhotep (c.2650)
Mycerinus (c.2500)
Hammurabi (1792–1750)
Akhenaten (*Amenhotep IV*, 1372–1358)
Ramesses II (1290–1223)

c.1000–300 B.C.

Homer (8th century)
Pythagoras (c.582–c.507)
● Psiax (second half of 6th century)
Euripides (c.480–406)
Socrates (469–399)
● Phidias (second half of 5th century)
Plato (c.427–c.347)
● Scopas (4th century)
● Praxiteles (4th century)
Alexander the Great (356–323)

c.300 B.C.–200 A.D.

Cicero (106–43 B.C.)
Julius Caesar (c.102–44 B.C.)
Vergil (70–19 B.C.)
Augustus (63 B.C.–14 A.D.)
Vitruvius (late 1st century B.C.–1st century
    A.D.)
Pliny the Elder (23–79 A.D.)
Trajan (53–117 A.D.)
Marcus Aurelius (121–180 A.D.)

200–600 A.D.

Diocletian (245-313)
Constantine the Great (288(?)–337)
Saint Benedict (died c.547)
Justinian (483–565)
● Anthemius of Tralles (6th century)
● Isidore of Miletus (6th century)
Saint Gregory the Great (*Pope Gregory I*,
    c.540–604)

600–1000

Charlemagne (742–814)
Otto I (912–973)
Otto II (955–983)
Bernward, Bishop of Hildesheim (died 1022)
Otto III (980–1002)

1000–1100

William the Conqueror (c.1027–1087)
Urban II (c.1042–1099)
● *Abbot Suger* (1081–1151)
Saint Bernard of Clairvaux (c.1090–1153)

1100–1200

■ Léonin of Paris (c.1160)
Richard the Lion-Hearted (1157–1199)
● Renier of Huy (12th century)
● Nicholas of Verdun (12th century)
■ Pérotin "the Great" (end of 12th century)
Frederick II (*von Hohenstaufen*, 1194–
    1250)

1200–1300

● Nicola Pisano (fl. 1258–1278)
● Giovanni Pisano (c.1245–after 1314)
● Master Honoré of Paris (late 13th century)
● Duccio di Buoninsegna (fl. 1278–1319)
Dante Alighieri (1265–1321)
● Giotto di Bondone (c.1266–c.1337)
● Lorenzetti Brothers (Pietro born c.1280;
    Ambrogio probably the younger; both
    died 1348)

1300–1350

■ Guillaume de Machaut (c.1300–1377)
Petrarch (1304–1374)
Giovanni Boccaccio (1313–1375)
■ Francesco Landini (1325–1397)
Geoffrey Chaucer (c.1340–1400)

1350–1400

● Claus Sluter (late 14th–15th century)
● Limbourg Brothers (late 14th–15th century)
● Gentile da Fabriano (c.1370–1427)
● Hubert van Eyck (c.1370–1426)
■ John Dunstable (c.1370–1453)
● Robert Campin (1375–1444)

- Filippo Brunelleschi (1377–1446)
- Lorenzo Ghiberti (c.1381–1455)
- Donatello (c.1386–1466)
- Jan van Eyck (c.1390–1441)
- Michelozzo Michelozzi (1396–1472)

1400–1420

- ■ Guillaume Dufay (c.1400–1474)
- Rogier van der Weyden (c.1400–1464)
- Masaccio (1401–c.1428)
- Conrad Witz (1400/10–1444/46)
- Leone Battista Alberti (c.1404–1472)
- Piero della Francesca (1410/20–1492)

1420–1440

- ■ Johannes Ockeghem (c.1420–1495)
- Andrea del Castagno (c.1421–1457)
- Antonio Rossellino (1427–1479)
- Giovanni Bellini (c.1430–1470/71)
- ■ Jakob Obrecht (c.1430–1505)
- Andrea Mantegna (c.1431–1506)
- Antonio del Pollaiuolo (1433–1498)
- ■ Johannes Tinctoris (c.1435/45–1511)
- Andrea del Verrochio (1436–1488)

1440–1450

- ■ Josquin Desprez (c.1440–1521)
  Julius II (1443–1513)
- Giuliano da Sangallo (1443–1516)
- Sandro Botticelli (c.1444–1510)
- Donato Bramante (c.1444–1514)
- Perugino (c.1445–1523(?))
  Lorenzo de' Medici (1449–1492)
- Domenico Ghirlandaio (1449–1494)

1450–1480

- Martin Schongauer (c.1450–1491)
- ■ Heinrich Isaac (c.1450–1517)
- Leonardo da Vinci (1452–1519)
- Jerome Bosch (c.1460–1516)
- Hans Holbein the Younger (1460/65–1524)
  Erasmus of Rotterdam (1469–1536)
- Albrecht Dürer (1471–1528)
  Ludovico Ariosto (1475–1533)
- Michelangelo Buonarroti (1475–1564)
  Baldassare Castiglione (1478–1529)

1480–1500

- Matthias Grünewald (c.1480–c.1530)
- Albrecht Altdorfer (c.1480–1538)
- Raphael Sanzio (1483–1520)
  Martin Luther (1483–1546)
- Titian (1489–1576)
  Henry VIII (1491–1547)

- Correggio (1494–1534)
- Rosso Fiorentino (1494–1540)

1500–1520

- Benvenuto Cellini (1500–1571)
- Parmigianino (1503–1540)
- Jean Goujon (c.1510–c.1565)
- Pierre Lescot (c.1510–1578)
- ■ Andrea Gabrieli (1510–1586)
- ■ Gioseffe Zarlino (1517–1590)
- Andrea Palladio (1518–1580)

1520–1540

- ■ Vincenzo Galilei (1520–1591)
- ■ Giovanni Pierluigi da Palestrina (c.1525–1594)
- Pieter Bruegel the Elder (c.1528–1569)
- Paolo Veronese (1528–1588)
- ■ Roland de Lassus (1532–1594)

1540–1560

- El Greco (1540/50–1614)
- ■ William Byrd (1543–1623)
- ■ Luca Marenzio (1553–1599)
- Carlo Maderno (1556–1629)
- ■ Thomas Morley (1557–1603)
- ■ Giovanni Gabrieli (1557–1612)

1560–1580

- ■ Prince Carlo Gesualdo of Venosa (c.1560–1613)
- Tintoretto (1560–1635)
- ■ John Dowland (1562–1626)
  William Shakespeare (1564–1616)
- Michelangelo da Caravaggio (1565–1609)
- ■ Thomas Campion (1567–1620)
- ■ Claudio Monteverdi (1567–1643)
  Marie de' Medici (1573–1642)
- Peter Paul Rubens (1577–1640)

1580–1600

- Frans Hals (c.1580–1666)
- Louis Le Nain (1593–1648)
- Nicolas Poussin (1594–1665)
- Gianlorenzo Bernini (1598–1680)
- Diego Velázquez (1599–1660)
- Francesco Borromini (1599–1667)

1600–1620

- Claude Lorraine (1600–1682)
- Rembrandt (1606–1669)
- Louis Le Vau (1612–1670)
- Claude Perrault (1613–1688)
- André Le Nôtre (1613–1700)
- Charles Lebrun (1619–1690)

1620–1630

Molière (1622–1673)
● Guarino Guarini (1624–1683)
■ Louis Couperin (c.1626–1661)
● Jan Steen (c.1626–1679)
● Jacob van Ruisdael (1628/29–1682)

1630–1640

● Jan Vermeer (1632–1675)
■ Jean Baptiste Lully (1632–1687)
● Sir Christopher Wren (1632–1723)
Louis XIV (1638–1715)
Jean Racine (1639–1699)
● Giovanni Battista Gaulli (1639–1709)

1640–1660

■ Antonio Stradivari (1644–1737)
● Jules Hardouin-Mansart (1646–1708)
■ Arcangelo Corelli (1653–1713)
● Johann Fischer von Erlach (c.1656–1723)
■ Henry Purcell (1659–1695)
■ Alessandro Scarlatti (1659–1725)

1660–1680

● Germain Boffrand (1667–1754)
■ François Couperin (1668–1733)
■ Antonio Vivaldi (c.1675–1741)

1680–1690

■ Georg Philipp Telemann (1681–1767)
■ Jean Philippe Rameau (1683–1764)
● Antoine Watteau (1684–1721)
■ Johann Sebastian Bach (1685–1750)
■ Domenico Scarlatti (1685–1757)
■ George Frideric Handel (1685–1759)
● Balthasar Neumann (1687–1753)

1690–1700

● Giovanni Battista Tiepolo (1692–1770)
Voltaire (1694–1778)
● William Hogarth (1697–1764)
● Jean-Baptiste Chardin (1699–1779)

1700–1720

■ Giovanni Battista Pergolesi (1710–1736)
Jean Jacques Rousseau (1712–1778)
Frederick II of Prussia (1712–1786)
● Jacques Germain Soufflot (1713–1780)
Denis Diderot (1713–1784)
■ Carl Philip Emmanuel Bach (1714–1788)
■ Christoph Willibald von Gluck (1714–1788)
● Etienne Maurice Falconet (1716–1791)
● Horace Walpole (1717–1797)
Johann Joachim Winckelmann (1717–1768)
● Alexander Cozens (c.1717–1786)

1720–1740

● Sir Joshua Reynolds (1723–1792)
● Jean-Baptiste Greuze (1725–1805)
● Thomas Gainsborough (1727–1788)
■ Franz Joseph Haydn (1732–1809)
■ Johann Christian Bach (1735–1782)
● John Singleton Copley (1738–1815)
● Benjamin West (1738–1820)

1740–1750

● Jean Antoine Houdon (1741–1828)
● Thomas Jefferson (1743–1826)
Johann Gottfried von Herder (1744–1803)
● Francisco José Goya (1746–1828)
● Jacques Louis David (1748–1825)
Johann Wolfgang von Goethe (1749–1832)

1750–1760

■ Wolfgang Amadeus Mozart (1756–1791)
● Antonio Canova (1757–1822)
● William Blake (1757–1827)
Johann Christoph Friedrich von Schiller (1759–1805)

1760–1780

■ Luigi Cherubini (1760–1842)
Napoleon I (1769–1821)
■ Ludwig van Beethoven (1770–1827)
● Joseph M. W. Turner (1775–1851)
● John Constable (1776–1837)

1780–1790

● Jean-Auguste Dominque Ingres (1780–1867)
● François Rude (1784–1855)
■ Carl Maria von Weber (1786–1826)
George Gordon, Lord Byron (1788–1824)
Arthur Schopenhauer (1788–1860)

1790–1800

● Théodore Géricault (1791–1824)
■ Jacob Meyerbeer (1791–1864)
■ Giacomo Rossini (1792–1868)
● Camille Corot (1796–1875)
■ Franz Schubert (1797–1828)
● Eugène Delacroix (1798–1863)

1800–1810

● Henri Labrouste (1801–1875)
Victor Hugo (1802–1885)
■ Hector Berlioz (1803–1869)
● Honoré Daumier (1808–1879)
■ Felix Mendelssohn (1809–1847)
Charles Darwin (1809–1882)

1810–1820

- Frédéric Chopin (1810–1849)
- Robert Schumann (1810–1856)
- George Caleb Bingham (1811–1879)
- Franz Liszt (1811–1886)
- Richard Wagner (1813–1883)
- Giuseppe Verdi (1813–1901)
  Karl Marx (1818–1883)
- Gustave Courbet (1819–1877)

1820–1830

  Charles Baudelaire (1821–1867)
- César Franck (1822–1890)
  Heinrich Schliemann (1822–1890)
- Anton Bruckner (1824–1896)
- Charles Garnier (1825–1898)

1830–1840

- Edouard Manet (1832–1883)
- Johannes Brahms (1833–1897)
- James Abbott McNeill Whistler (1834–1903)
- Edgar Degas (1834–1917)
- Winslow Homer (1836–1910)
- Georges Bizet (1838–1875)
- Modest Mussorgsky (1839–1881)
- Paul Cézanne (1839–1906)

1840–1850

- Peter Tchaikovsky (1840–1893)
- Auguste Rodin (1840–1917)
- Claude Monet (1840–1926)
- Antonin Dvořák (1841–1904)
- Auguste Renoir (1841–1919)
- Edvard Grieg (1843–1907)
  Friedrich Wilhelm Nietzsche (1844–1900)
- Nicolai Andreyevich Rimsky-Korsakov (1844–1908)
- Henri Rousseau (1844–1910)
- Paul Gauguin (1848–1903)

1850–1860

- Vincent van Gogh (1853–1890)
- Louis Sullivan (1856–1924)
- Giacomo Puccini (1858–1924)
- Georges Seurat (1859–1891)

1860–1870

- Gustav Mahler (1860–1911)
- Edward Alexander MacDowell (1861–1908)
- Aristide Maillol (1861–1944)
- Claude Debussy (1862–1918)
- Edvard Munch (1863–1944)
- Henri de Toulouse-Lautrec (1864–1901)
- Richard Strauss (1864–1949)

- Jean Sibelius (1865–1957)
- Erik Satie (1866–1925)
- Wassily Kandinsky (1866–1944)
- Emil Nolde (1867–1956)
- Frank Lloyd Wright (1867–1959)
- Henri Matisse (1869–1954)

1870–1880

- Georges Rouault (1871–1958)
- Julio Gonzalez (1872–1942)
- Piet Mondrian (1872–1944)
- Sergei Rachmaninoff (1873–1943)
- Arnold Schoenberg (1874–1951)
- Raymond Duchamp-Villon (1876–1918)
- Constantin Brancusi (1876–1957)
- Vincenzo Tommasini (1878–1950)
- Paul Klee (1879–1940)

1880–1890

- Joseph Stella (1880–1946)
- Marcel Duchamp (1880–   )
- Béla Bartók (1881–1945)
- Pablo Picasso (1881–   )
- Umberto Boccioni (1882–1916)
- Georges Braque (1882–1963)
- Igor Stravinsky (1882–   )
- Anton Webern (1883–1945)
- Walter Gropius (1883–   )
- Max Beckmann (1884–1950)
- Alban Berg (1885–1936)
- Ludwig Mies van der Rohe (1886–   )
- Oskar Kokoschka (1886–   )
- Le Corbusier (1887–1965)
- Giorgio de Chirico (1888–   )
- Marc Chagall (1889–   )

1890–1900

  Jean Cocteau (1891–1963)
- Max Ernst (1891–   )
- Joan Miró (1893–   )
- Chaim Soutine (1894–1943)
- Paul Hindemith (1895–1963)
- Roger Sessions (1896–   )
- Alexander Calder (1898–   )

1900–1920

- Aaron Copland (1900–   )
- Alberto Giacometti (1901–1966)
- Jackson Pollock (1912–1956)
- John Cage (1912–   )

1920–1930

- Roy Lichtenstein (1923–   )
- Pierre Boulez (1925–   )
- Karlheinz Stockhausen (1928–   )

301

BOOKS FOR
FURTHER READING ON ART

This list is primarily a practical one, devoted not so much to standard scholarly sources as to works which the reader of this book should consult for the next stage of his exposure to the materials of art history. Most of these books contain bibliographies that may be consulted for more specialized readings. Not listed individually, but also generally recommended as a point of departure for further study are the books in the series, The Pelican History of Art, published by Penguin Books (Baltimore). Primary sources in English translation—covering most of the periods discussed in this book—are collected in the series, Sources and Documents in the History of Art, published by Prentice-Hall (Englewood Cliffs, N. J.).

Books relevant to several chapters are listed under the first heading only. Titles marked with an asterisk (*) are available in paperback editions. Consult Books in Print, U. S. A. for titles and publishers of the paperbacks.

GENERAL WORKS

*HOLT, E. B., *Literary Sources of Art History,* Princeton University Press, 1947.
*PANOFSKY, E., *Meaning in the Visual Arts,* Anchor Books, Garden City, N. J., 1955.

PART ONE: ART IN THE ANCIENT WORLD

1. THE ART OF PREHISTORIC MAN

LEROI-GOURHAN, A., *Treasures of Prehistoric Art,* Abrams, New York, 1967.
WINGERT, P. S., *The Sculpture of Negro Africa,* Columbia University Press, 1959.

2. EGYPT AND THE ANCIENT NEAR EAST

LANGE, K., and HIRMER, M., *Egypt,* 3rd rev. ed., Phaidon, London, 1961.
STROMMENGER, E., and HIRMER, M., *5000 Years of the Art of Mesopotamia,* Abrams, New York, 1964.

3. GREEK AND ROMAN ART

ARIAS, P., and HIRMER, M., *A History of 1000 Years of Greek Vase Painting,* Abrams, New York, 1963.

BERVE, H., GRUBEN, G., and HIRMER, M., *Greek Temples, Theaters, and Shrines,* Abrams, New York, 1962.
BRENDEL, O. J., "Prolegomena to a Book on Roman Art," *Memoirs of the American Academy in Rome,* vol. 21, 1953.
DINSMOOR, W. B., *The Architecture of Ancient Greece,* rev. ed., Batsford, London, 1950.
KÄHLER, H., *The Art of Rome and Her Empire,* Crown, New York, 1963.
MACDONALD, W. L., *The Architecture of the Roman Empire,* Yale University Press, New Haven, 1965.
MARINATOS, S., and HIRMER, M., *Crete and Mycenae,* Abrams, New York, 1960.
RICHARDSON, E., *The Etruscans, Their Art and Civilization,* University of Chicago Press, 1964.
RICHTER, G. M. A., *A Handbook of Greek Art,* 2nd rev. ed., Phaidon, London, 1960.

4. EARLY CHRISTIAN AND BYZANTINE ART

DEMUS, O., *Byzantine Mosaic Decoration,* Kegan Paul, Trench, Trubner, London, 1941.
SIMSON, O. G. VON, *Sacred Fortress,* University of Chicago Press, 1948.
VOLBACH, W. F., and HIRMER, M., *Early Christian Art,* Abrams, New York, 1961.

PART TWO: ART IN THE MIDDLE AGES

1. EARLY MEDIEVAL ART

GRABAR, A., and NORDENFALK, C., *Early Medieval Painting,* Skira, New York, 1957.
*KITZINGER, E., *Early Medieval Art,* Indiana University Press, Bloomington, Ind., 1964.
*PEVSNER, N., *An Outline of European Architecture,* 6th (Jubilee) ed., Penguin Books, Baltimore, 1960.

2. ROMANESQUE ART

CRICHTON, G. H., *Romanesque Sculpture in Italy,* Routledge & Kegan Paul, London, 1954.
GARDNER, A., *Medieval Sculpture in France,* Russell & Russell, New York, 1931.
MARLE, R. VAN, *The Development of the Italian Schools of Painting,* 19 vols., Nijhoff, The Hague, 1923–38.
NORDENFALK, C., *Romanesque Painting,* Skira, New York, 1958.

3. GOTHIC ART

Abbot Suger on the Abbey Church of St.-Denis and its Art Treasures, tr. by Erwin Panofsky, Princeton University Press, 1946.

*KATZENELLENBOGEN, A., *The Sculptural Programs of Chartres Cathedral,* Johns Hopkins Press, Baltimore, 1959.

*PANOFSKY, E., *Gothic Architecture and Scholasticism,* Archabbey Press, Latrobe, Pa., 1951.

POPE-HENNESSY, J., *Introduction to Italian Sculpture,* 3 vols., Phaidon, London, 1955–62.

PART THREE: ART IN THE RENAISSANCE

1. THE FIFTEENTH CENTURY

BORSOOK, E., *The Mural Painters of Tuscany,* Phaidon, London, 1960.

DEWALD, E. T., *Italian Painting, 1200–1600,* Holt, Rinehart, and Winston, New York, 1961.

*HIND, A. M., *History of Engraving and Etching,* 3rd rev. ed., Houghton Mifflin, Boston, 1927.

KRAUTHEIMER, R., and KRAUTHEIMER-HESS T., *Lorenzo Ghiberti,* Princeton University Press, 1956.

PANOFSKY, E., *Early Netherlandish Painting,* 2 vols., Harvard University Press, 1954.

2. THE SIXTEENTH CENTURY

ACKERMAN, J. S., *The Architecture of Michelangelo,* 2 vols. (vol. 2, rev. ed., 1966), Viking, New York, 1961.

FREEDBERG, S. J., *Painting of the High Renaissance in Rome and Florence,* 2 vols., Harvard University Press, 1961.

GOULD, C., *The 16th Century Venetian School,* National Gallery Publications, 3rd ed., London, 1959.

PANOFSKY, E., *Albrecht Dürer,* 2 vols., Princeton University Press, 1948.

VASARI, G., *The Lives of the Painters, Sculptors, and Architects,* tr. by A. B. Hind, 4 vols., Dutton, New York, 1927.

*WITTKOWER, R., *Architectural Principles in the Age of Humanism,* Random House, New York, 1965.

WÖLFFLIN, H., *Classic Art,* 2nd ed., Phaidon, London, 1953.

3. THE BAROQUE

FRIEDLAENDER, W. F., *Caravaggio Studies,* Princeton University Press, 1955.

McCOMB, A. K., *The Baroque Painters of Italy,* Harvard University Press, 1934.

ROSENBERG, J., *Rembrandt,* rev. ed., Phaidon, London, 1964.

SCHÖNBERGER, A., and SOEHNER, H., *The Rococo Age,* McGraw-Hill, New York, 1960.

WITTKOWER, R., *The Sculptures of Gian Lorenzo Bernini,* rev. and enl. ed., Phaidon, London, 1966.

PART FOUR: ART IN THE MODERN WORLD

1. ENLIGHTENMENT AND REVOLUTION

FRIEDLAENDER, W. F., *From David to Delacroix,* Harvard University Press, 1952.

ROSENBLUM, R., *Ingres,* Abrams, New York, 1967.

ROTHENSTEIN, J. K. M., *An Introduction to English Painting,* Cassell, London, 1933.

2. ROMANTICISM AND IMPRESSIONISM

BARKER, V., *American Painting, History and Interpretation,* Macmillan, New York, 1953.

BRION, M., *Romantic Art,* McGraw-Hill, New York, 1960.

REWALD, J., *History of Impressionism,* rev. and enl. ed., Museum of Modern Art, New York, 1962.

———, *Post-Impressionism from Van Gogh to Gauguin,* Museum of Modern Art, New York, 1958.

SCHMUTZLER, R., *Art Nouveau,* Abrams, New York, 1964.

3. THE TWENTIETH CENTURY

BARR, A. H., JR., ed., *Picasso, Fifty Years of His Art,* Museum of Modern Art, New York, 1946.

GIEDION-WELCKER, C., *Contemporary Sculpture,* 3rd rev. ed., Wittenborn, New York, 1961.

*GROPIUS, W., *Scope of Total Architecture,* Harper, New York, 1955.

*HAFTMANN, W., *Painting in the Twentieth Century,* new ed., 2 vols., Praeger, New York, 1965.

HITCHCOCK, H.-R., *In the Nature of Materials: The Buildings of Frank Lloyd Wright, 1887–1941,* Duell, Sloan & Pearce, New York, 1942.

LE CORBUSIER (pseud. for JEANNERET-GRIS, C. E.), *Towards a New Architecture,* tr. by F. Etchells, Praeger, New York, 1959.

RITCHIE, A. C., *Abstract Painting and Sculpture in America,* Museum of Modern Art, New York, 1951.

*ROSENBLUM, R., *Cubism and Twentieth-Century Art,* Abrams, New York, 1961.

SELZ, P., *German Expressionist Painting,* University of California Press, Berkeley, 1957.

BOOKS FOR
FURTHER READING ON MUSIC

This list is first and foremost a practical one, devoted not so much to standard scholarly sources as to works which the reader of this book should consult for the next stage of his exposure to the materials of music history. The bibliographies contained in these works may be referred to for more specialized readings.

Books relevant to several chapters are listed under the first heading only. Titles marked with an asterisk (*) are available in paperback editions. Consult Books in Print, U. S. A. for titles and publishers of the paperbacks.

GENERAL WORKS

*APEL, W., and DANIEL, R. T., *The Harvard Brief Dictionary of Music,* Harvard University Press, 1960 (under a dollar in paperback).

BLOM, E., ed., *Grove's Dictionary of Music and Musicians,* 5th ed., 10 vols., St. Martin's Press, New York, 1954 (use only the 5th edition; articles on composers are recommended).

*DART, T., *The Interpretation of Music,* 4th ed., Hutchinson, London, 1967 (the problems of performing old music).

GROUT, D. J., *A History of Western Music,* Norton, New York, 1960 (one-volume survey, widely used in colleges).

HARRISON, F. L., and RIMMER, J., *European Musical Instruments,* Norton, New York, 1965 (with excellent illustrations).

*KÁROLYI, O., *Introducing Music,* Penguin Books, Baltimore, 1965 (elements of music).

LÁNG, P. H., *Music in Western Civilization,* Norton, New York, 1941 (the role of music in cultural history).

*STRUNK, O., *Source Readings in Music History,* Norton, New York, 1950.

*WESTRUP, J. A., *An Introduction to Musical History,* 4th ed., Hutchinson, London, 1963.

*WESTRUP, J. A., and HARRISON, F. L., *The New College Encyclopedia of Music,* Norton, New York, 1960.

PART ONE: MUSIC IN THE ANCIENT WORLD

APEL, W., *Gregorian Chant,* Indiana University Press, Bloomington, Ind., 1957.

SACHS, C., *The Rise of Music in the Ancient World, East and West,* Norton, New York, 1943.

WELLESZ, E., ed., *The New Oxford History of Music,* vol. 1 (*Ancient and Oriental Music*), Oxford University Press, 1957.

PART TWO: MUSIC IN THE MIDDLE AGES

CROCKER, R. L., *A History of Musical Style,* McGraw-Hill, New York, 1966.

*ROBERTSON, A., and STEVENS, D., eds., *The Pelican History of Music,* vol. 1 (*Ancient Forms to Polyphony*), Penguin Books, Baltimore, 1963.

*SEAY, A., *Music in the Medieval World,* Prentice-Hall, Englewood Cliffs, N. J., 1965.

PART THREE: MUSIC IN THE ERA OF THE RENAISSANCE

1. THE FIFTEENTH AND SIXTEENTH CENTURIES

ARNOLD, D., *Marenzio,* Oxford University Press, 1965.

*BLUME, F., *Renaissance and Baroque Music: A Comprehensive Survey,* tr. by M. D. Herter Norton, Norton, New York, 1967.

LOWINSKY, E. E., "Music in the Culture of the Renaissance," *Journal of the History of Ideas,* XV, 1954, pp. 509–53.

PATTISON, B., *Music and Poetry of the English Renaissance,* Methuen, London, 1948.

*ROBERTSON, A., and STEVENS, D., eds., *The Pelican History of Music,* vol. 2 (*Renaissance to Baroque*), Penguin Books, Baltimore, 1964.

2. THE BAROQUE

ARNOLD, D., *Monteverdi,* J. M. Dent, London, 1963.

GEIRINGER, K., *The Bach Family: Seven Generations of Creative Genius,* Oxford University Press, 1954 (includes Johann Sebastian, Johann Christian, and Carl Philip Emmanuel).

GROUT, D. J., *A Short History of Opera,* 2nd ed., 2 vols., Columbia University Press, 1965.

GRUNFELD, F. V., *The Baroque Era,* Time Inc., New York, 1966 (with excellent illustrations; accompanied by records).

STREATFEILD, R. A., *Handel*, Da Capo, New York, 1964.

TOVEY, D. F., *Essays in Musical Analysis*, 6 vols., Oxford University Press, 1935–9 (valuable on individual compositions from the time of Bach to Brahms).

PART FOUR: MUSIC IN THE MODERN WORLD

1. ENLIGHTENMENT AND REVOLUTION

BLOM, E., *Mozart*, 6th ed., Dutton, New York, 1966.

*DENT, E. J., *Mozart's Operas*, 2nd ed., Oxford University Press, 1947.

GRUNWALD, H. A., *The Age of Elegance*, Time Inc., New York, 1966 (with excellent illustrations; accompanied by records).

*HUGHES, R., *Haydn*, rev. ed., Farrar, Straus & Cudahy, New York (n. d.; after 1950).

*PAULY, R. G., *Music in the Classic Period*, Prentice-Hall, Englewood Cliffs, N. J., 1965.

RIEZLER, W., *Beethoven*, tr. by G. D. H. Pidcock, Dutton, New York, 1938.

2. ROMANTICISM AND AFTER

ABRAHAM, G., *A Hundred Years of Music*, rev. ed., Aldine, Chicago, 1964 (on the period 1830–1930).

*BARZUN, J., *Berlioz and his Century: An Introduction to the Age of Romanticism*, 6th rev. ed., Peter Smith, Gloucester, Massachusetts, 1966.

*SCHUMANN, R., *On Music and Musicians*, tr. by P. Rosenfeld, ed. by K. Wolff, Pantheon, New York, 1946 (anthology of Schumann's critical essays from 1834–44).

*TOYE, F., *Giuseppe Verdi, His Life and Works*, Vintage, New York, 1959.

*WHITE, C., *An Introduction to the Life and Works of Richard Wagner*, Prentice-Hall, Englewood Cliffs, N. J., 1967.

3. THE TWENTIETH CENTURY

AUSTIN, W., *Music in the Twentieth Century*, Norton, New York, 1966.

HITCHCOCK, H. W., *Music in the United States: A Historical Introduction*, Prentice-Hall, Englewood Cliffs, N. J. (forthcoming).

LANG, P., ed., *Problems of Modern Music*, Norton, New York, 1962.

*LOCKSPEISER, E., *Debussy; Life and Mind*, 2 vols., Macmillan, New York, 1962–65.

MEYER, L. B., "The End of the Renaissance?", *The Hudson Review*, XVI, 1963, pp. 169–86.

PERLE, G., *Serial Composition and Atonality: An Introduction to the Music of Schoenberg, Berg, and Webern*, University of California Press, Berkeley, 1962 (though technical, the best discussion of this important subject).

*SALZMAN, E., *Twentieth-Century Music: An Introduction*, Prentice-Hall, Englewood Cliffs, N. J., 1967 (the best concise survey).

STEVENS, H., *The Life and Music of Béla Bartók*, rev. ed., Oxford University Press, 1964.

*STUCKENSCHMIDT, H. H., *Arnold Schoenberg*, 2nd ed., tr. by E. T. Roberts and H. Searle, Hutchinson, London, 1964.

WHITE, E. W., *Stravinsky: The Composer and His Works*, University of California Press, Berkeley, 1966.

INDEX

317

LIST OF CREDITS

The authors and publisher wish to thank the libraries, museums, and private collectors for permitting the reproduction in black-and-white of paintings, prints, and drawings in their collections. Photographs have been supplied by the owners or custodians of the works of art except for the following, whose courtesy is gratefully acknowledged.

Alinari (incl. Anderson and Brogi), Florence (45, 48, 49–51, 60, 79, 95–97, 104–106, 110, 111, 113, 123–127, 129, 131, 132, 135, 136, 138, 142–147, 150–154, 157, 164, 167, 169, 170, 173, 204, 207); American Museum of Natural History, New York (8); Andrews, Wayne (199); Copyright Archives Centrales Iconographiques, Brussels (82, 114); Archives Photographiques, Paris (18, 80, 103, 107, 188, 192, 220, 227); Arland, Jean, Geneva (117); Baker, Oliver, Museum of Modern Art, New York (232); Bildarchiv Oesterr. Nationalbibliothek, Vienna (56); Bijebier, Paul, Brussels (245); Borsig, Arnold von, Berlin (94); Bruckmann, A.-G. (159); Bulloz, J.-E., Paris (81, 203, 212); Bundesdenkmalamt, Vienna (86); Burstein, Barney, Boston (239); Castelli, Leo, New York (258); Chapman, William, New York (1); Chevojon, Paris (210); Copyright Country Life, London (208); Devinoy, Pierre, Paris (85); Deutsche Fotothek, Dresden (224); Deutscher Kunstverlag, Munich (3; former Staatliche Bildstelle, Berlin, 67, 200); Fotocielo, Rome (54, 168); Copyright Fotocommissie Rijksmuseum, Amsterdam (179, 184); Fototeca, Unione Internazionale degli Istituti . . . , Rome (38, 39, 149); Frantz, Alison, (21, 29, 30); Copyright Frick Collection (137); Gabinetto Fotografico Nazionale, Rome (37); German Archaeological Institute, Rome (43); Giraudon, Paris (75, 84, 112, 166, 191, 198, 201, 205, 206, 226); Gundermann, Würzburg (176); Hedrich-Blessing, Chicago (269, from Bill Engdahl); Hervé, Lucien, Paris (271, 273, 274); Hirmer, Max, Verlag, Munich (11–14, 23, 25, 26, 31–36, 47, 57, 59); Horn, Walter, Berkeley, California (68); Institut Géographique, National Ministry of Public Works and Transport, Saint-Mande, France (190); Istituto Centrale del Restauro, Rome (109); Kersting, A. F., London (77, 93); Kidder-Smith, G. E., New York (27, 41, 58, 78, 89, 171, 174); Kleinhempel, Hamburg (241); Knoedler, M., New York (231); Kuhn, Herbert, Mainz (2); Lange, Kurt (9); Levy, Et., and Neurdein Réunis, Paris (91); Galerie Louise Leiris, Paris (264); Foto-Marburg (70, 98, 100, 101, 211); Mas, A. and R., Barcelona (116, 120–122, 155, 178, 218); McKenna, Rollie, New York (128, 158); Ministry of Public Works, London, Crown Copyright (5); Nathan, Dr. F. and Dr. P., Zurich (223); Copyright National Buildings Record, London (195, 209); Nickel, Richard, Park Ridge, Illinois (268); Oriental Institute, University of Chicago (16); Pasta, Fernando, Milan (139); Penguin Press, Baltimore (72, from K. J. Conant, Carolingian and Romanesque Architecture: 850–1200); Piaget, St. Louis (255); Commissione Pontificia d'Archeologia Sacra, Rome (53); Powell, Josephine, Rome (61); Rheinisches Bildarchiv, Kölnisches Stadtmuseum, Cologne (102); Roubier, Jean, Paris (74, 76, 88, 89); Royal Library, Windsor Castle, Crown Copyright (141, photo George Spearman); Schmidt-Glassner, Helga, Stuttgart (175); Copyright Sir John Soane's Museum, London (196); Smith, Edwin, London (19, 92); Soprintendenza alle Antichità, Roma (44, Scavi di Ostia); Staatliche Graphische Sammlung, Munich (118); Stoller, Ezra, Mamaroneck, New York (272); Sunami, Soichi, Museum of Modern Art, New York (236, 242–244, 250–252, 257, 259, 261, 262, 265–267); Thames and Hudson, Ltd., London (193, from Martin Hürliman, Moscow and Leningrad); UNESCO (4, from UNESCO World Art Series, Australia, plate XXII); Copyright Universitetets Oldsaksamling, Oslo (64); Vaering, Otto, Oslo (234); Victoria and Albert Museum, London, Crown Copyright (83, 130); Viollet, H. Roger, Paris (140); Vizzavona, Paris (189, 221, 238); Ward, Clarence, Oberlin, Ohio (87, 90); Wehmeyer, Hildesheim (71); Yan Photo Reportage (73); Yugoslav State Tourist Office, New York (42).

Acknowledgment is made with thanks to Harcourt, Brace & World, Inc., for permission to use the quotation on page 115 from "The Love Song of J. Alfred Prufrock" by T. S. Eliot from his volume Collected Poems 1909–1935, copyright 1936, by Harcourt, Brace & World, Inc.

Grateful acknowledgment is also made to Theo Presser, Inc., for permission to reproduce on page 286 the excerpt from Wozzeck by Alban Berg.